Inside Out with
GADGET

A FIRESIDE BOOK
PUBLISHED BY SIMON & SCHUSTER
New York London Toronto Sydney Tokyo Singapore

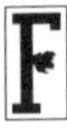

Fireside
Simon & Schuster Inc.
Rockefeller Center
1230 Avenue of the Americas
New York, NY 10020

Copyright © 1995 SYNERGY, Inc. All rights reserved.

Graphics by HARUHIKO SHONO
Text by HIROKAZU NABEKURA
Translated by david
Book and Cover Design by ISAO KONAKA

Edited by MASANORI AWATA and SYNERGY, Inc.

No part of this publication may be reproduced or transmitted in any form or by any means, electronic or mechanical, including photocopy, recording, or any information storage and retrieval system, without permission in writing from the publisher.

Fireside and colophon are registered trademarks of Simon & Schuster Inc.

Conceived and Produced by
SYNERGY, Inc.
Takadanobaba 1-24-16
Shinjuku, Tokyo, Japan 169

10 9 8 7 6 5 4 3 2 1

ISBN 0-684-82396-9
Library of Congress Cataloging-in-Publication data is available.

LVT by East West, Inc.
Printed in Japan by DAI NIPPON PRINTING CO., LTD.

...and in the end a comet collided with the planet

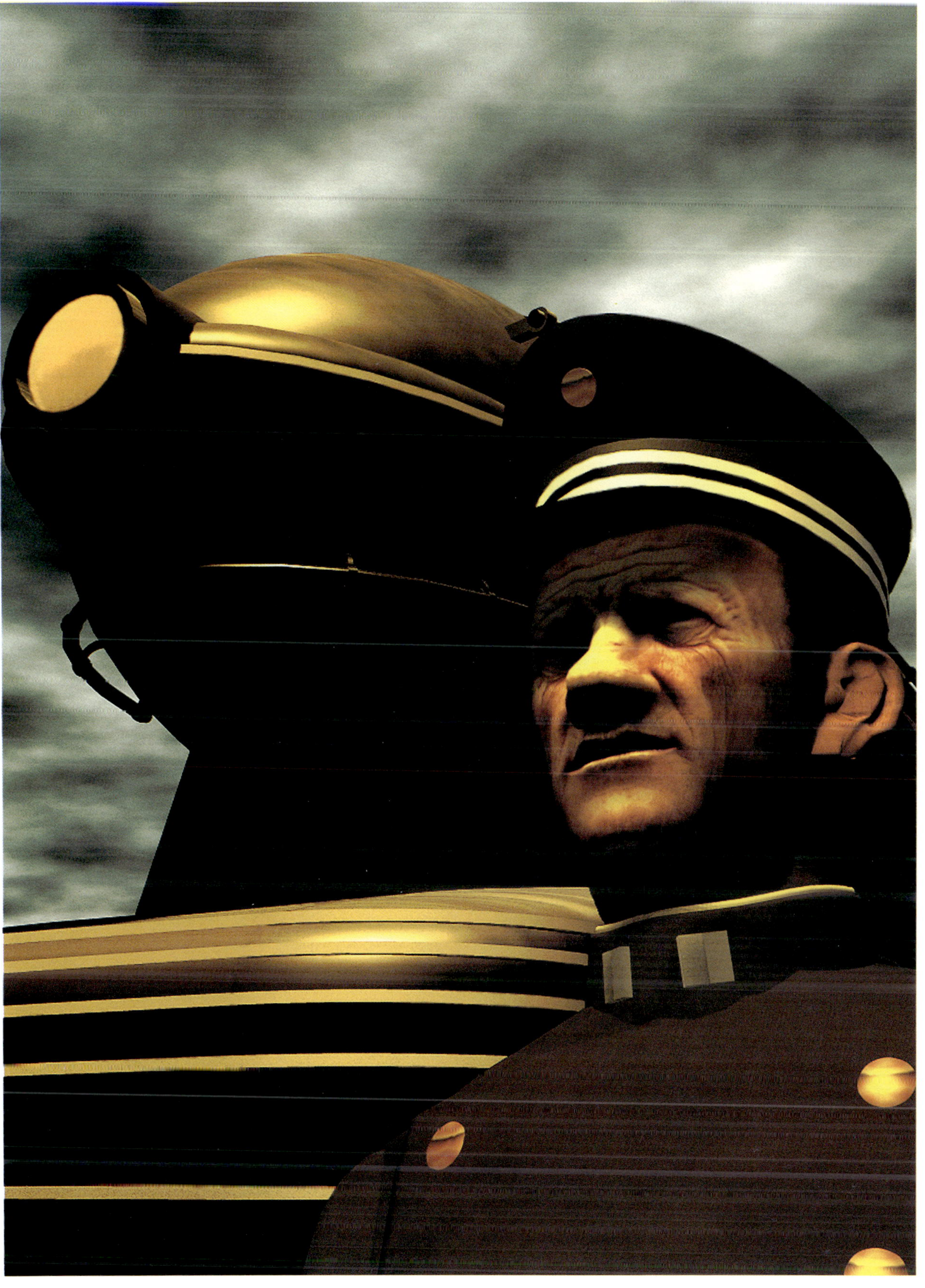

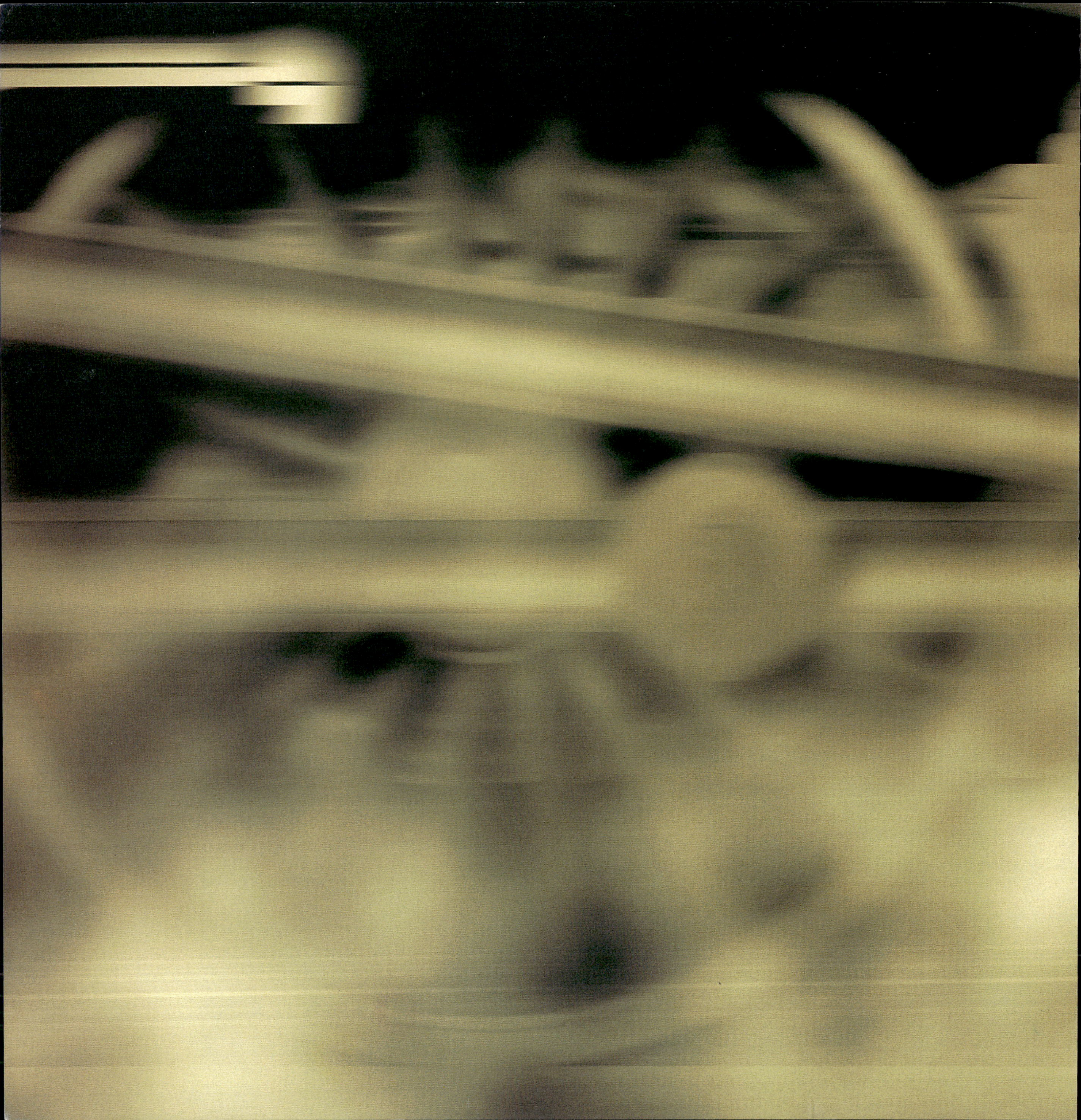

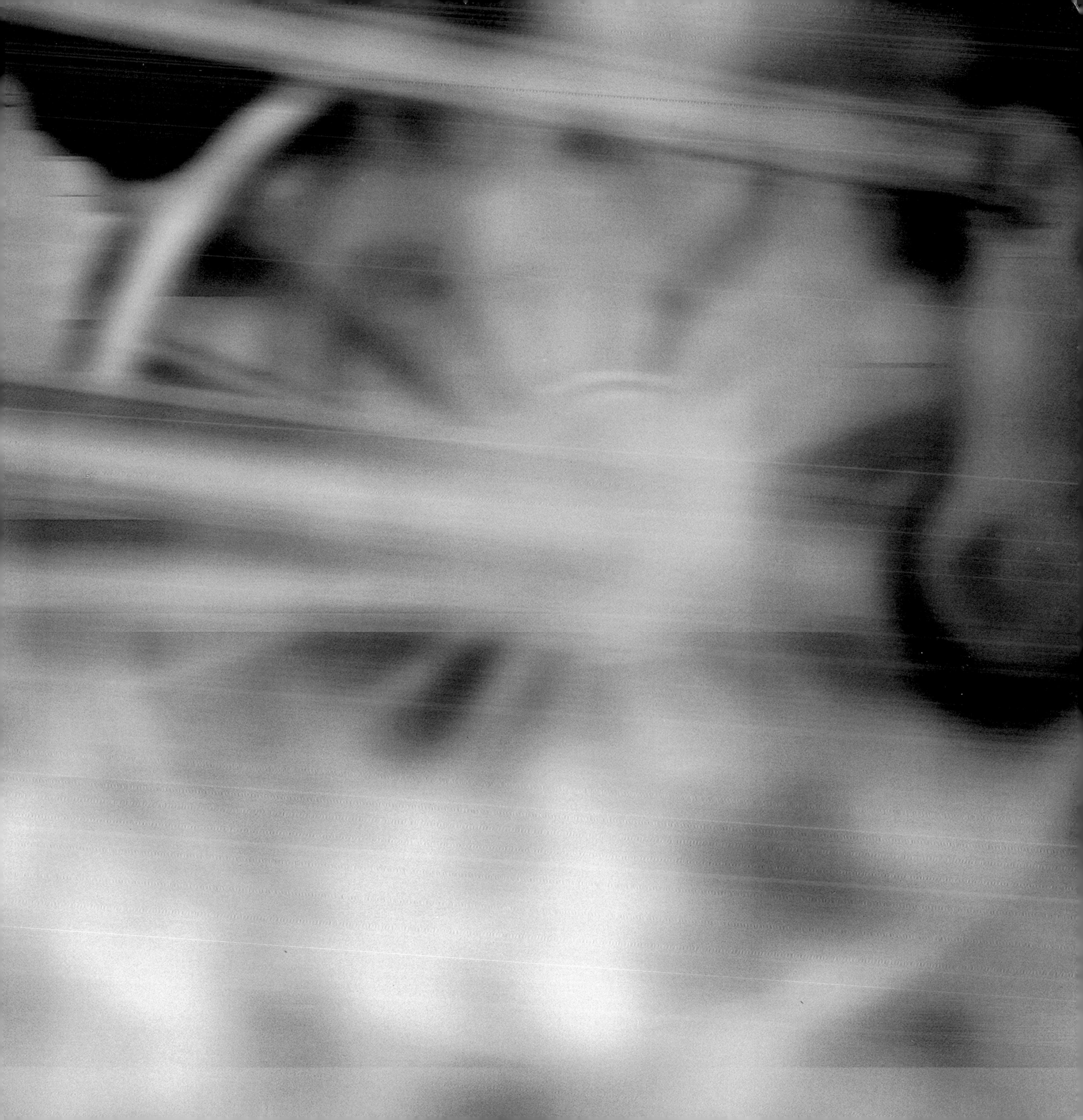

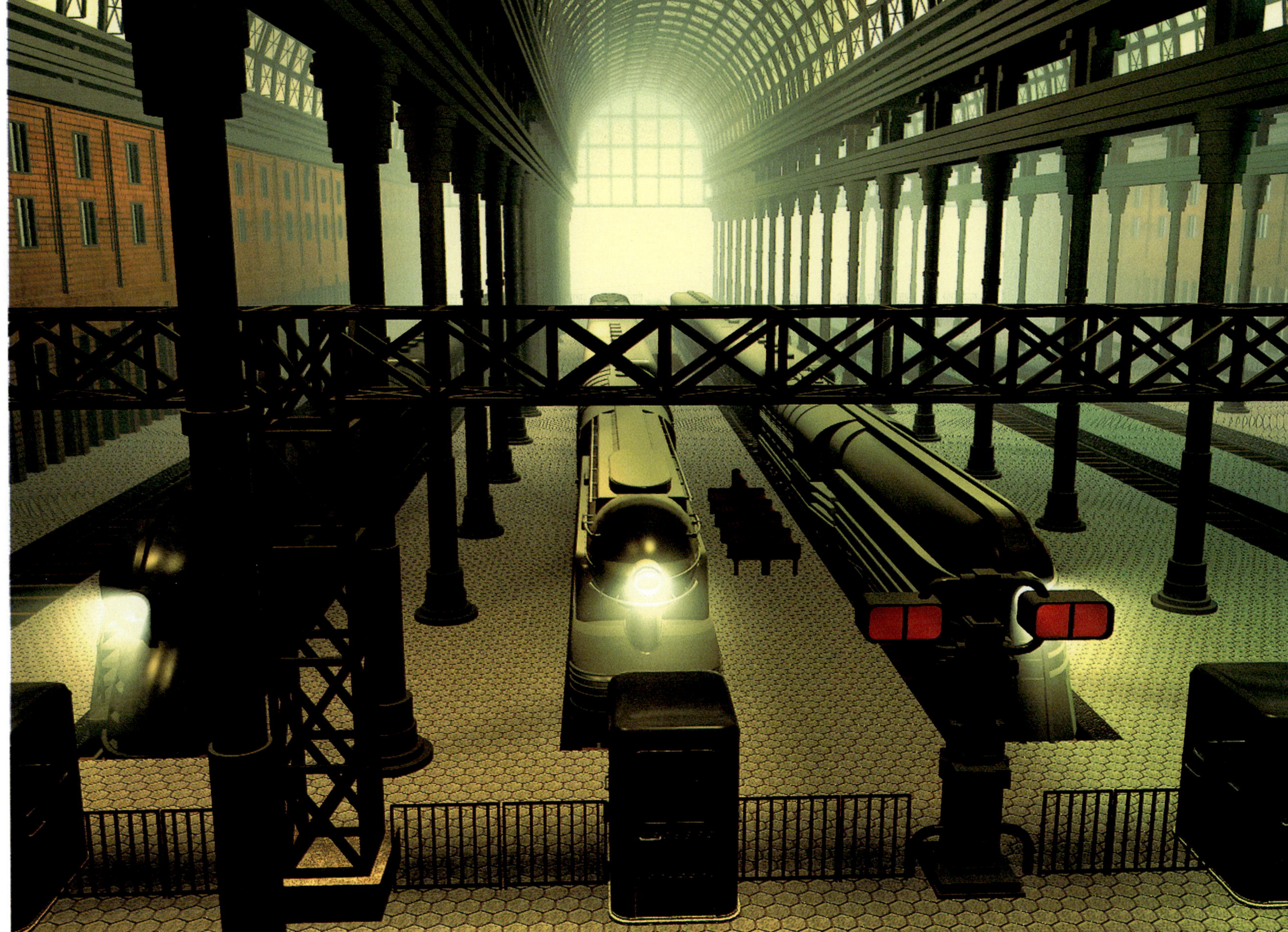

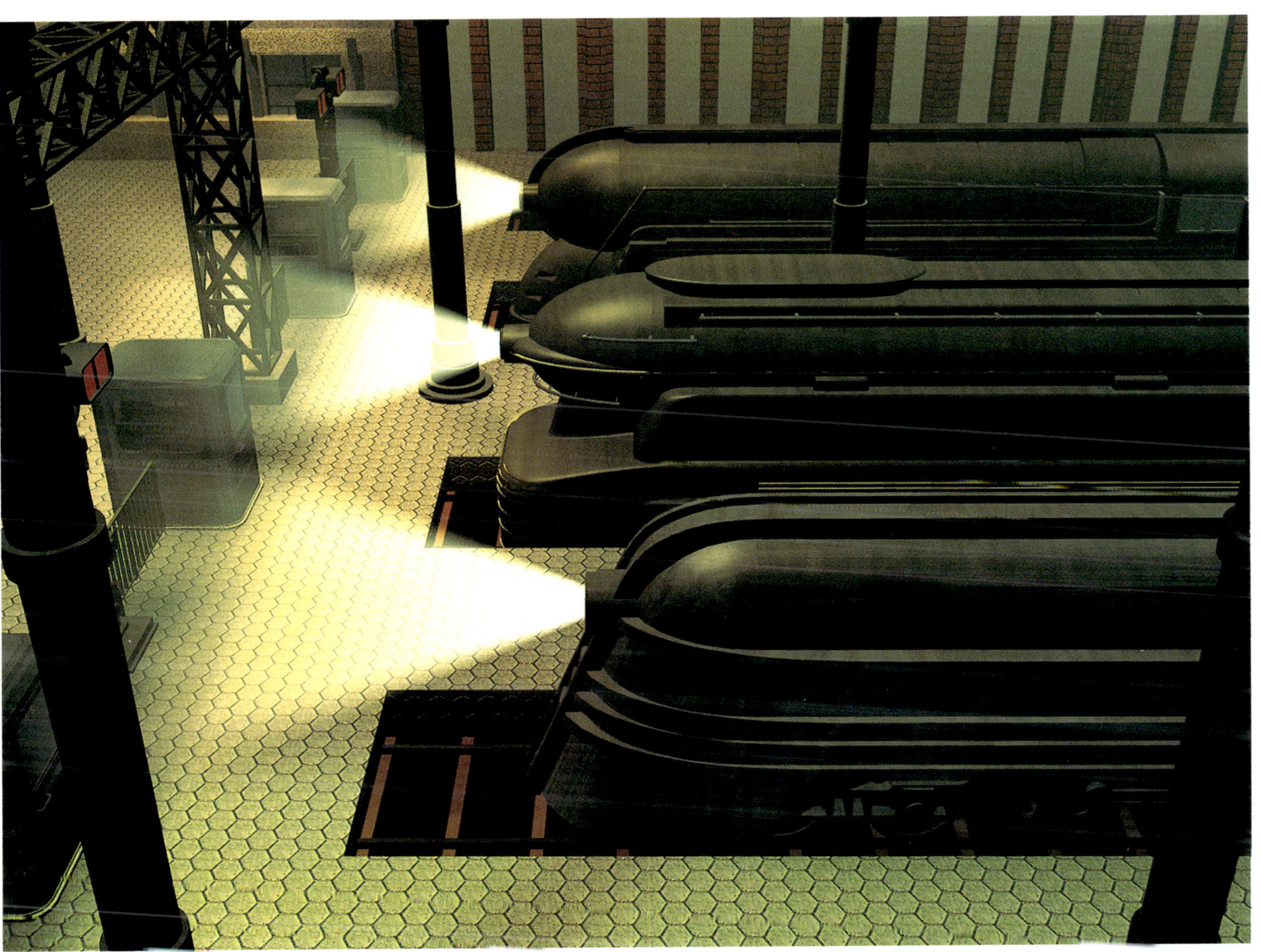

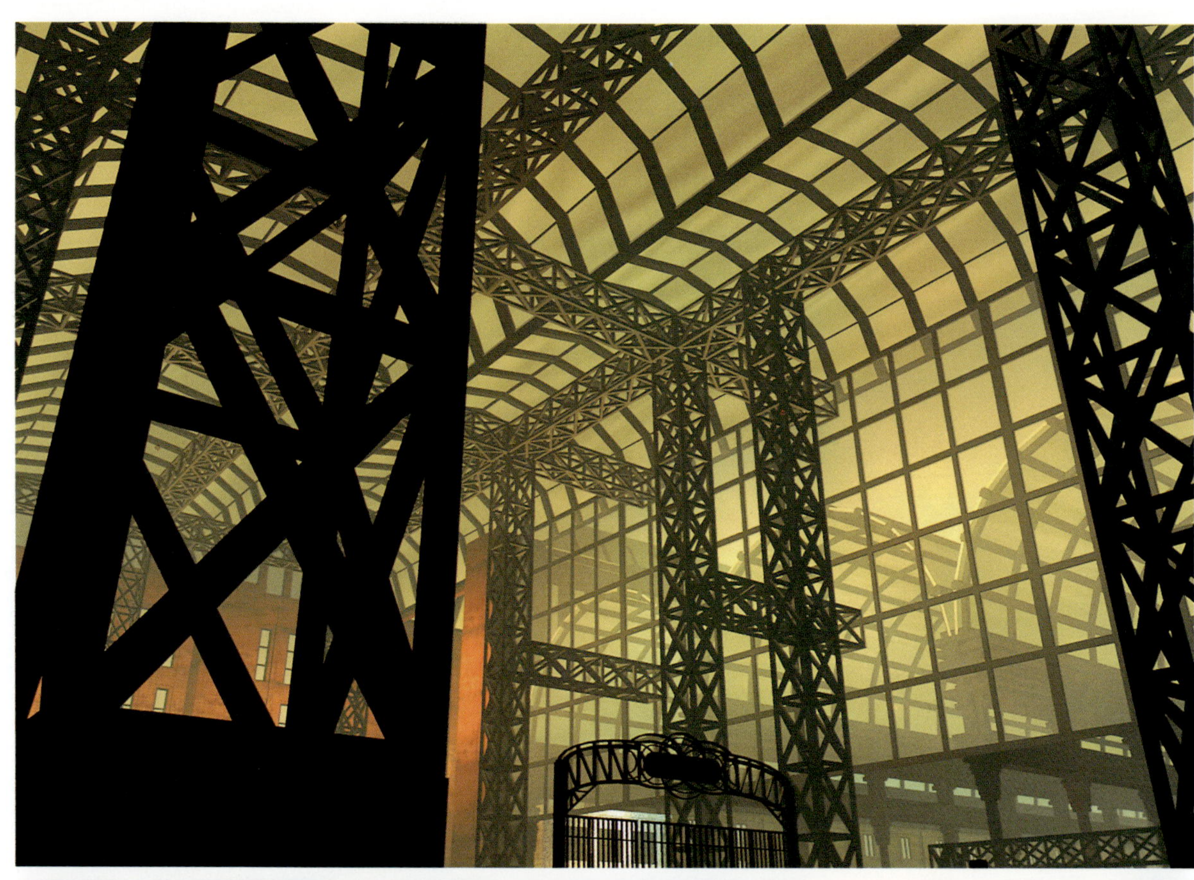

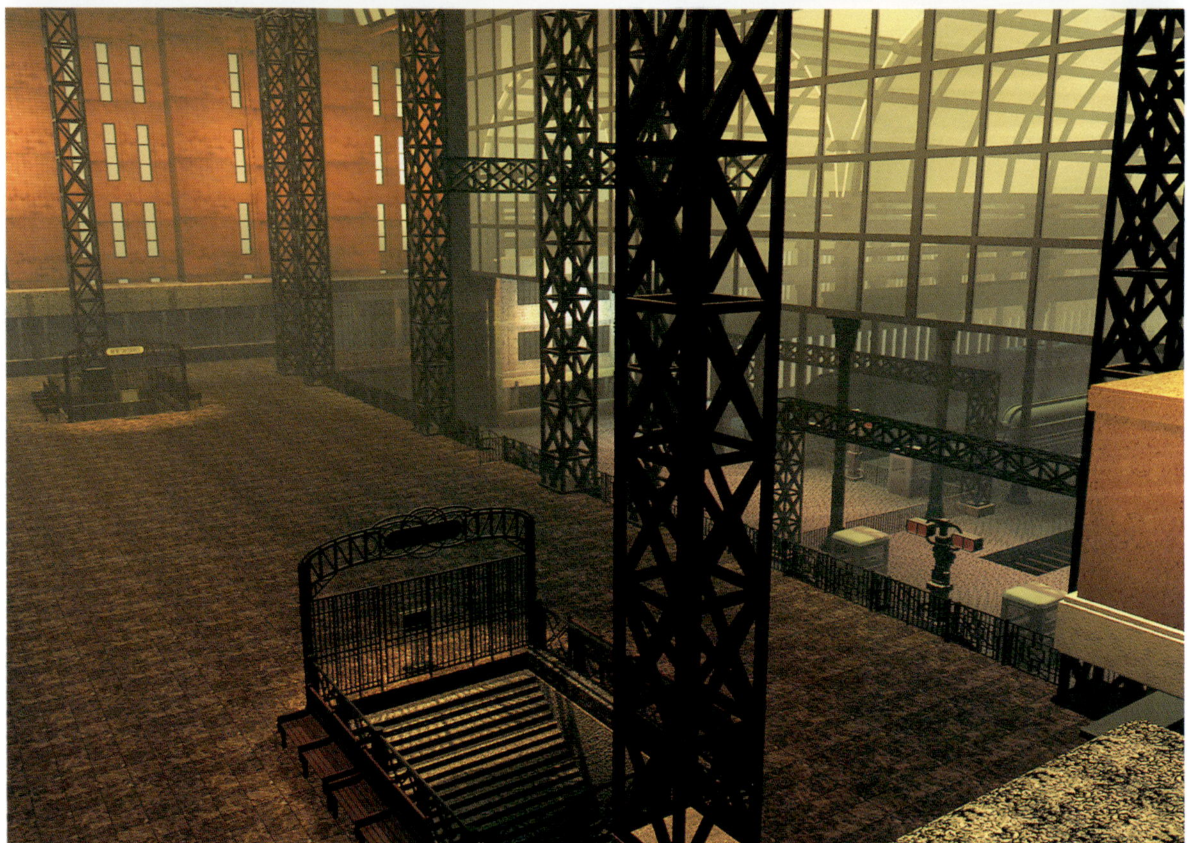

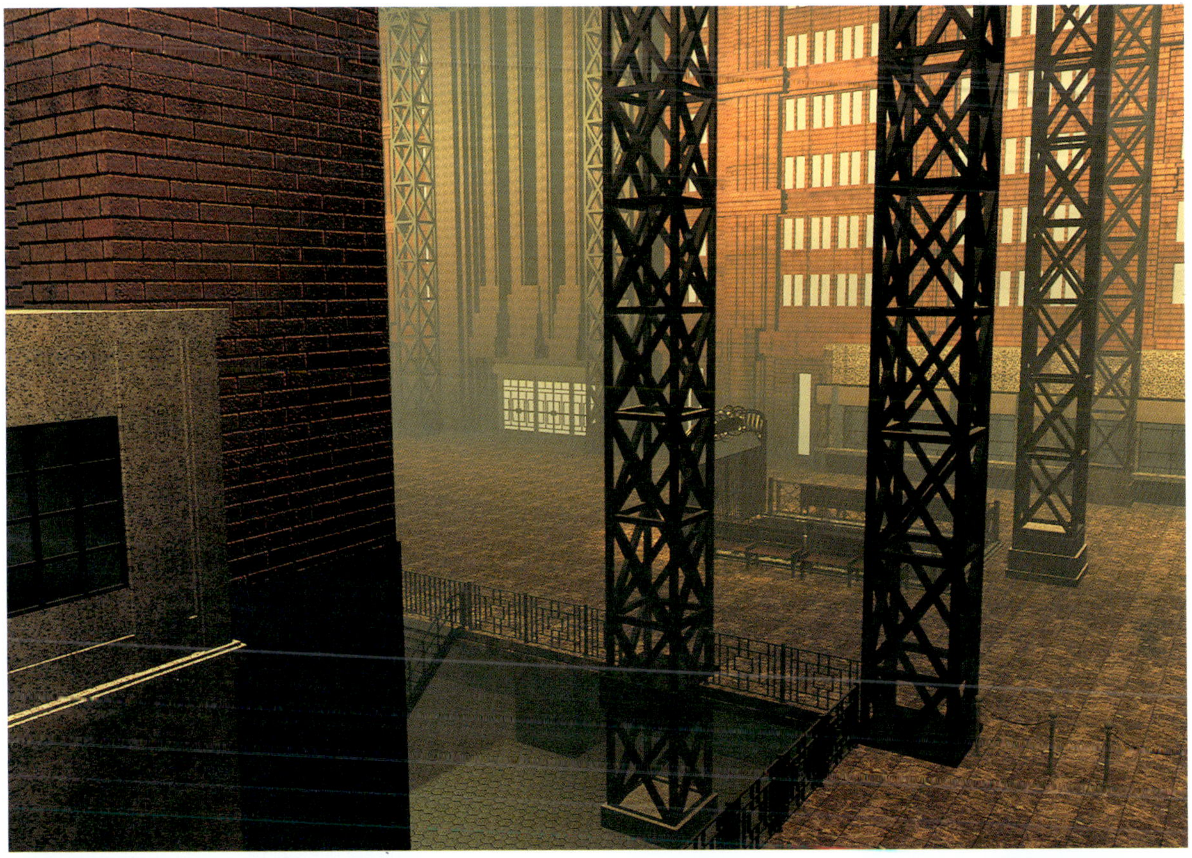

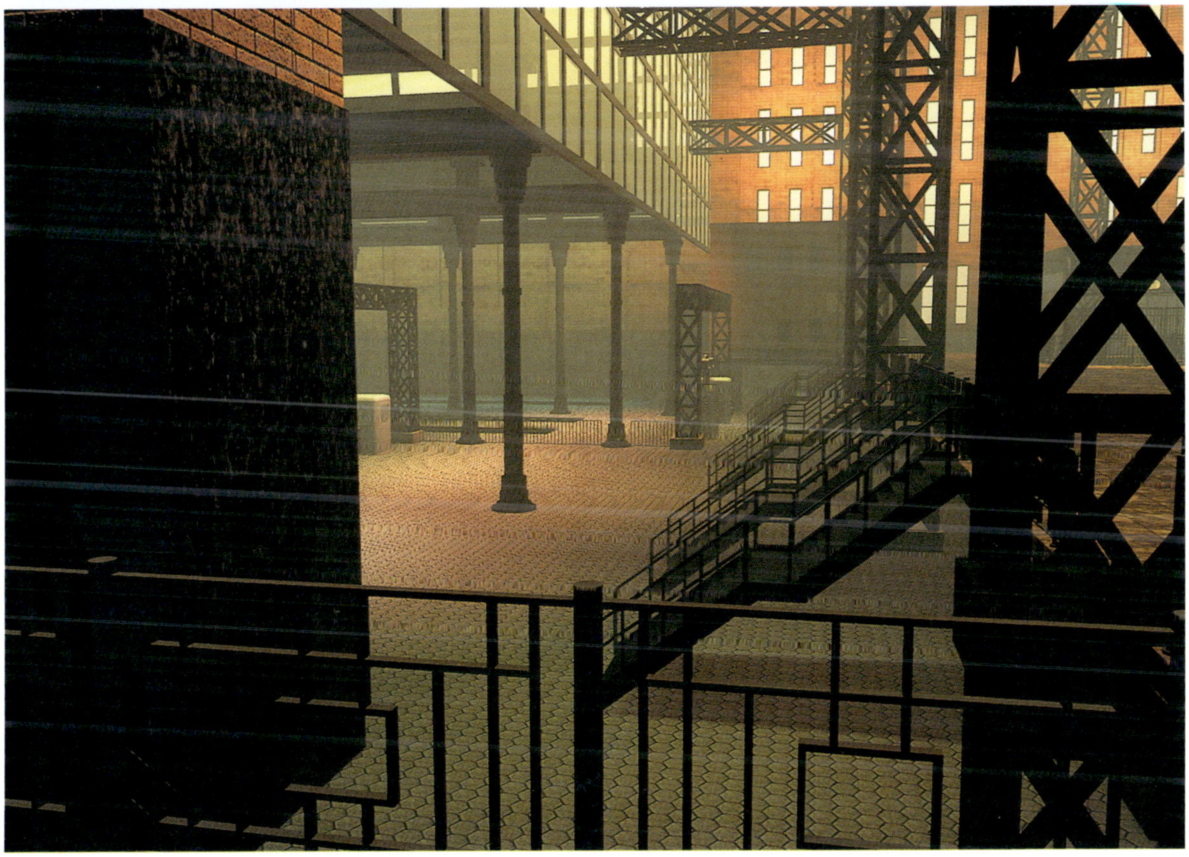

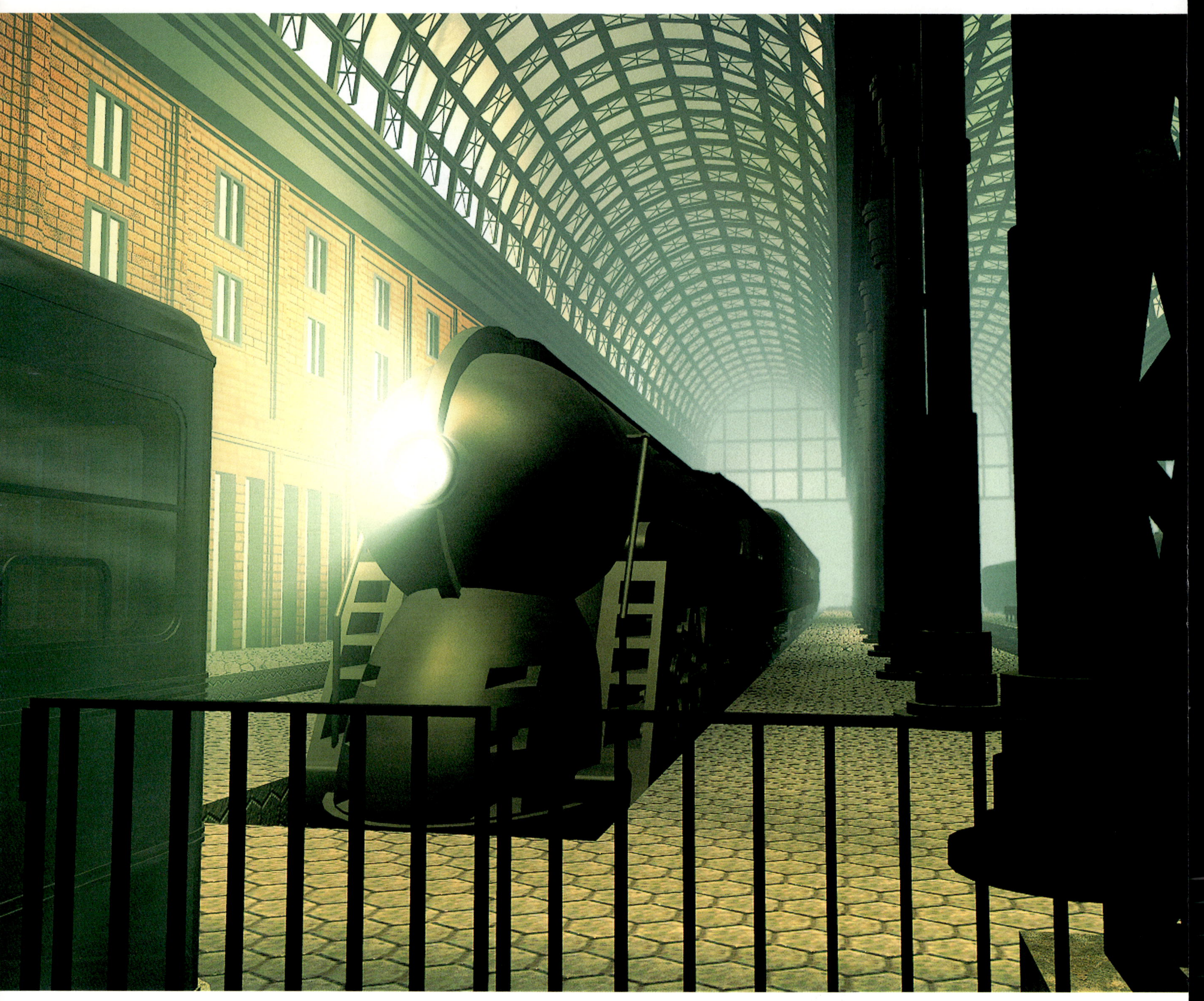

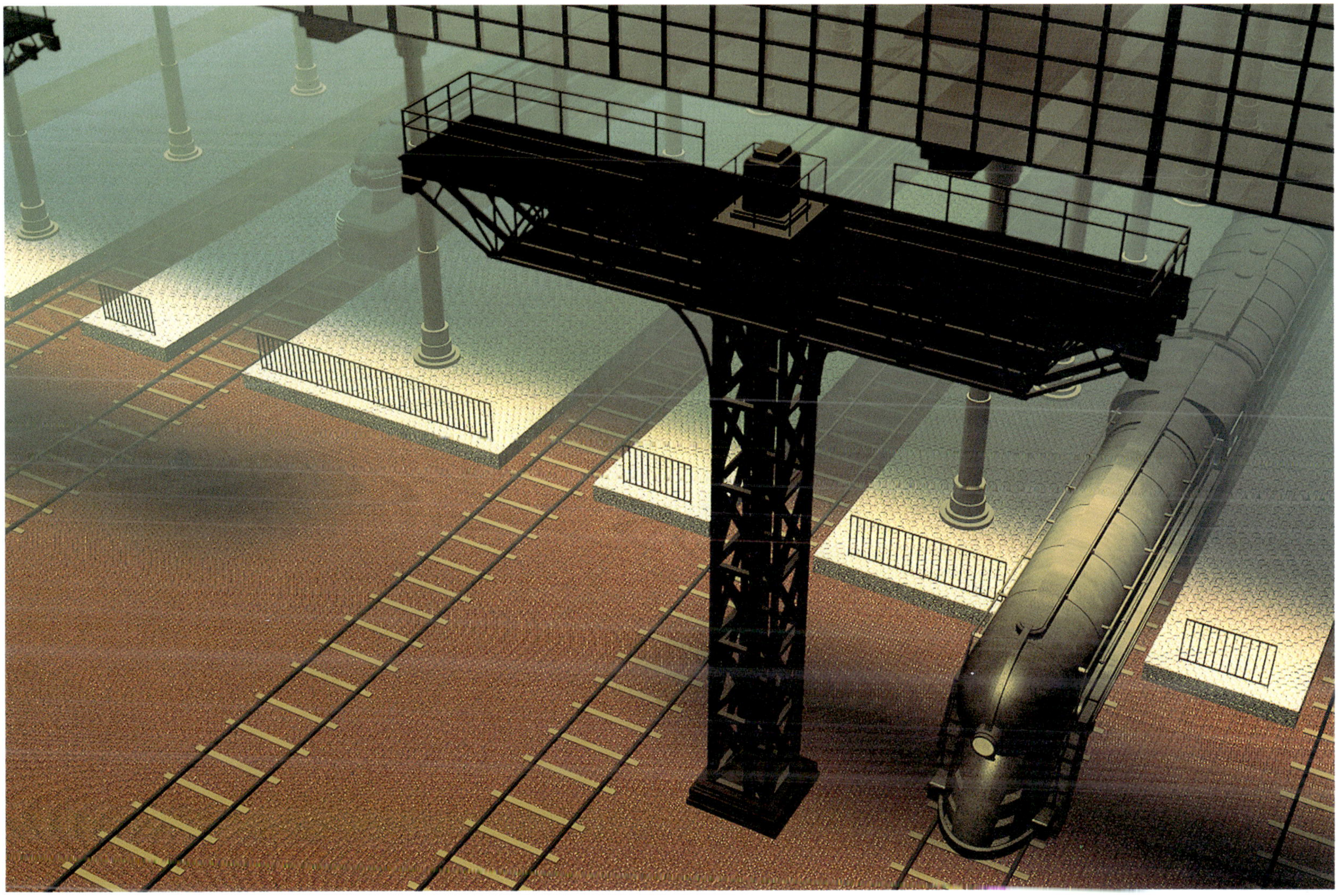

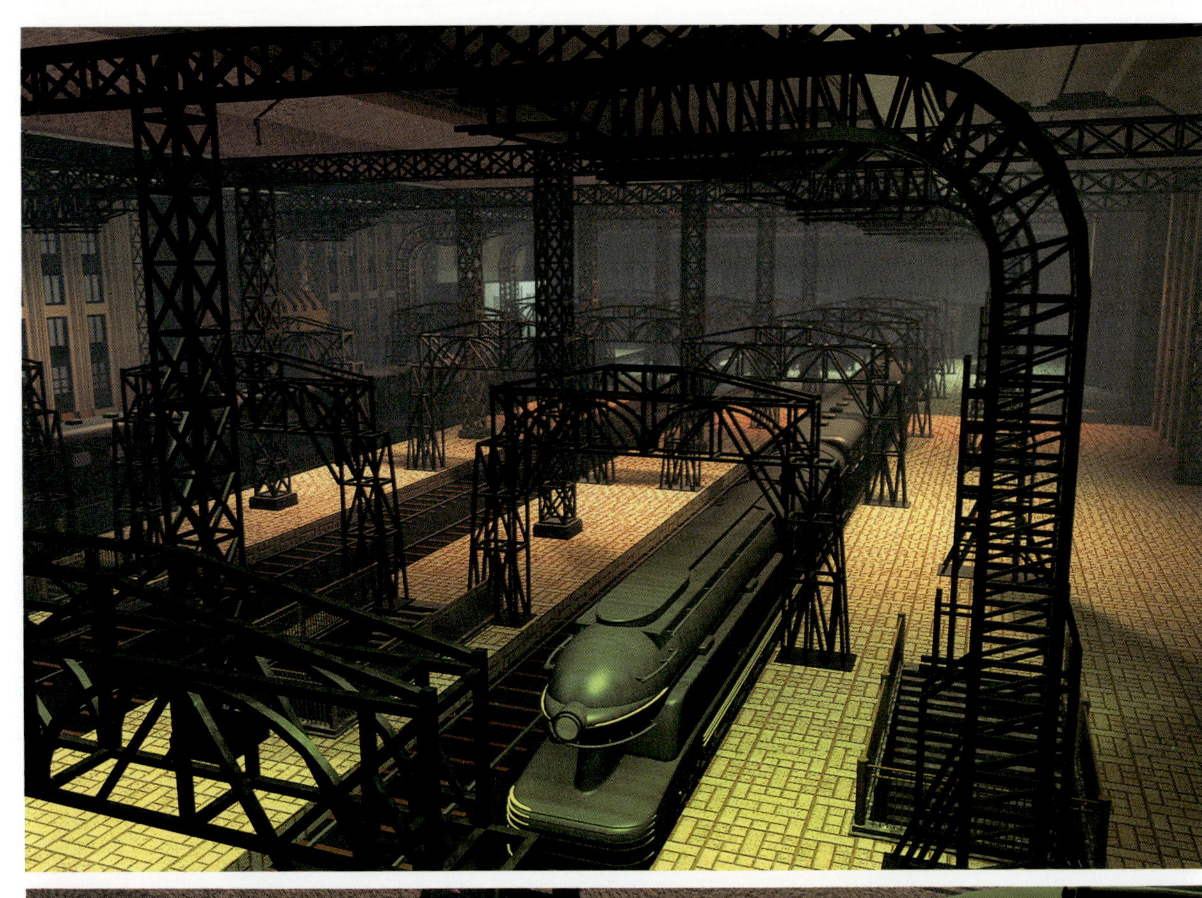

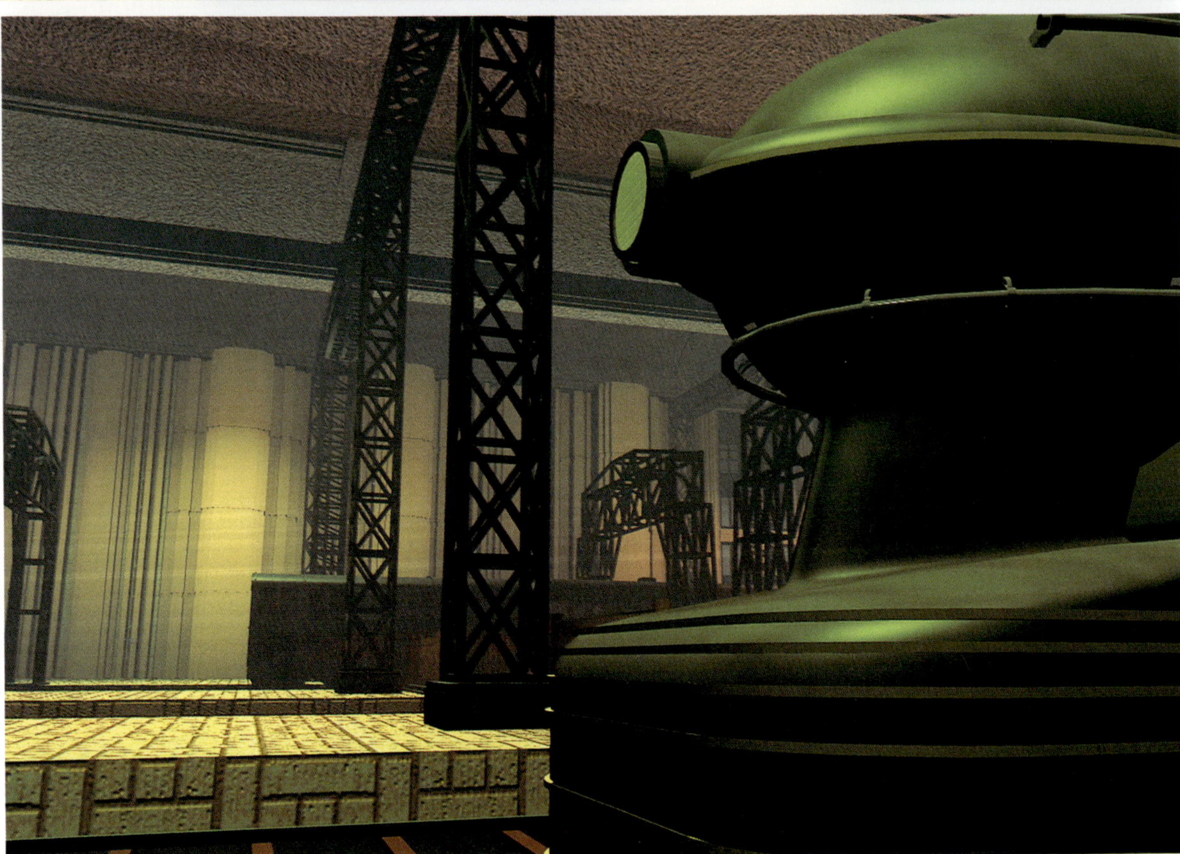

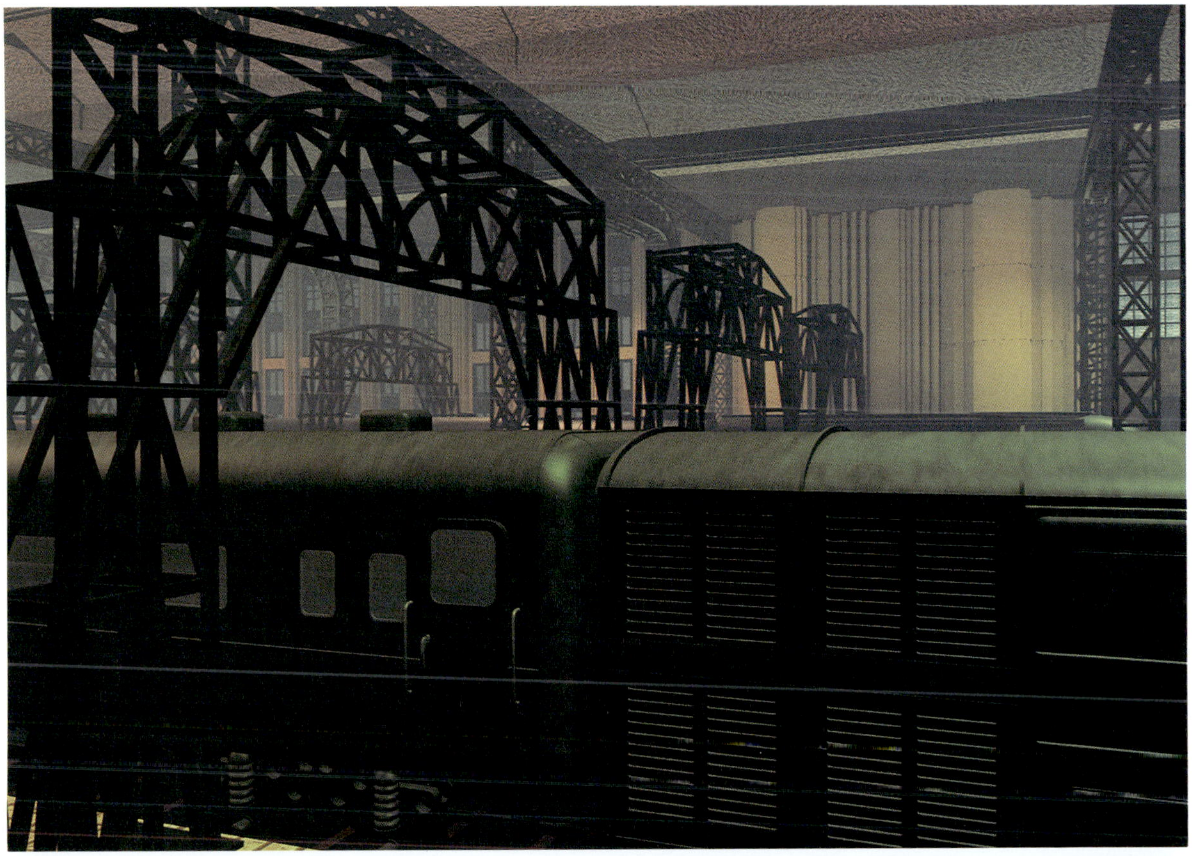

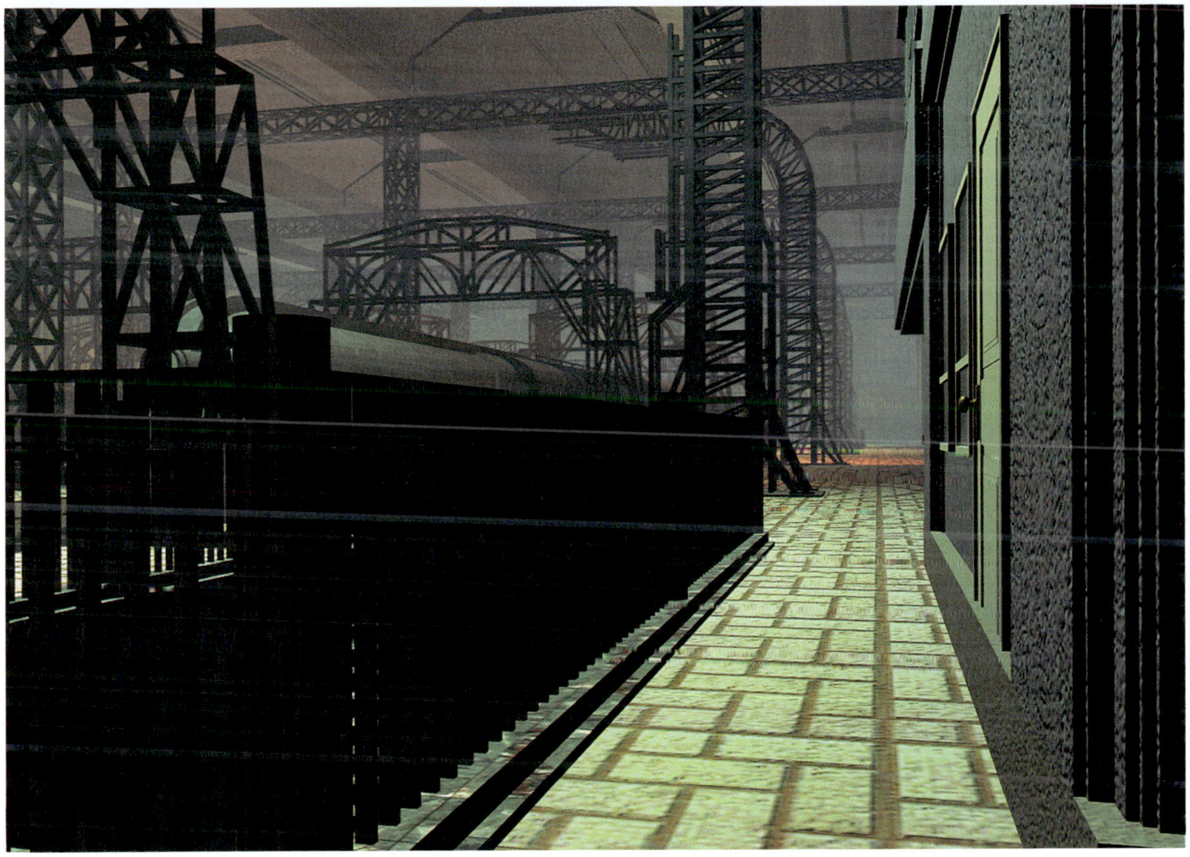

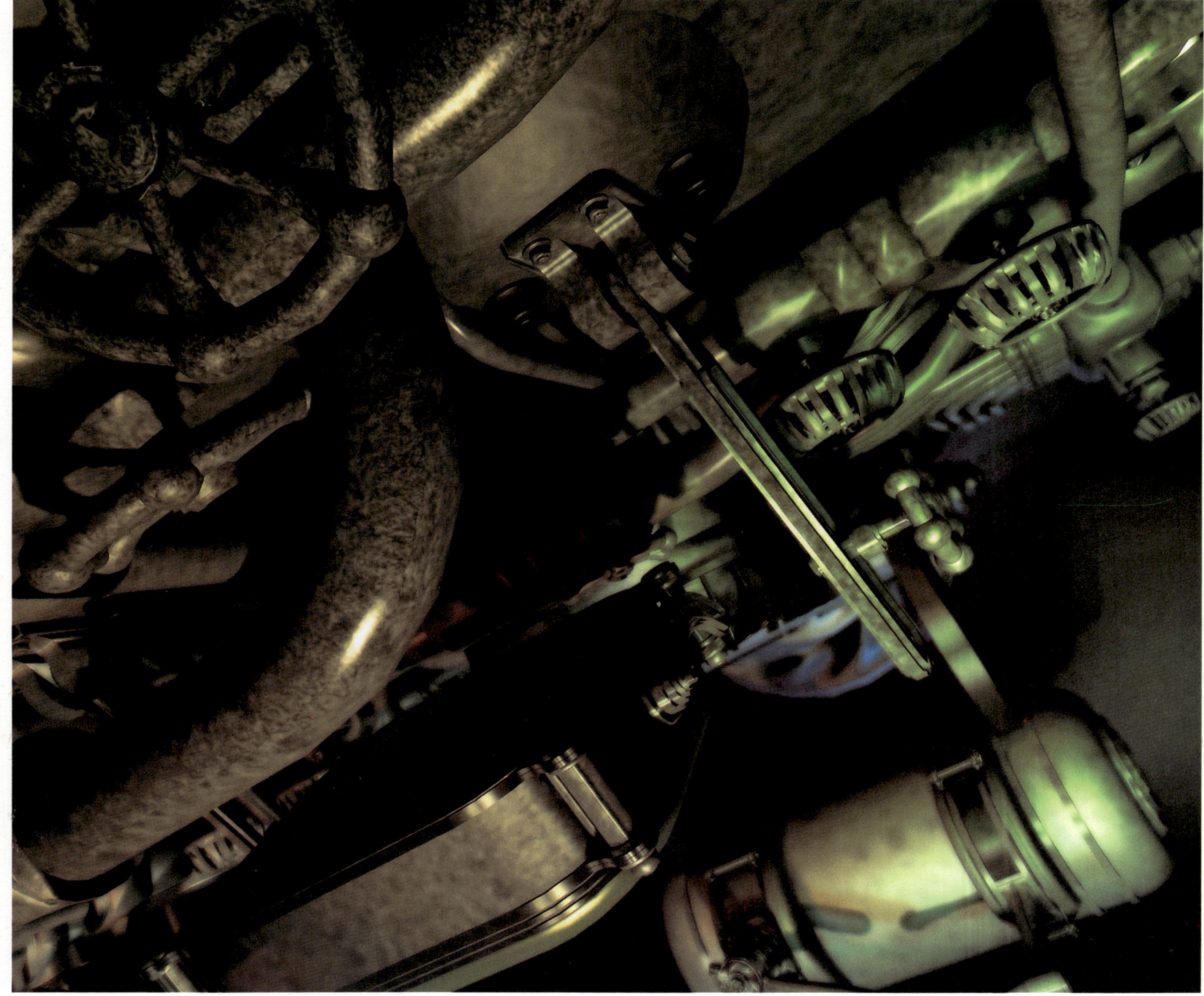

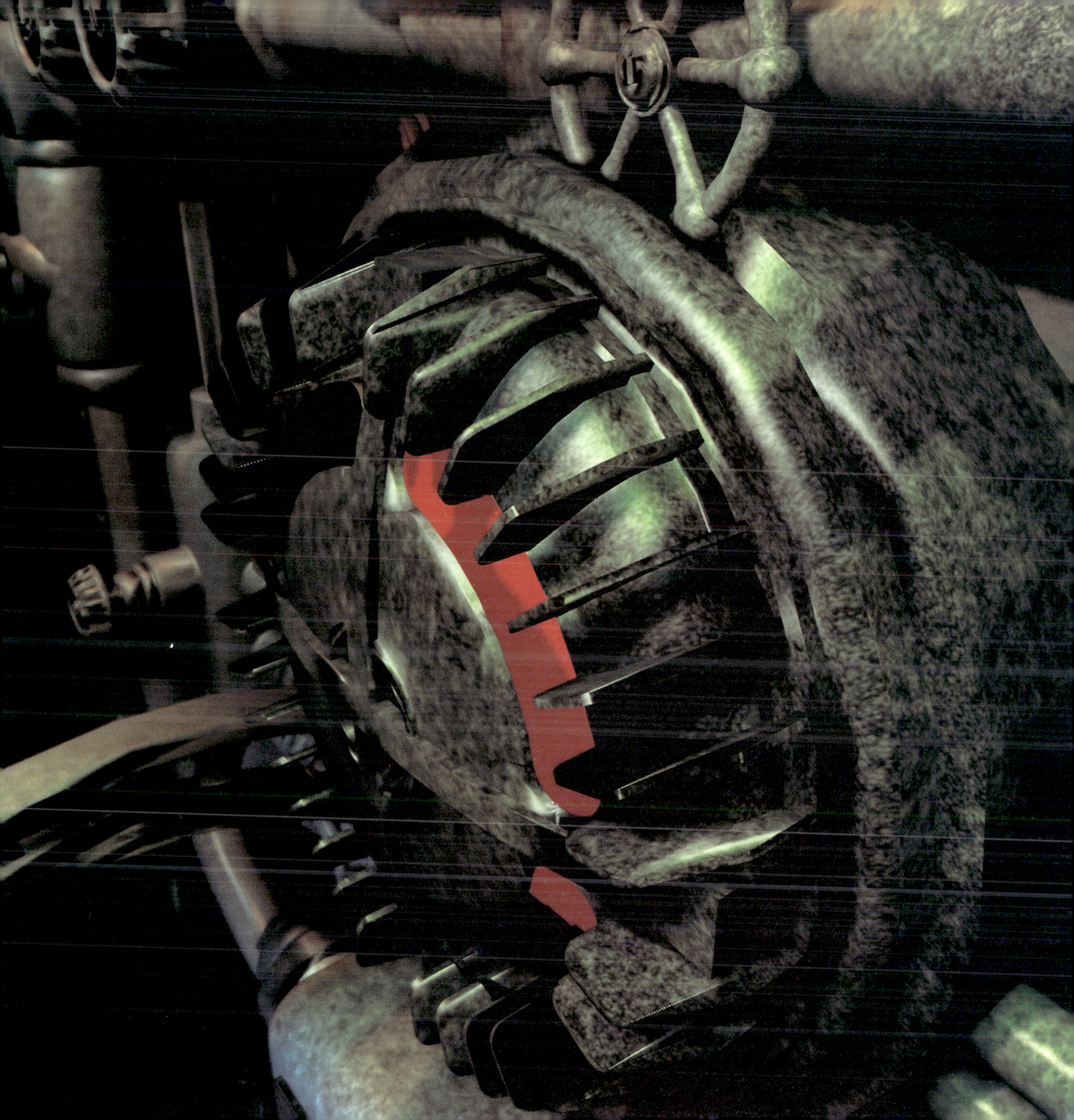

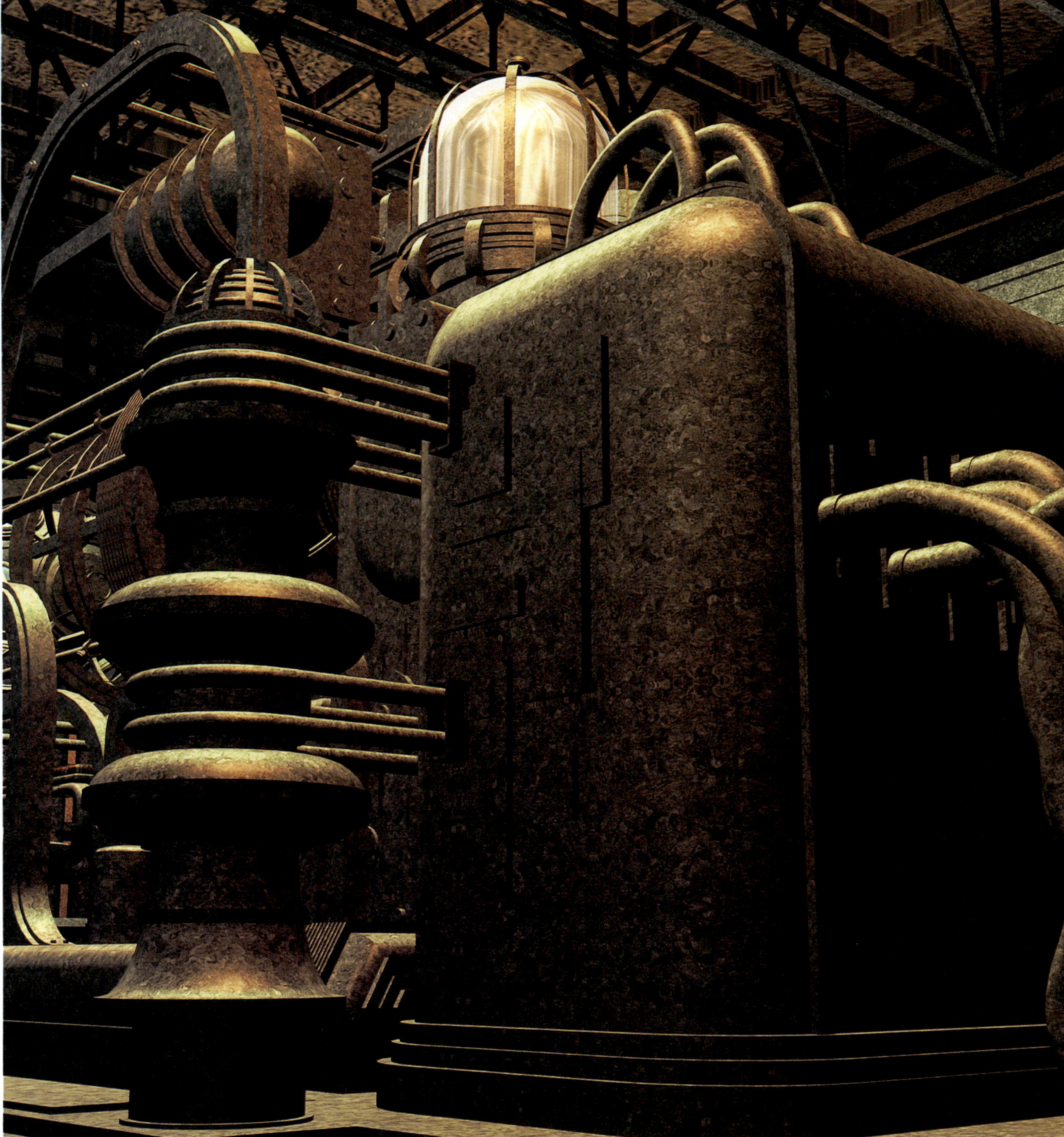

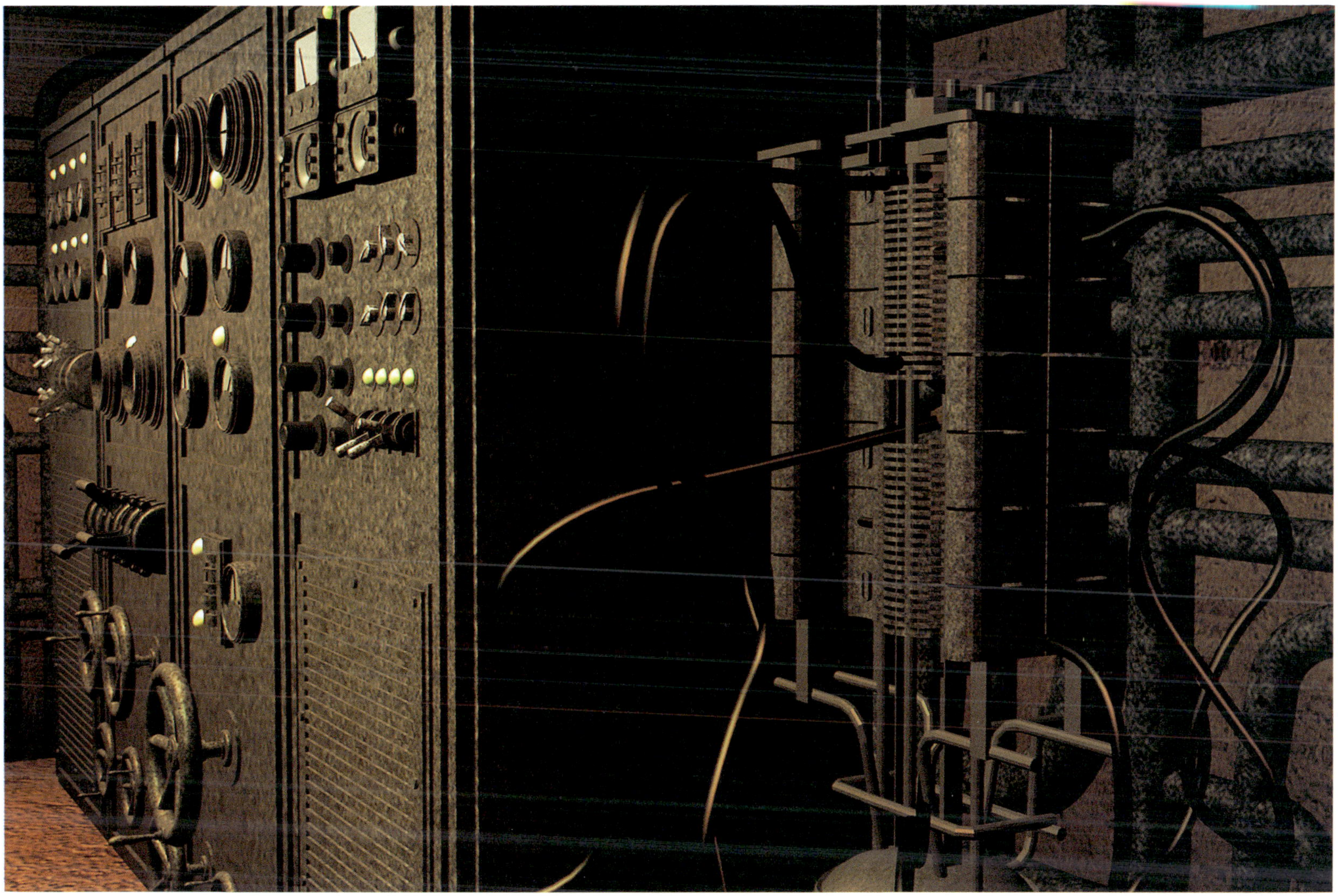

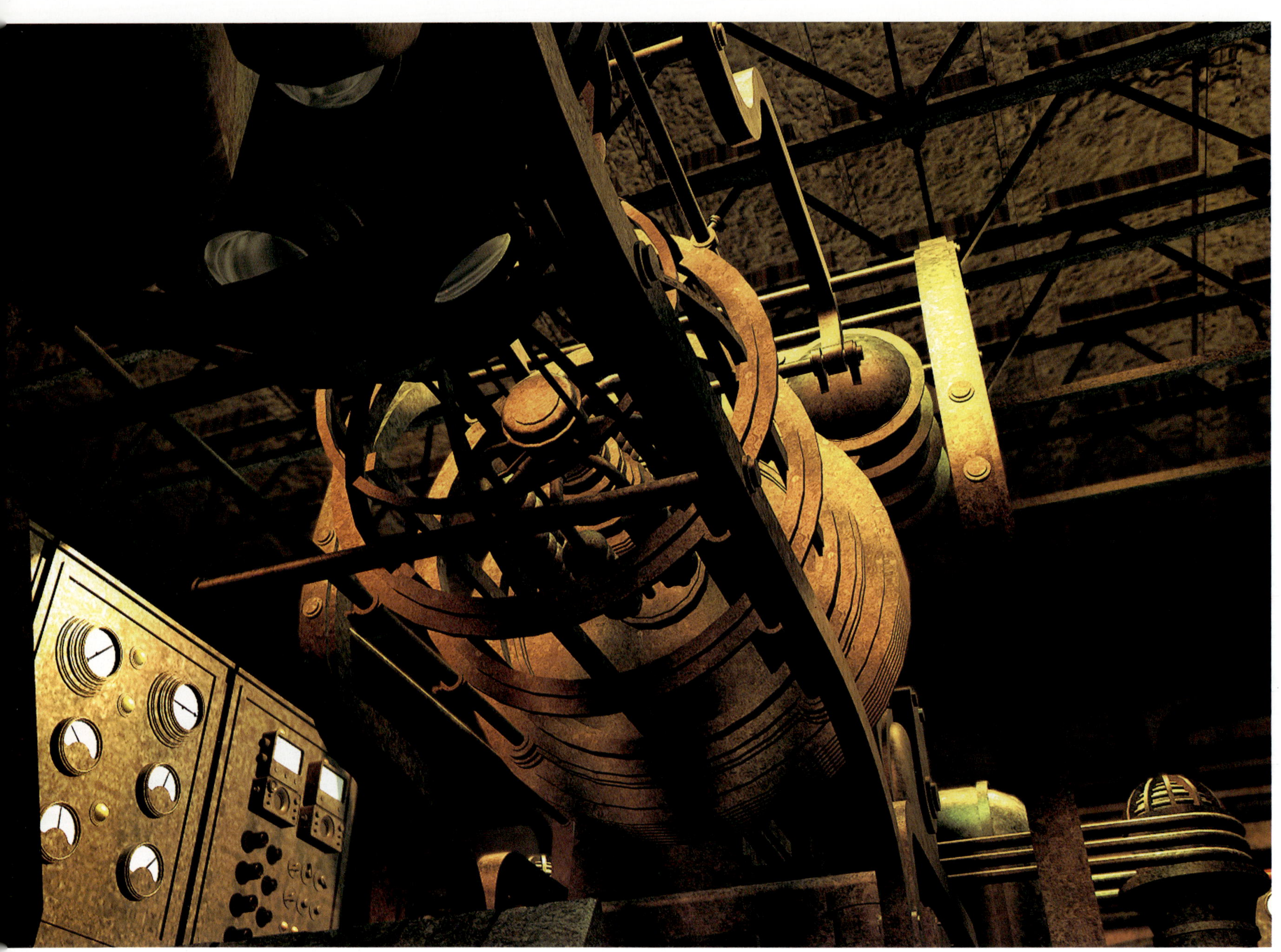

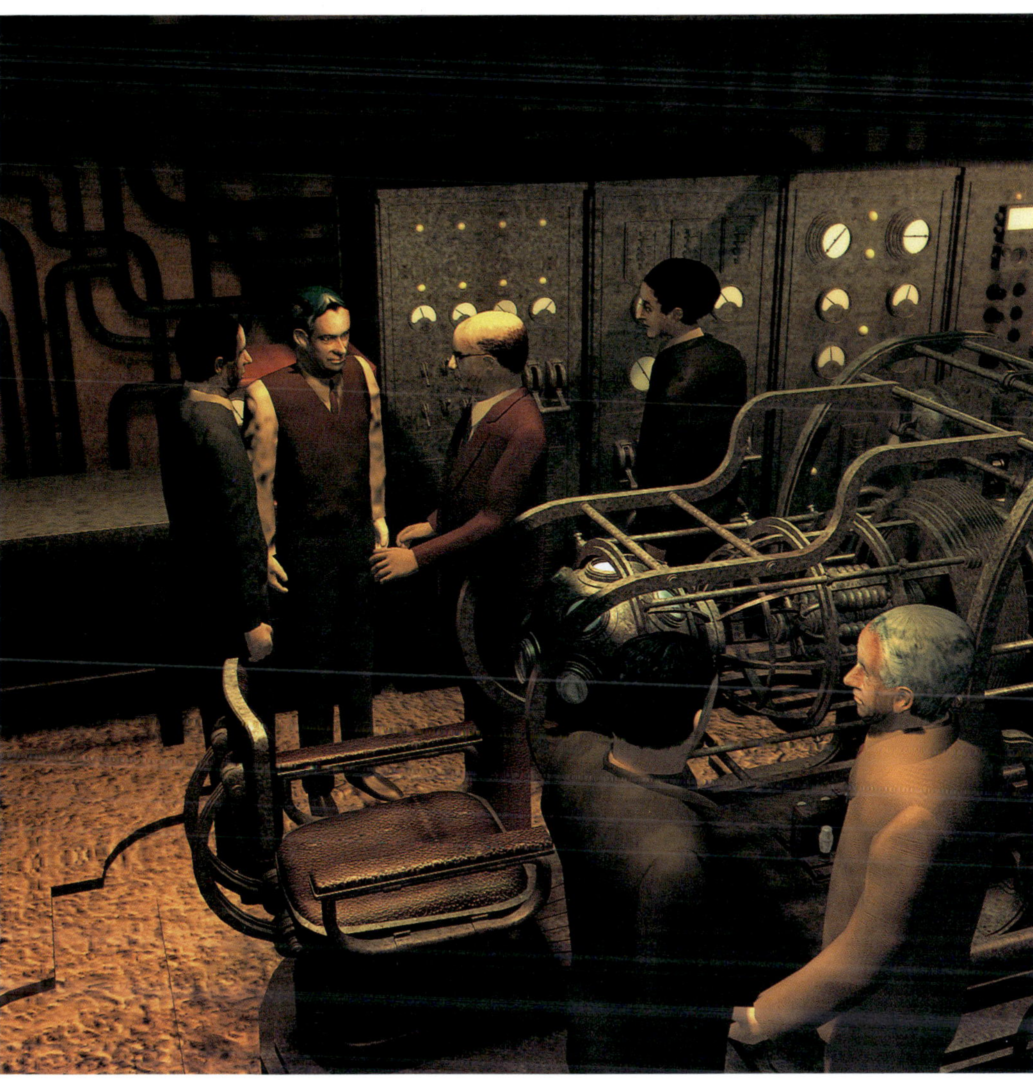

A day that will not be forgotten. On this great day our researches have borne fruit. We have accomplished an abrupt leap forward, such as on countless occasions humankind has achieved in its advance with the progress of science. I am confident that we, the research associates of the National Academy of Science, have today conducted an unprecedented experiment which will open a new chapter in the history of science.

Physics, neurophysiology, optics, and pharmacology. Untiring investigation into each of these fields has eventuated in an astounding discovery.

This tremulous lump of tissue, so similar in texture to a spongy testicle. This unknown field in which the only means of drawing a conclusion has been to drill a hole in the skull and excise a portion of the cerebrum. This terra incognita that defies analysis and analogy.

All is condensed in the brain of man. Through our researches, we have for the first time in human experience breached the walls of this long inviolable sanctum sanctorum.

Images imprinted on the retinae pass as neural impulses through the optic nerve to the back of the brain—the so-called visual area. In the first stage of our research we have directed our attention to this part of the cerebrum; our purpose: to transmit an artificial image to the visual area using a range of electromagnetic wavelengths, or 'beams.' Images produced by our Beam Machine give off light, change colors, and assume distorted shapes in the process of enlargement.

This experiment derives from an application of electromagnetic waves conceived and developed by George Tessera. Excision, reflection, mutation...adjustment of wave frequency and duration of radiation can work a range of influences upon subject matter. Based on George's documentation concerning electromagnetic waves, we have planned and carried out an experiment in which multiple beams of differing frequency were trained on the posterior portion of the cerebrum. Through a series of steps we were able not only to effect changes in images registered on the retinae, but also succeeded in transmitting images of non-existent objects to the visual area.

The Beam Machine: a device for registering artificial images within the brain. Unfortunately, we are not yet able to predict in what directions our research will lead from here.

This observation alone I wish to record: outdated abuses such as the implanting of electrodes in the back of the head or the removal of the pituitary are none other than emanations of the devil himself. I and my associates in the Beam Machine project have maintained a strict scientific objectivity and have carried out our researches in a manner congruent with absolute respect for the integrity of the human body. It is my deepest desire that throughout subsequent investigations this humanist stance should be preserved.

(From the diary of Horselover—set down on a day 20 years before the End)

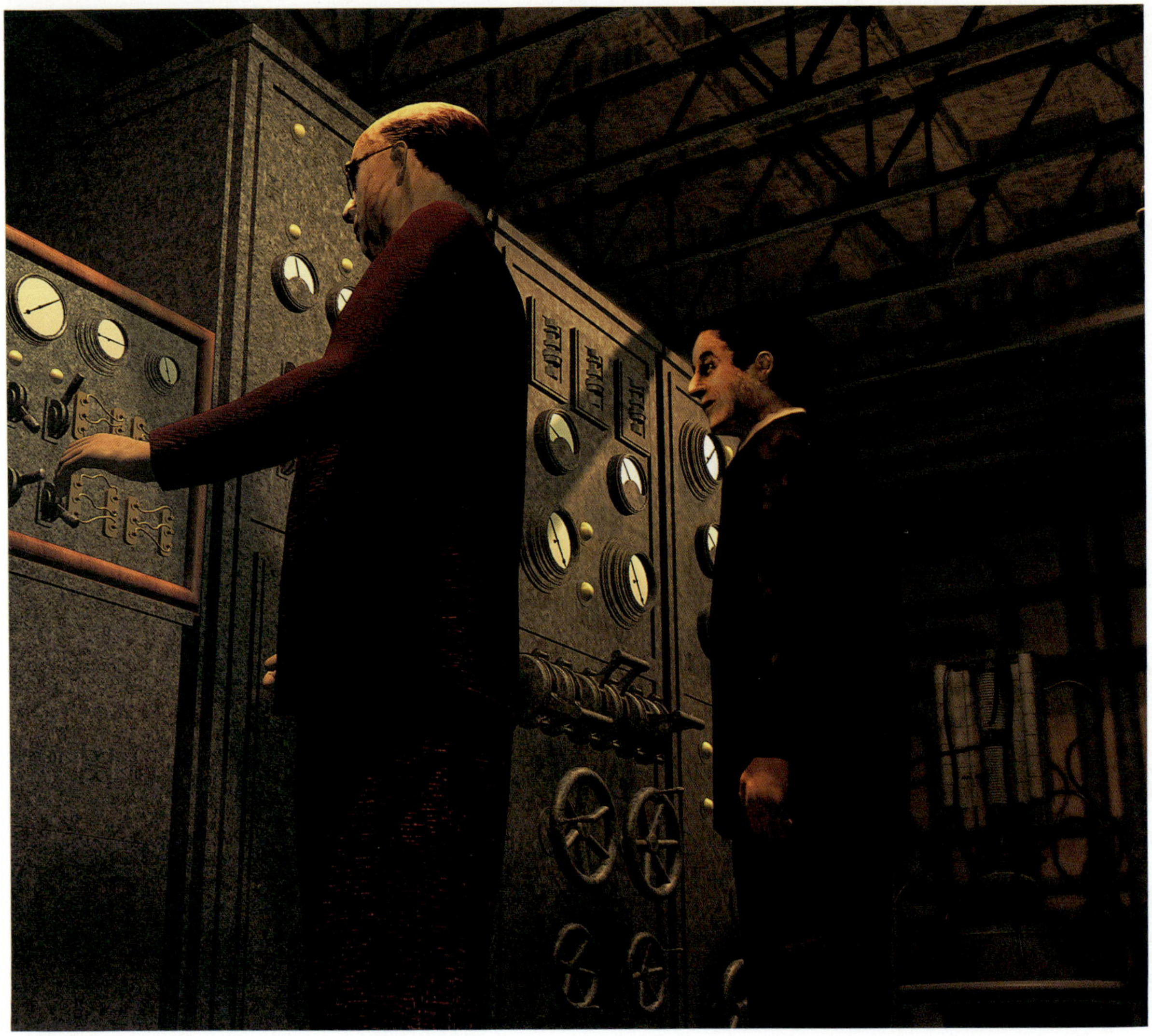

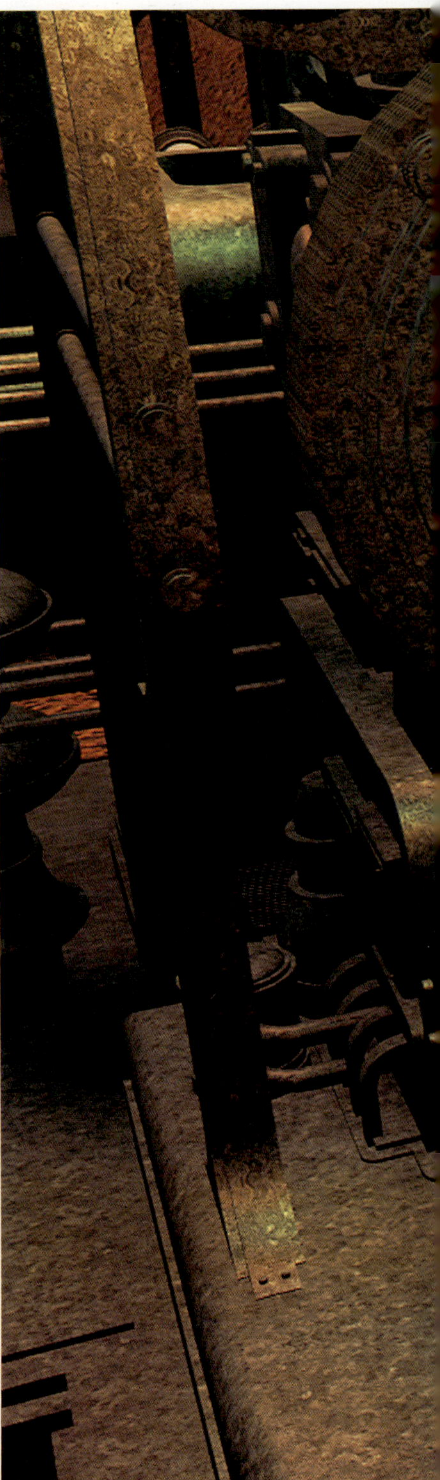

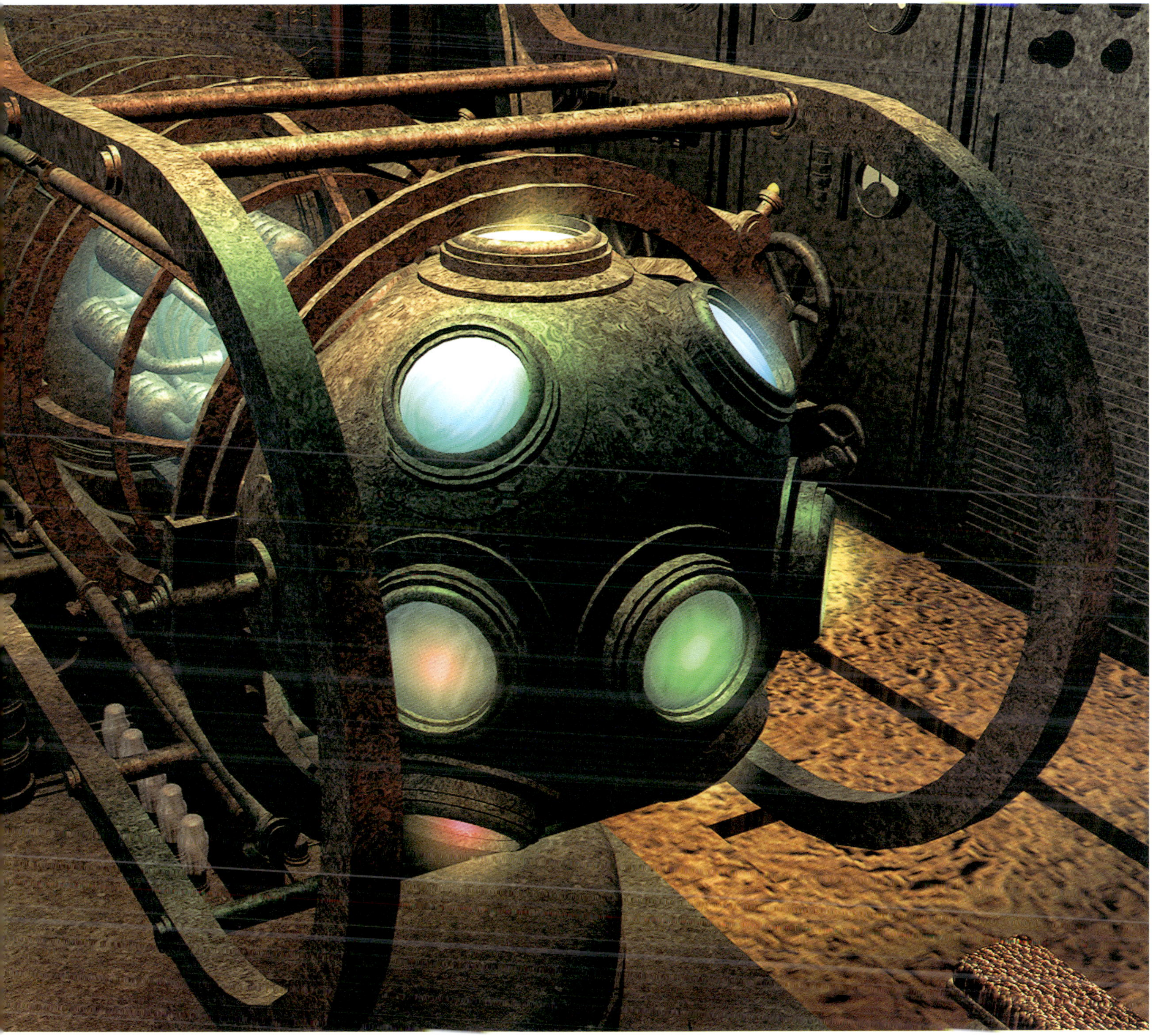

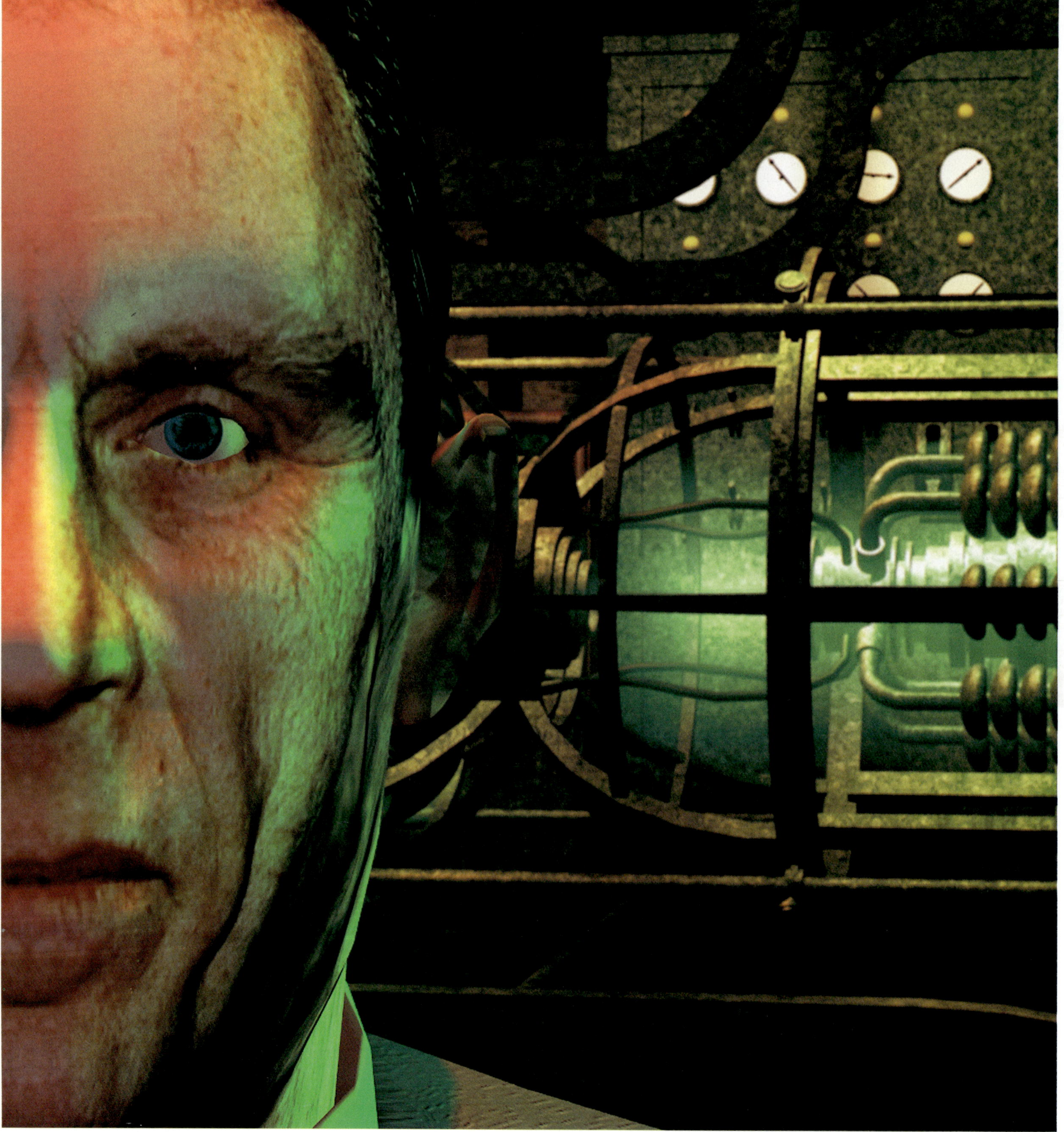

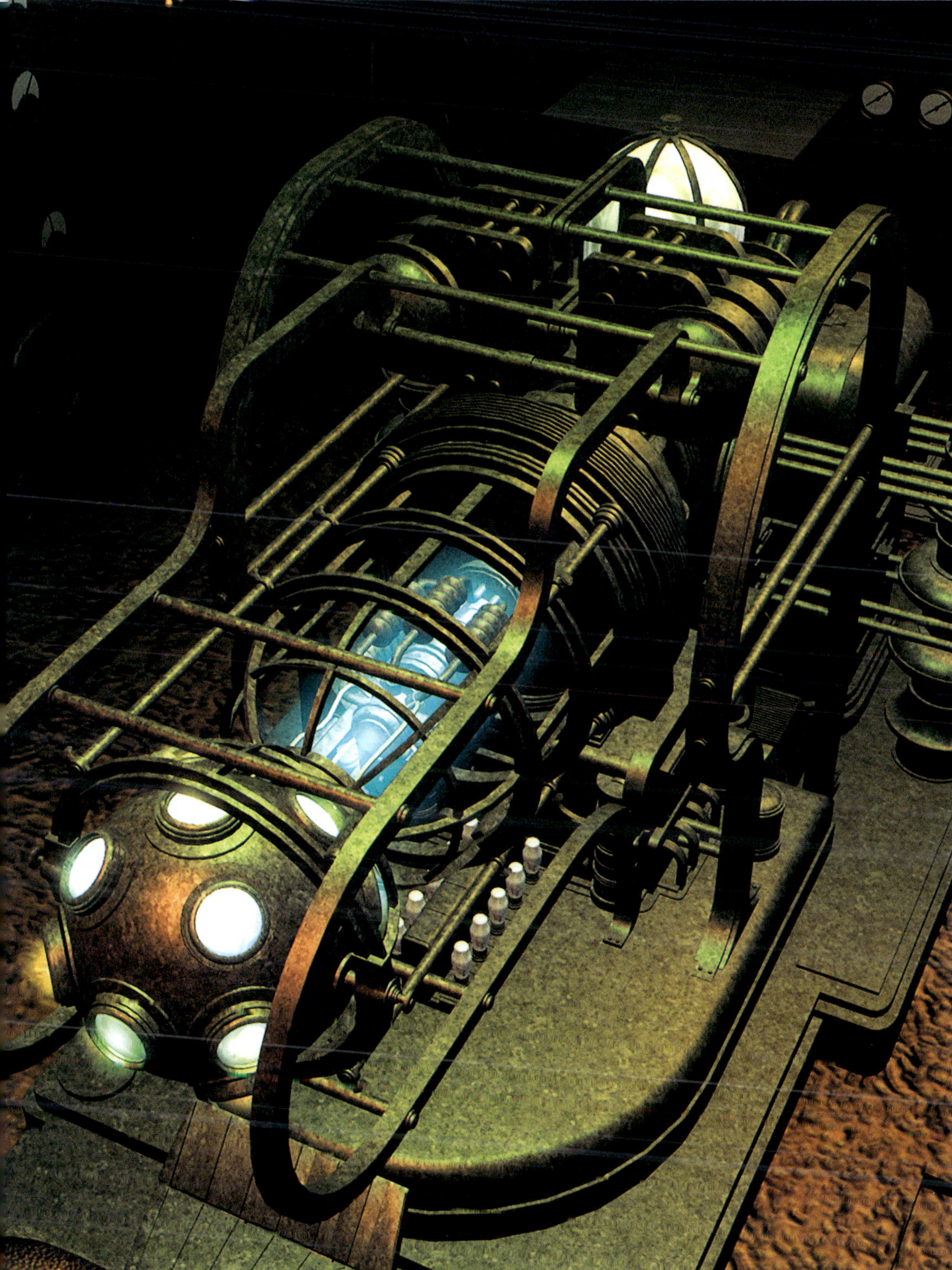

Beam Machine Irradiation Experiment

Site: a laboratory of the National Academy of Science

Research Team: George Tessera
Wilhelm Draun
Charles Reif
Thomas Reich
John MacNaughton
Constantine Wallace

Supervisor of Experiment: Charles Reif

Experimentee: Horselover Frost

Procedure

Upon termination of the radiation experiment George recorded the essentials of Horselover's description.

" Mild vertigo for some 30 seconds. A thin mist settles over my mind. An image of countless drifting clouds. An unfamiliar forest, the green of trees. Scattered pieces of machines and other mechanical gadgets. Rusting pieces of iron. A lightplane abandoned in a shallow pool. A face reflected in the water. A wind blows, wavelets rise, the margins crumble. The surface of the water bends."

Consciousness restored. Duration: 300 seconds.

Conclusions

Following the experiment the research team discussed what inferences could be drawn. Abstracted by Charles.

It is evident—as was not the case with previous radiation experiments—that we have succeeded this time in inducing representational images. It is hypothesized that if the electromagnetic wave frequency that aroused the image of a forest in the testee can be determined, it will then be possible to formulate a basic law.

As a consequence of these findings, it is posited that if we can induce the perception of images through electromagnetic wave radiation, it may also be possible to extract personal memories. For example, if we can determine the precise electromagnetic waves that evoke the image of 'forest,' we can collect individual memories related to forests—even fragments of memories that the testee himself is unable to recall. We must proceed with radiation experimentation and assemble a corpus of documentation relating to memory.

It is presumed that restrictions limiting duration of beam emission will become an issue of subsequent radiation experimentation. The problem is we don't have a power source capable of satisfying the Beam Machine's radical load demands. Electrical power alone is insufficient to sustain the motor's energy requirements. The testee's return to consciousness is a direct result of diminishing beam output.

(From Academy documents—entered on a day 18 years before the End)

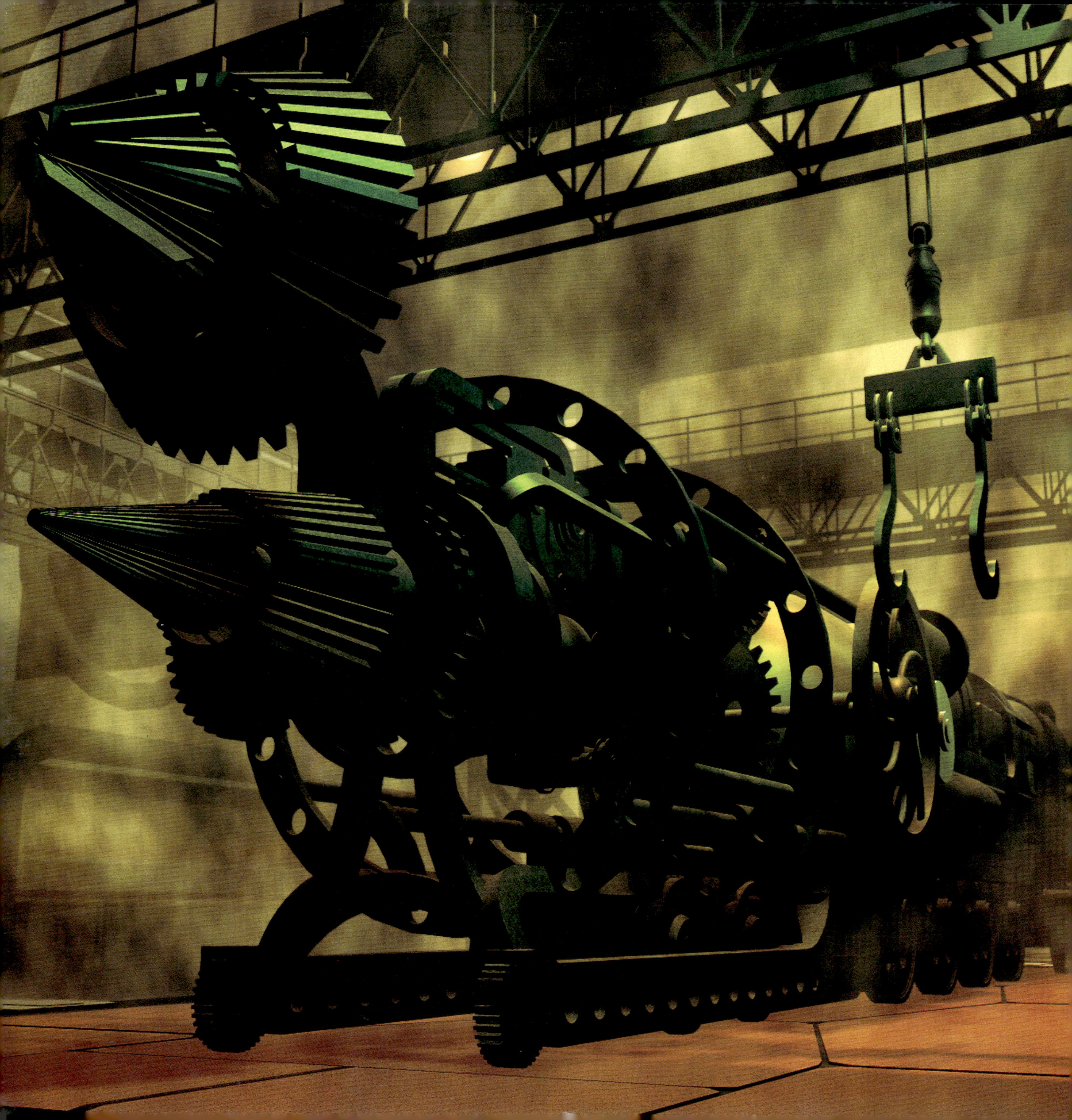

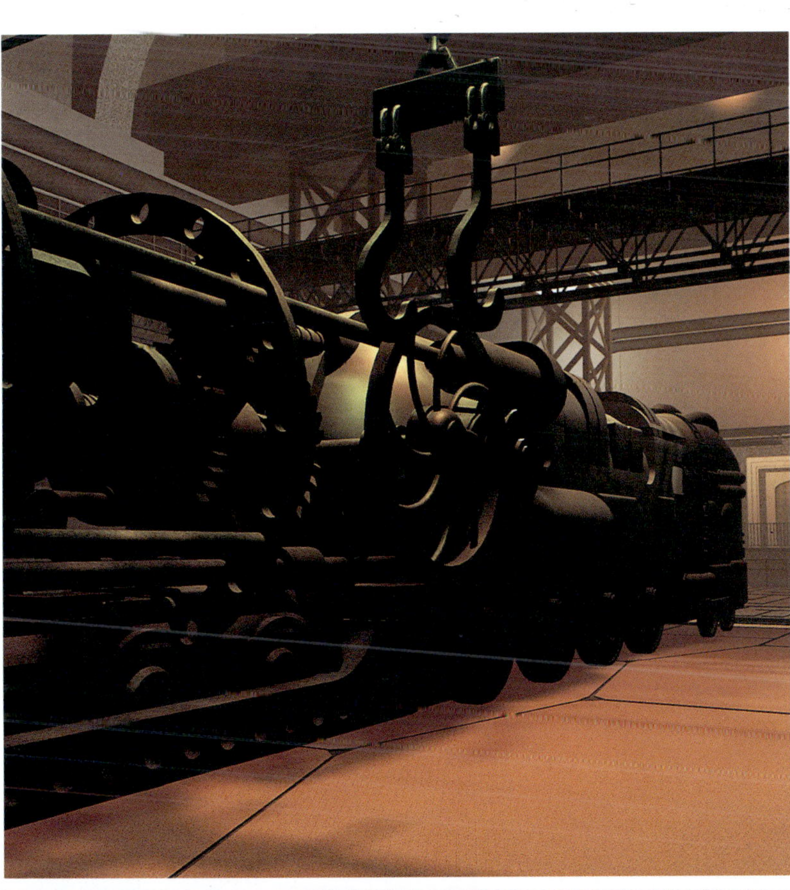

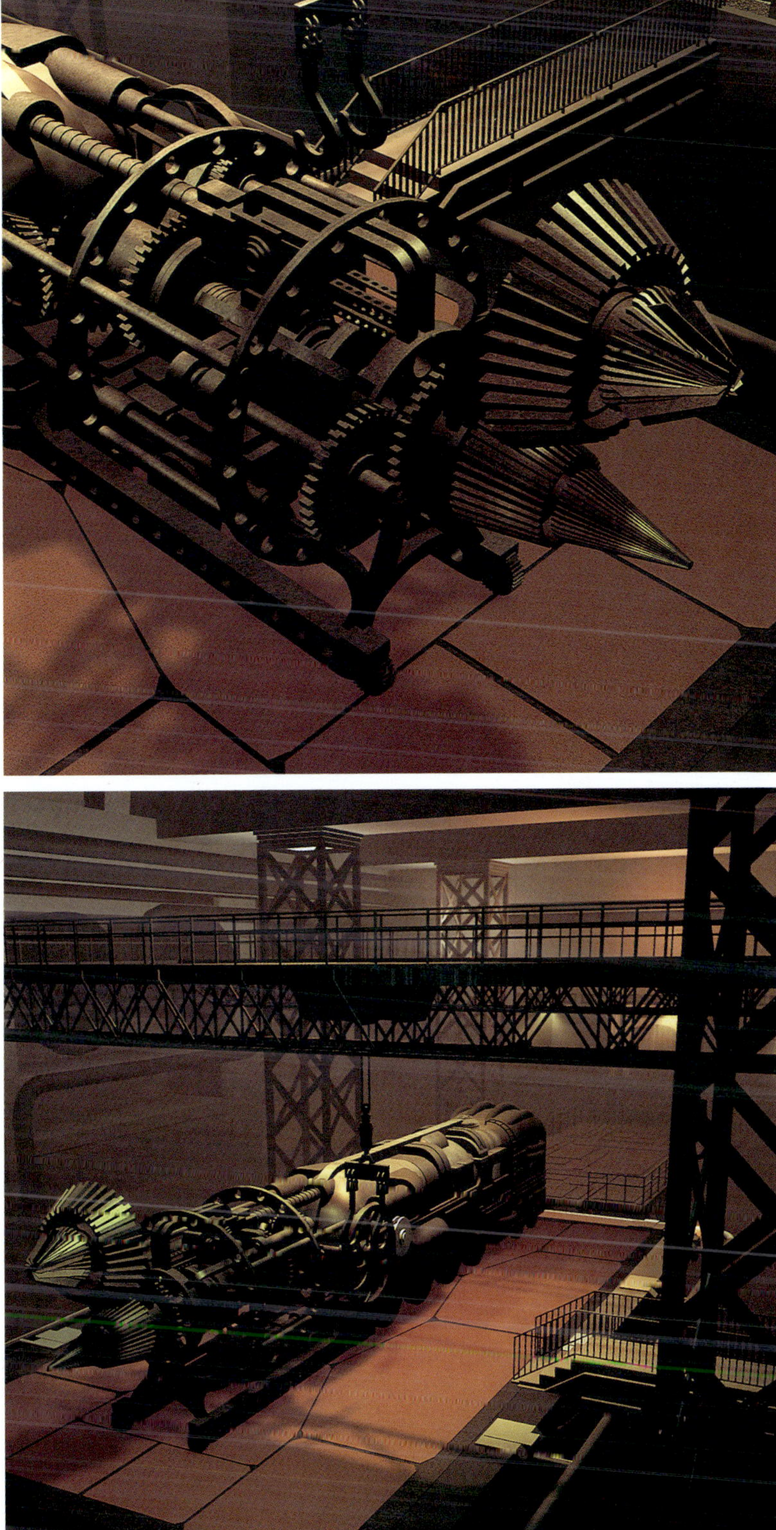

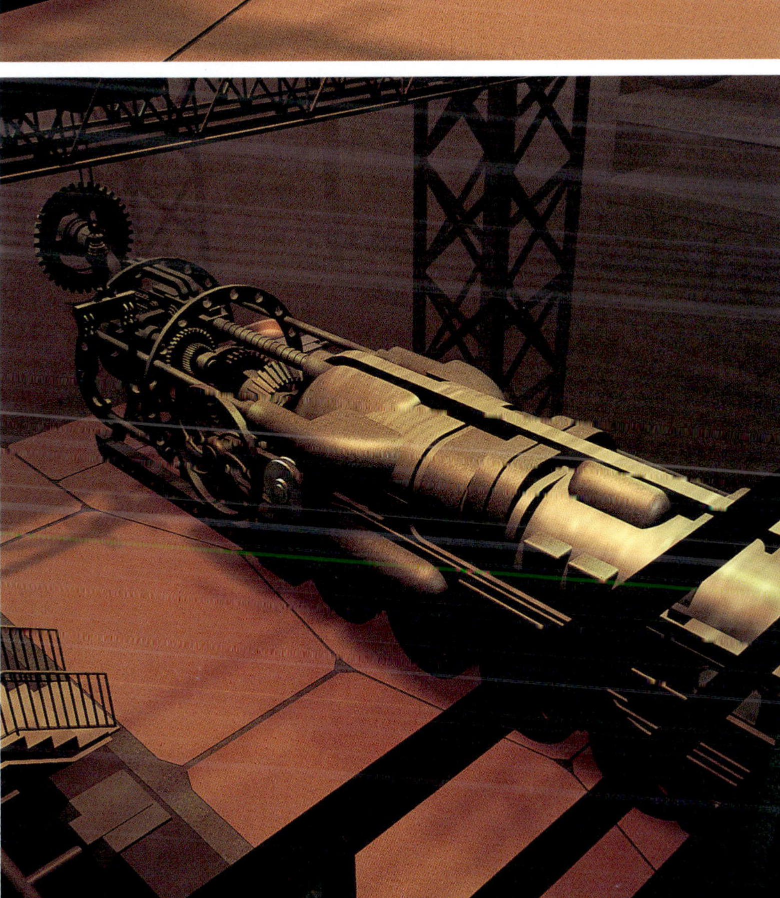

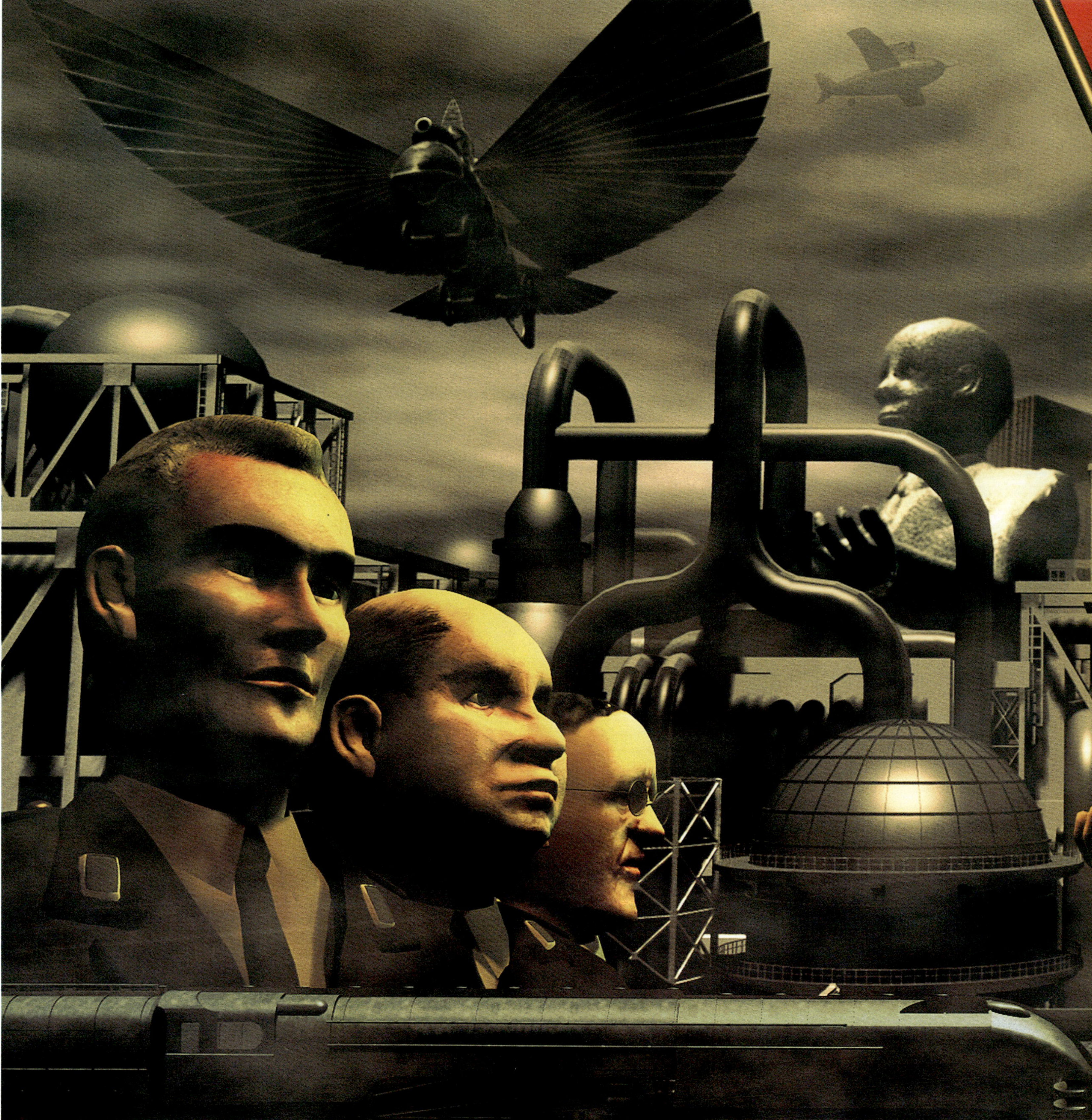

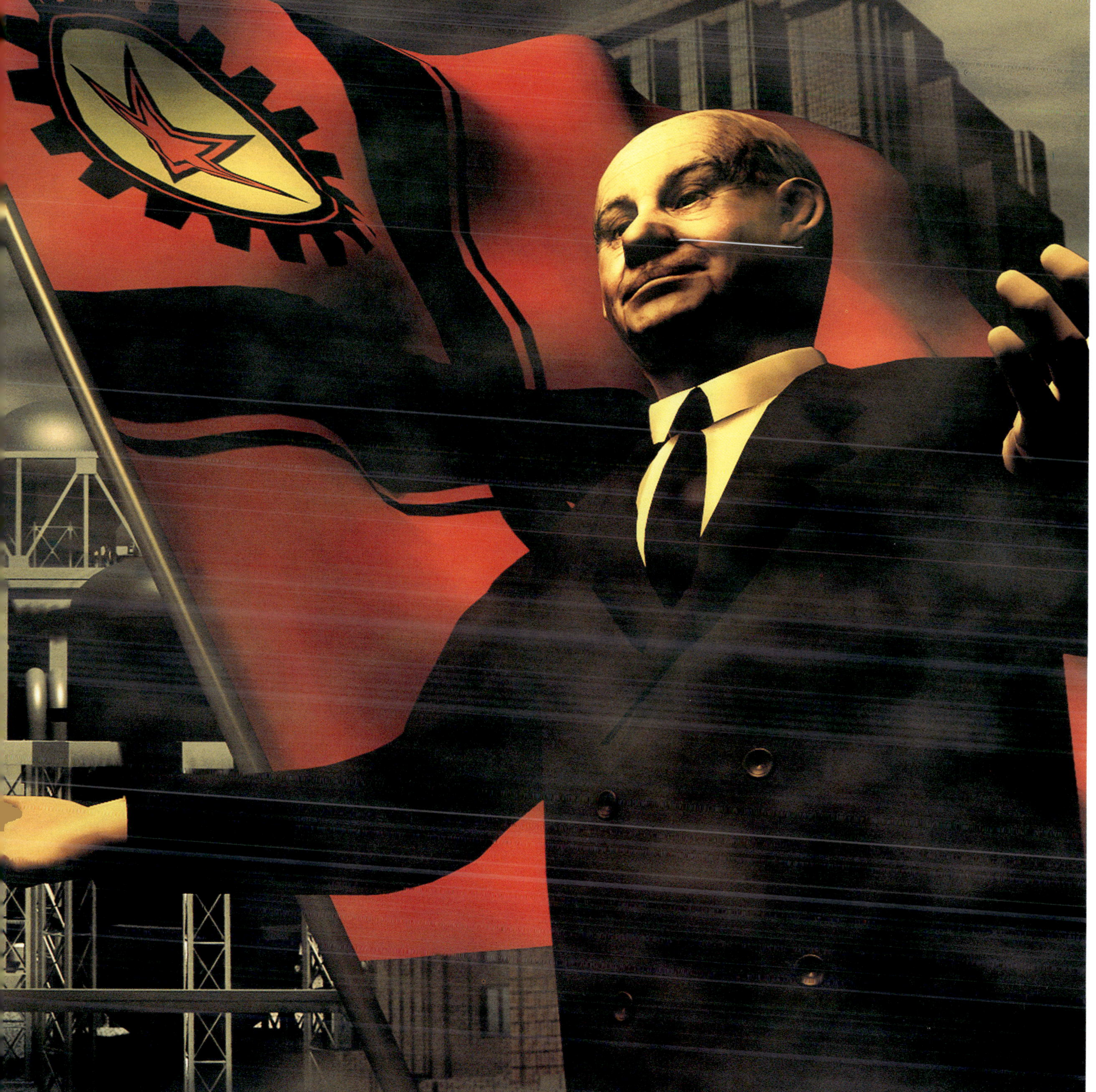

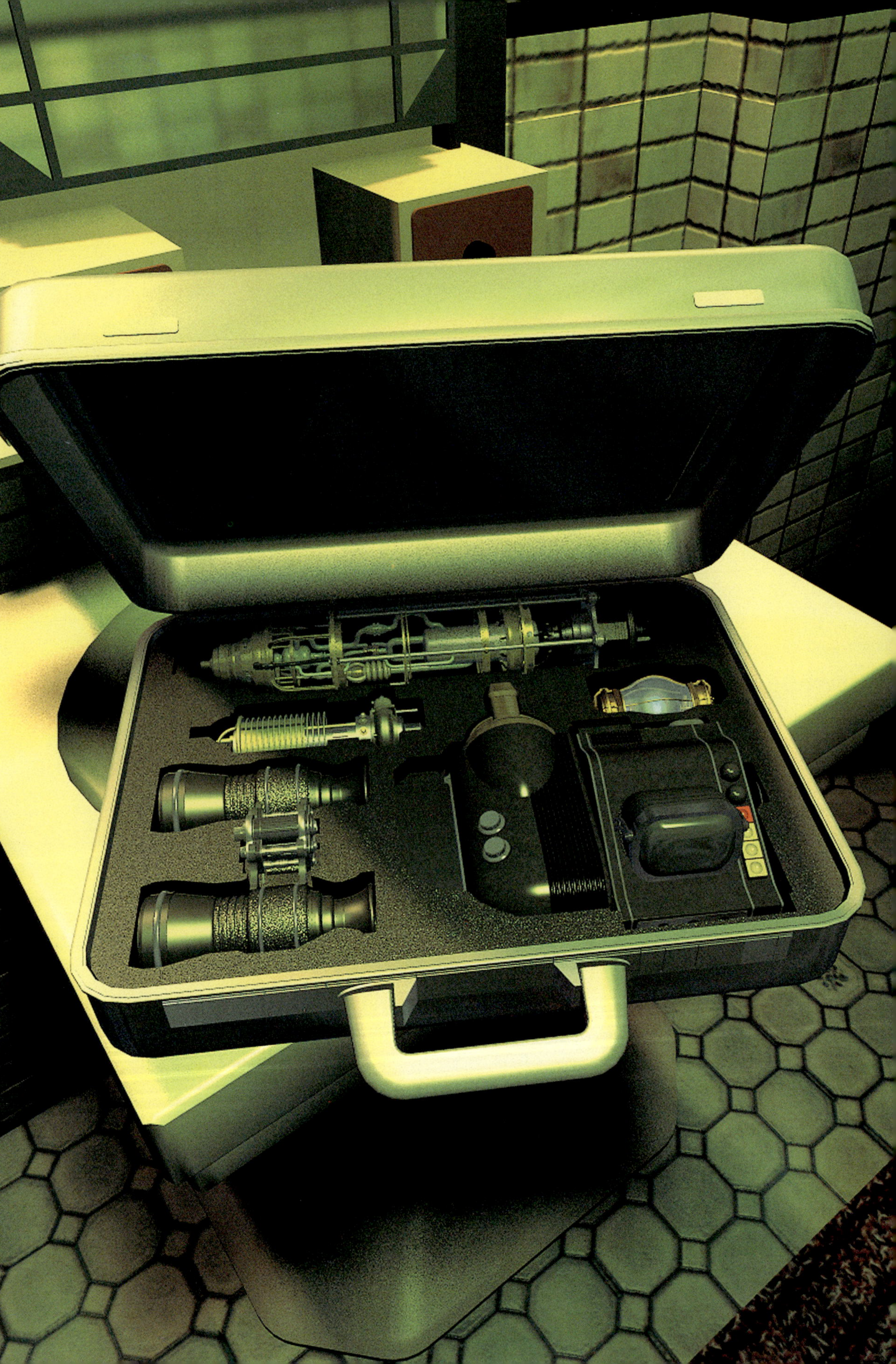

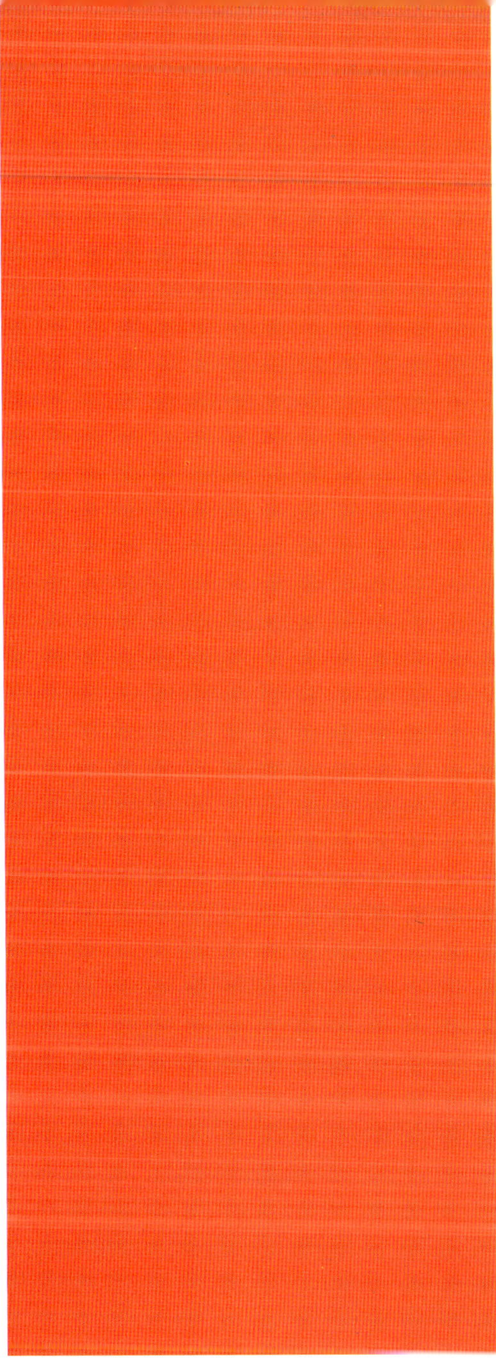

Resounding roar of cheers
A time for iron and arms
The Dictator and the Leader of the Party
Those who must stay and those who won't return
The flags of two nations sway
Likeminded scientists
Analysis and solution
Lead-gray stones rain down on earth
Research, experiment, development: one leads to the next

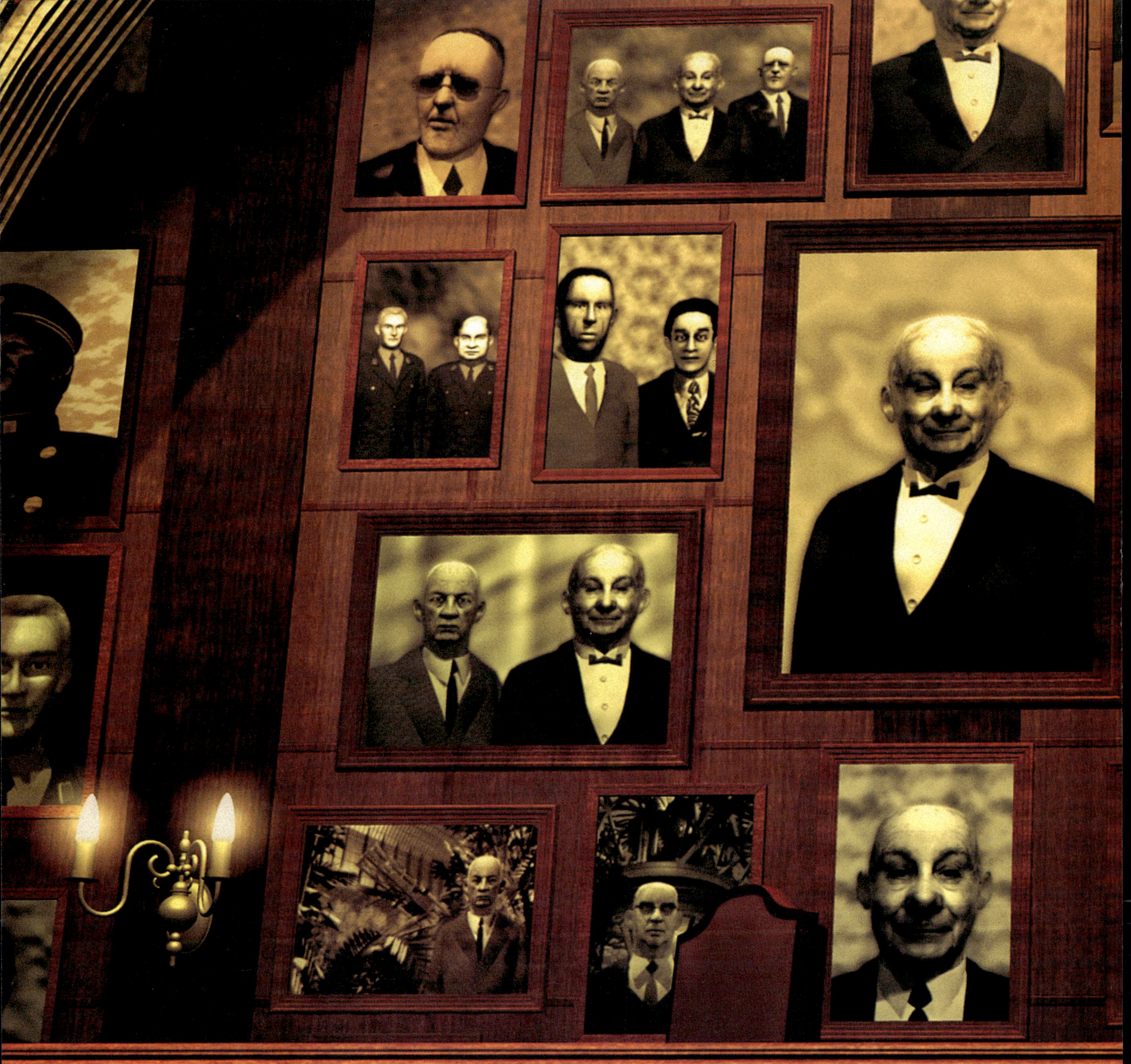

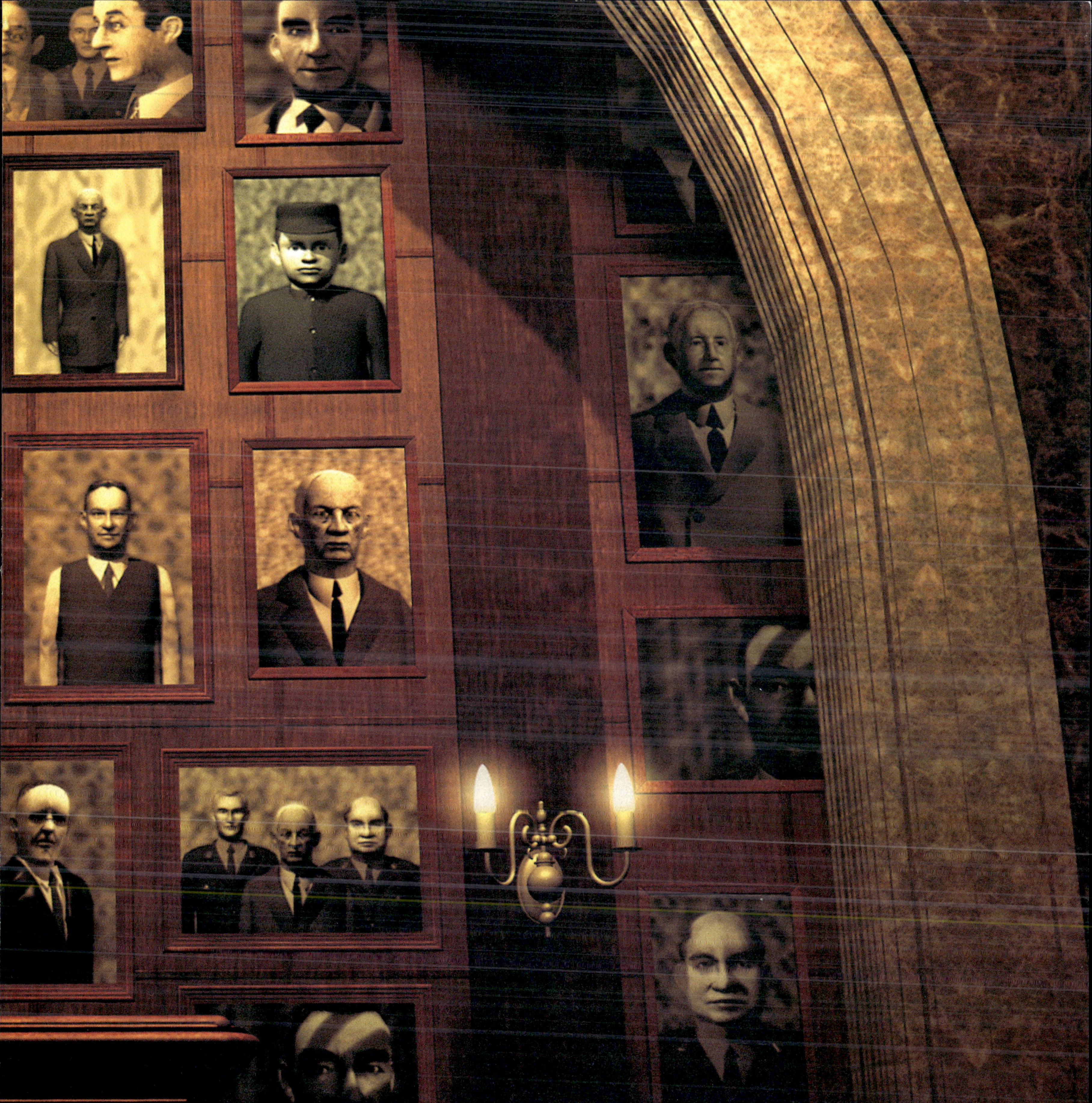

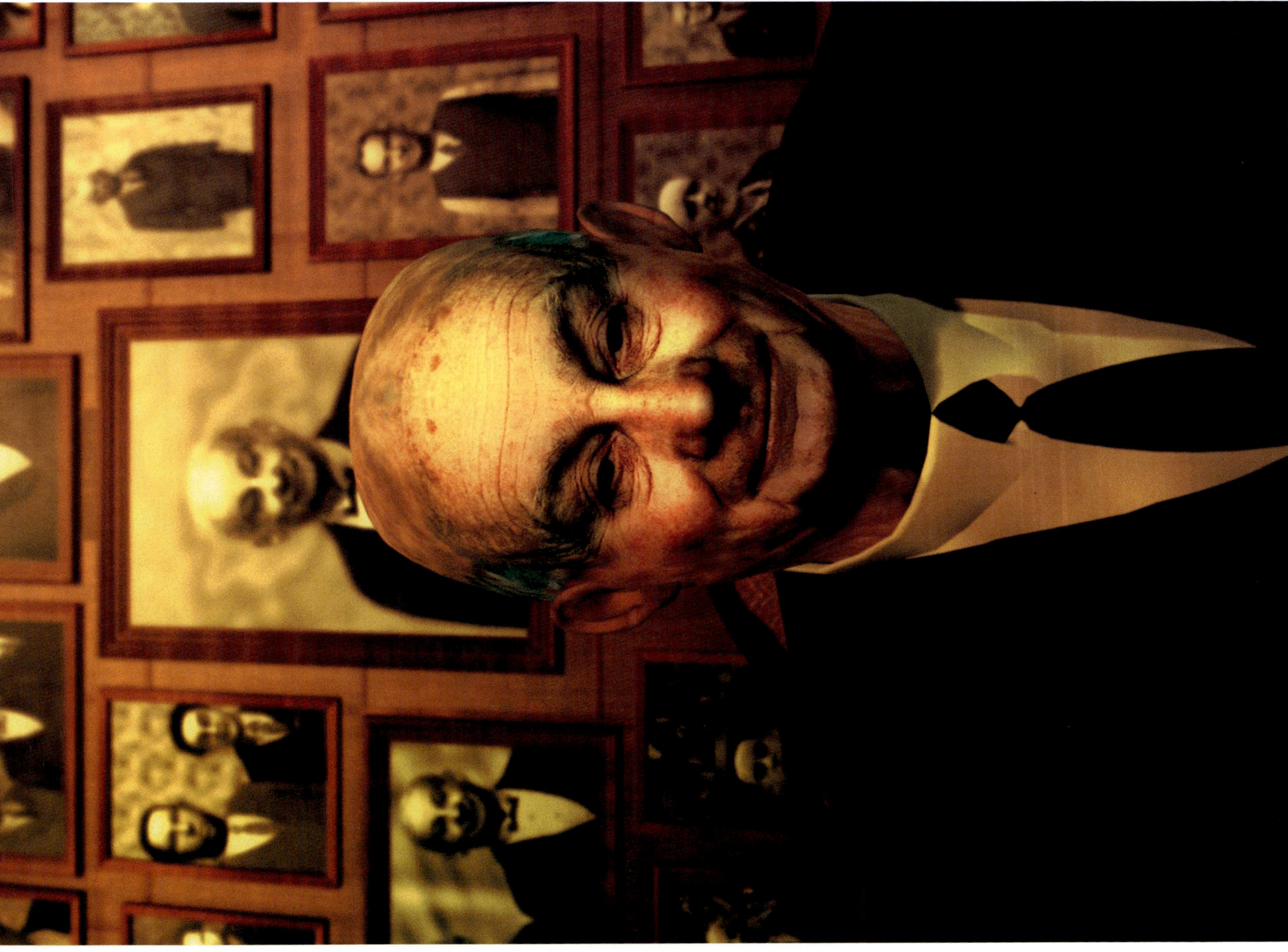

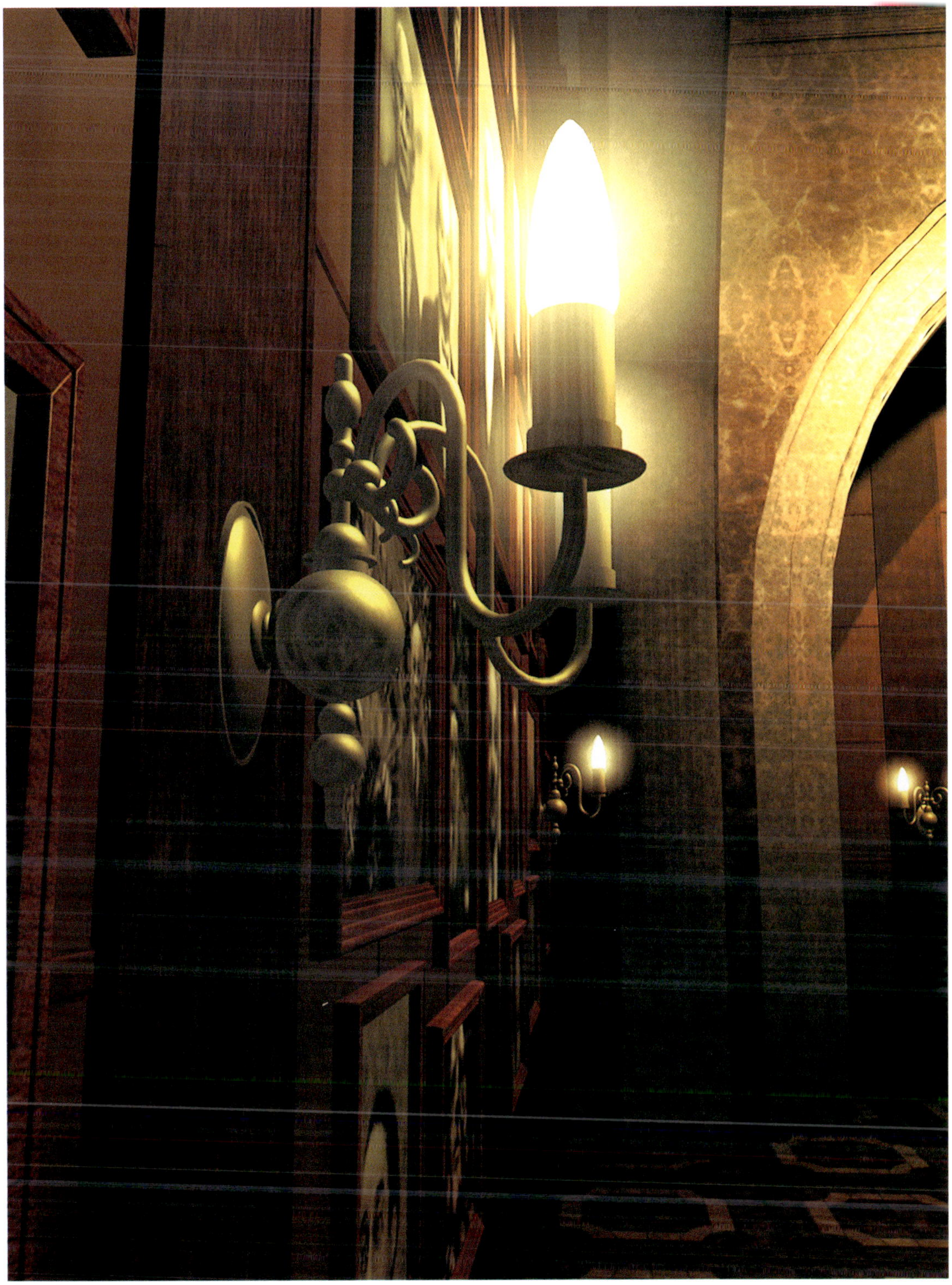

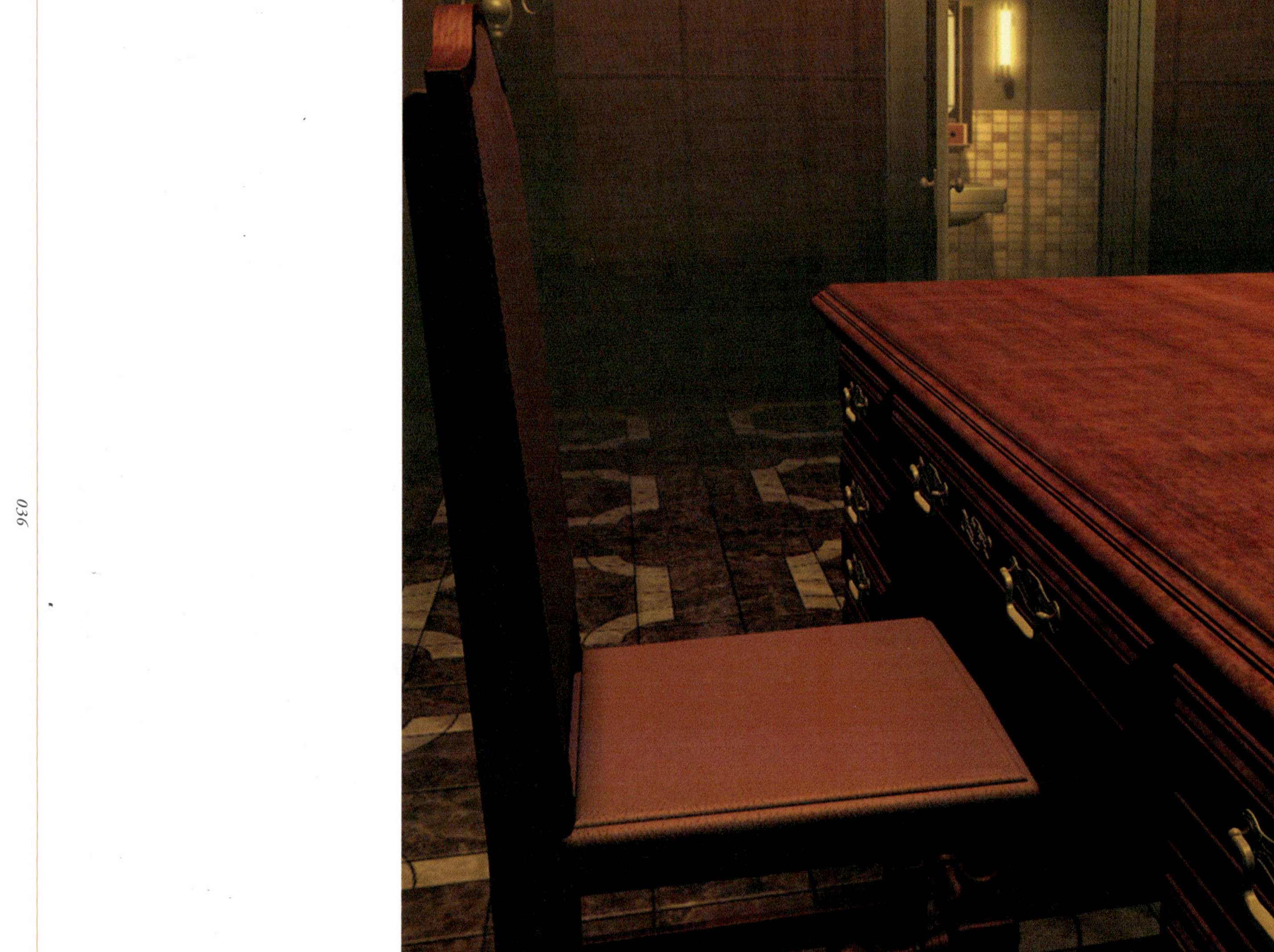

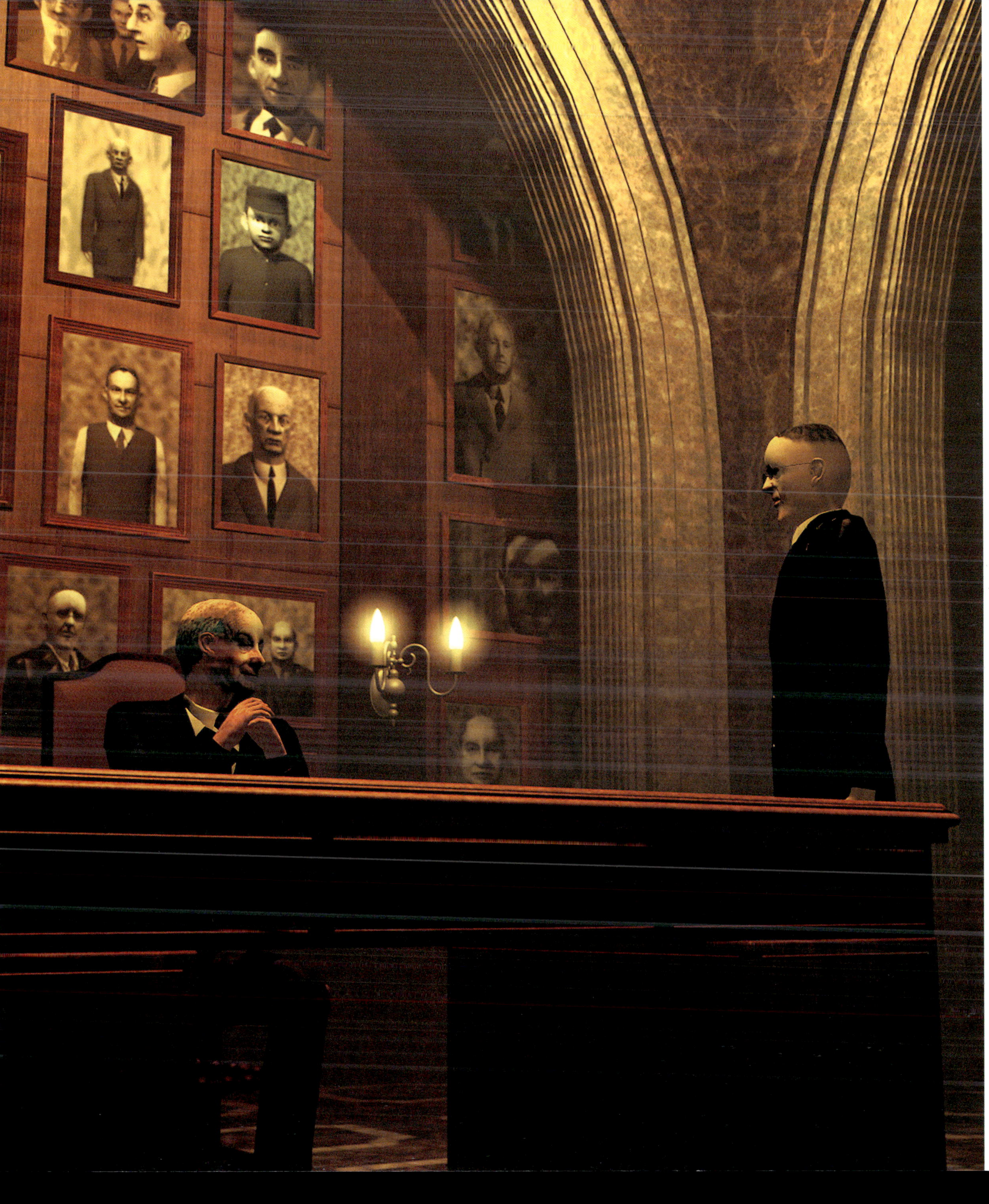

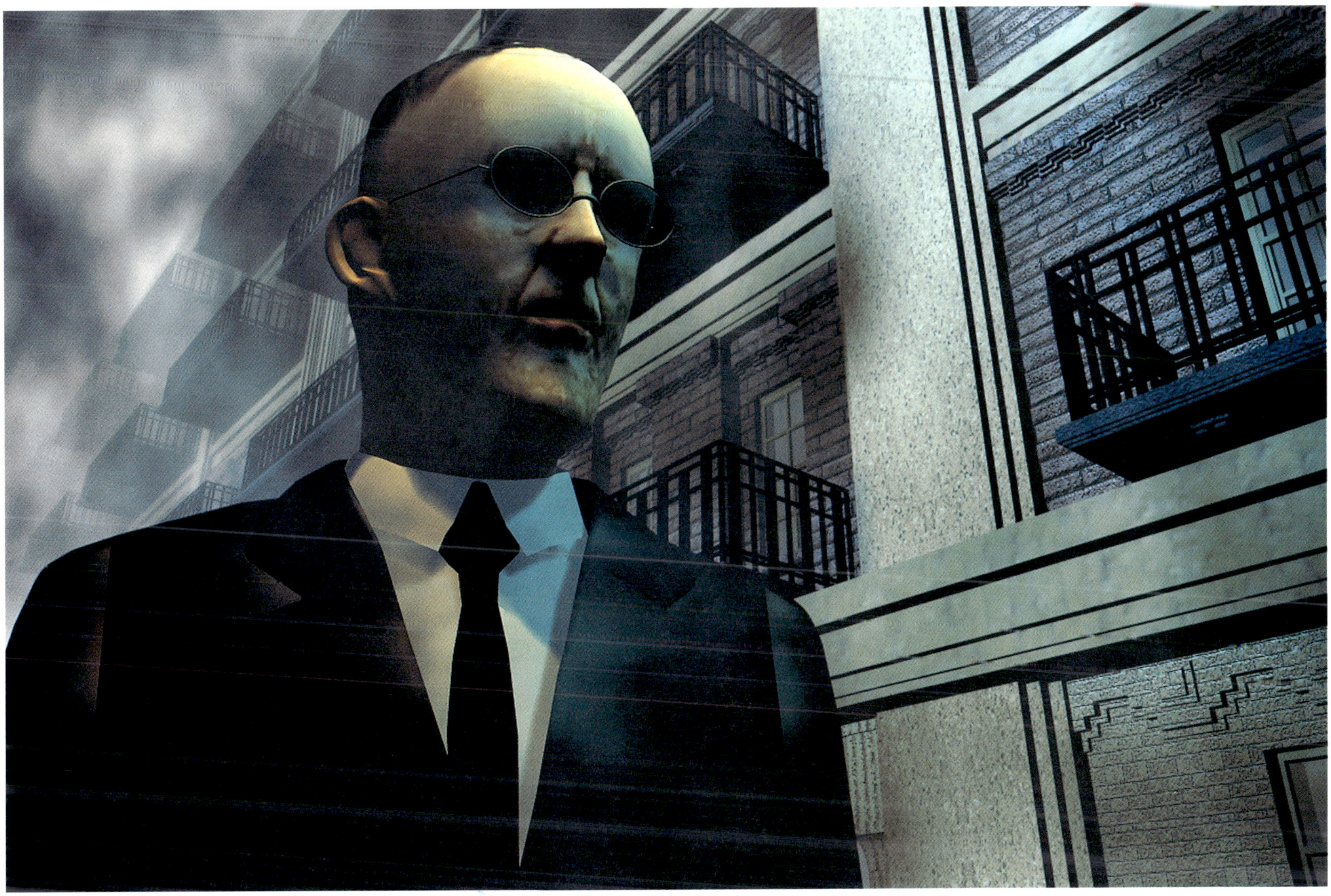

Years 1 and 2 of the Imperial Age

Resounding roar of cheers

Revolution succeeds. Dictatorship established. Orlovsky stands in West End Square. His voice on the loudspeaker reverberates in the Square. The Imperial colors raised. Anthem chorused. A call for military expansion. Waves of applause, ringing cries of support.

A time for iron and arms

Orlovsky's foreign policy posits armed conflict with the Republic. Resumption of military conscription. Development of an ultimate weapon. Natural resources stockpiled. Railway laid for Army use. Supreme Commander of the Army Slowslop builds arms factories.

The Dictator and the Leader of the Party

Party Chairman Onegin awaits Orlovsky's move. A directive issued to intelligence agent Gondarev: orders to infiltrate the Imperial Guards. Communication maintained by radio and written report. Time is ripe for gathering in the state secrets of the new Empire.

Those who must stay and those who won't return

Lofty Command Tower of the Republic. A huge receiver activated. Information is collected by monitoring Imperial transmissions. Onegin awaits events. A mingling of light and shadow. Attack or defend. A compulsion to power or a premonition of doomsday.

The flags of two nations sway

Grand Central Railway runs the full length of the new Empire. Army Intelligence agent Hausmann heads for the former West End Hotel, where Supreme Commander Slowslop awaits him. Abetment follows appeasement. One man's order is another man's mission.

Likeminded scientists

Meteors shower down upon Imperial soil. An abandoned mine, entrance forbidden. George and Wilhelm sent to investigate. A disused crane. Rusting iron machinery. Ground subsidence. Light is radiated; it scatters in shimmering whorls and shafts.

Analysis and solution

In the suburbs of East End stands a temporary research lab. Repeated experiments in electromagnetic radiation conducted by George and Wilhelm. Laser beam trained. Frequency adjusted. Structure analyzed. A mystery substance. Report submitted.

Lead-gray stones rain down on earth

Abandoned iron-ore mine. Disused heavy equipment. A rusty barrow on rails. The mine tunnel has settled into quiet ruin. But now plans for restoration. Slowslop takes charge of things. Thomas is set to the construction of an all-purpose excavator.

Research, experiment, development: one leads to the next

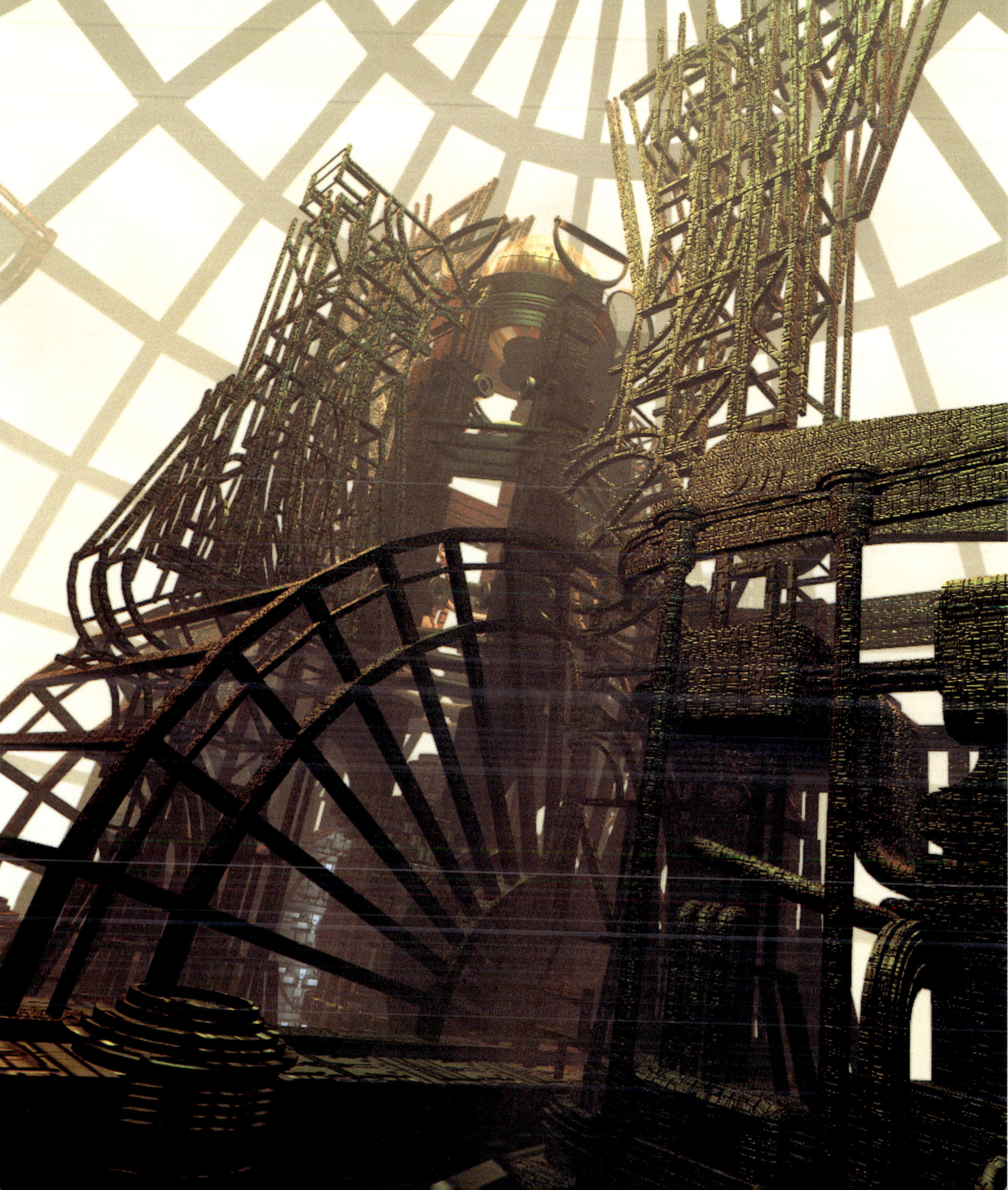

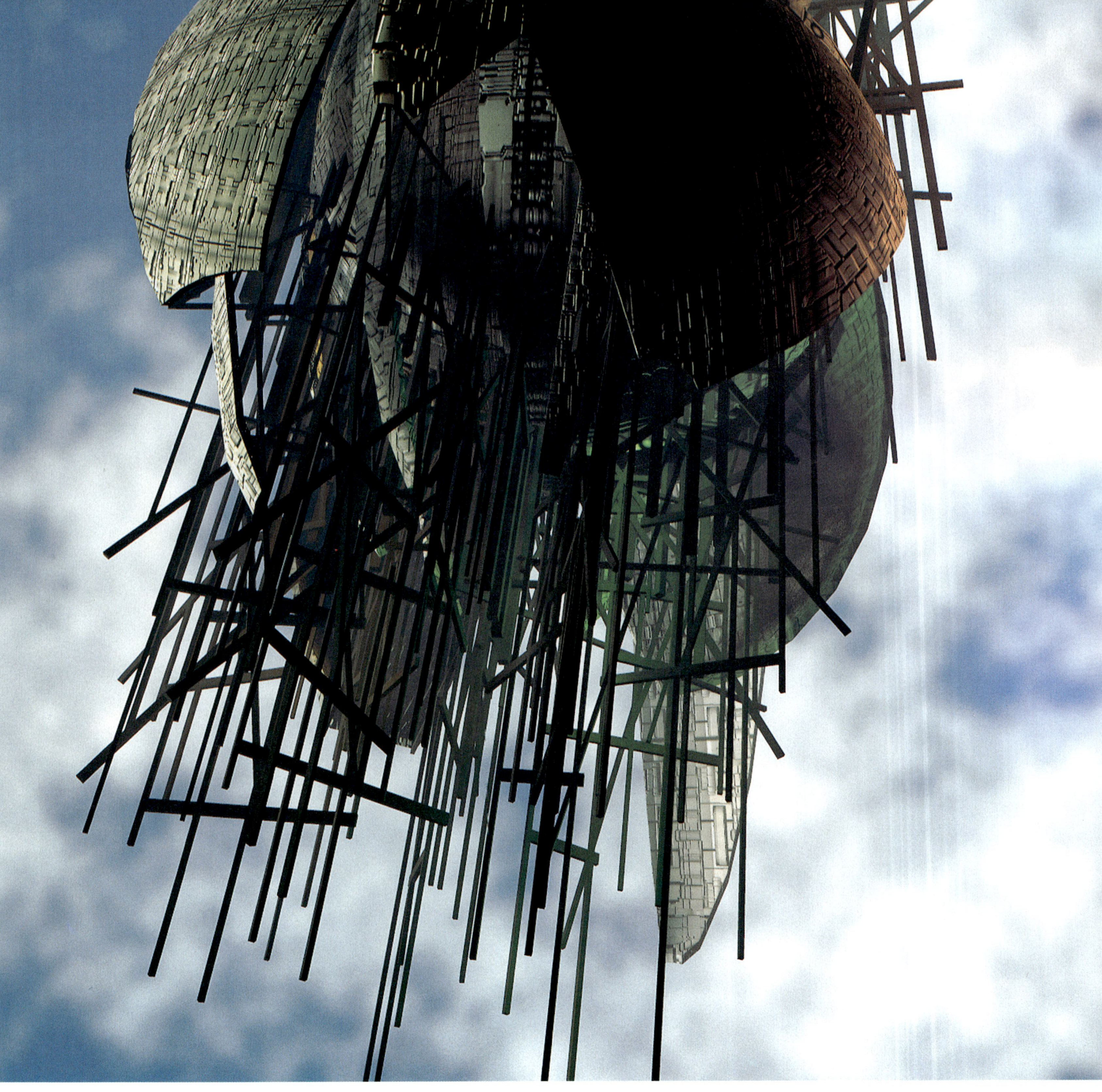

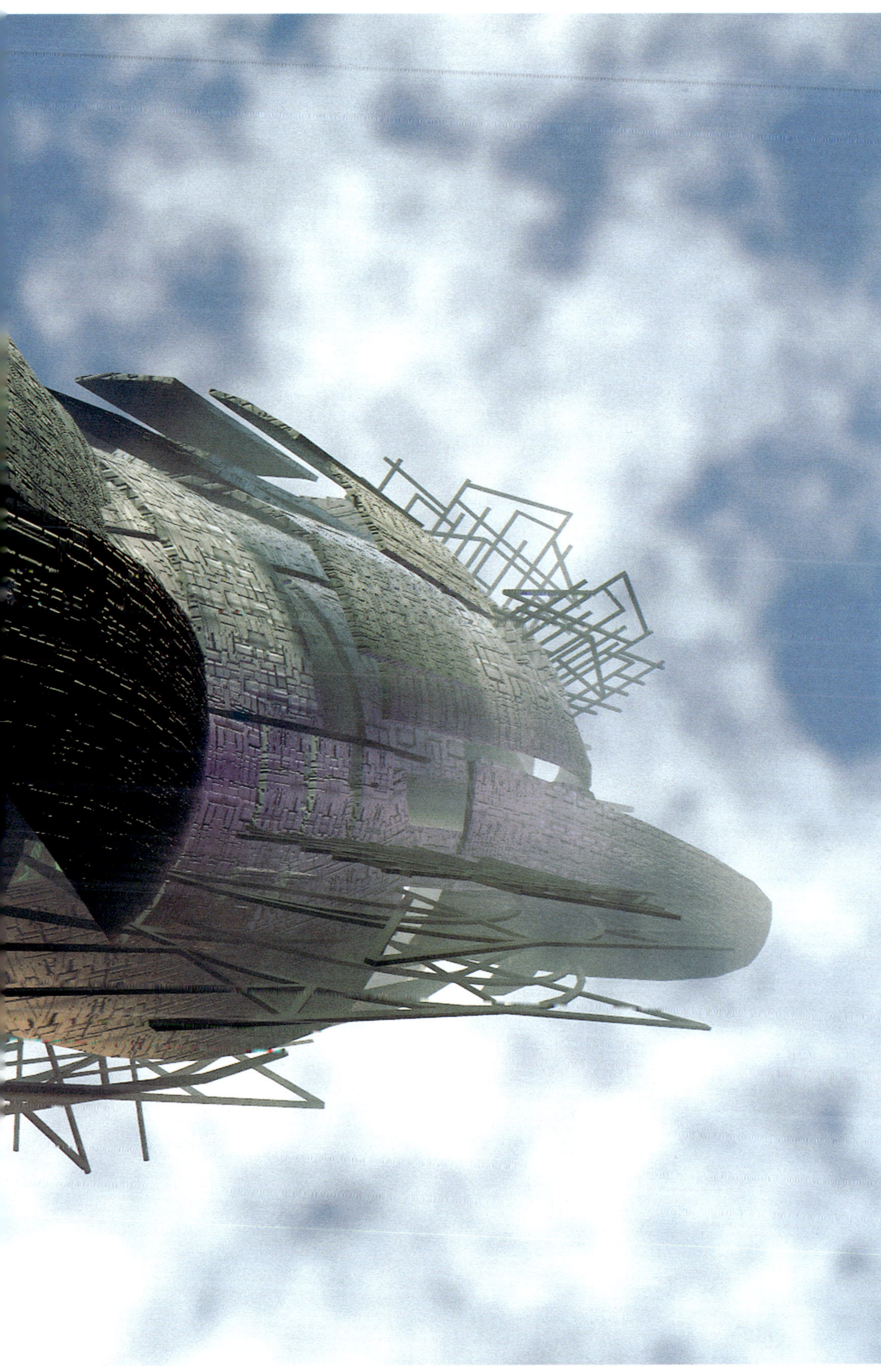

There is a knock on the office door. Onegin sits in an outsized chair with his back to the far wall. Gondarev, director of the Socialist-Republican Party's Intelligence Office awaits permission to enter.

— Come in!
— If I may.
— You've read my directive, have you?
— Yes, sir, I have.
— And what do you think.
— ....
— Come now! You can be frank with me. Your mission will have a decisive influence on the future of our Party and on the nation as a whole.
— I am aware of that.
— In the very near future the Socialist-Republican Party will take the reins of government into its hands.
— Inevitable, I'm sure.
— The problem is the new Empire. Orlovsky's policy of military expansion threatens the present delicate balance of power.
— ....
— The worst-case scenario would conclude with the opening of hostilities. Intelligence operations inside the Empire are indispensable to an accurate reading of future developments.
— ....
— Several members of your organization have already infiltrated the Empire.
— Yes.
— Use them to help you burrow into Imperial Army Headquarters. The paperwork has already been prepared.
— Very well, sir.
— I expect results.

(Conversation between Onegin and Gondarev on 14 August, Year 1 of the Imperial Age)

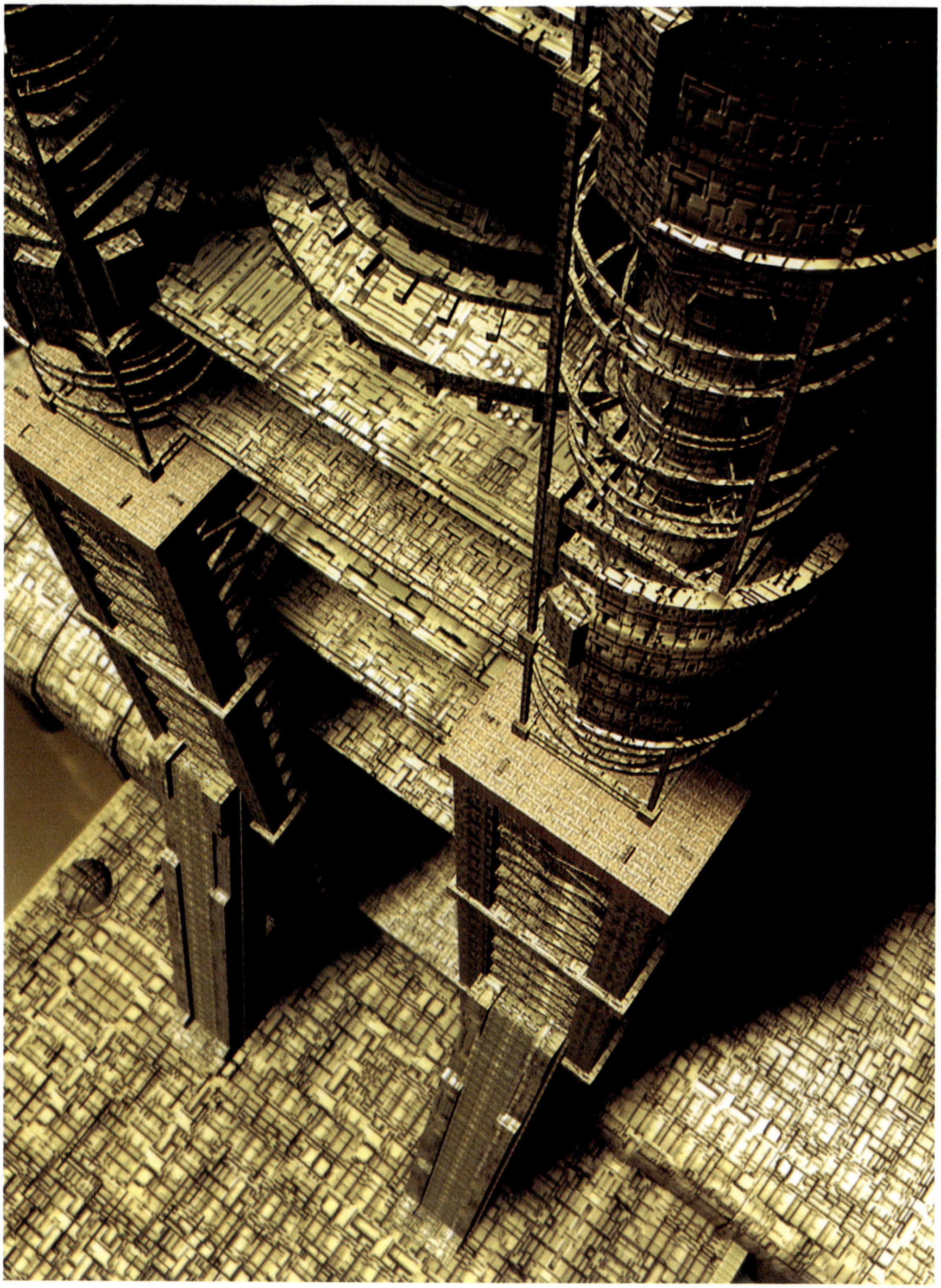

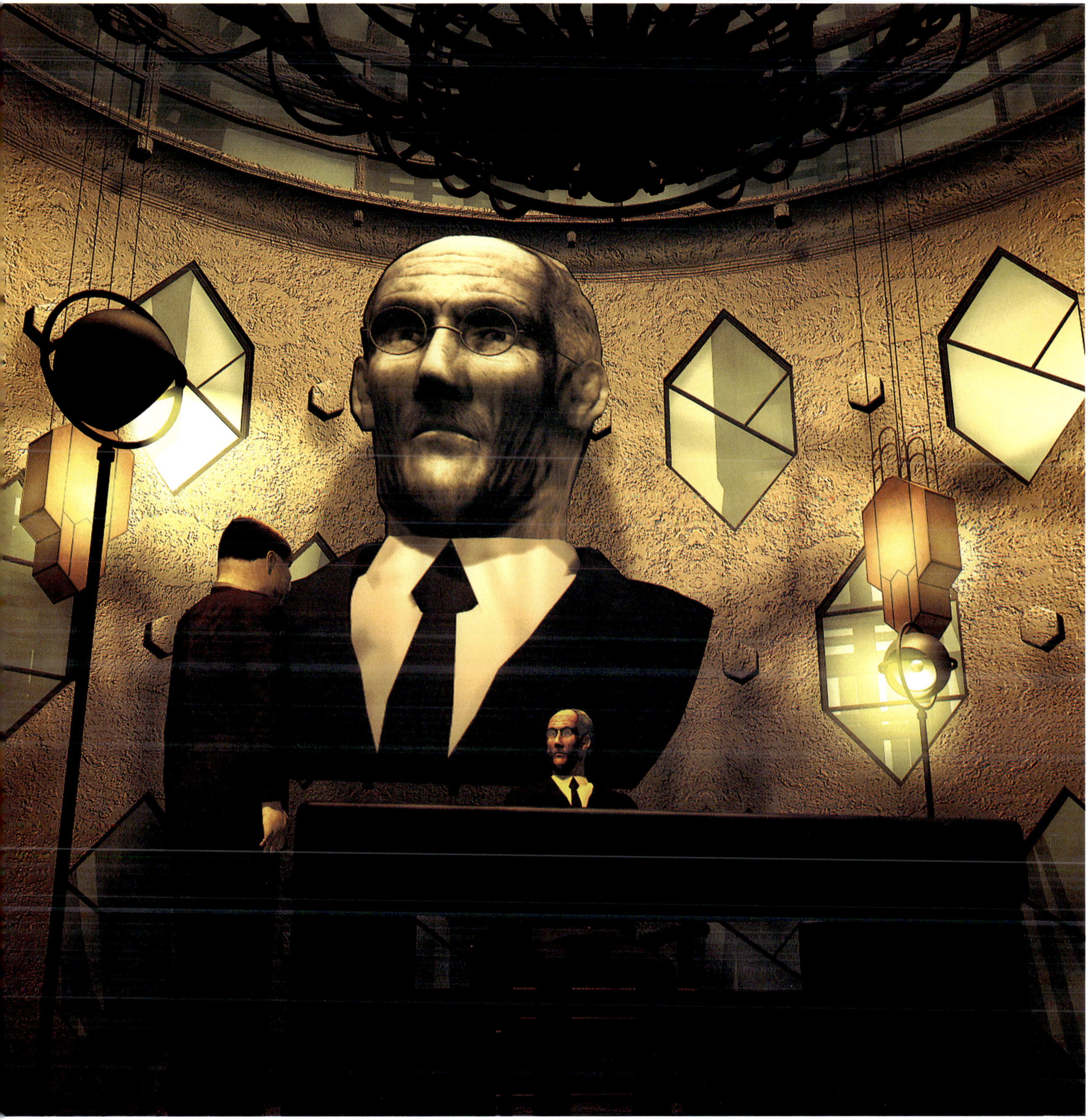

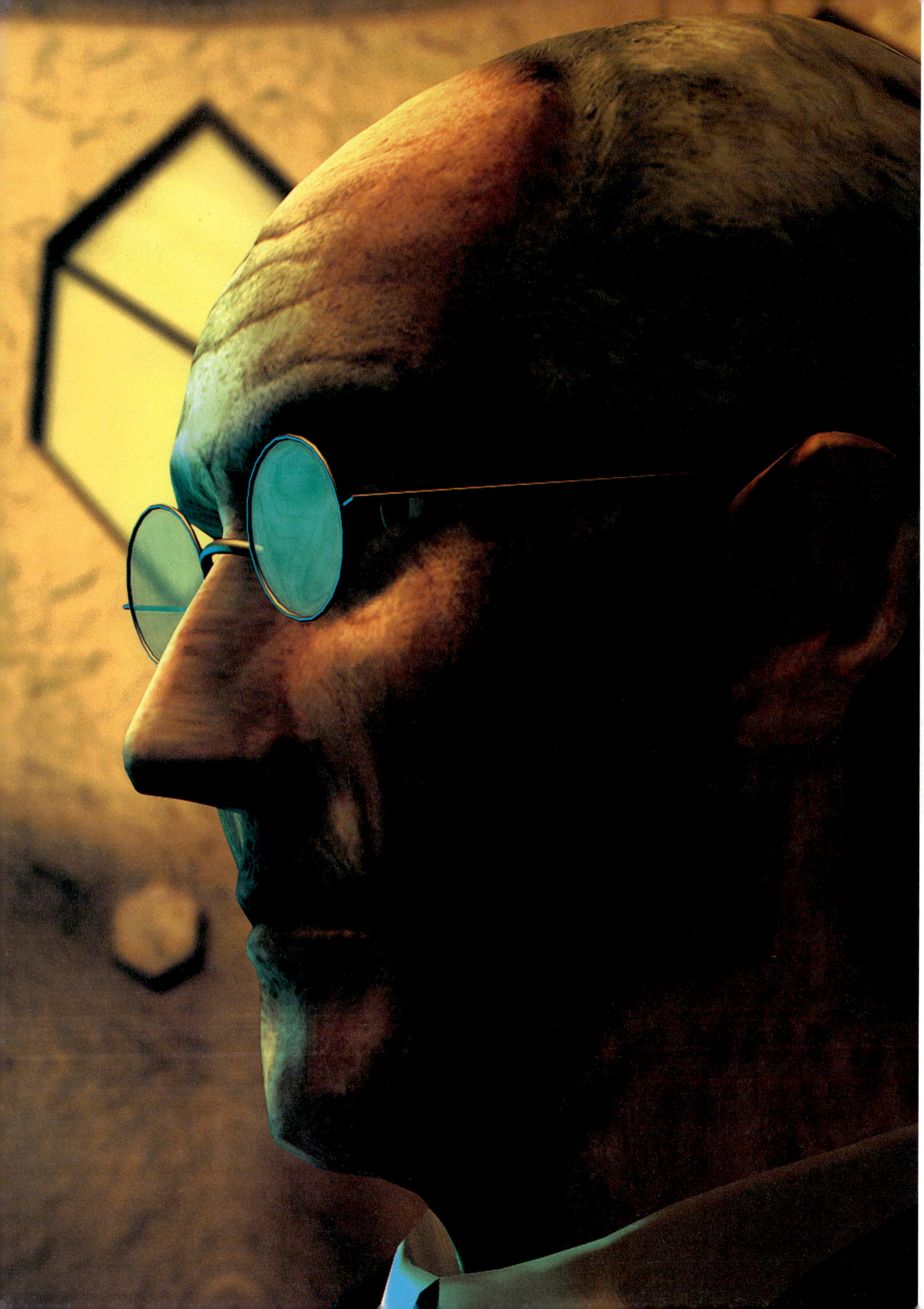

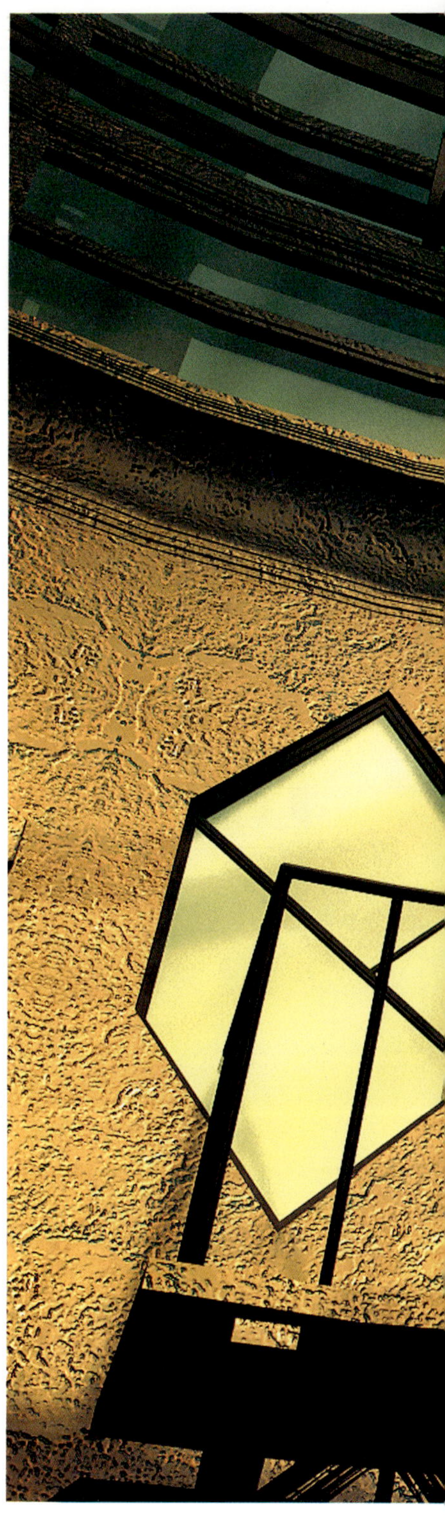

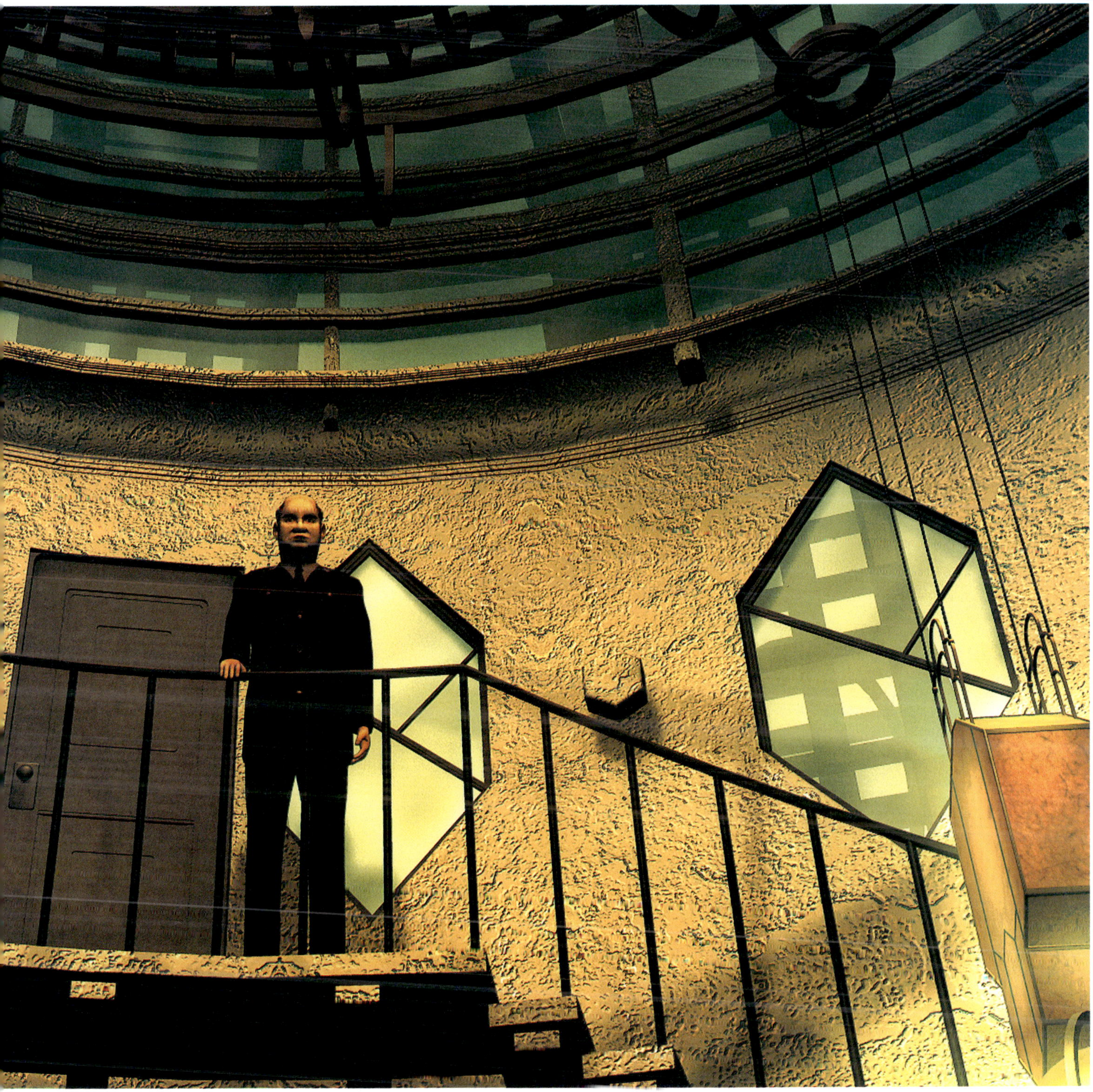

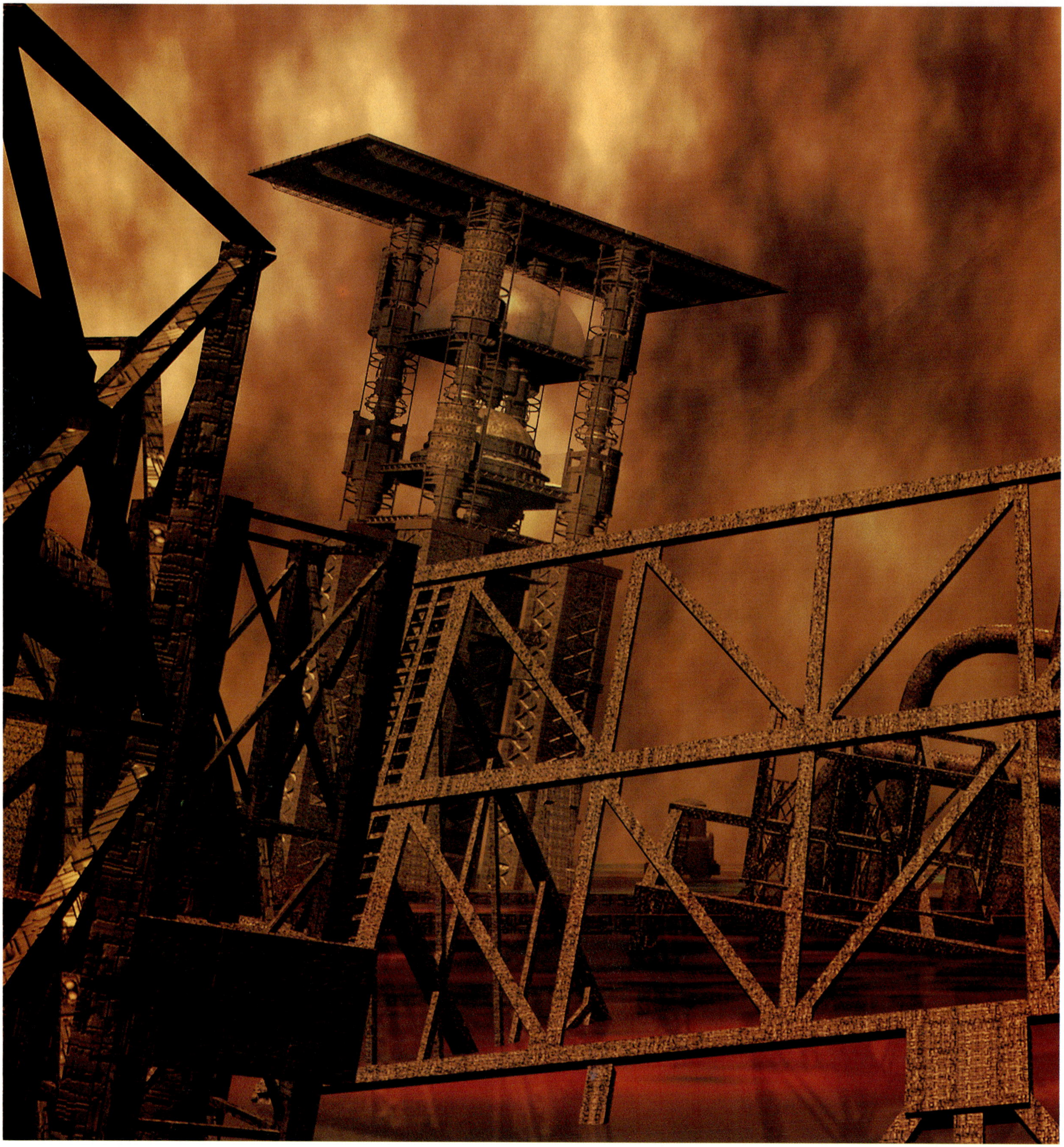

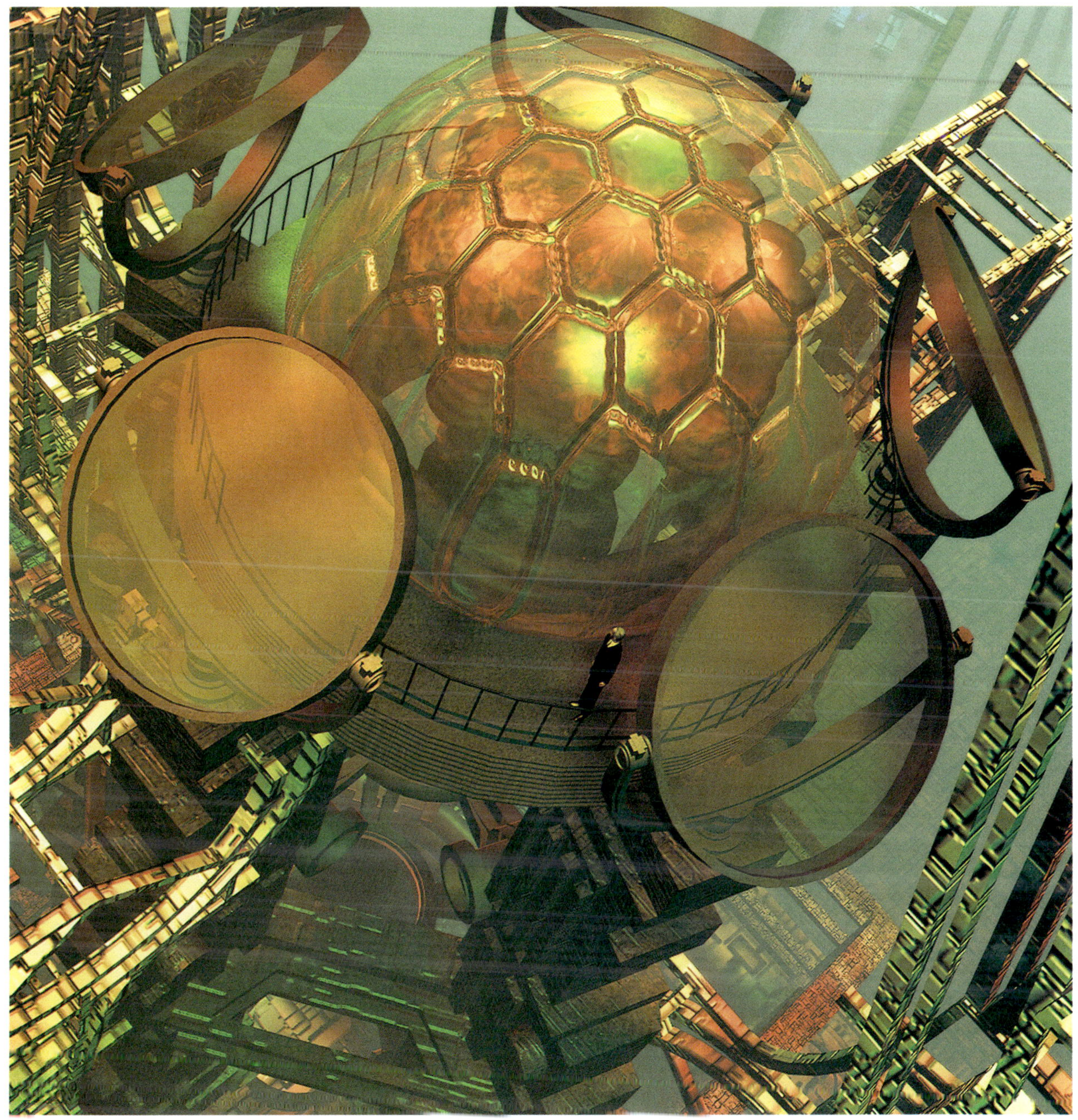

In an underground office at Imperial Army Intelligence Headquarters Slowslop reports to Orlovsky, who is seated in a chair.

— My Lord, I have something of signal importance to show you.
— ....
— You recall the shower of meteors that fell in the area of the old mine.
— ....
— I've asked two scientists who used to be with the academy to analyze the composition of the meteors. This is their report.
— Found some new substance?
— They've extracted what they call 'lumps of thermal energy.'
— Is there a potential for energy conversion?
— They insist that energy is emitted with no decrease in mass. In essence, the substance is a storable energy resource of apparently inexhaustible potency.
— Mind-boggling, to be sure.
— Shall I have them report to you, My Lord?
— No need. Get me the results of a detailed analysis as fast as you can.
— Yes, My Lord. Is there anything else?
— Get a lock on those meteors. There's an old mine in the restricted area, right?
— ....
— Use a mechanical excavator and dig out every last one of those beggars.
— I understand.
— And keep the matter under wraps.
— Yes, My Lord.

(Conversation between Orlovsky and Slowslop on 23 November, Year 1 of the Imperial Age)

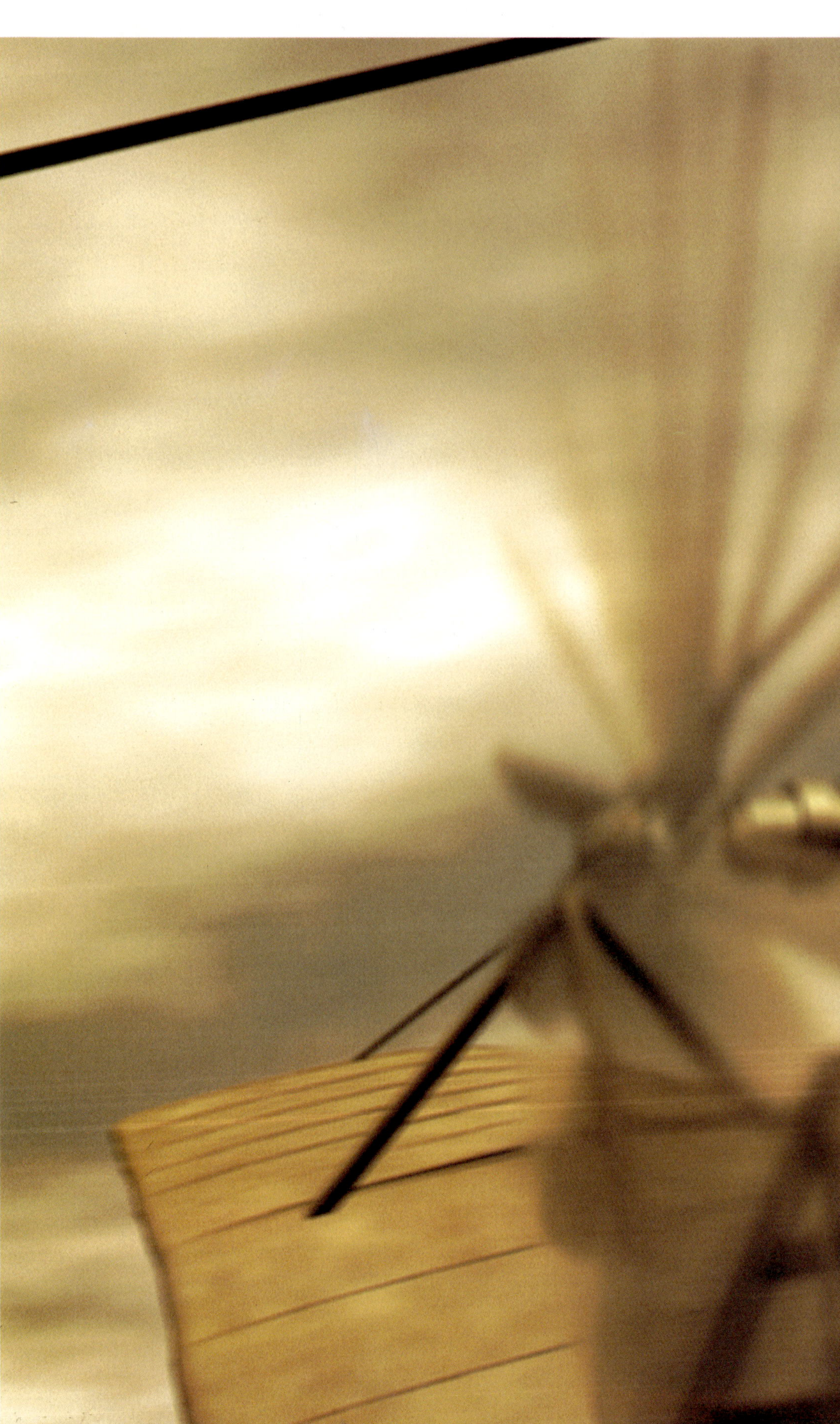

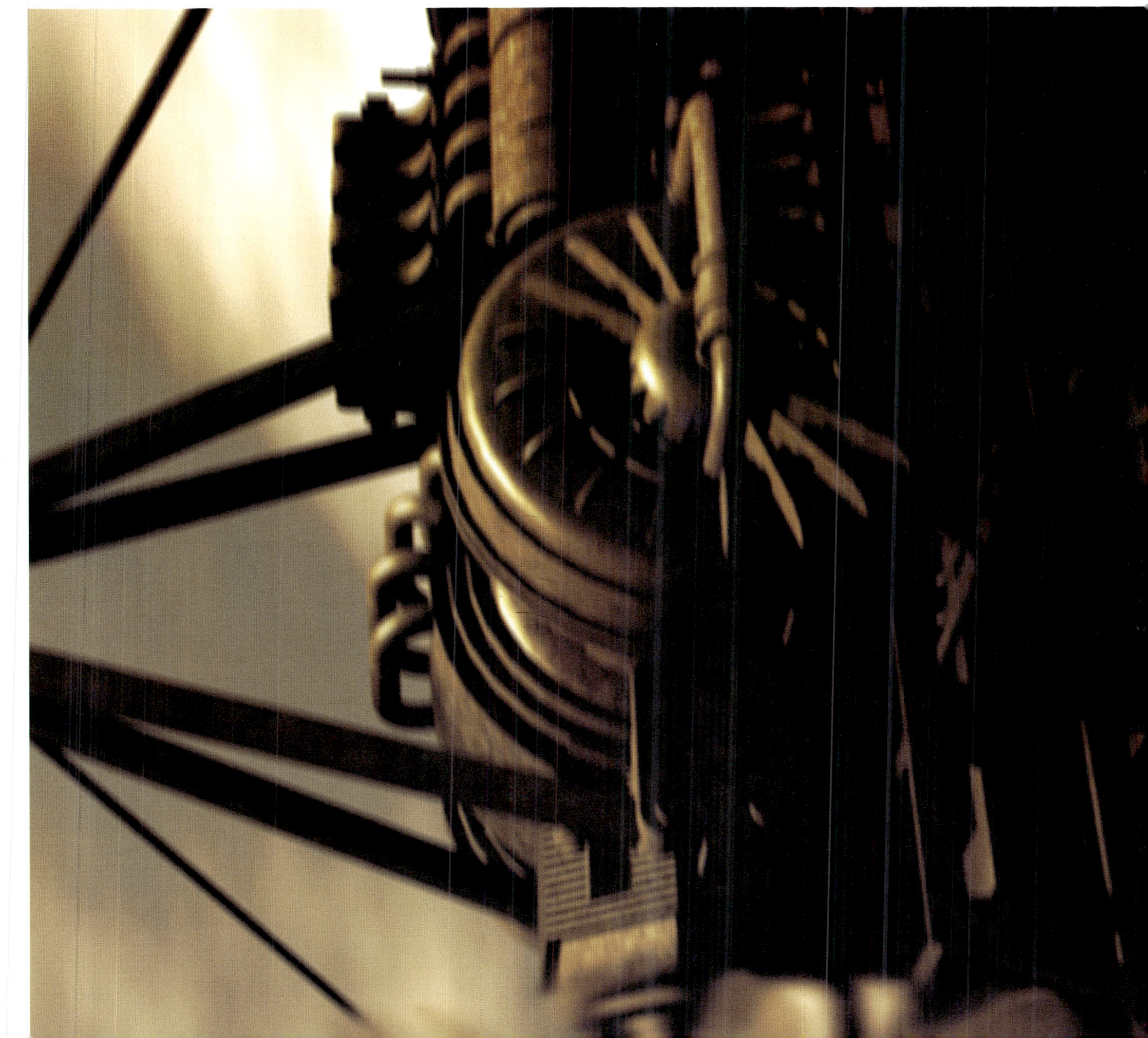

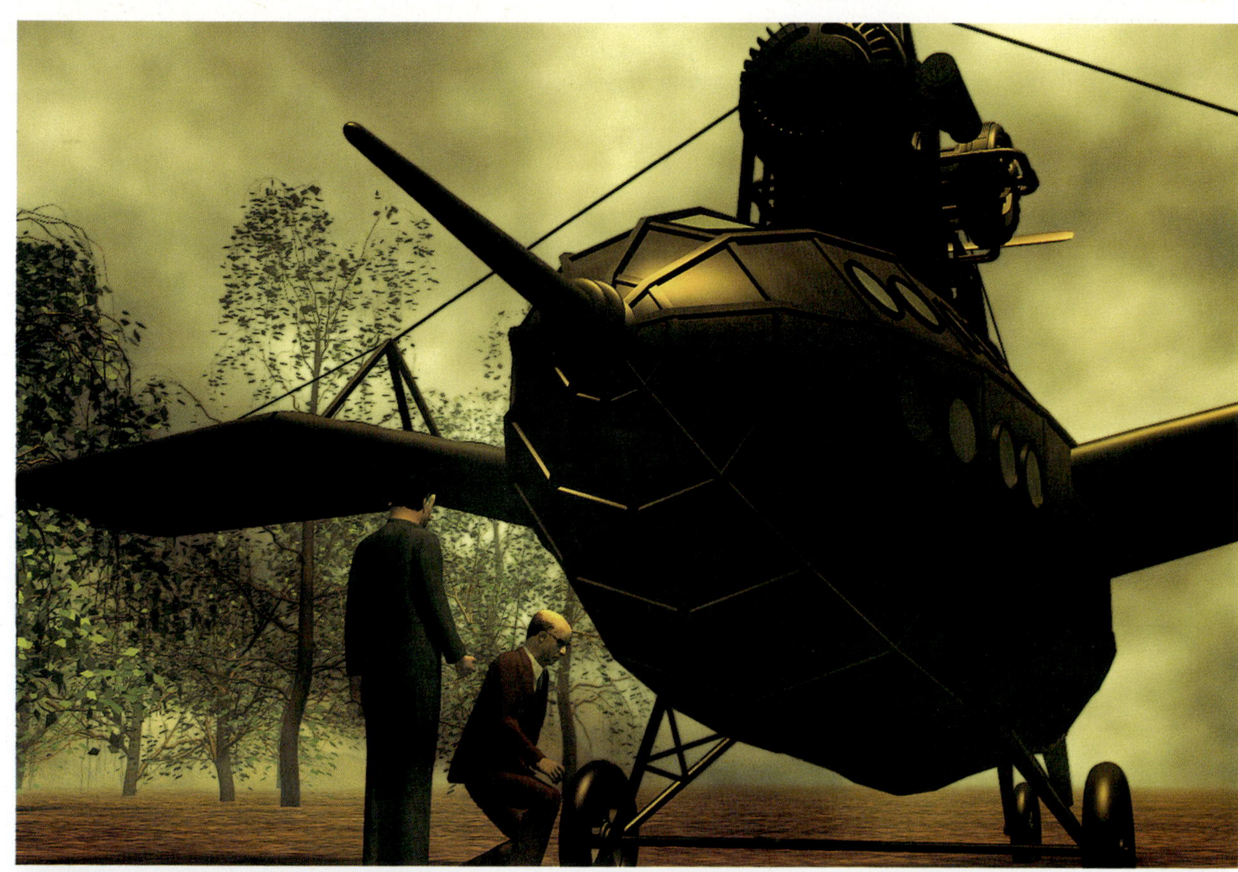

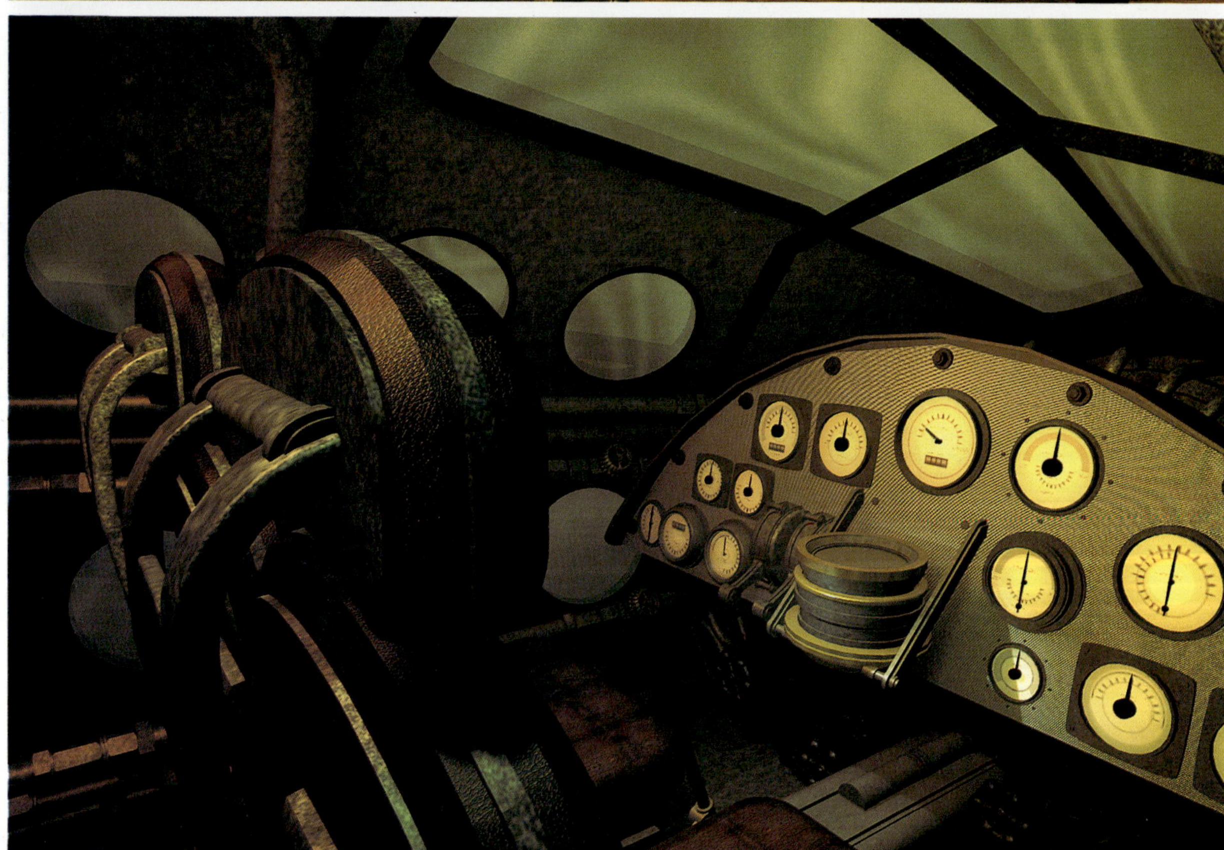

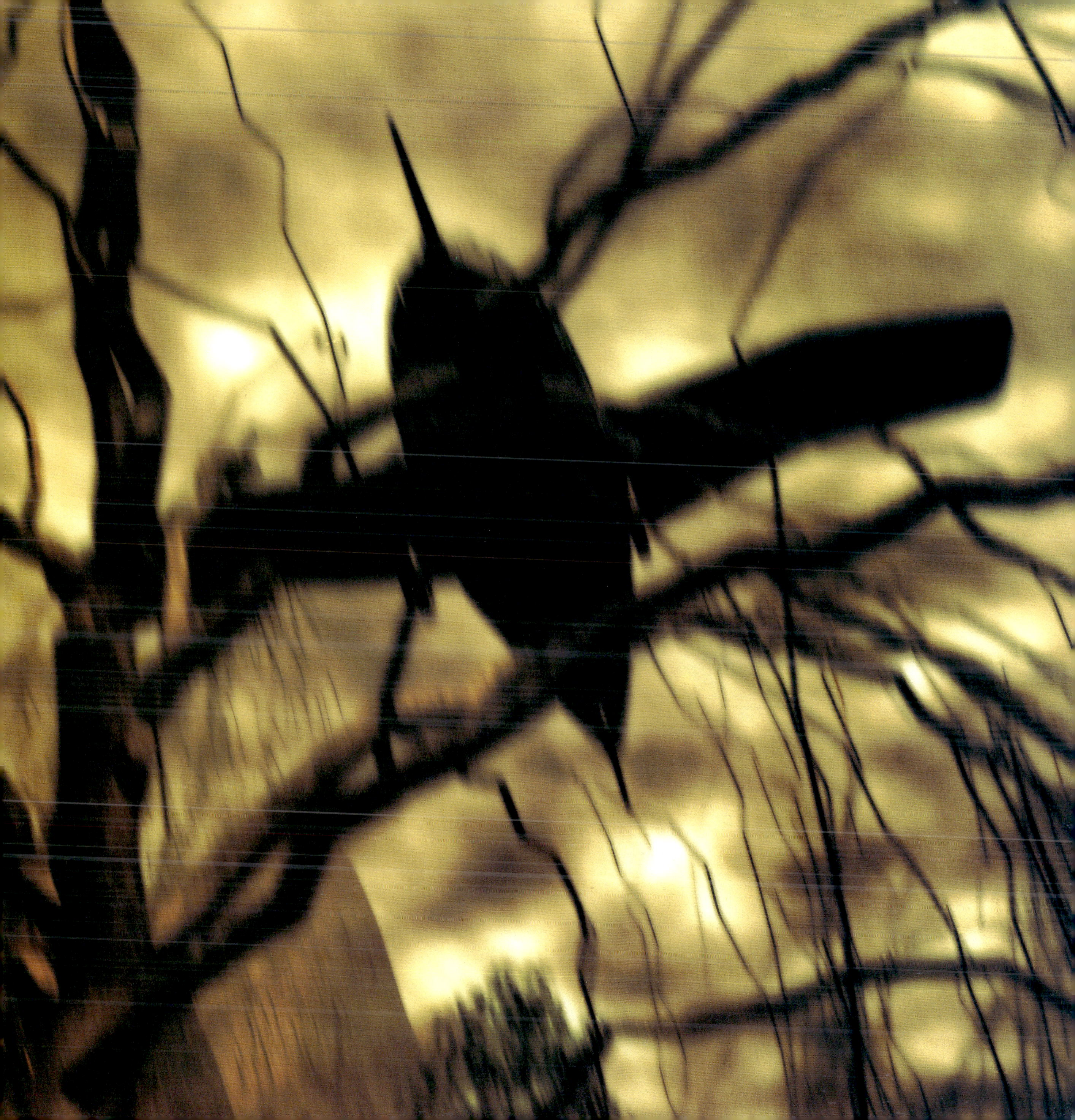

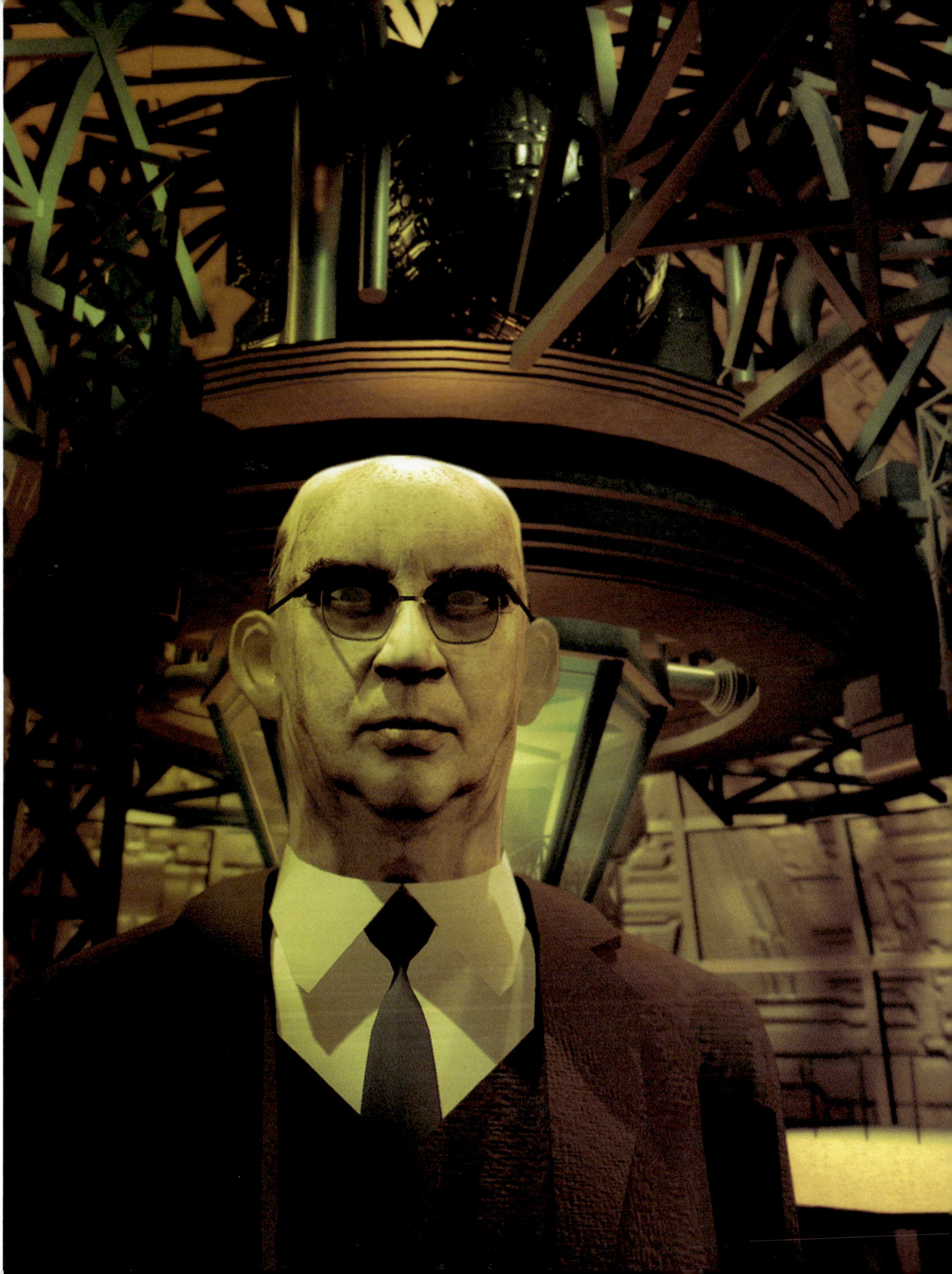

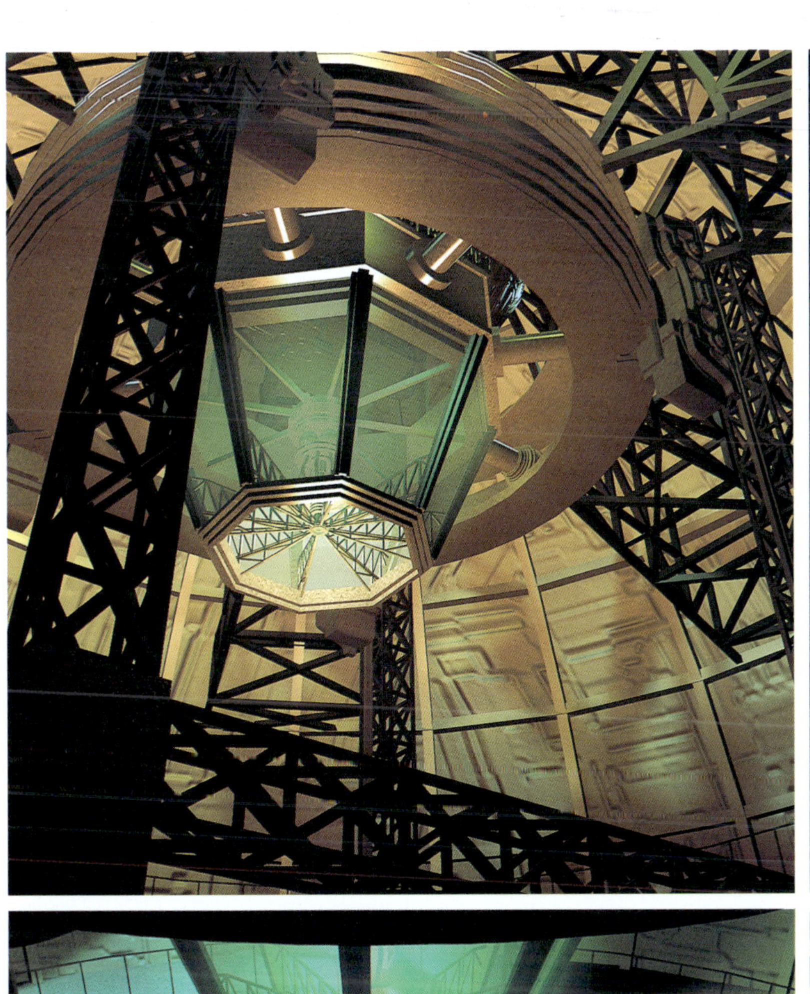
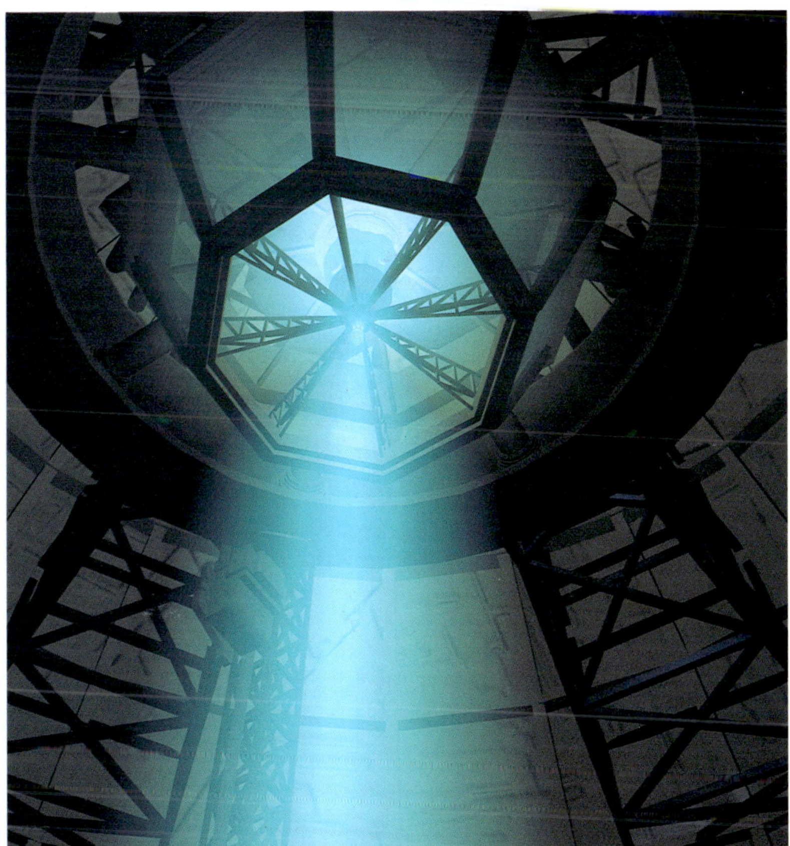
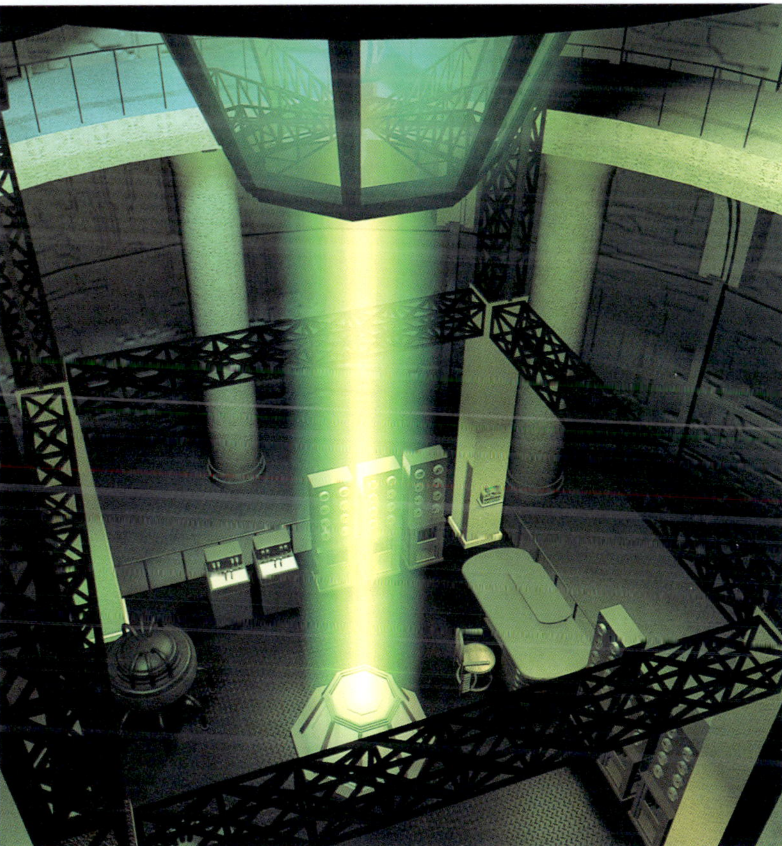
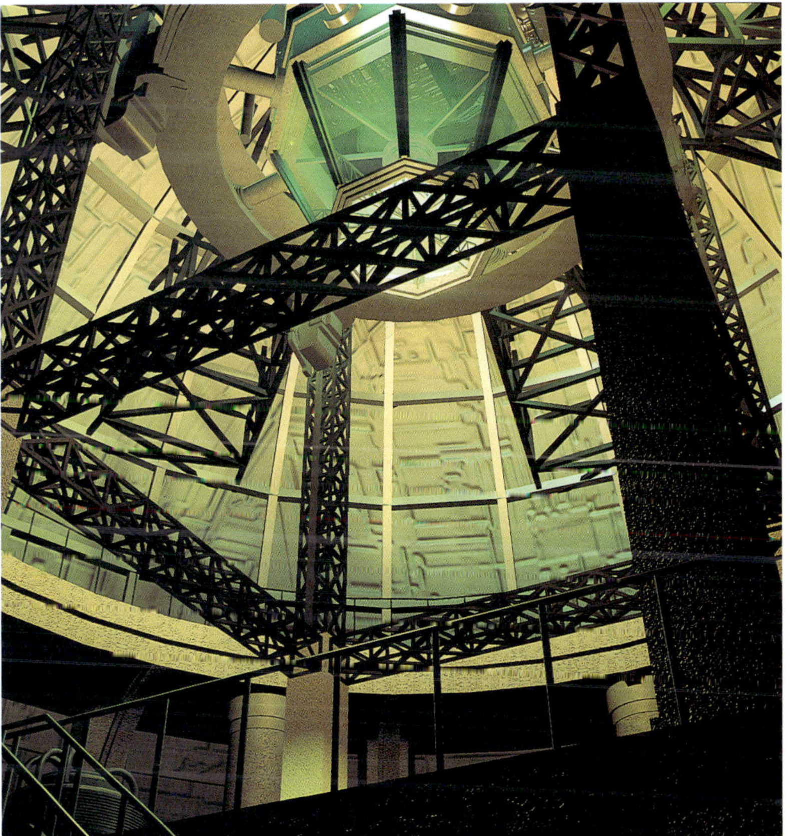

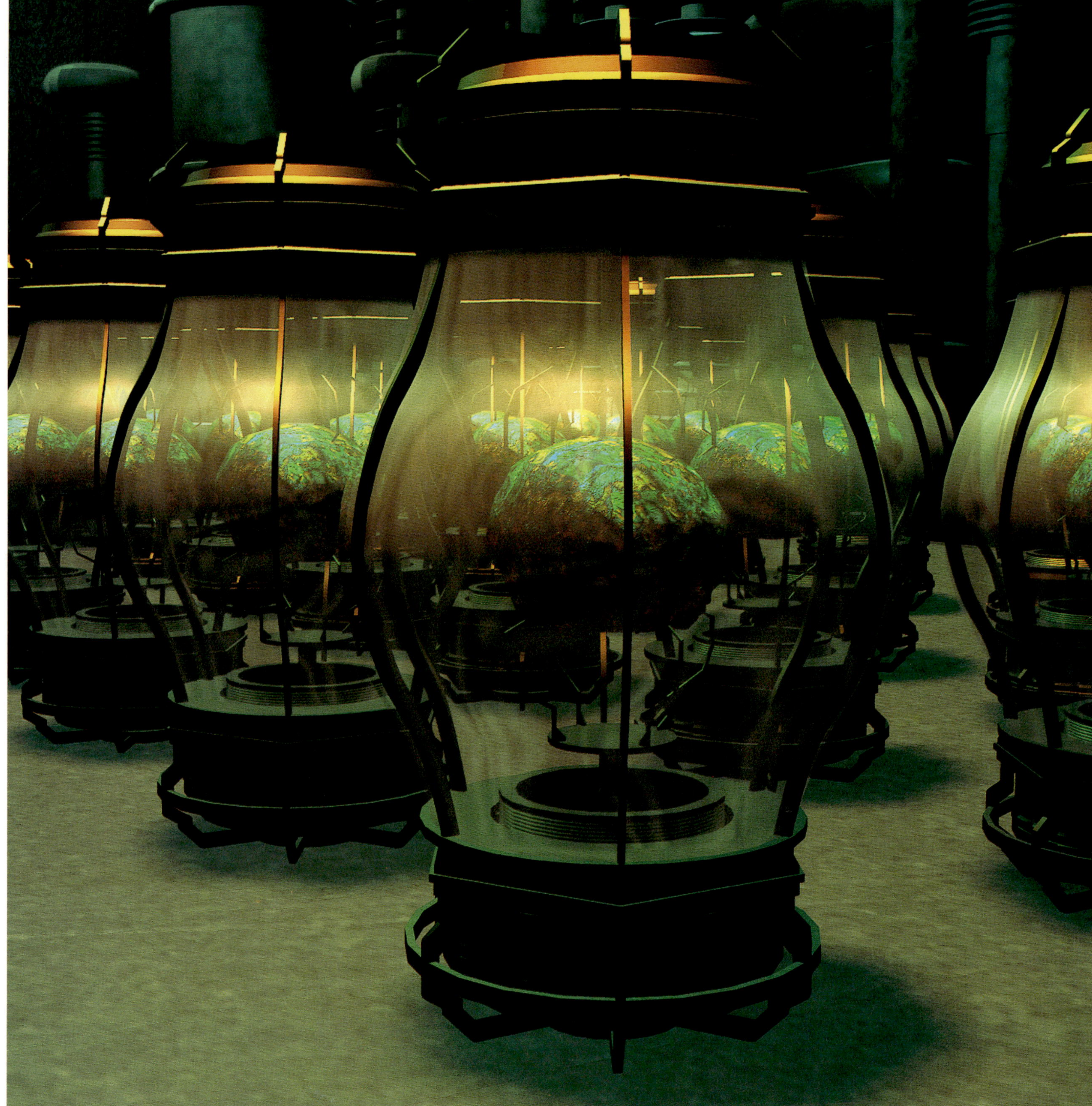

23 November, Year 1 of the Imperial Age

My Dear Professor Horsclover,

Permit me to turn directly to the matter in hand.

We are now at a research facility situated some three miles north of East End Station. Pursuant to Empire orders we made our way to the meteor field and gathered fragments which we are now analyzing. After three weeks of intensive investigation we made a startling discovery.

But let me explain events in the order of their occurrence.

The meteor field, which has been designated a restricted area by the Imperial Army, is at the site of a disused iron-ore mine. Mining equipment has been abandoned to the elements and there are towering heaps of red earth that has been excavated from the mine. As you know there was a heavy rain on the day the meteors fell, so on reaching the site our first task was to dig up meteorites out of the mud.

I have no idea how many there are altogether, but the pieces we've found so far are rather small, none being larger than a yard in diameter.

The meteorites are a greenish brown, quite similar in structure to garnet. (In appearance quite like andradite, do you take my point?)

After three days of analysis we had identified 98 percent of its constituents. Like andradite the chief elements are iron and calcium. Up to this point results coincided with our expectations.

The problem was the remaining 2 percent.

Wilhelm and I did tests for any number of suppositional constituents, but we were unable to identify that last 2 percent. We conclude that it is not a substance found on earth and, furthermore, confess our astonishment at having no idea what its composition is.

Training a laser on a meteorite produced high temperatures. The ferrous and calcareous constituents melted away, leaving the mysterious 2 percent whose mass remained constant. A second and a third time we aimed a laser beam at this irreducible residue, but the results were the same. The process of oxidation caused an inevitable reduction in mass of the iron and calcium, but there was no change at all in the mass of our "anomalous substance." We went through the same process with other meteorites but the outcome was the same.

We still have no idea what the composition of this material is. We have, however, verified the paradoxical fact that directing a laser beam at the substance causes it to release thermal energy on a semi-permanent basis.

My quick-witted colleague surely realizes the consequences, does he not?.

We have been directed to analyze the constituents of the meteors by Supreme Commander Slowslop of the Imperial Army. There is, I suspect, no need for me to explain things further in light of Orlovsky's recent embarkation on a policy of military expansion.

We have filed a formal report with Army authorities concerning the properties of this unique meteoritic substance. It is now our wish to continue our researches outside the reach of Imperial notice.

In this we humbly implore your assistance.

Sincerely yours,

George Tessera

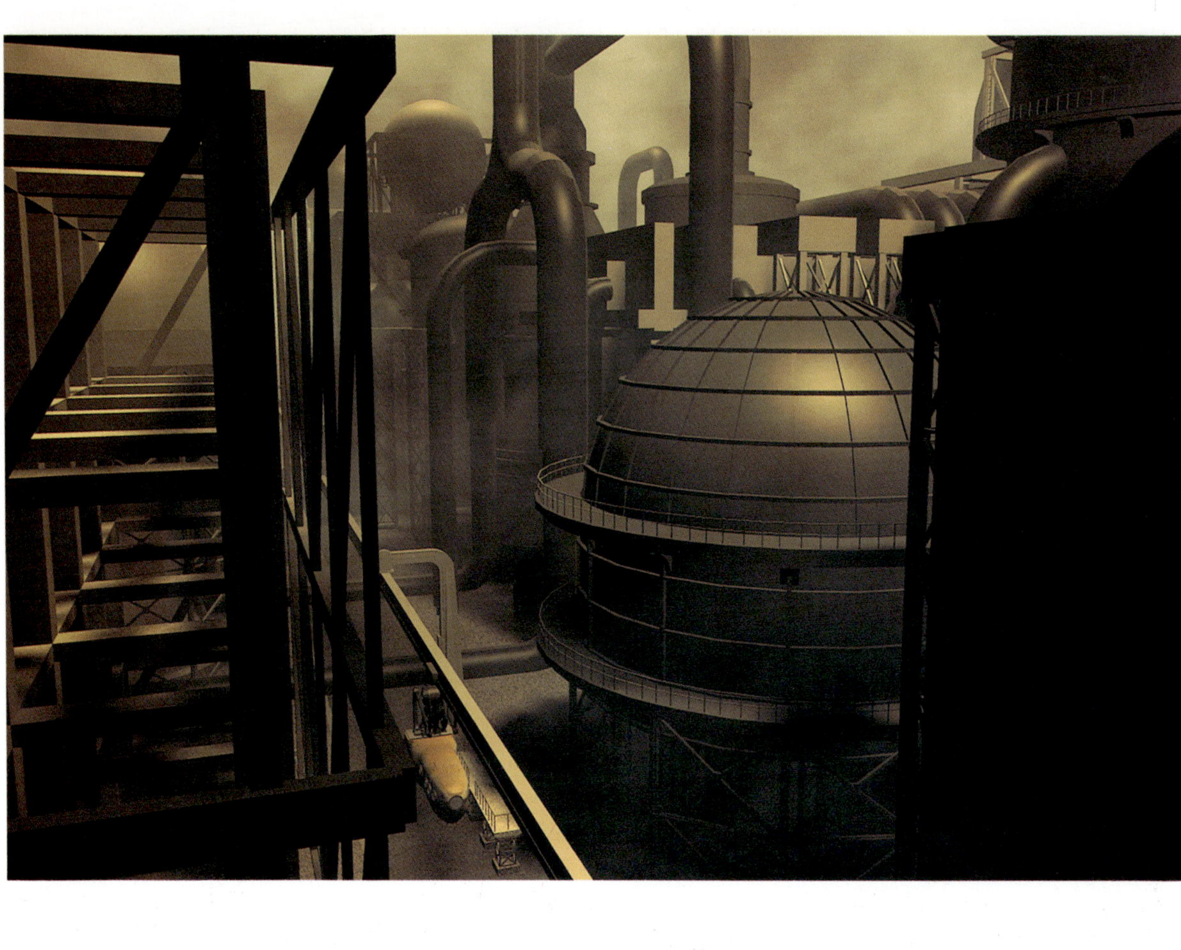

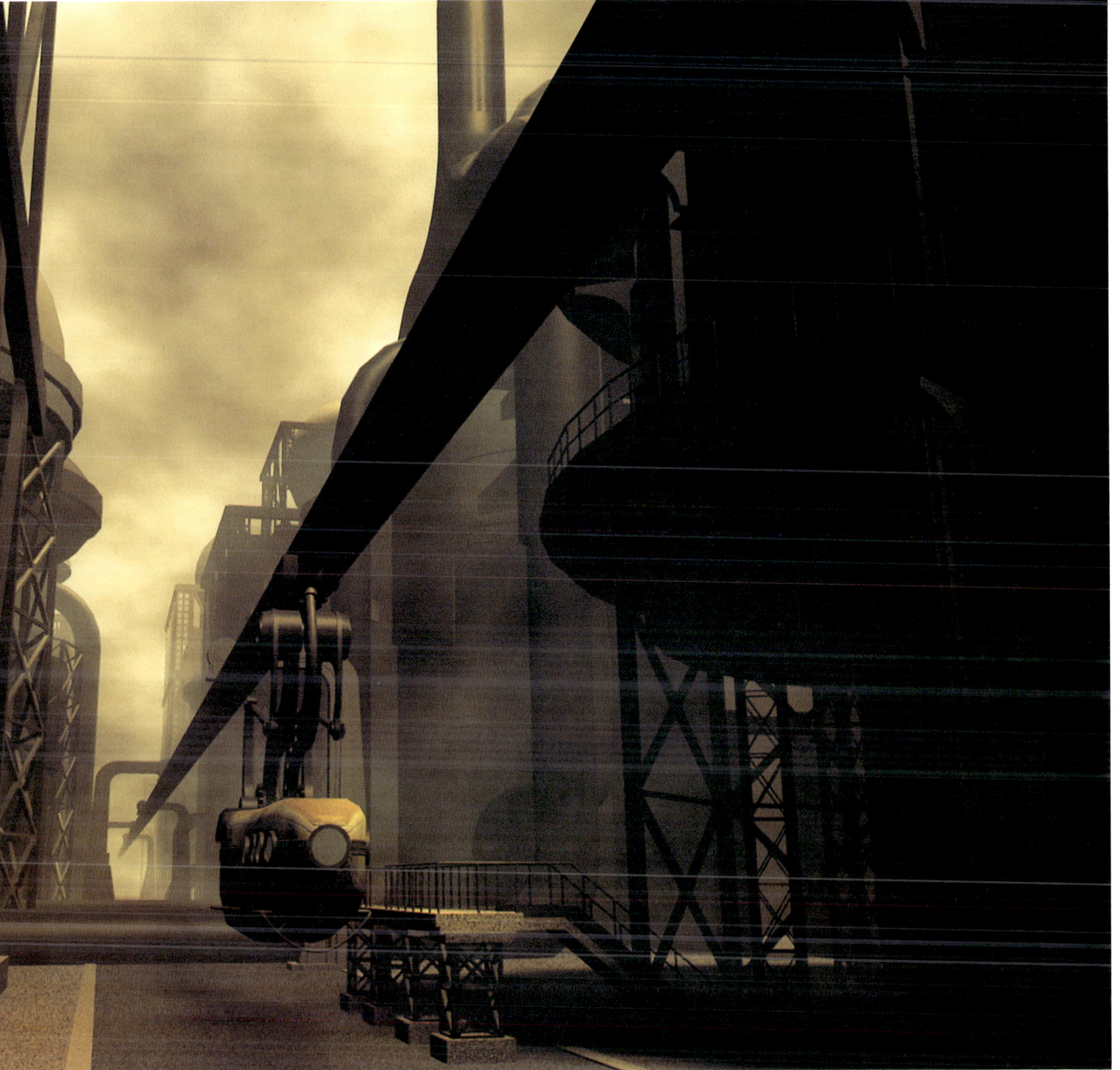

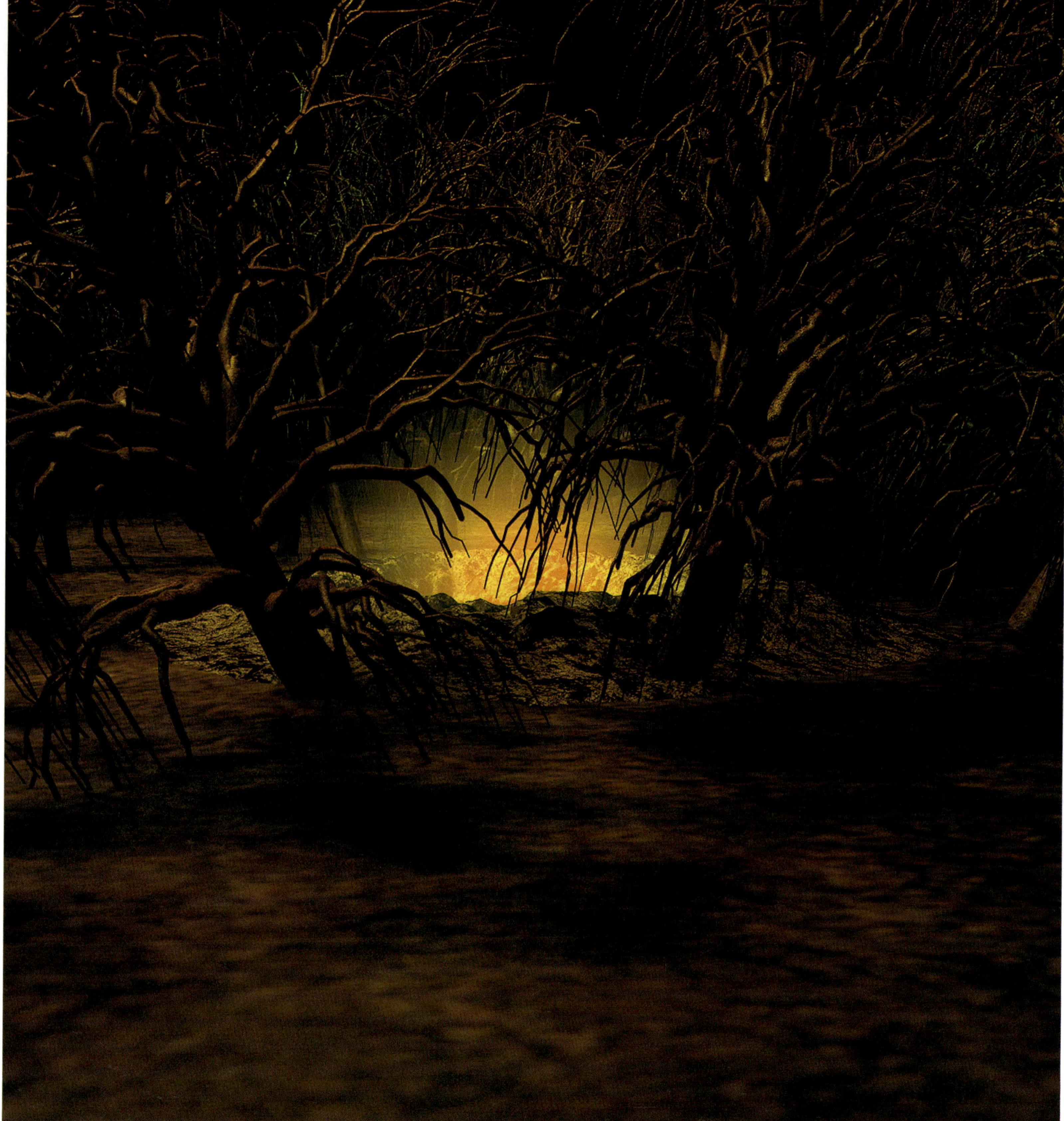

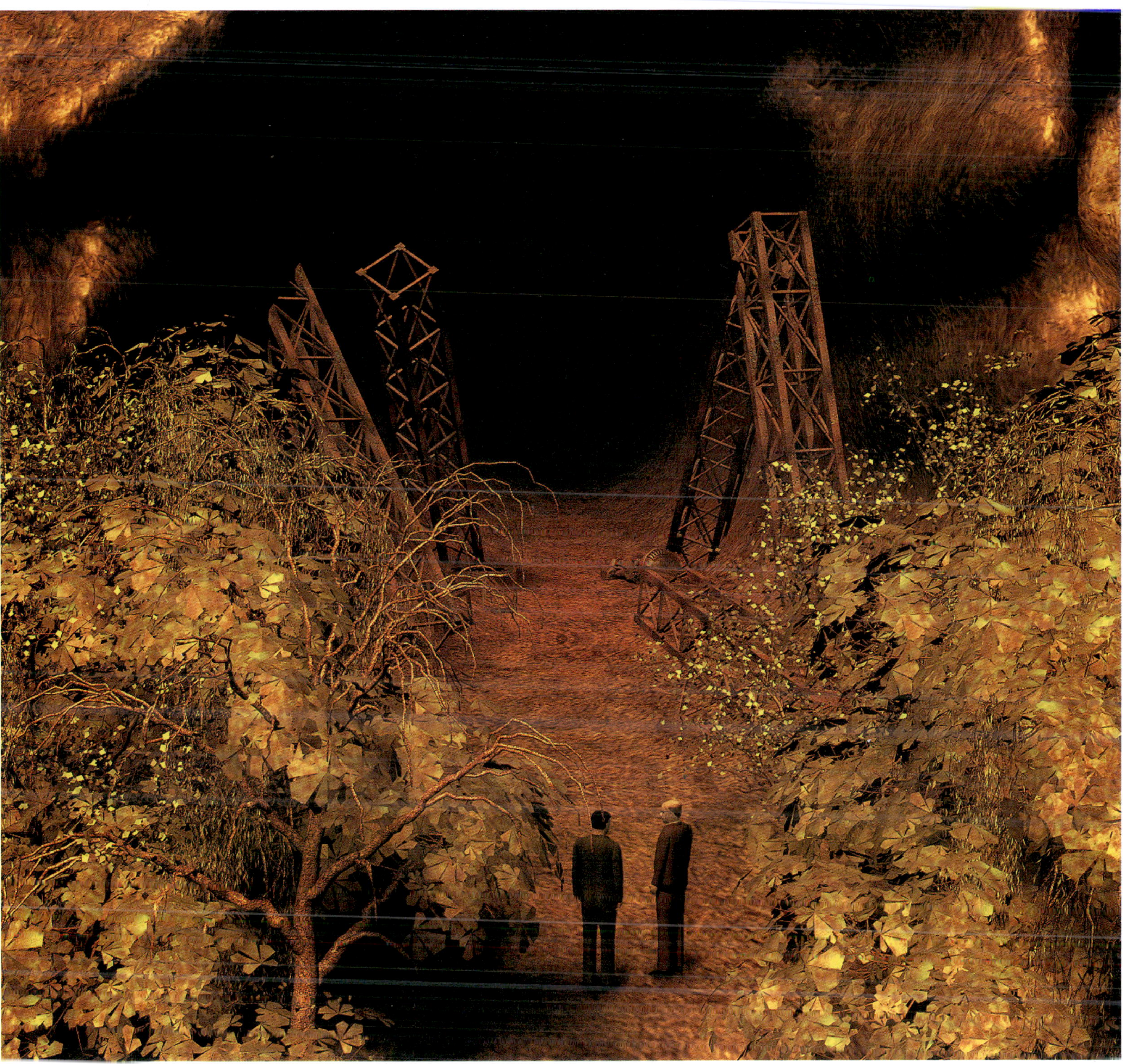

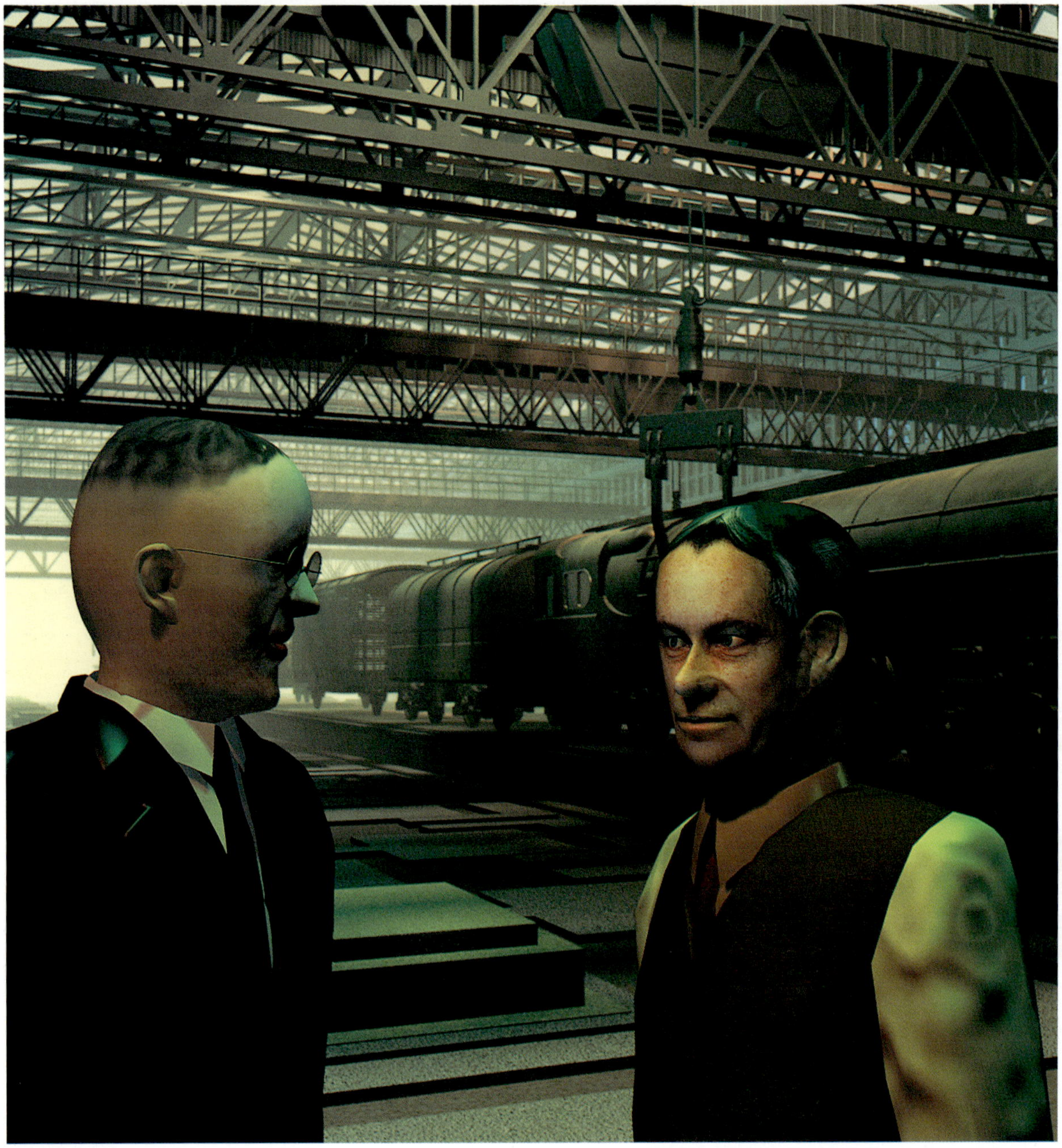

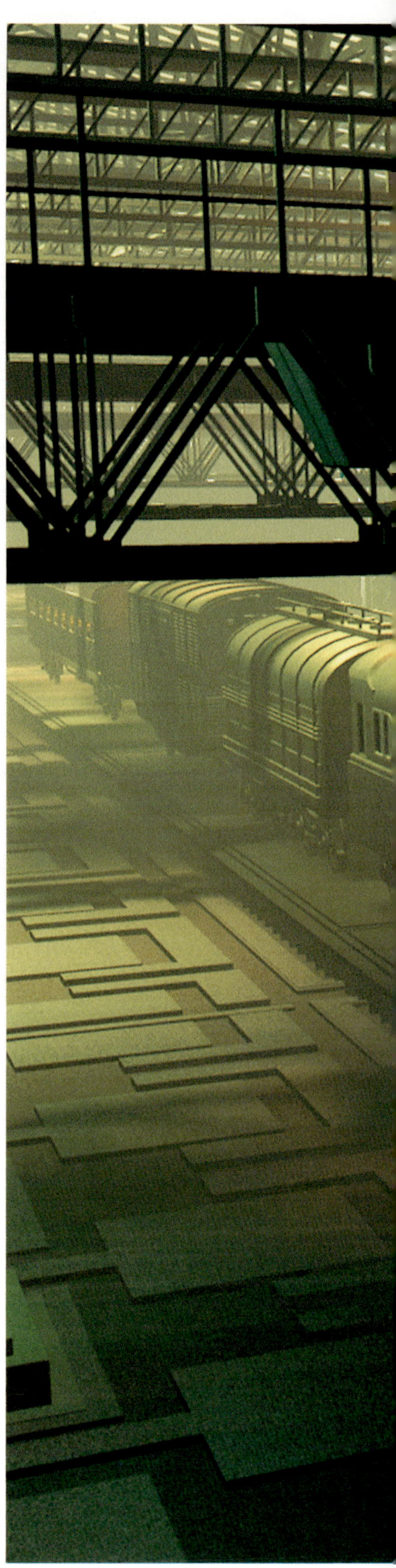

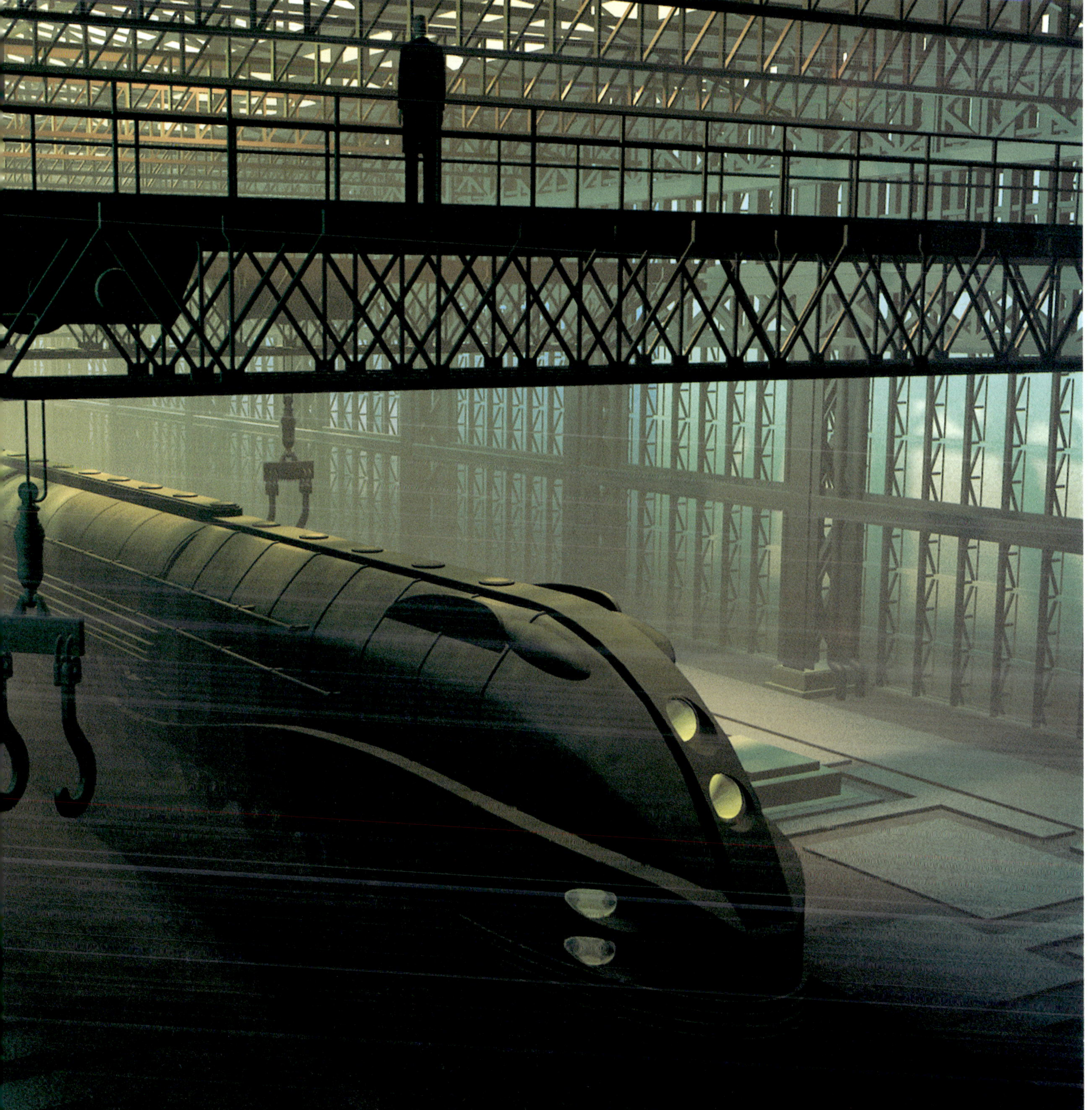

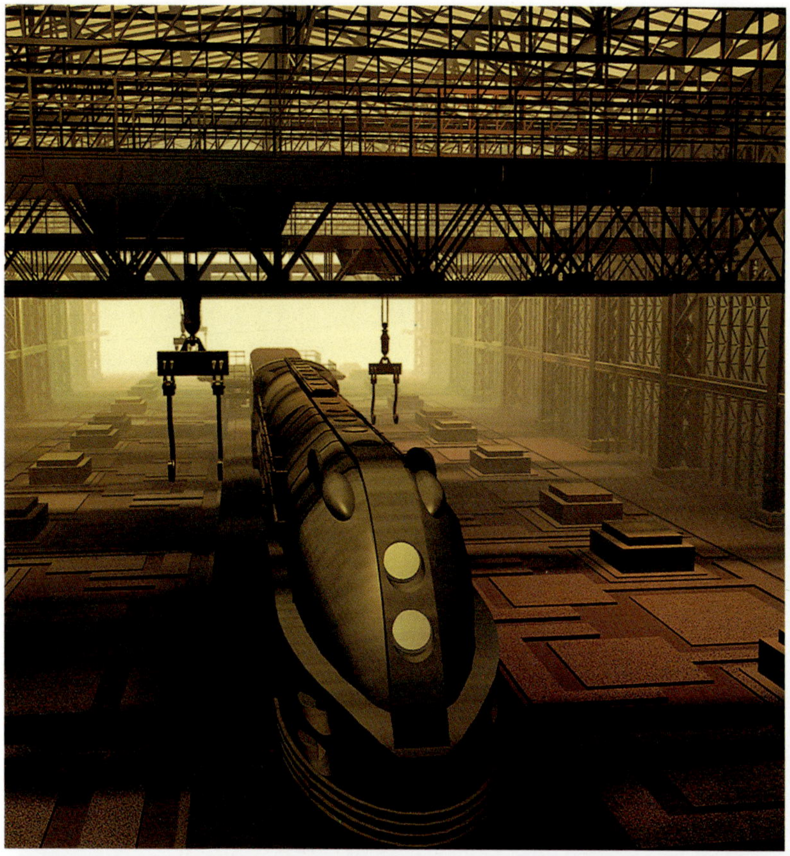

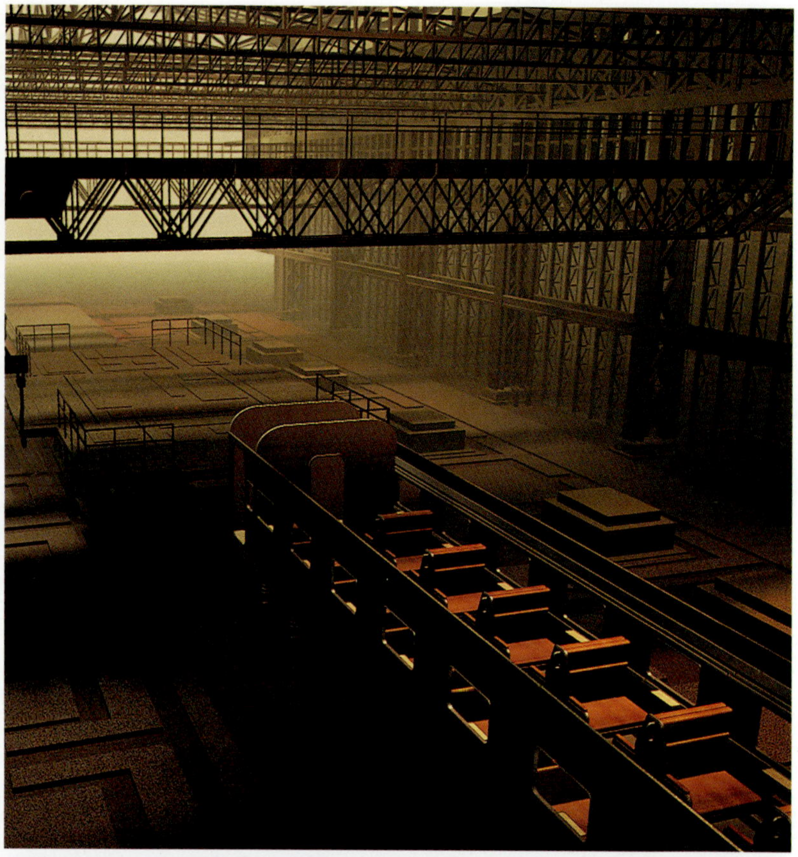

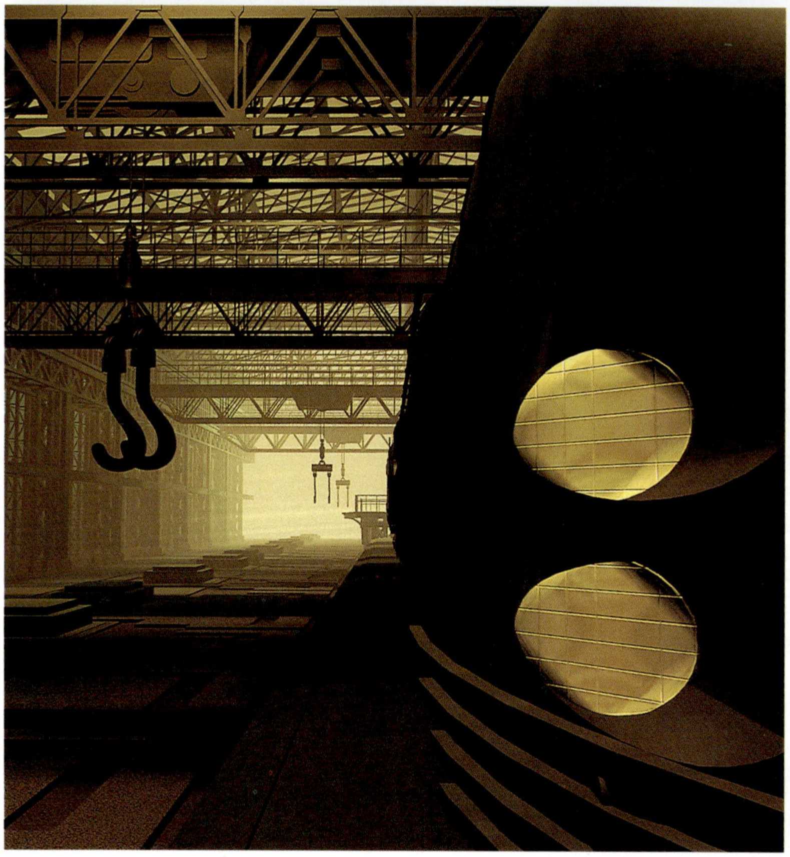

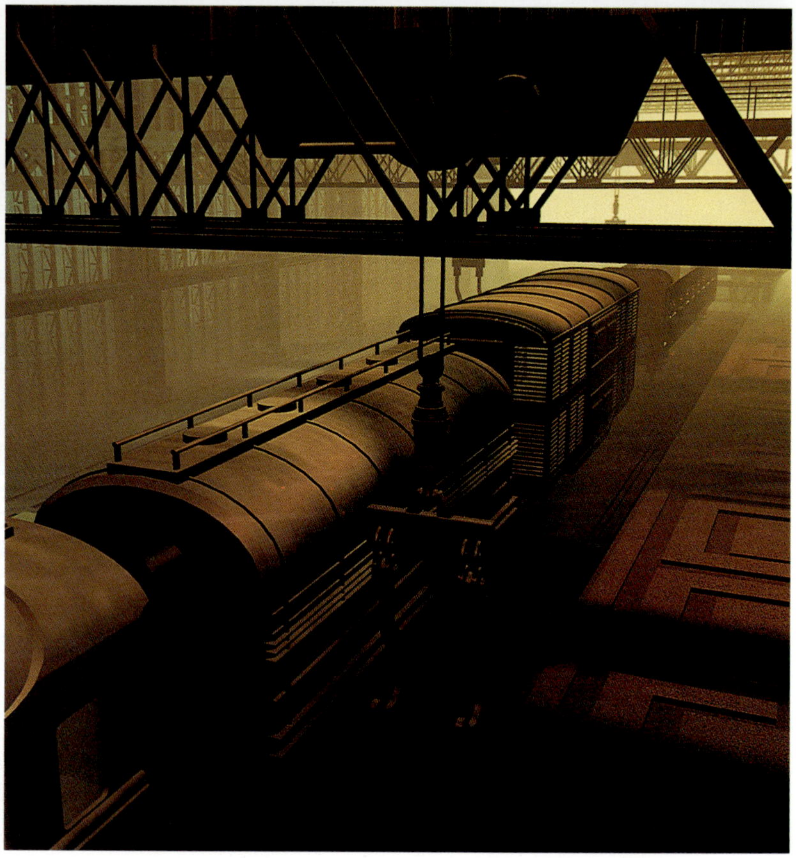

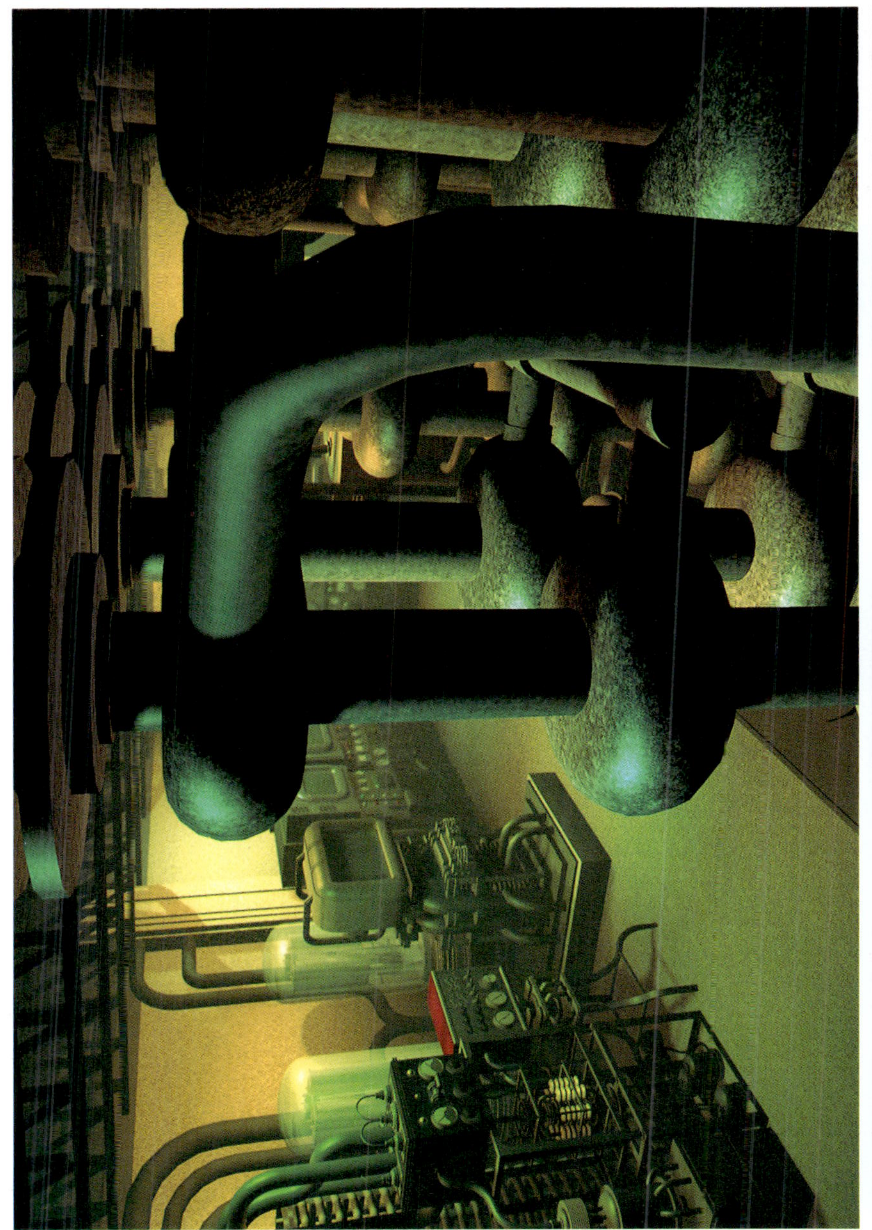

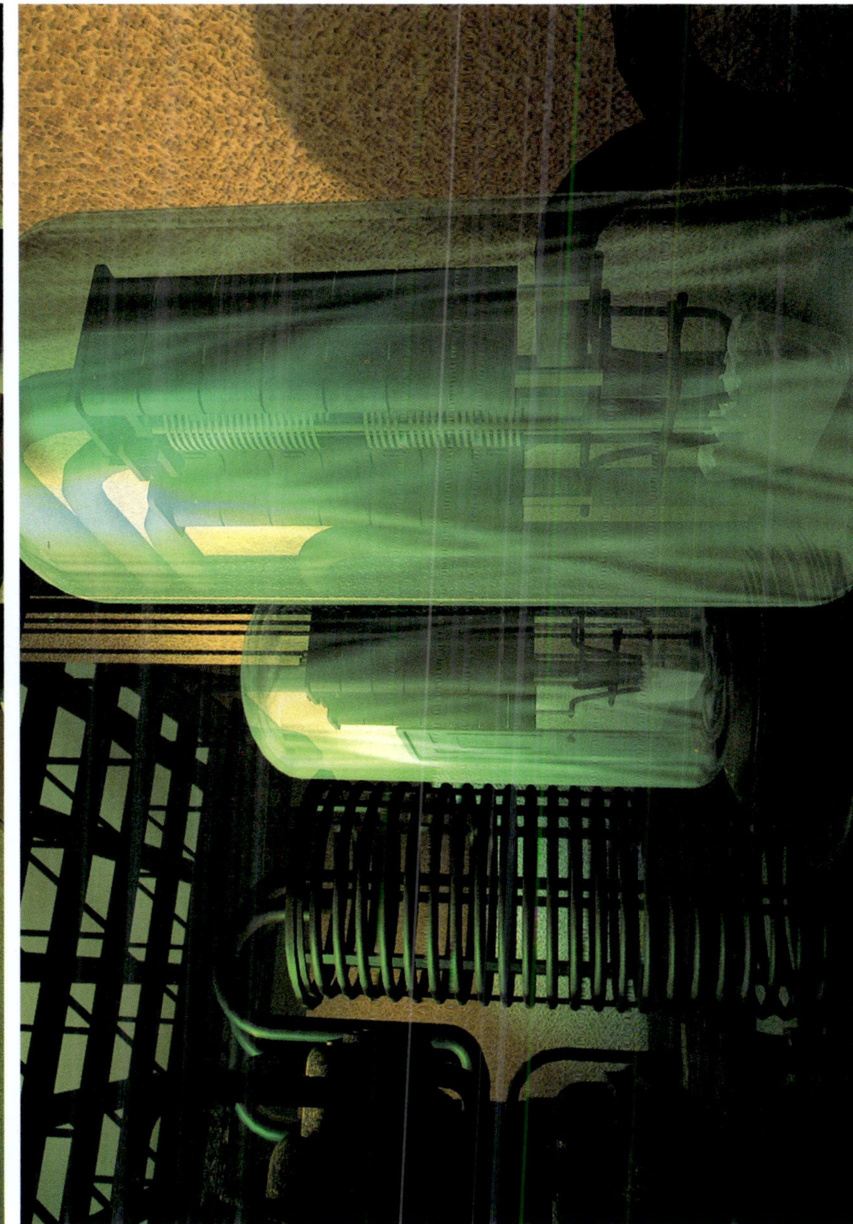

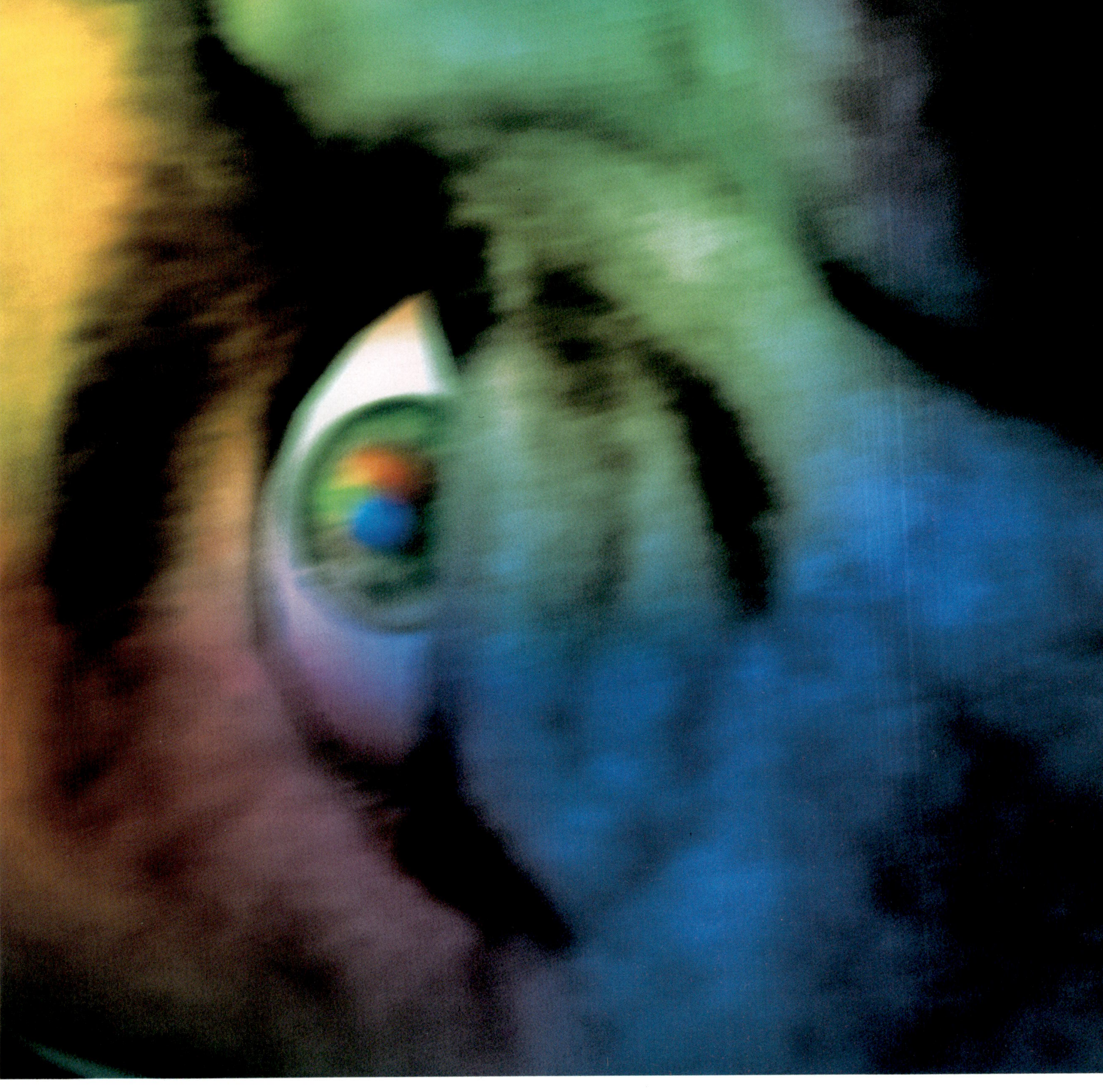

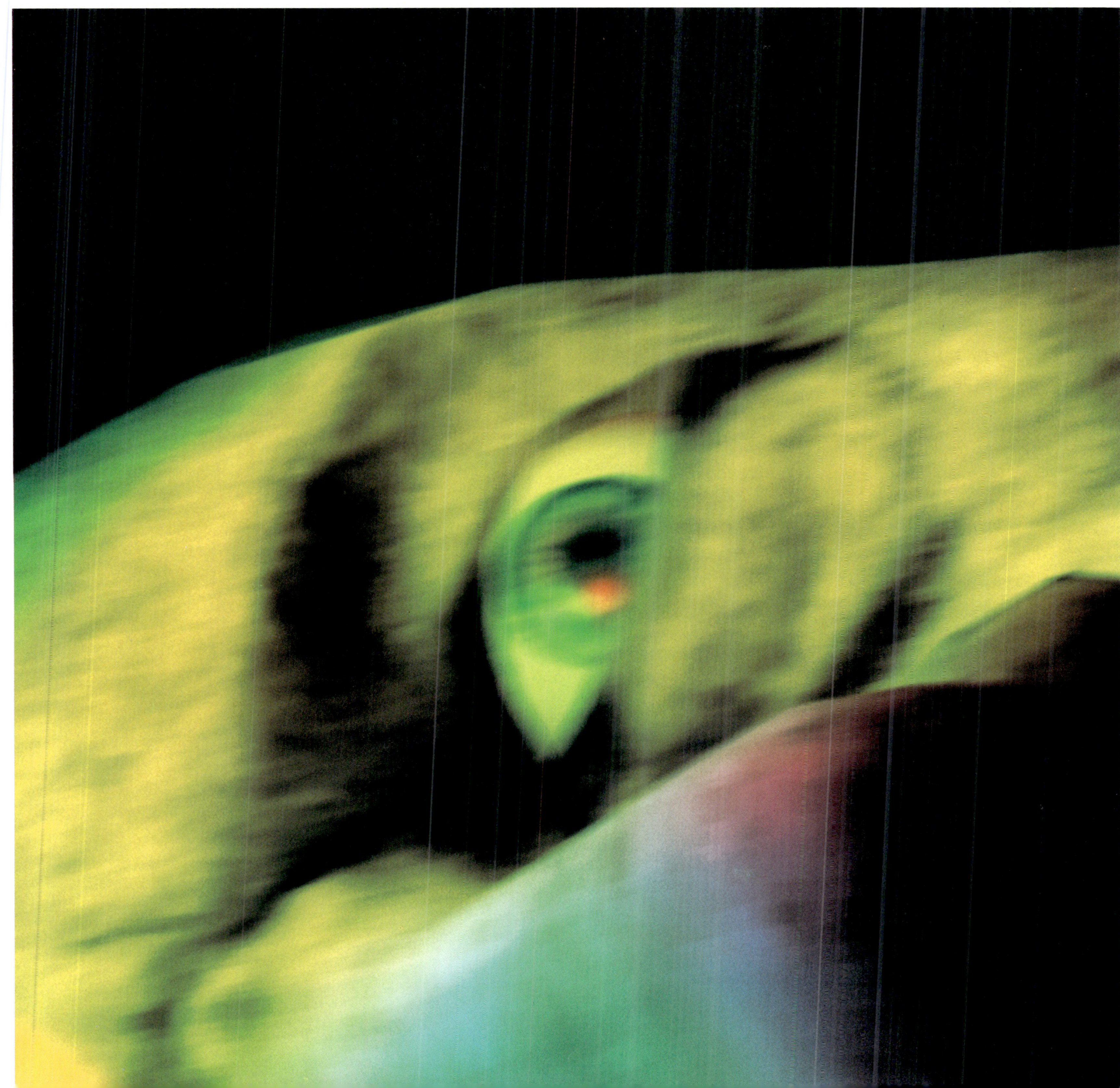

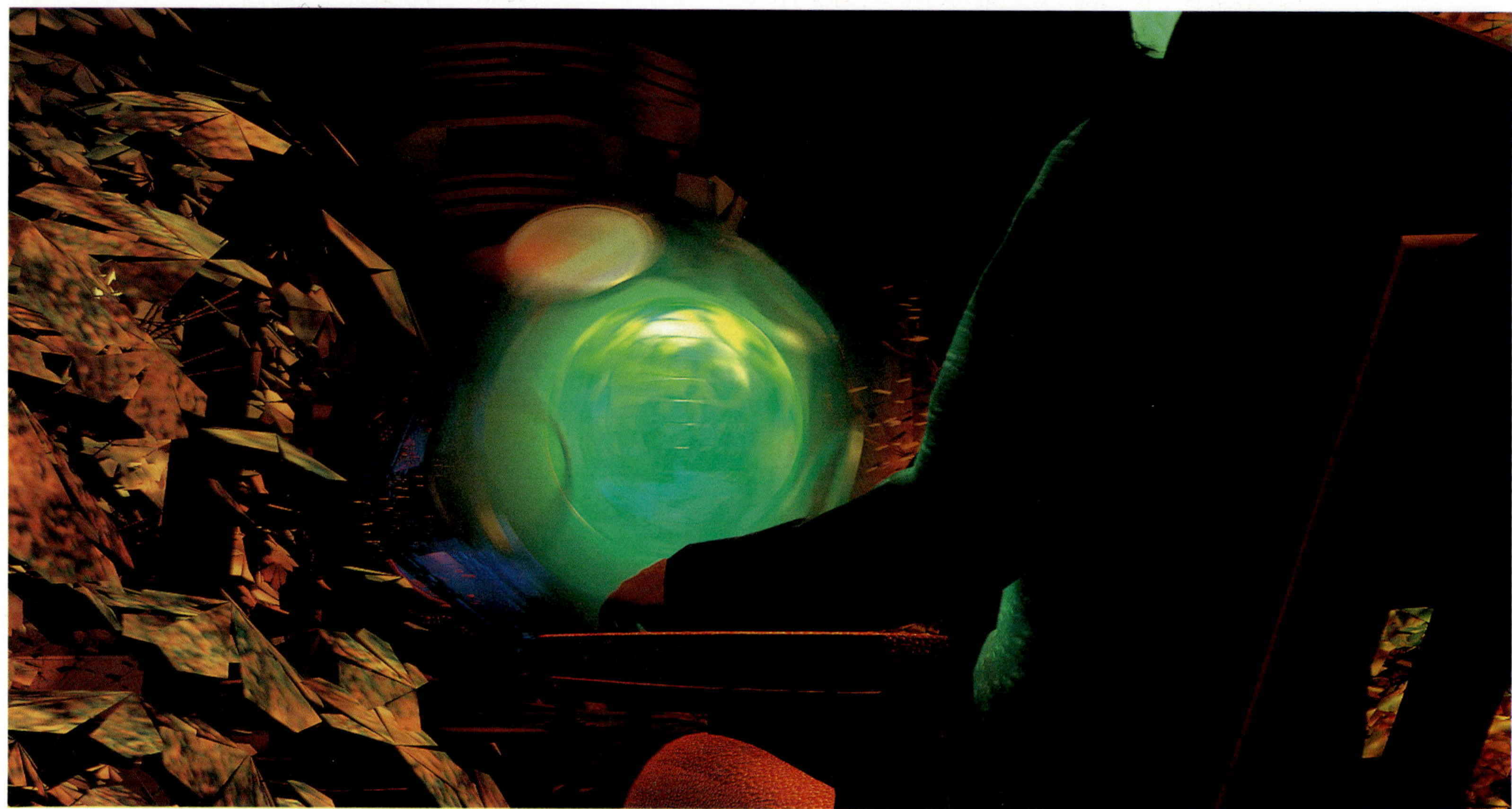

12 December, Year 2 of the Imperial Age

Charged the intelligence operative Hausmann with the task of gathering information concerning the Sensorama project now underway at the Imperial Museum. I'll detail another agent to keep an eye on the water tower where George and Wilhelm are continuing research on the composition of the meteorites.

14 December

A report has arrived from Hausmann. I now have details on the careers of the men working on the Sensorama—what was at one time called the "Beam Machine." According to the records accompanying the report there are seven scientists working on the project.

George Tessera and Wilhelm Draun are the two in the private research facility in the water tower. Thomas Reich and Charles Reif work at the Imperial Museum. John MacNaughton and Constantine Wallace are on the staff of the Imperial Army Hospital. We still haven't tracked down Horselover Frost.

21 December

If we find out where Horselover is, we'll learn all there is to know about the Sensorama project. The quickest way to get the facts is to put him behind bars and apply a little painful persuasion. I'll have Hausmann mount a search.

26 December

Put Thomas in custody...a technician, formerly of the Academy. We've arranged in strictest secrecy for the manufacture of an excavator. We can use the excavator for transport from the restricted area to the Army Ordnance Factory.

29 December

A report has arrived from George at the research facility in the tower regarding the constituents of the meteorites. I'm pressing him about the inconsistencies between his report and information in a letter of his to Horselover, which has come into my hands through Hausmann. I've ordered him to resubmit his report with special reference this time to military applications.

(From the diary of Slowslop)

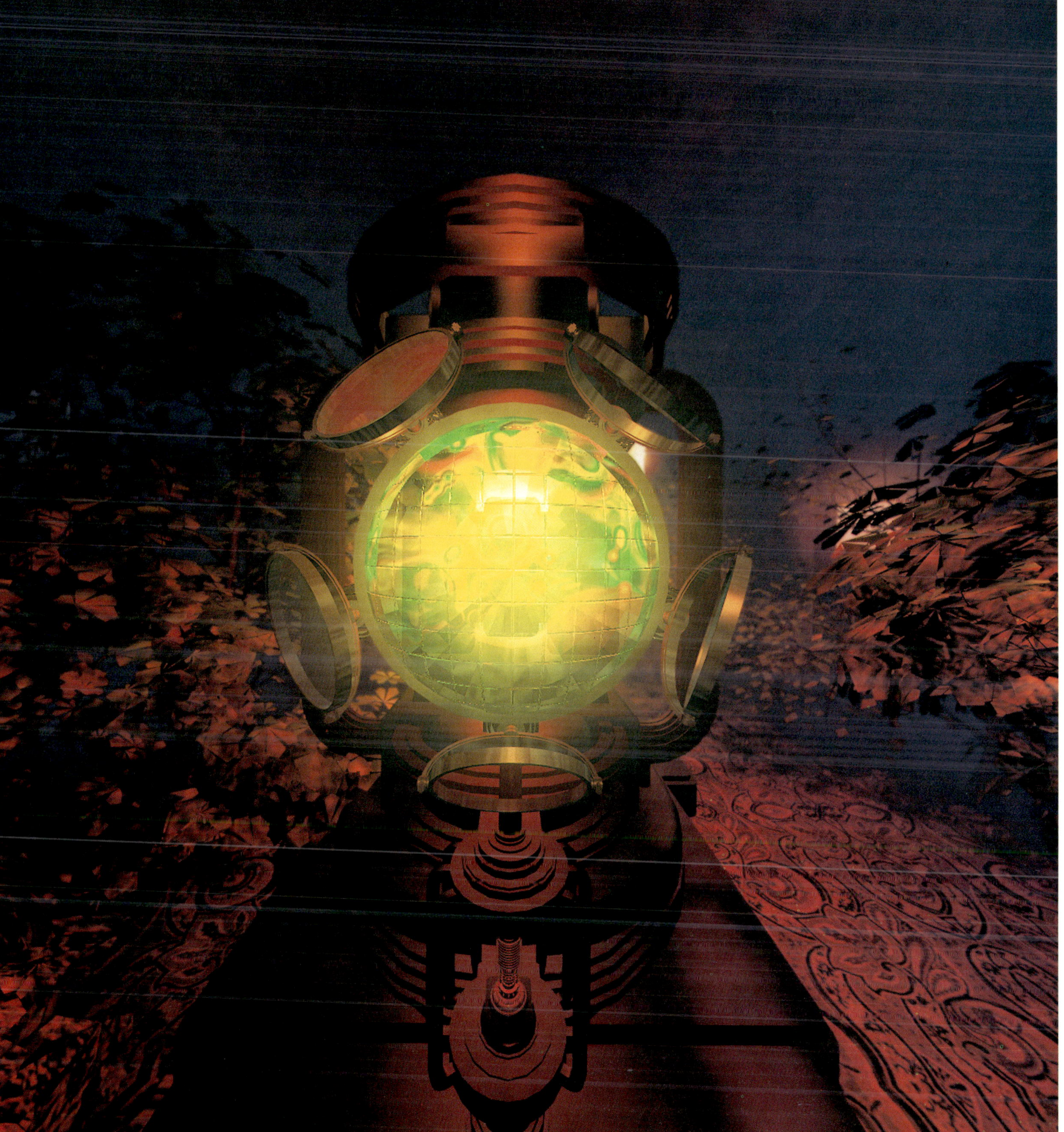

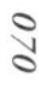

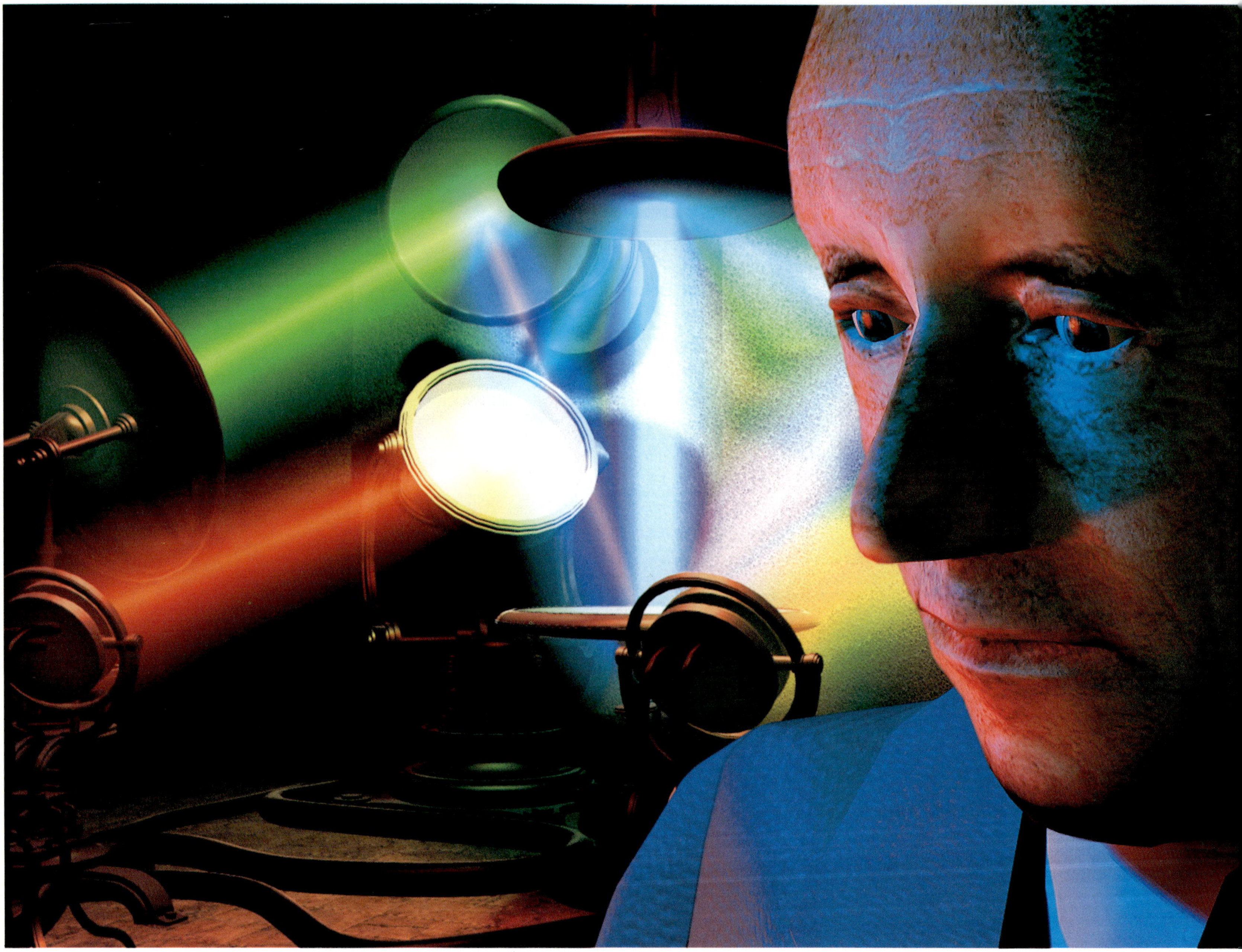

Six scientists, or maybe seven
Ascent, or is it descent
Para-experience or precognition
The past extends into the future
The scientists' daily labors
A machine that doesn't work
Investigation by Army Intelligence
Unusual activity at the Museum
The Sensorama goes round and round

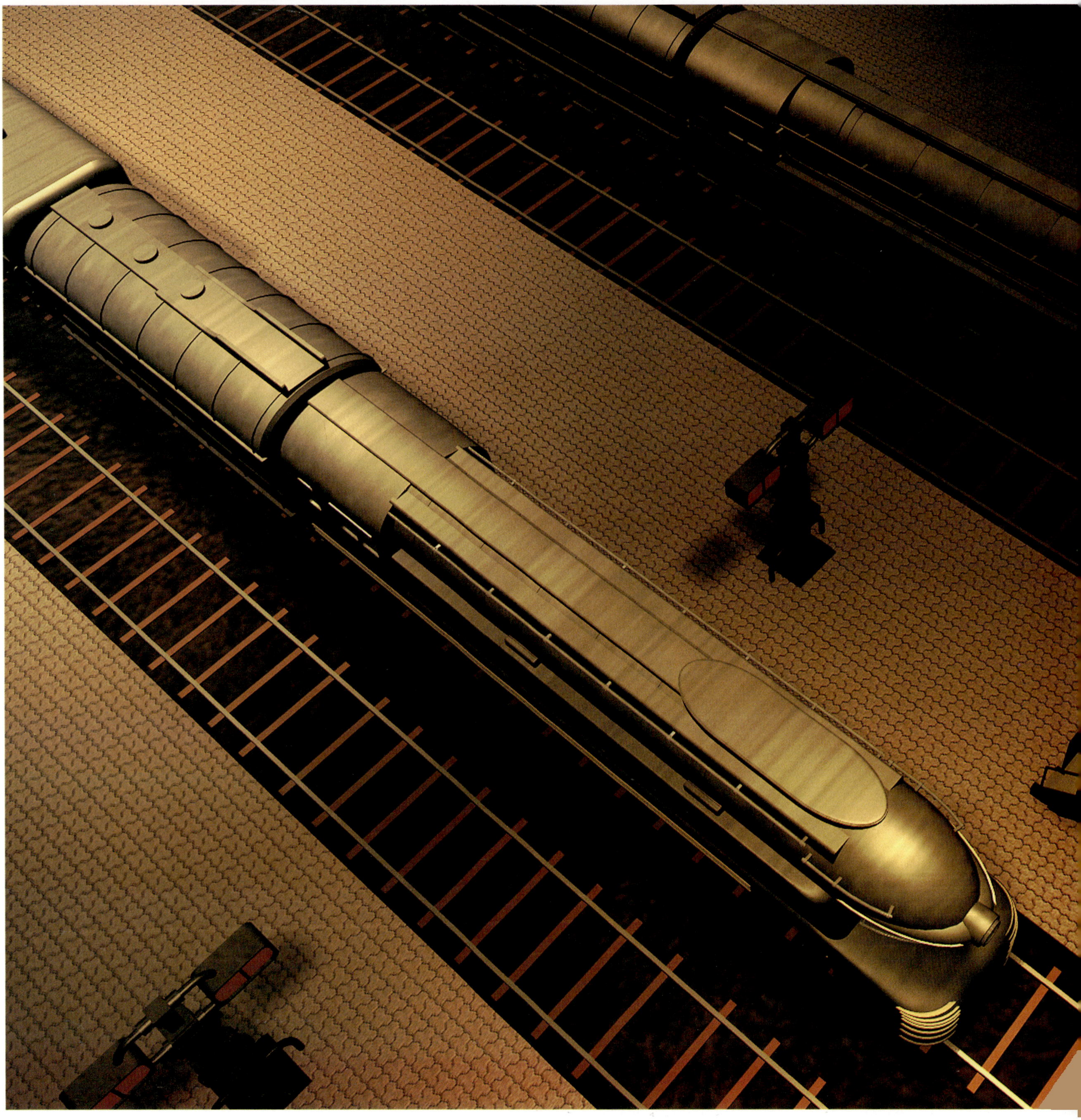

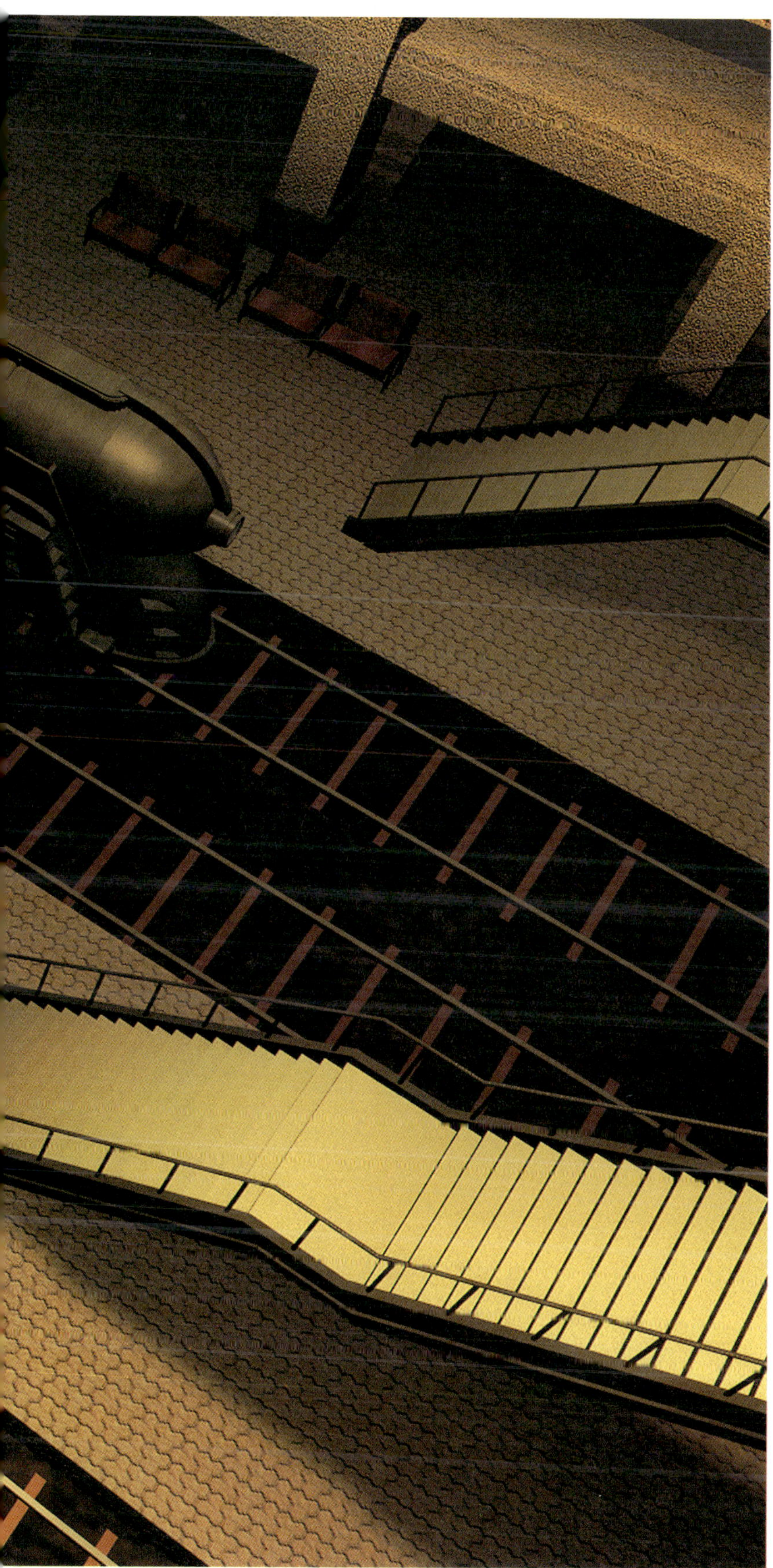

Years 3 and 4 of the Imperial Age

Six scientists, or maybe seven

The scientists, once associates at the Academy, reassemble at the Imperial Museum. A new Beam Machine set up in the research lab. The resumption of tests. Rush of light and electricity. Noise of motor and coils. A surge of excitement, a feeling light as air.

Ascent, or is it descent

A needle-like protuberance stimulates the nerves. Cactus spines sprout on the cerebral cortex. Feeling in pain spots is lost, images real and illusory on the fundus of the eye. Voice in the distance. Hazy outline. A cosmos extends from retina to cortex.

Para-experience or precognition

Congealing blood. Heartbeats captured by sea horses. Irregular pulse. Dilating pupils. Leaden clouds. The tall man who stands at the top of the tower. Flight of the mother ship. Collision with a comet. The end of the world, or has it just disappeared.

The past extends into the future

Infiltration of the Imperial Army. With the aid of the Republic's underground, Gondarev infiltrates the Imperial Guards. Submission of a report to Onegin. It contains secret information concerning a meteor shower and a series of tests with electromagnetic waves.

The scientists' daily labors

Horselover and six scientists. Repeated radiation experiments at the Imperial Museum. Adjustment of frequency. Response of the human body to patterns of electromagnetic waves. Oral reports delivered by experimentees. Thorough documentation made on film.

A machine that doesn't work

Archaic tools stored in glass showcases. Industrial machinery frozen with rust. A holographic device that gathers light in circular mirrors. Film unspooled on the projection-room floor. A lightplane is shut away in the darkness of the second storey.

Investigation by Army Intelligence

Inquiries made at the Imperial Museum by Hausmann. Response of the six scientists amenable. Goal, method, and progress of the radiation experiments established through rigorous interrogation. Information sifted and organized. Report submitted to Slowslop.

Unusual activity at the Museum

Electromagnetic wave radiation device activated. Madness captured on film. Spasmodic muscle tissue. Pairs of eyes gaze deep into the void. Blinding beams of light. The sounds of the machine in operation. Subjects and scientists repeat coma and consciousness.

The Sensorama goes round and round

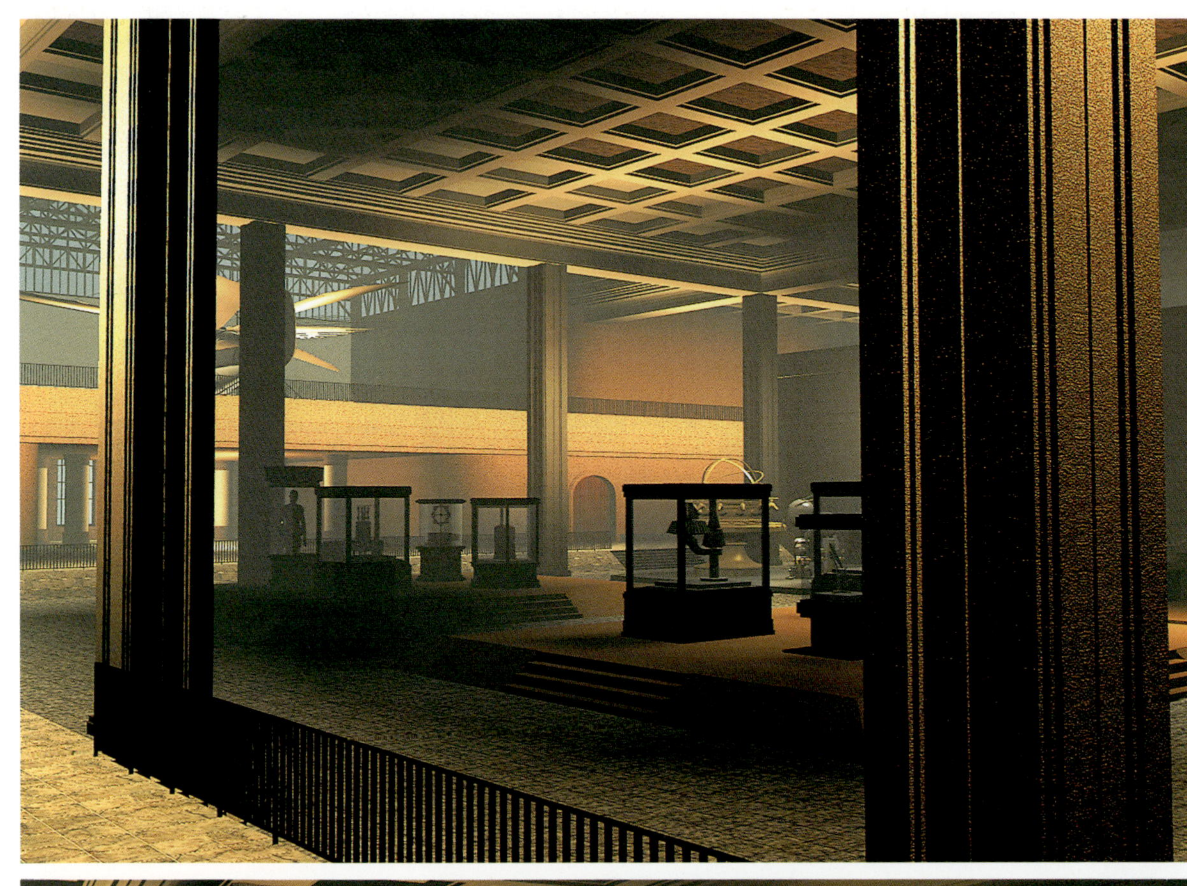

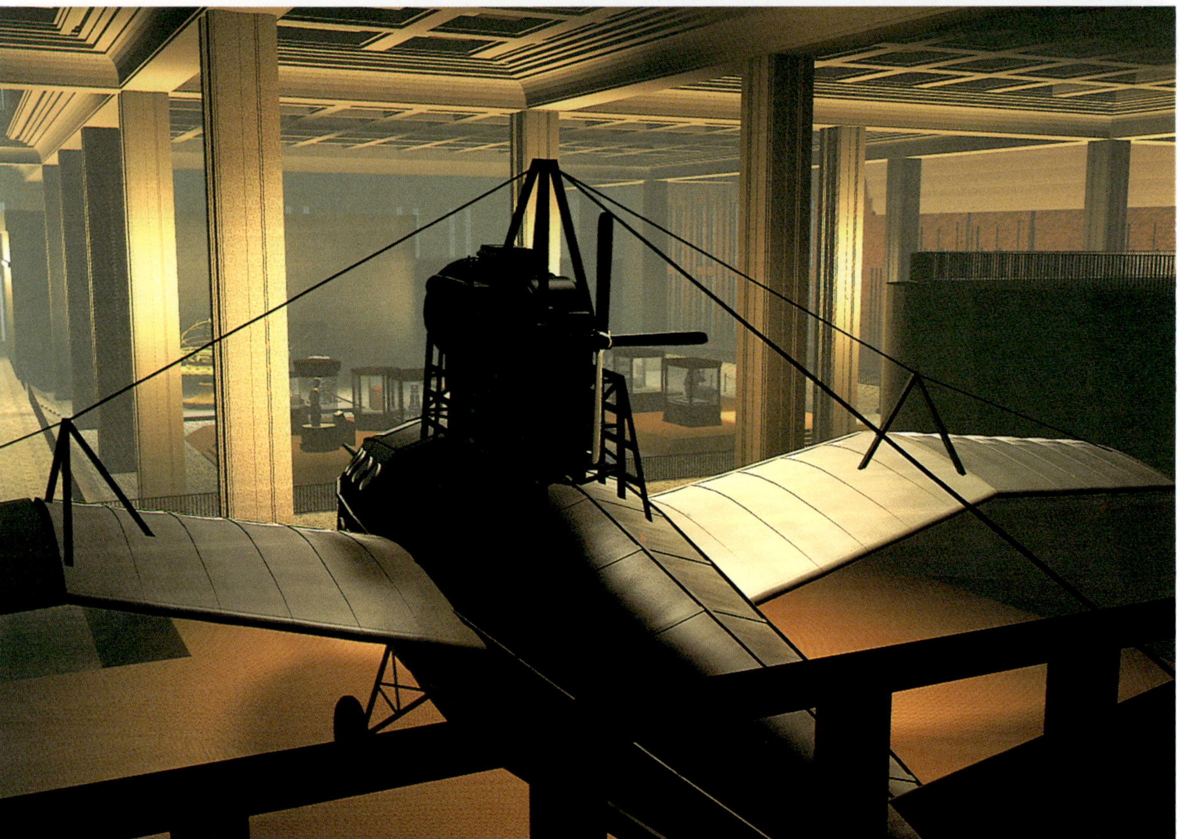

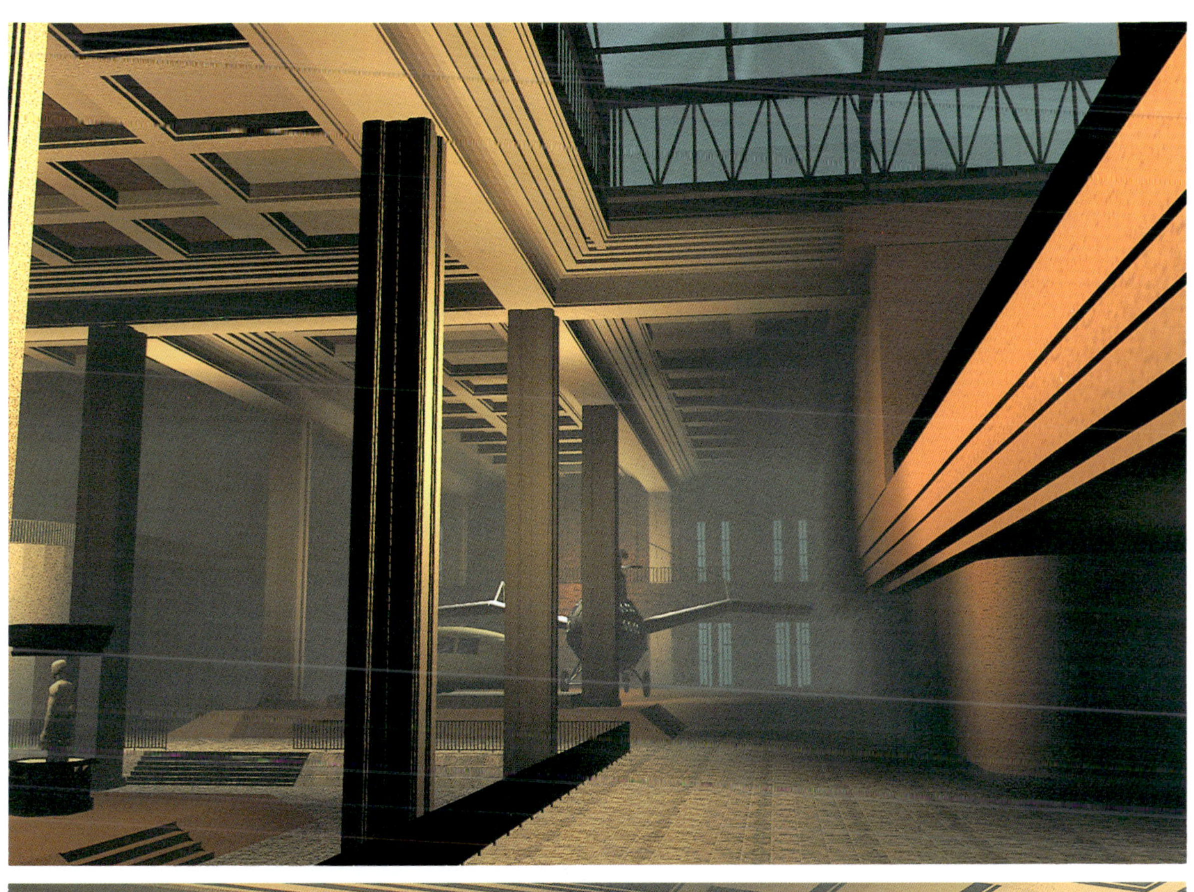

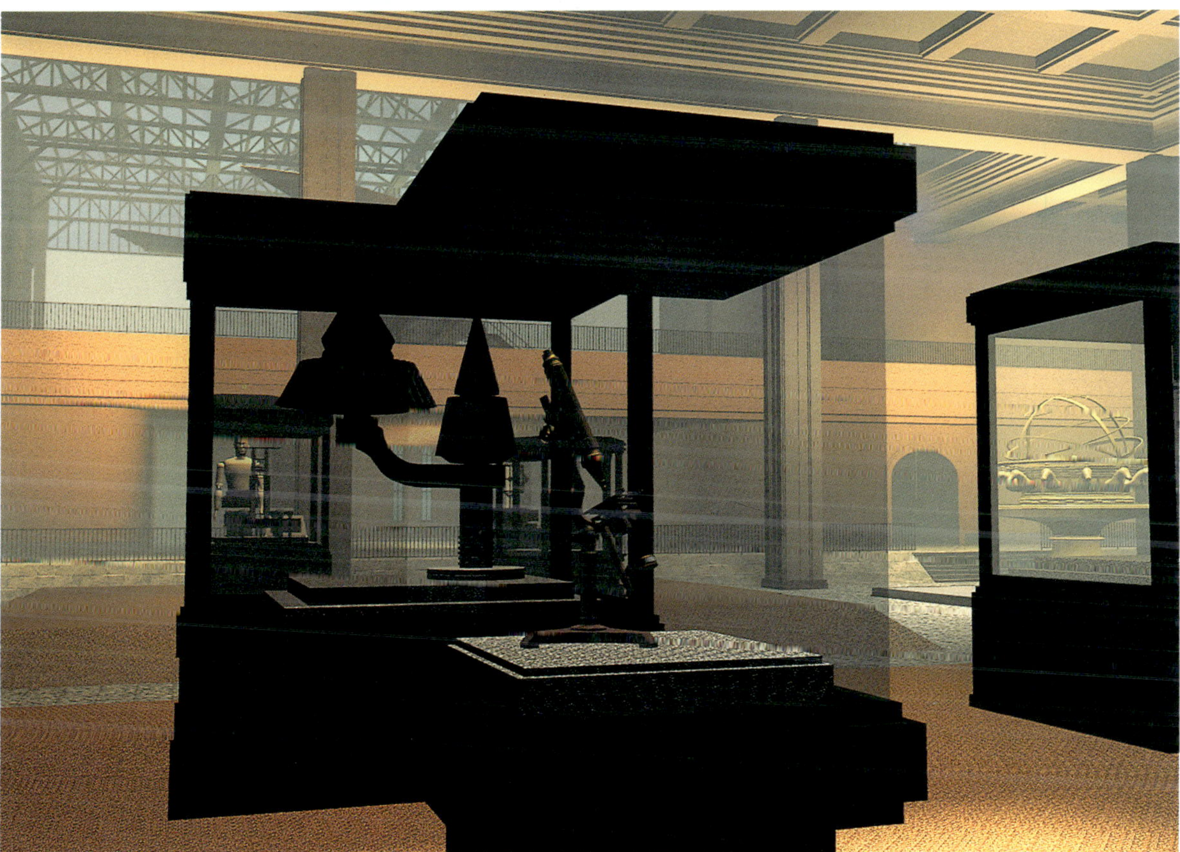

Sensorama Irradiation Experiment

Site: Imperial Museum

Research Team: Wilhelm Draun
George Tessera
John MacNaughton
Constantine Wallace

Supervisor of Experiment: Charles Reif

Experimentee: George Tessera

Statement concerning the Resumption of Experiments:
(The following remarks by George Tessera have been preserved as an attachment to the records.)

At the request of Horselover, research associates of the former National Academy of Science gathered at the Imperial Museum and laid plans to resume irradiation experiments. Through the efforts of my associates, Charles and Thomas, dramatic improvements have been made on the device once known as the Beam Machine. Introduction of redesigned vacuum tubes and a new condenser have enhanced regulation of motor revolutions and a new device has improved output capacity. It is now possible to maintain radiation for 60 minutes or more. We have christened this renovated radiation machine Sensorama. The accompanying document records the results of the first experimental operation of the Sensorama conducted on this memorable day.

Progress of Experiment:
(This record was abstracted by the experiment supervisor, Charles, from an account given by the testee, George Tessera, upon conclusion of the experiment.)

"Some 30 seconds of faint dizziness and nausea. Receding consciousness. Mechanical apparatus scattered in a forest. Scanner, binoculars, neon laser, vacuum tube, condenser, the wreckage of a communications satellite. A boy's face reflected in a pool. The boy's face disappears, and again consciousness recedes.

"A speeding train. A silver suitcase. Gadgets scattered in the forest. A rhythmic series of explosions. Through binoculars an unfamiliar tower, abandoned and eerie. A huge ship like a silkworm's cocoon draws near. The ship comes to a halt at the pinnacle of the tower, and I awake."

(9 January, Year 3 of the Imperial Age)

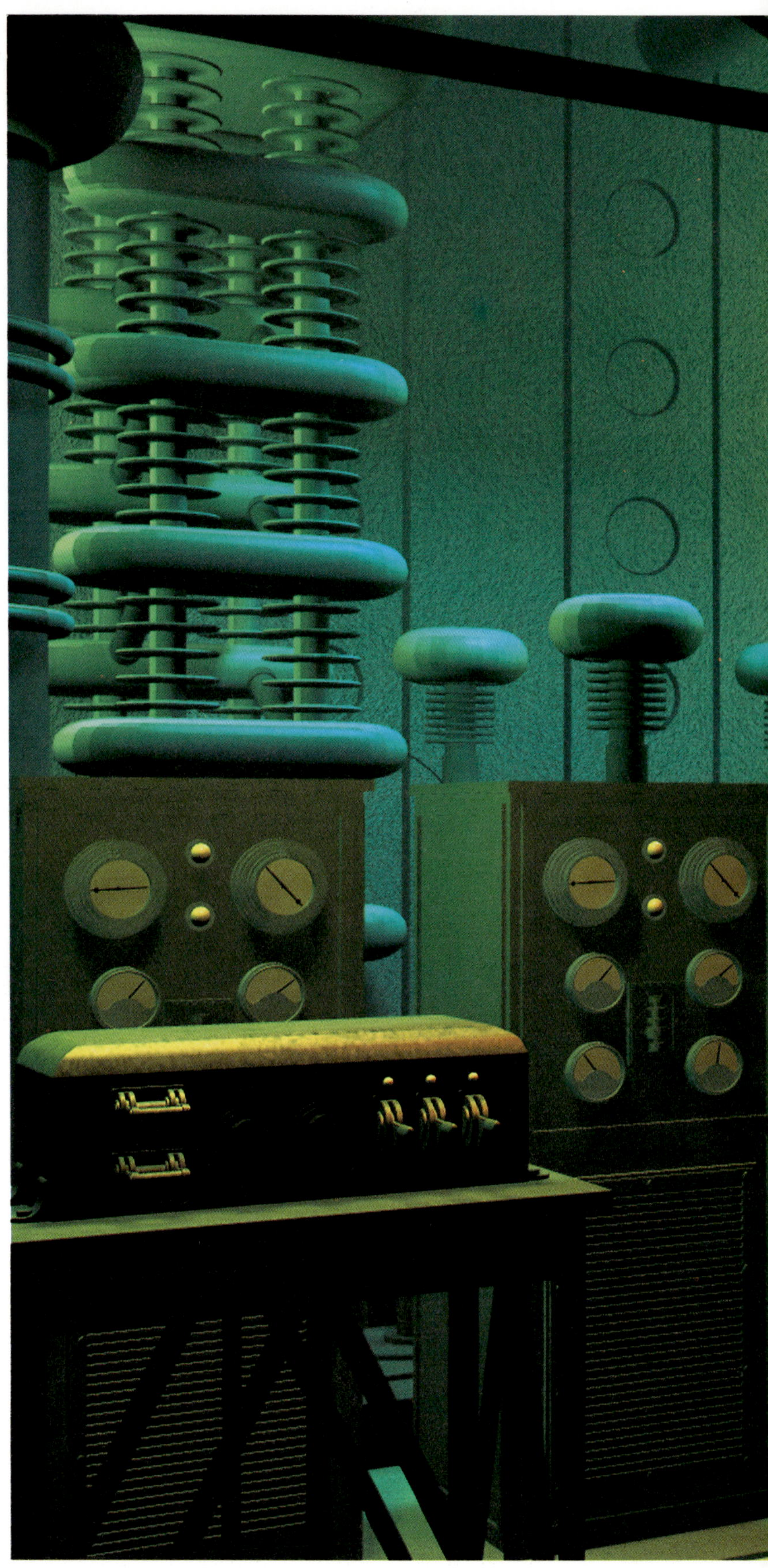

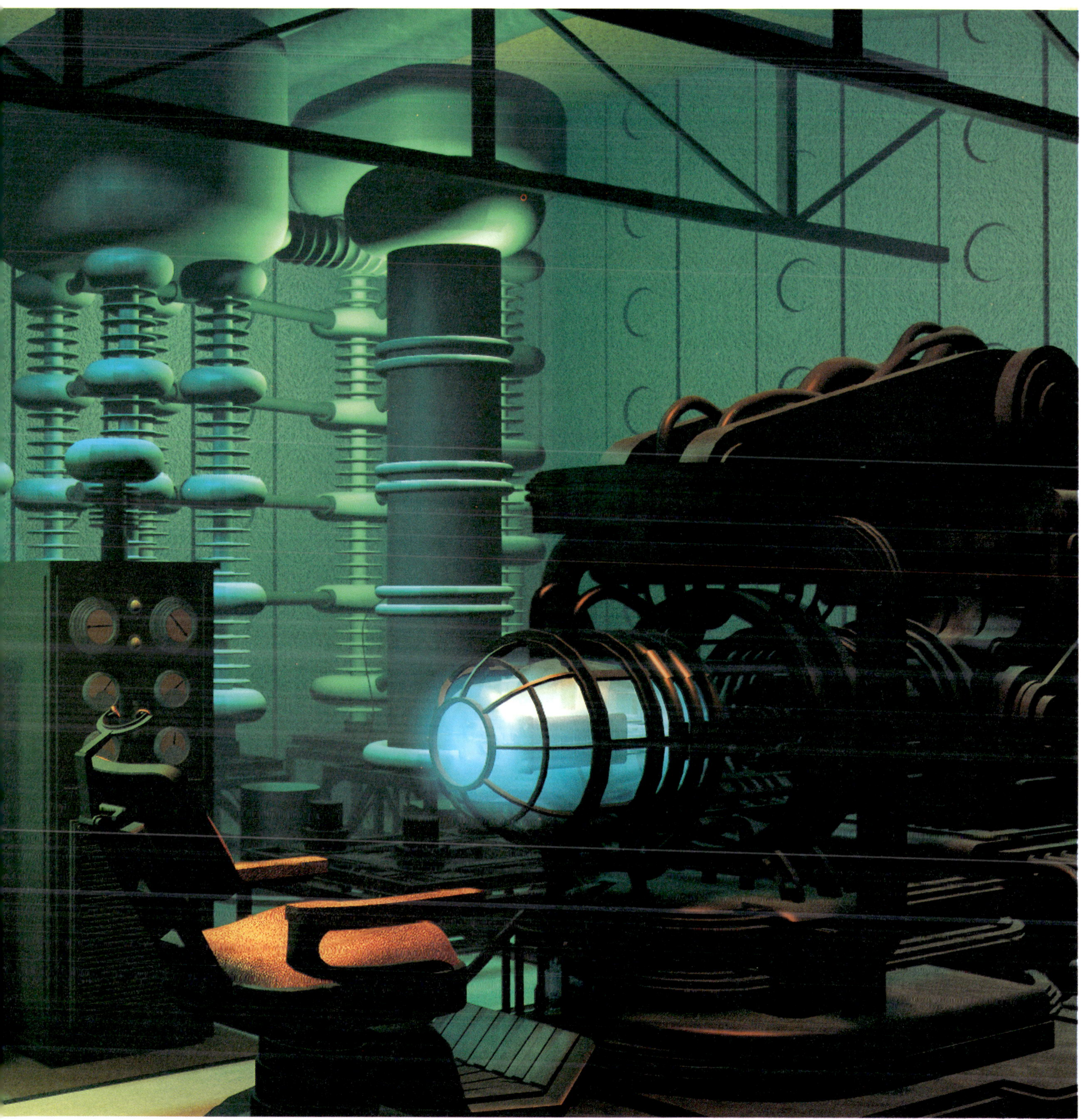

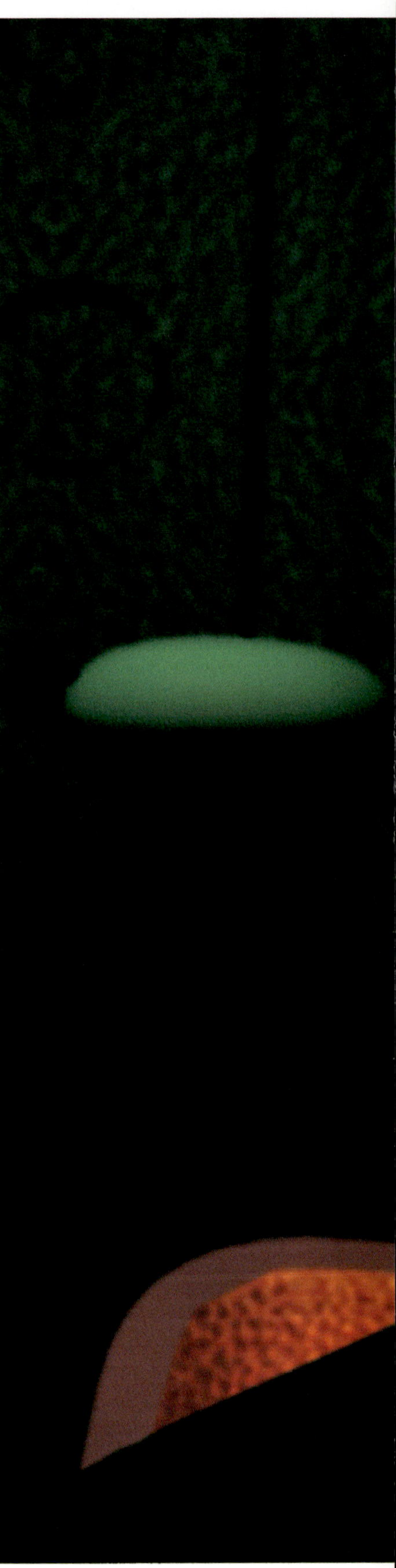

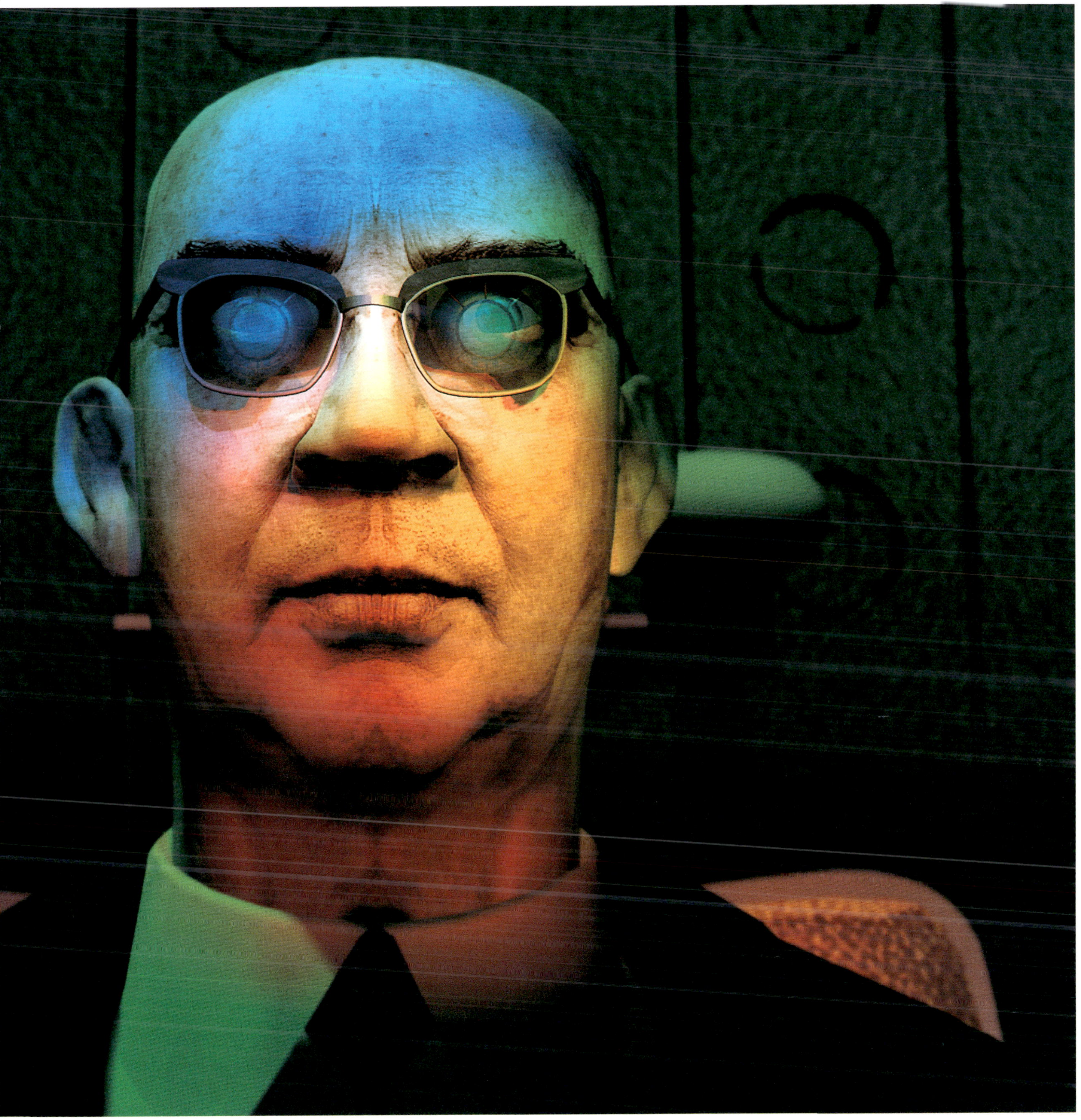

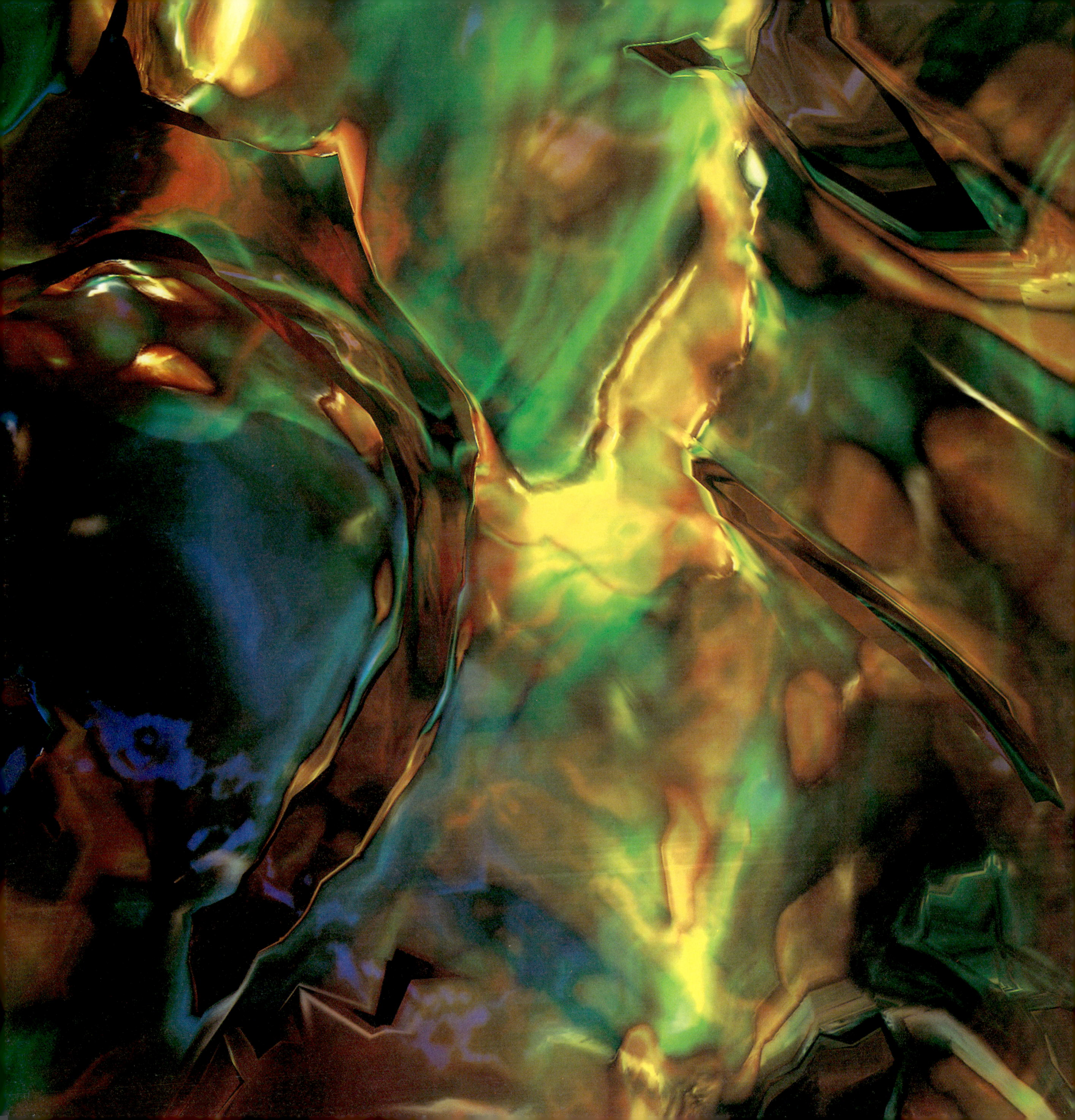

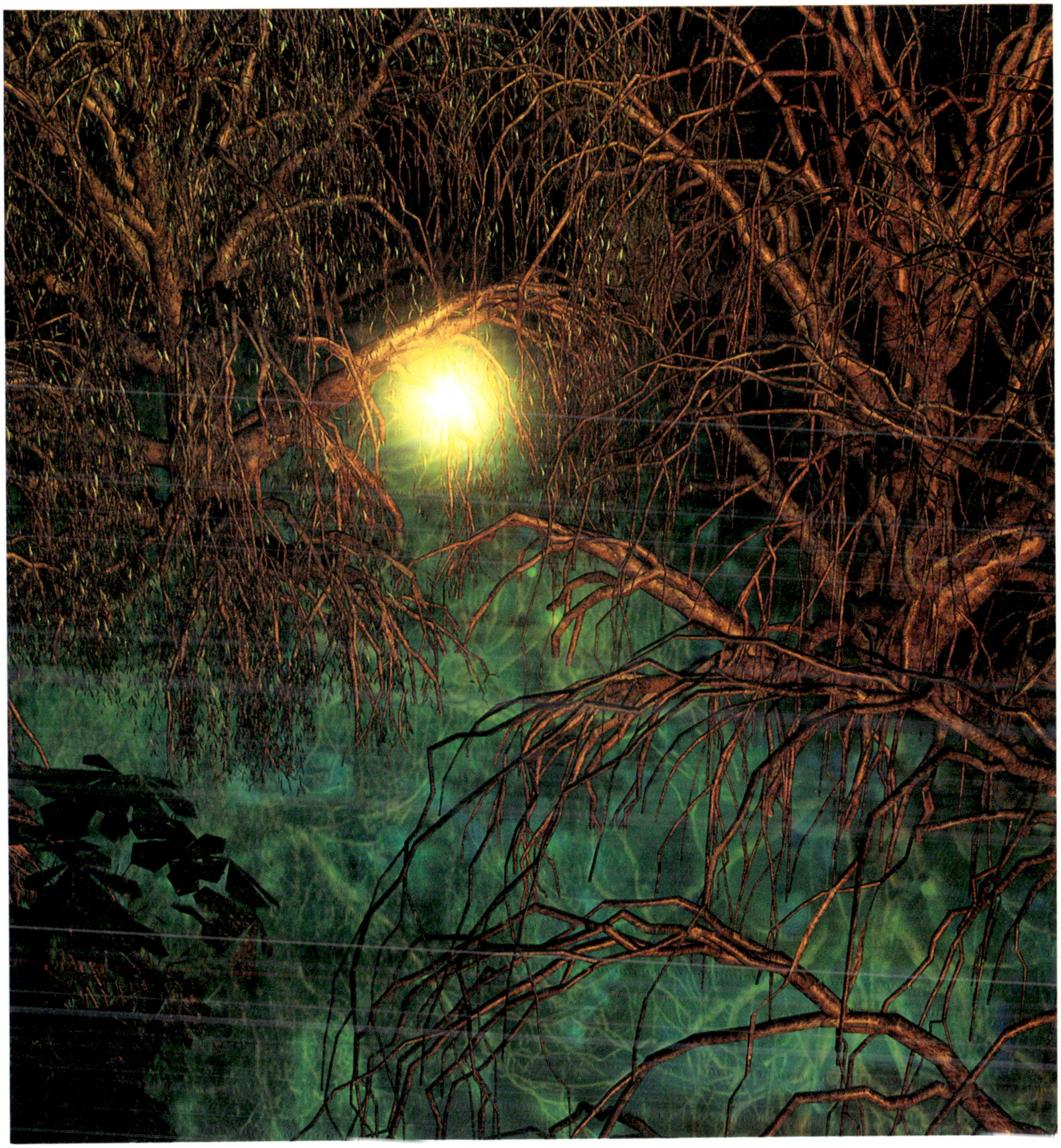

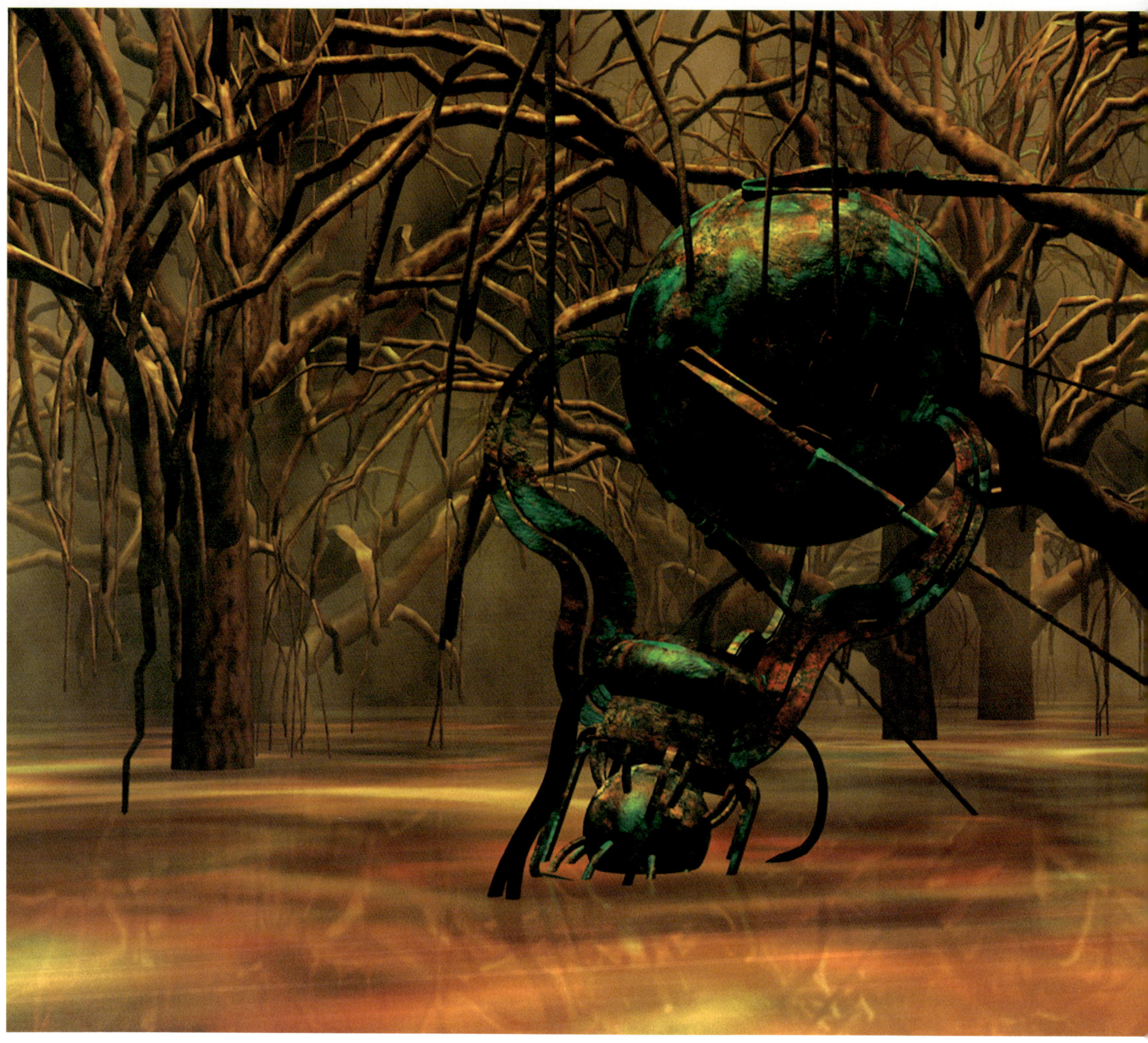

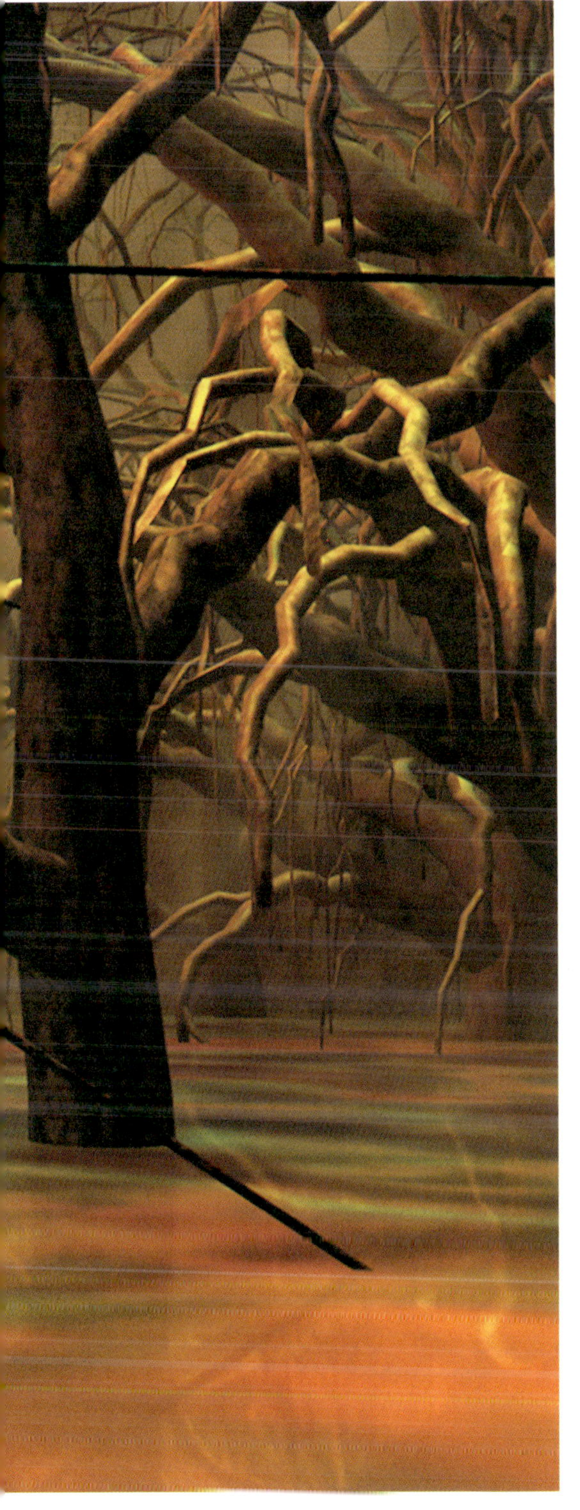

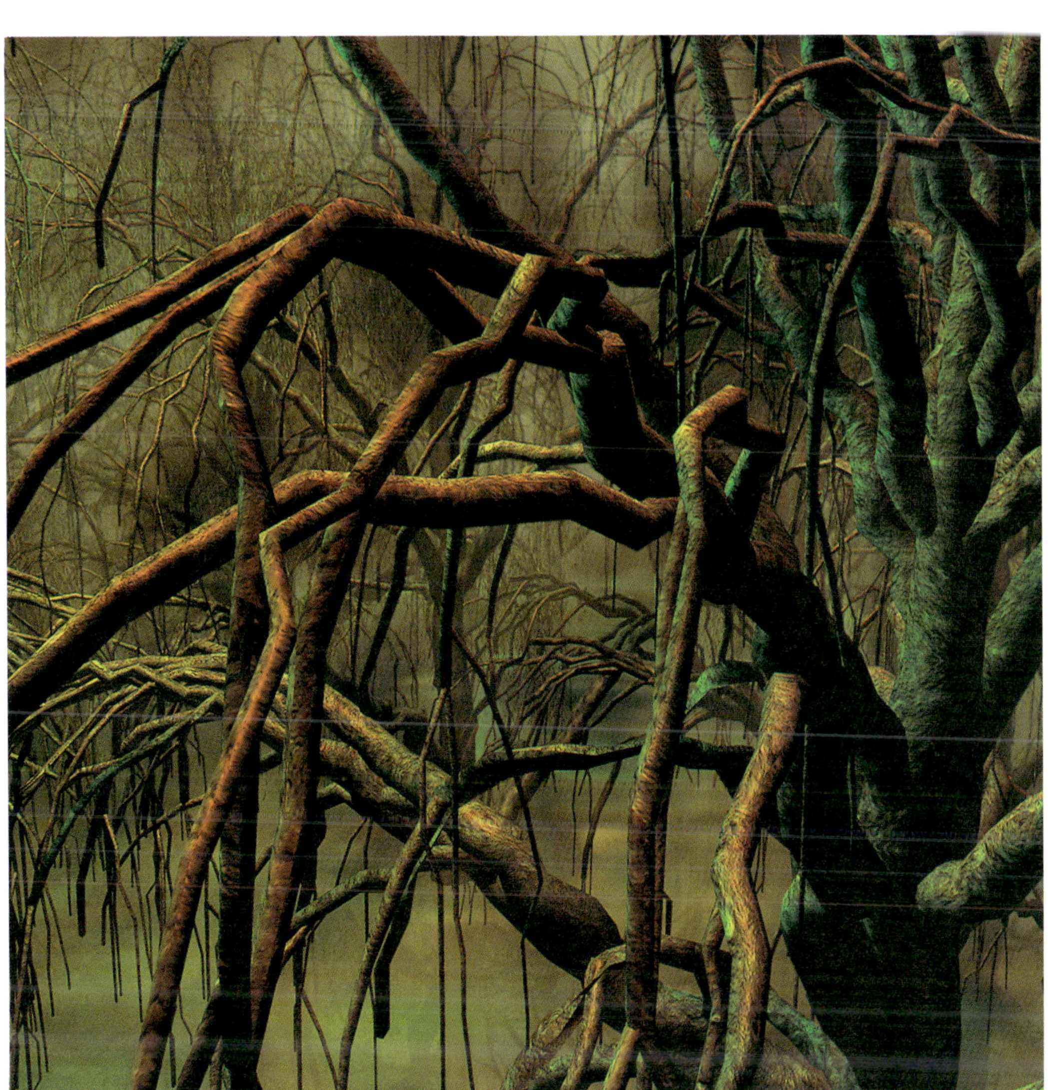

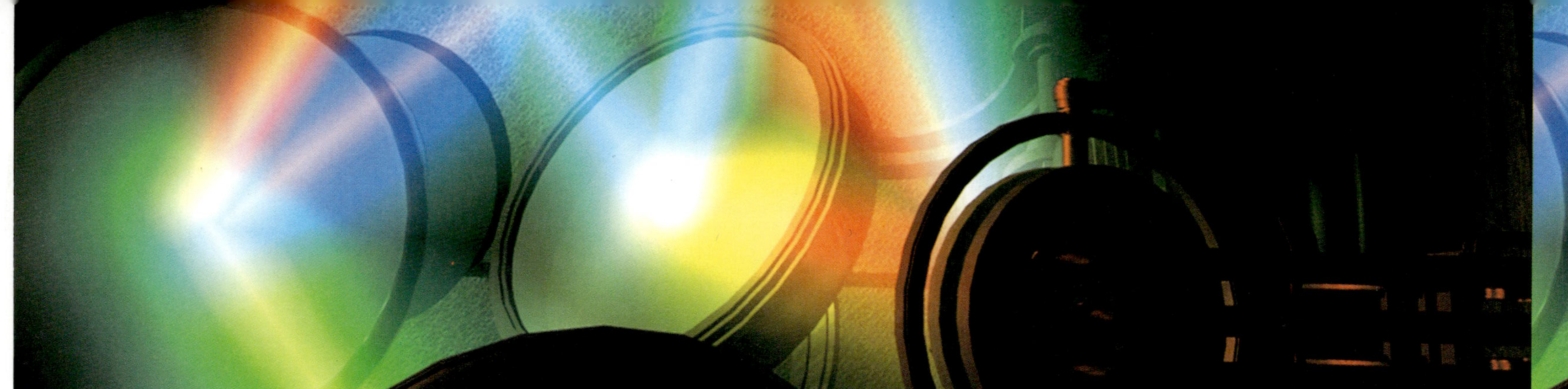

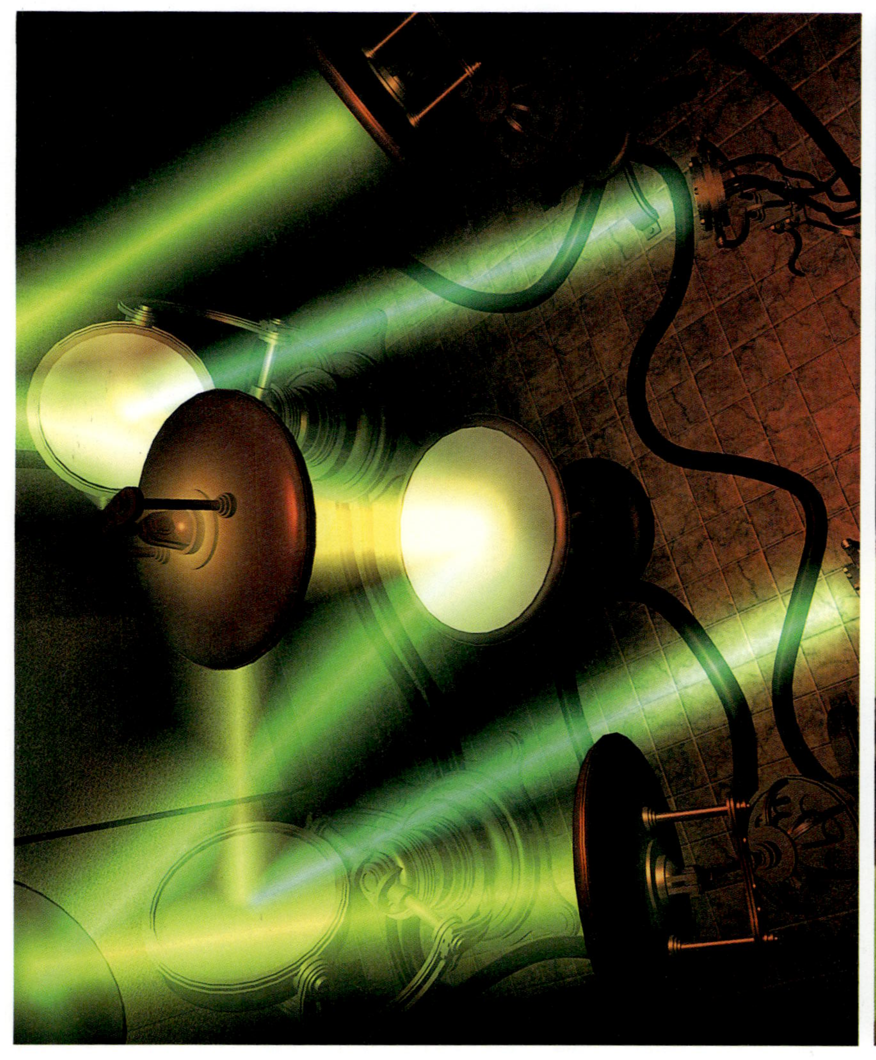

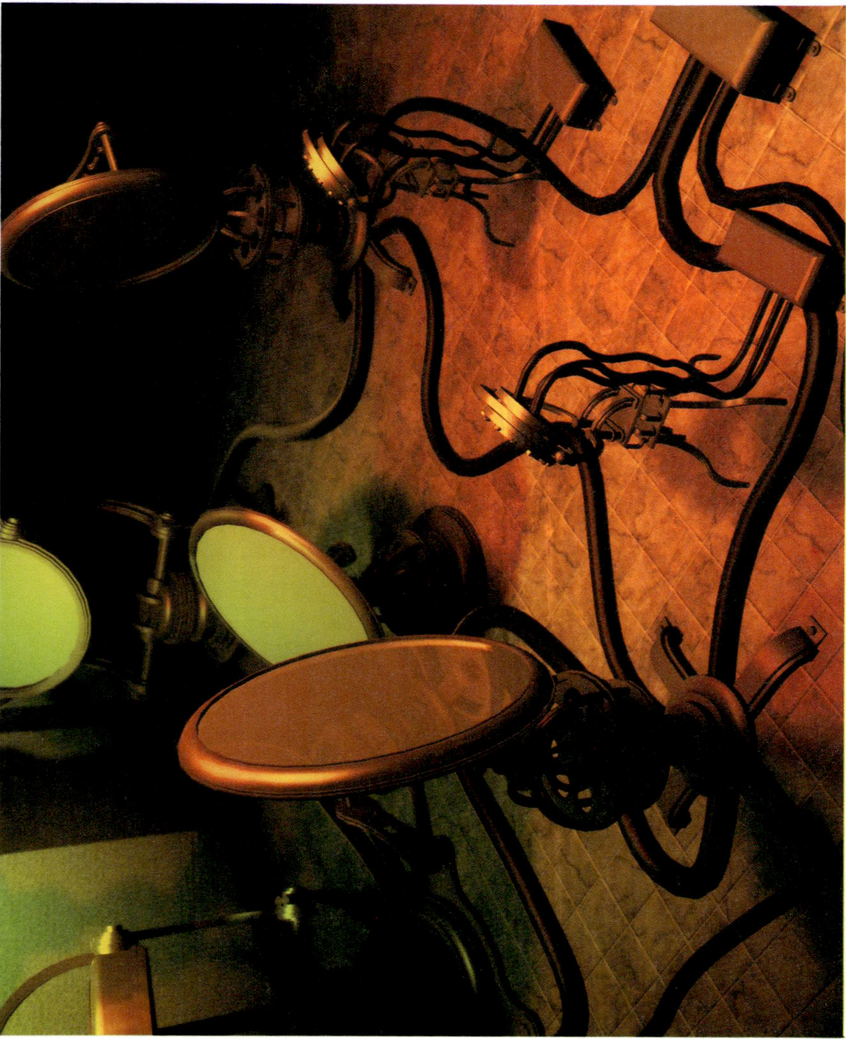

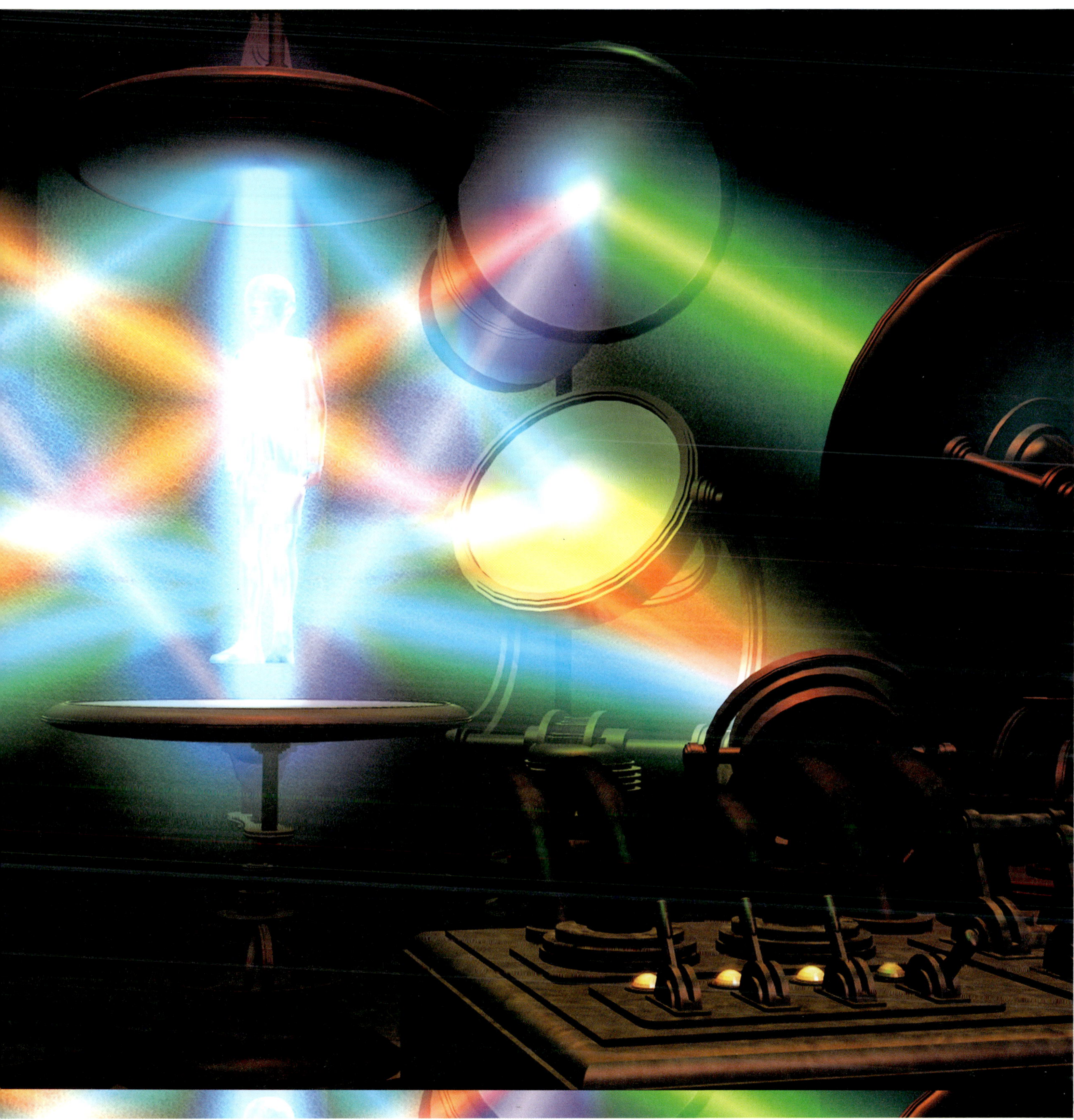

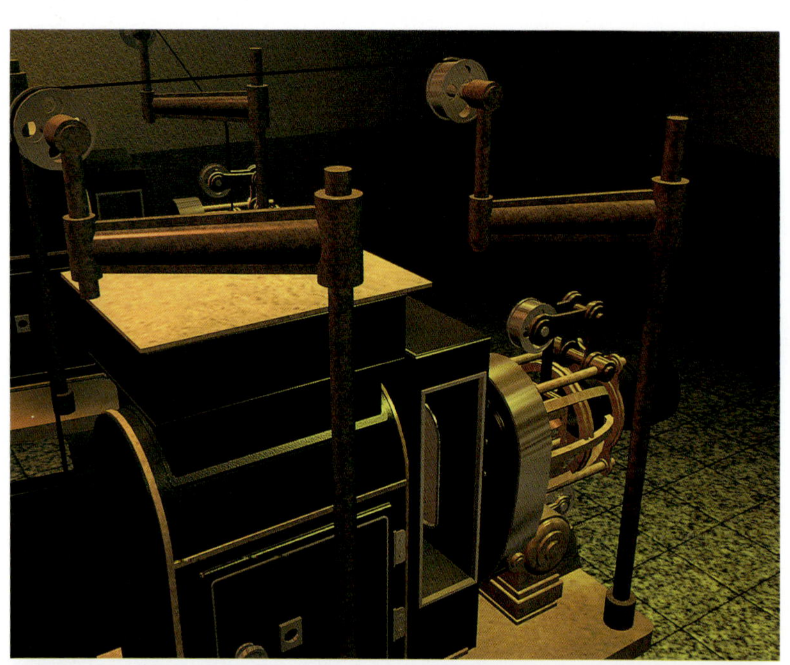

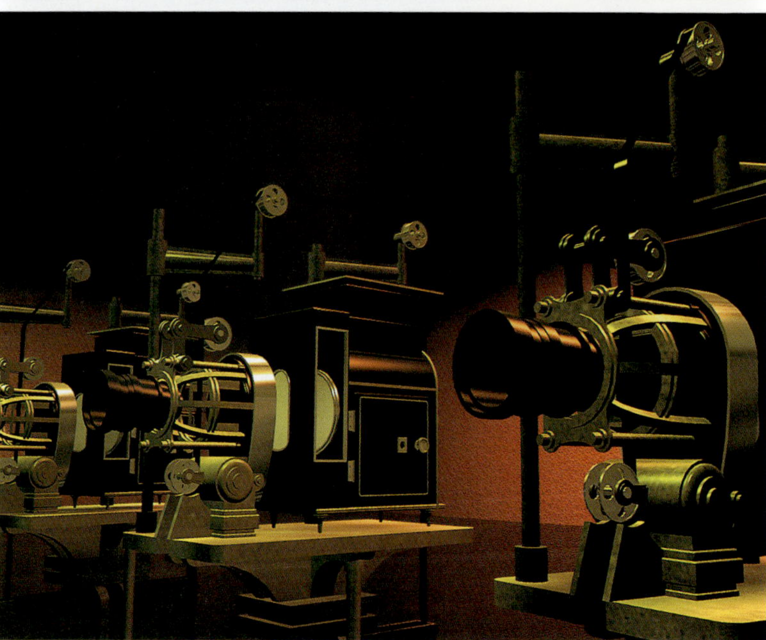

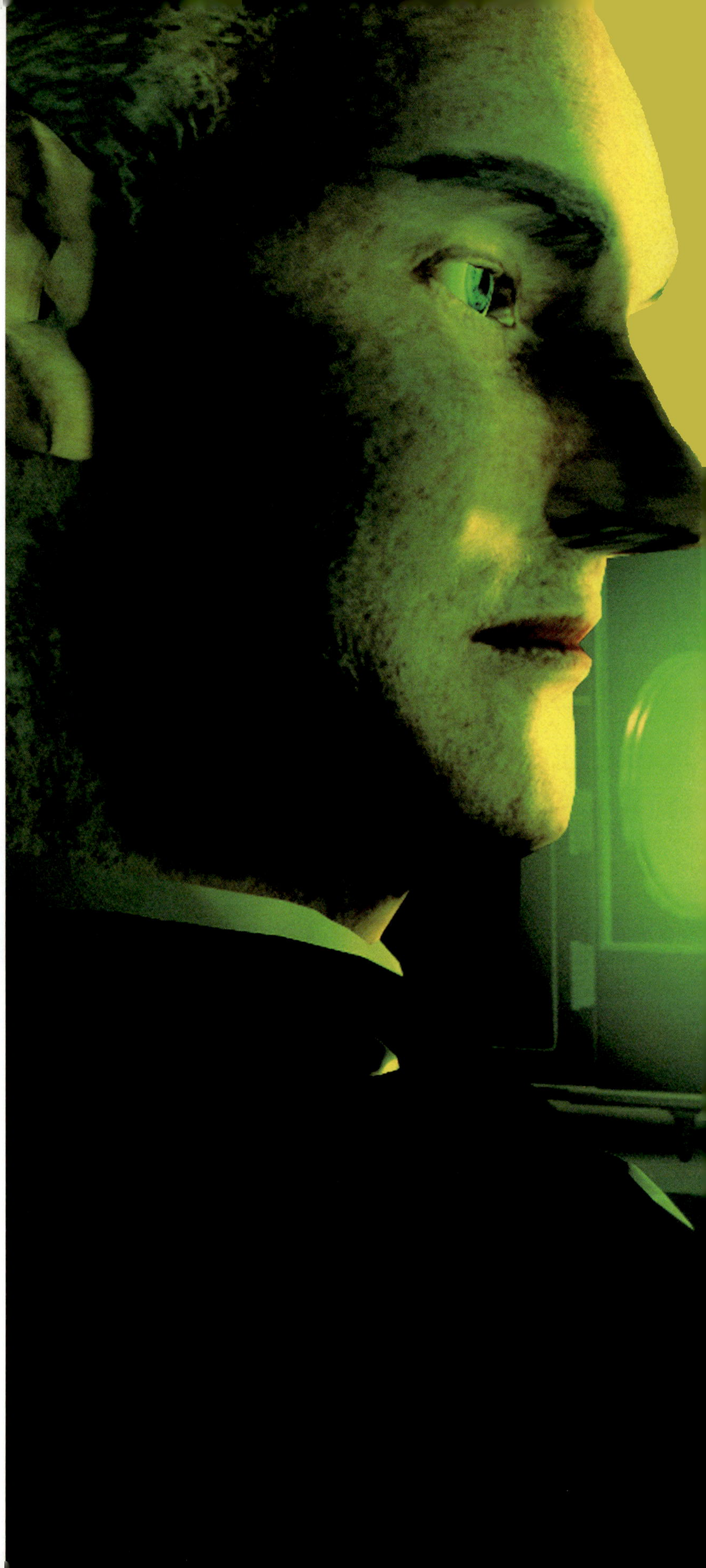

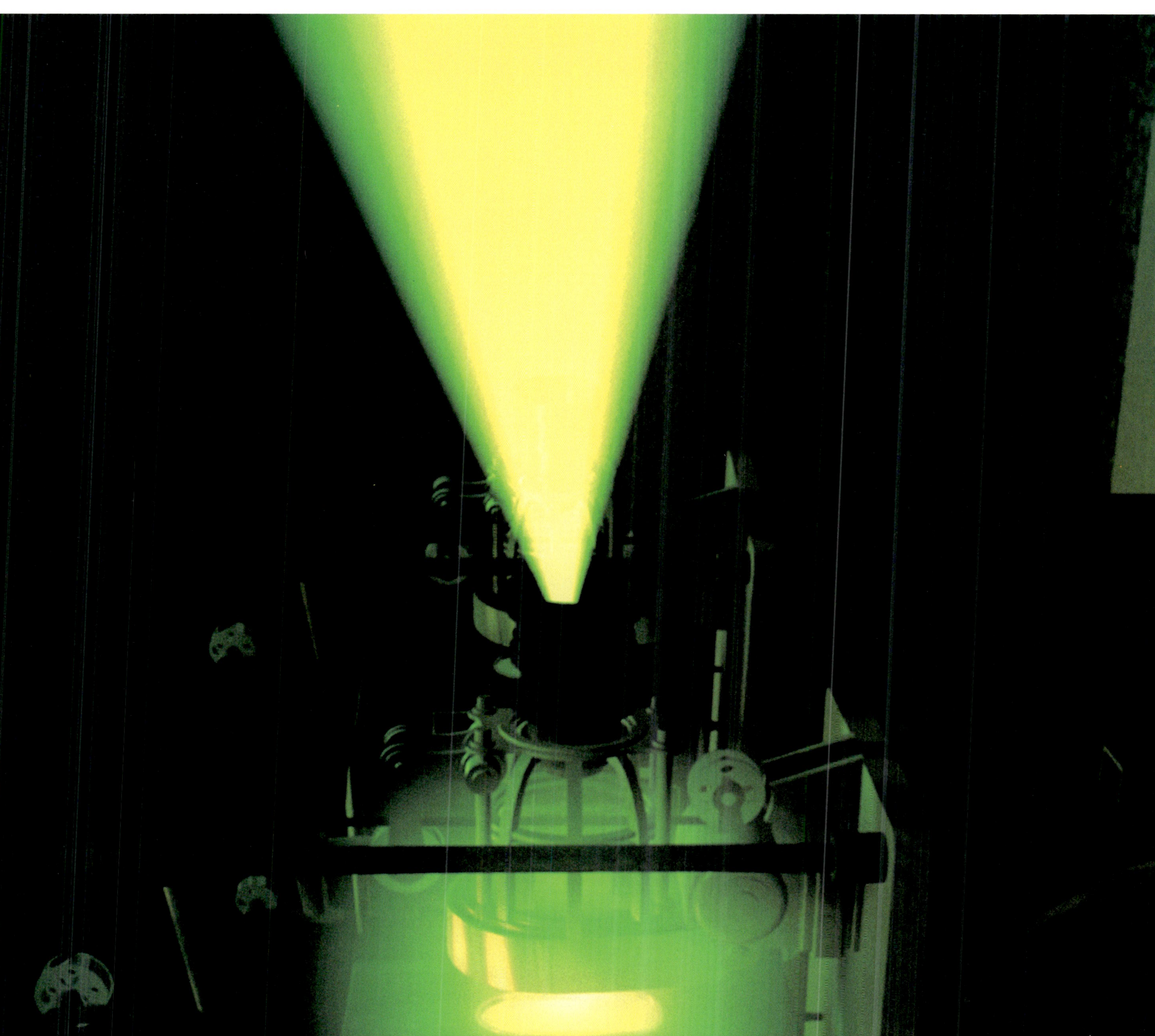

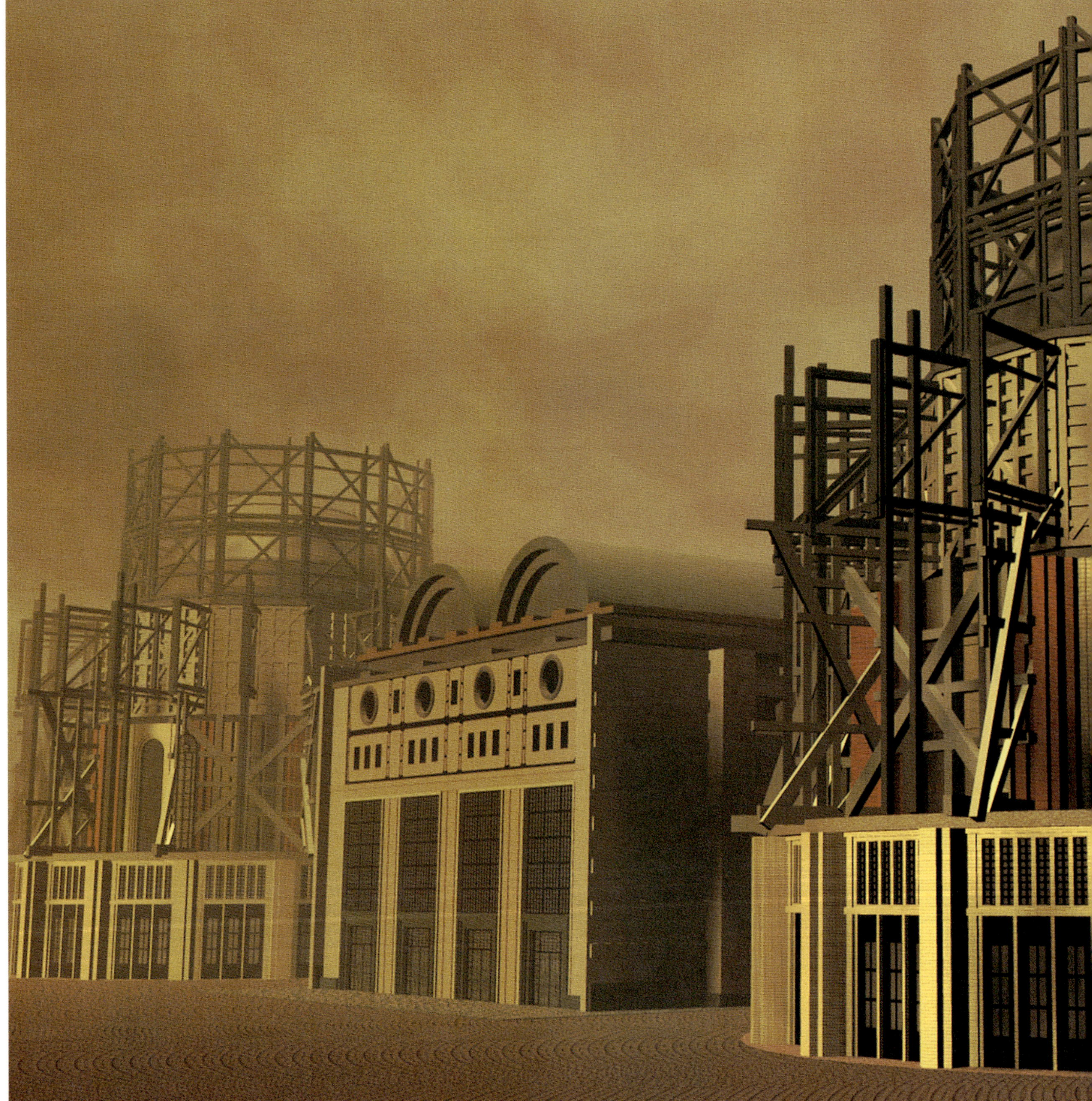

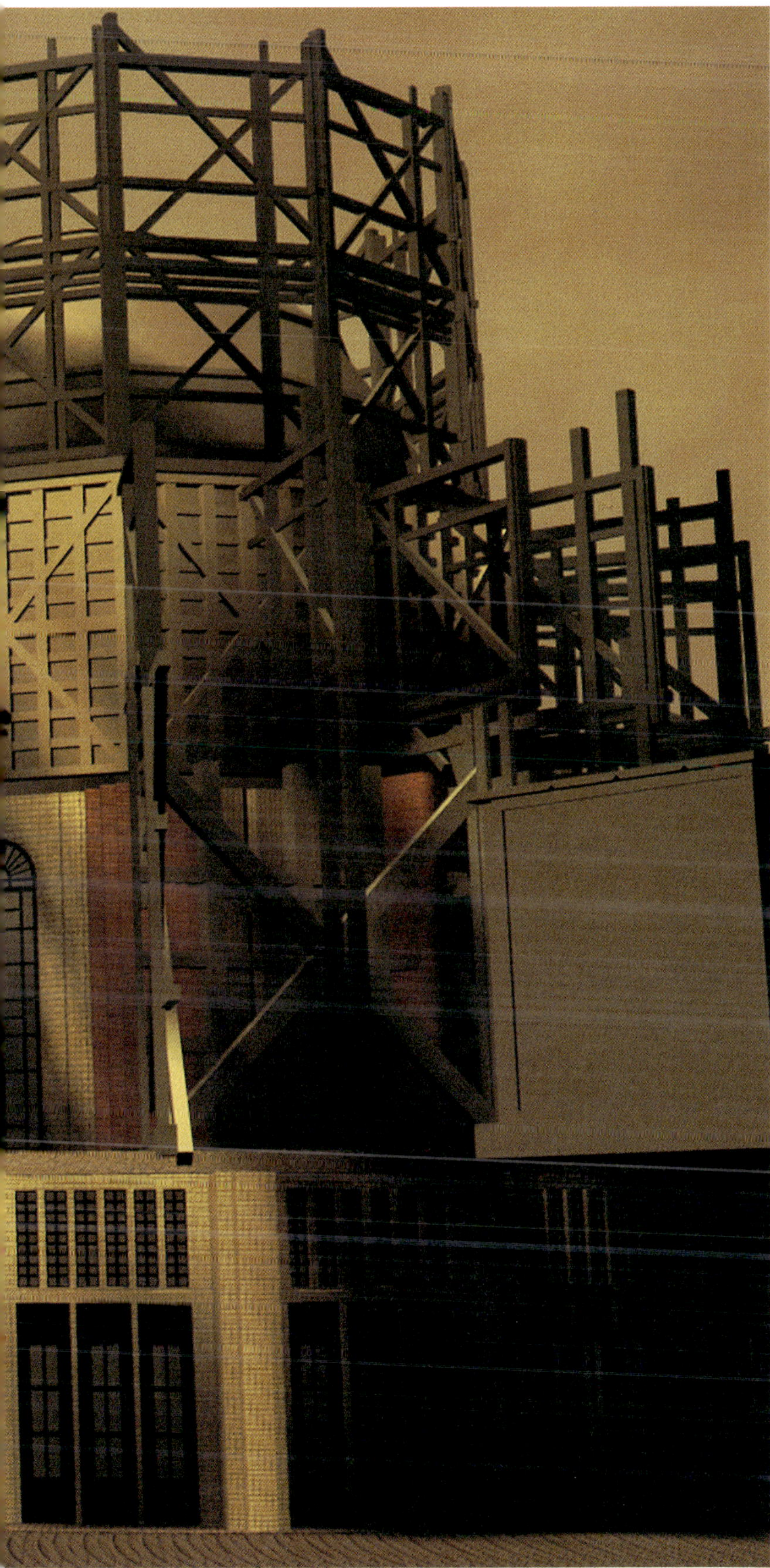

11 February, Year 4 of the Imperial Age

I observed an experiment conducted at the Imperial Museum by scientists of the former National Academy of Science. A machine called a Sensorama directed electromagnetic waves at a human subject. I also studied film footage of past experiments. If tests performed at the Academy on a prototype device known as the Beam Machine are included, more than a hundred such experiments have been conducted. The device is intended as a therapeutic apparatus for the treatment of psychological disorders and works by inducing hallucinations in subjects through radiation with electromagnetic waves. Although my inspection appears to substantiate that the radiation experiments represent no threat to the interests of the Empire, there are suspicious aspects and I intend to keep the scientists' activities under surveillance.

Notes on the Scientists

George Tessera

Physicist; a leading scholar in the fields of radiation and electromagnetic wave theory. He's a member of the faculty of the Department of Physics at the Imperial University, but he spends all his time doing research at a private facility in the suburbs of East End. He was the leader of the three-man team that conducted the experiment I observed.

Wilhelm Draun

Prominent geologist and mineralogist; chairman of the Department of Geology at the Imperial University. He and George Tessera were sent by the Army to analyze the composition of the meteorites.

Charles Reif

Specialist in radiation and electromagnetic waves; works as George's assistant; member of the staff of the Imperial Museum. The Sensorama is kept at the Museum and it's Charles's job to keep it in running order. He has detailed documentation of the effects of electromagnetic wave frequencies on human subjects.

Thomas Reich

Widely respected mechanical engineer; faculty member at the University. He is now under contract to the Army and is making an excavator at the Ordnance Factory. He didn't participate in the recent experiment.

John MacNaughton

Student of astronomy at the old National Science Academy. He later turned to pharmacology and is now on the staff of the Army Hospital. He's Constantine Wallace's assistant.

Constantine Wallace

Clinician who has treated patients using electromagnetic waves and radiation; member of the staff of the Army Hospital. At present he engages chiefly in research but sees patients referred by the Army.

(From the diary of Hausmann)

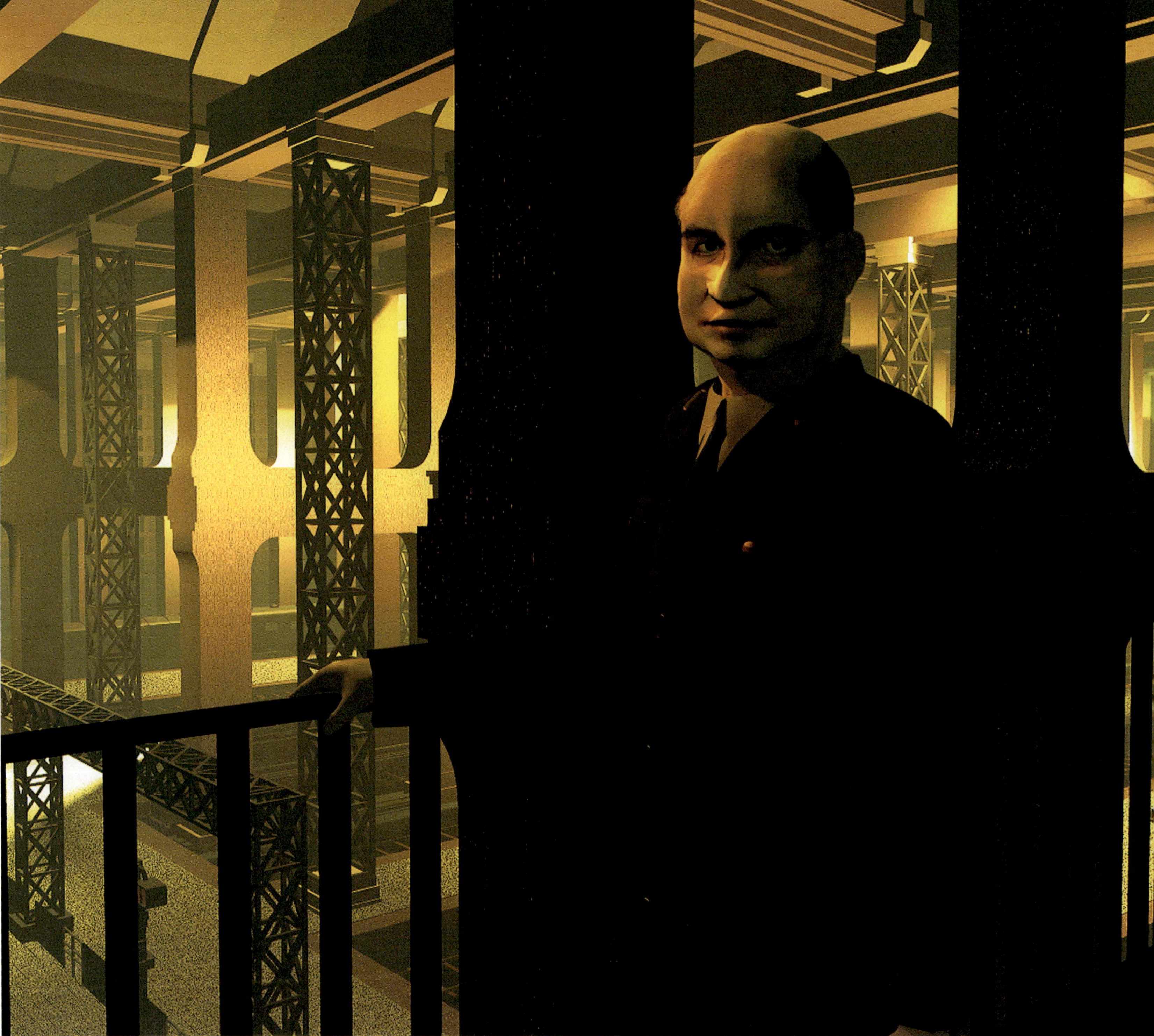

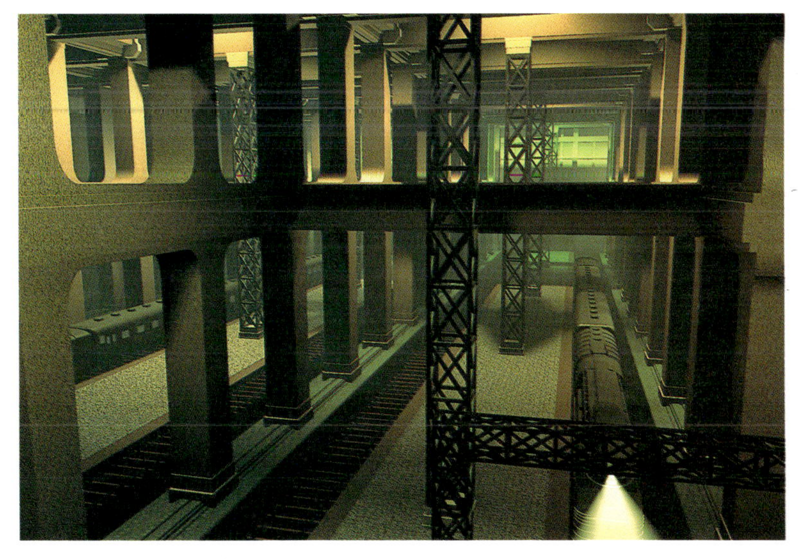

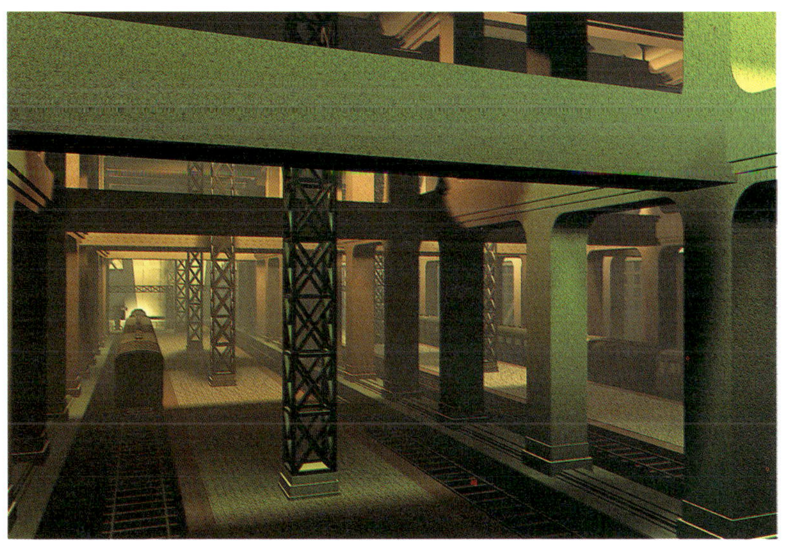

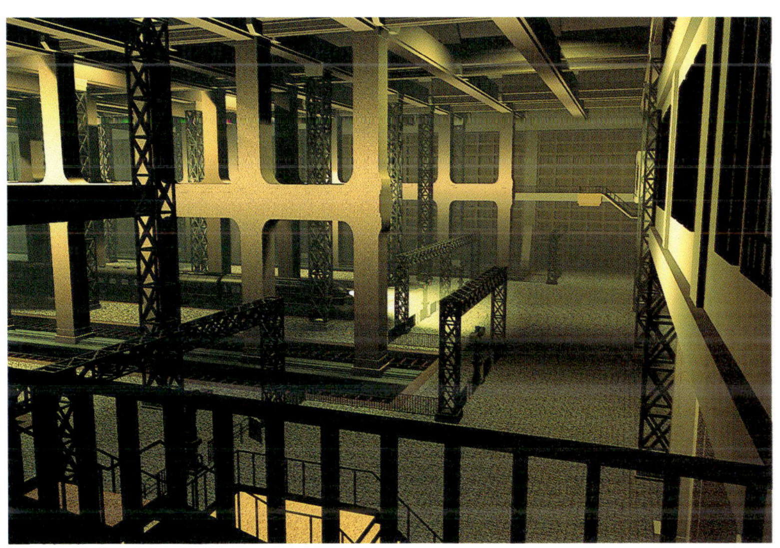

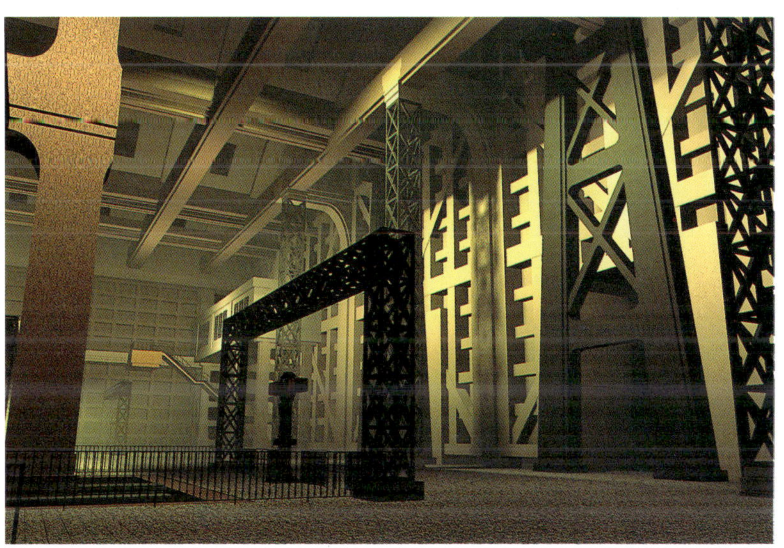

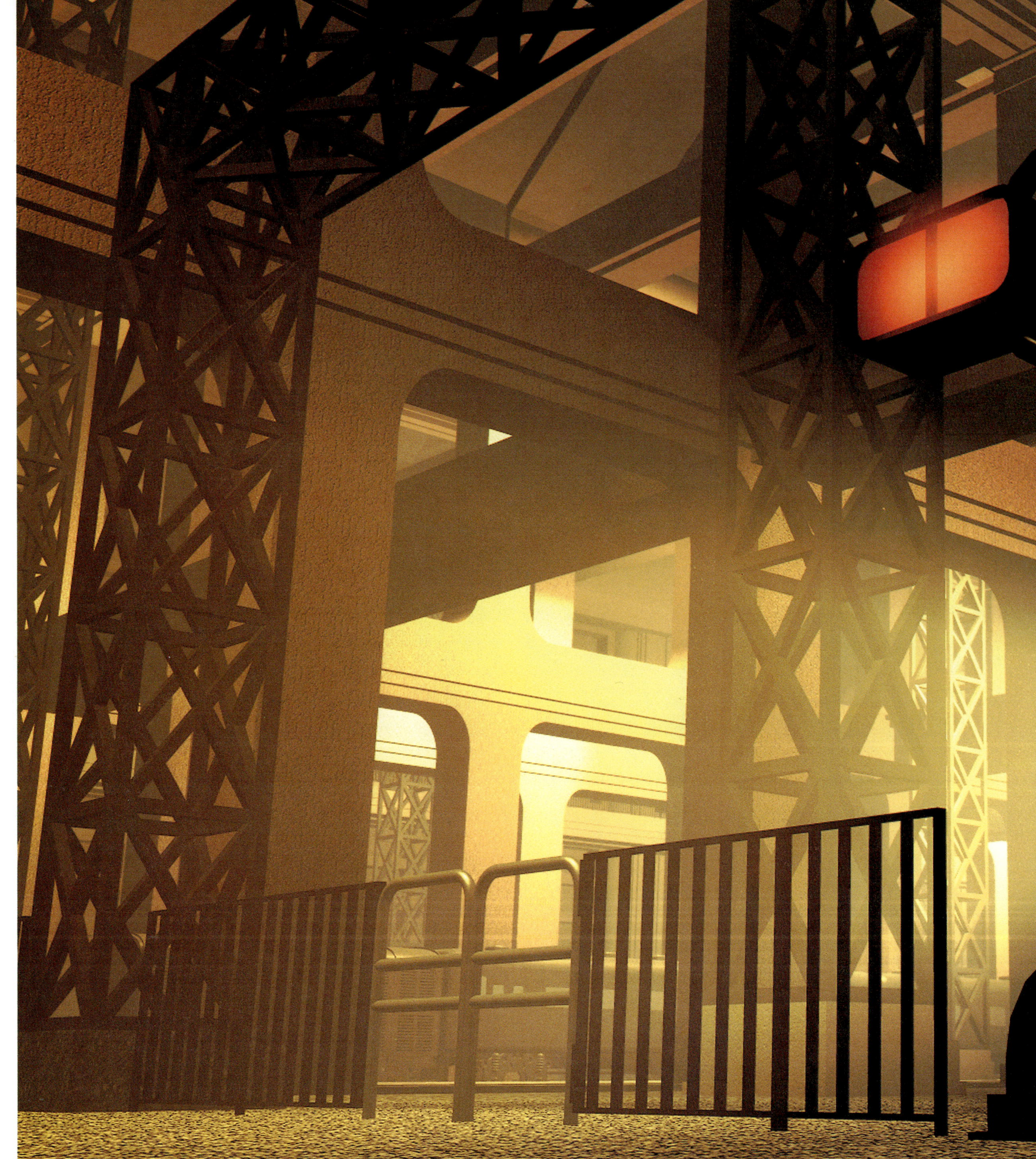

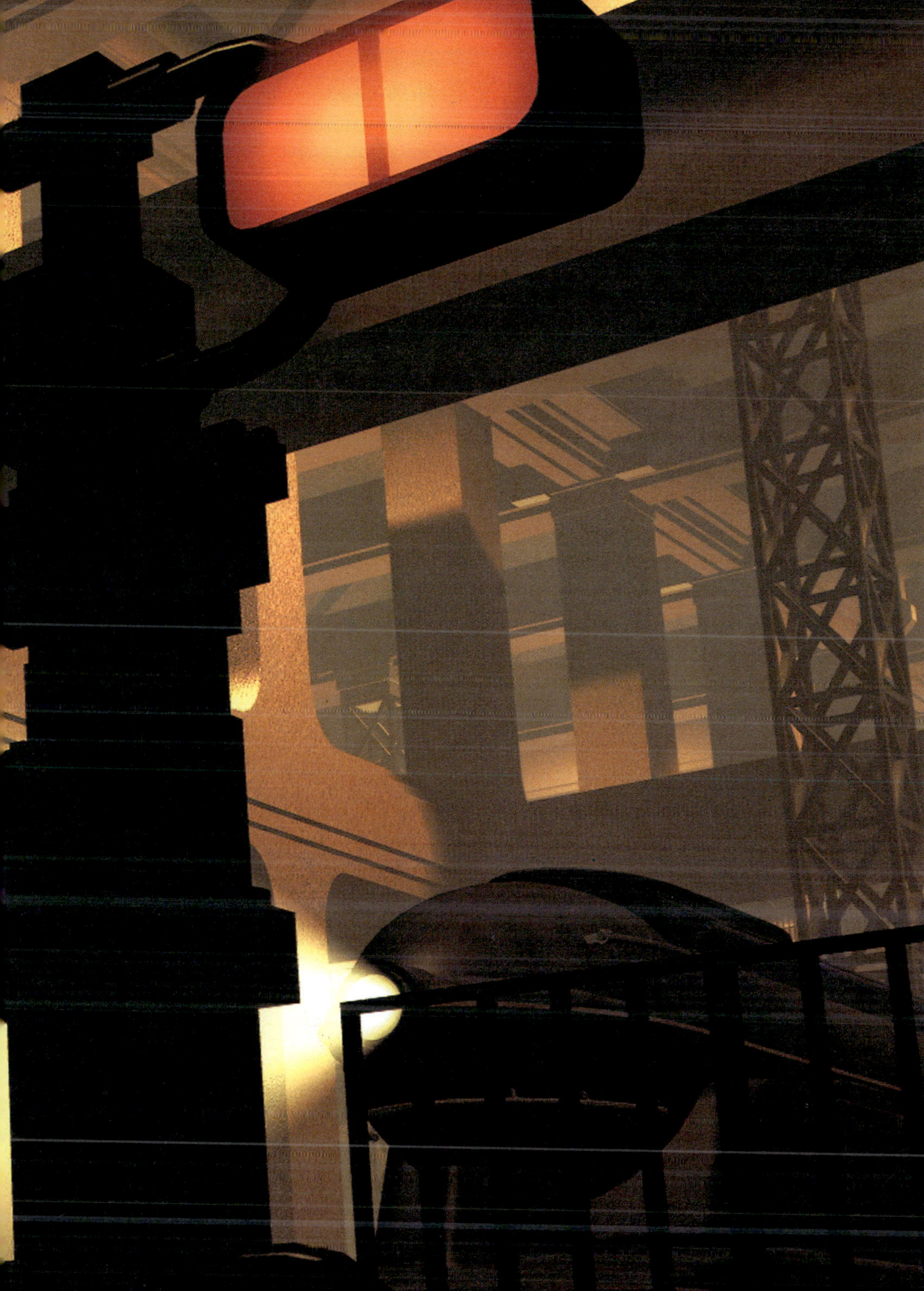

26 February, Year 4 of the Imperial Era

Chairman Onegin,

Through the assistance of my comrades I have received a special three-rank promotion. I am now commanding officer of the Imperial Guards and report directly to Supreme Commander Slowslop. Responsibility for the Army's daily operations and for the elaboration of strategies has been entrusted entirely to Slowslop. You may rest assured that appointment to a position as his immediate subordinate has put me in an extremely advantageous situation for gathering intelligence.

That much said, allow me to brief you on the present situation.

As I informed you the other day, Slowslop has, at Orlovsky's command, begun to excavate the meteorites. His plan is to repair an abandoned mine tunnel and to store the meteorites at the Army Ordnance Factory.

At present he is still working on repair of the tunnel, and, as no date has yet been set for completion of the excavator, meteorite recovery is not likely to begin until sometime next year. But more important than the excavations themselves is the use to which the Empire plans to put this source of energy, and I will spare no effort to find that out.

I have one further piece of information to report.

Seven scientists of the former National Academy of Science have built a mysterious device known as a Sensorama that is powered by the meteorites. The scientist's activities are now being investigated by Army Intelligence. This machine they call the Sensorama uses electromagnetic wave radiation to induce artificial optical images in the minds of human subjects. Why Empire leaders are so concerned about this machine I am unable to say at the moment, but I intend to keep close track of subsequent developments.

Enclosed please find pertinent documents. I await your instructions.

Your ever faithful servant,
O. Gondarev

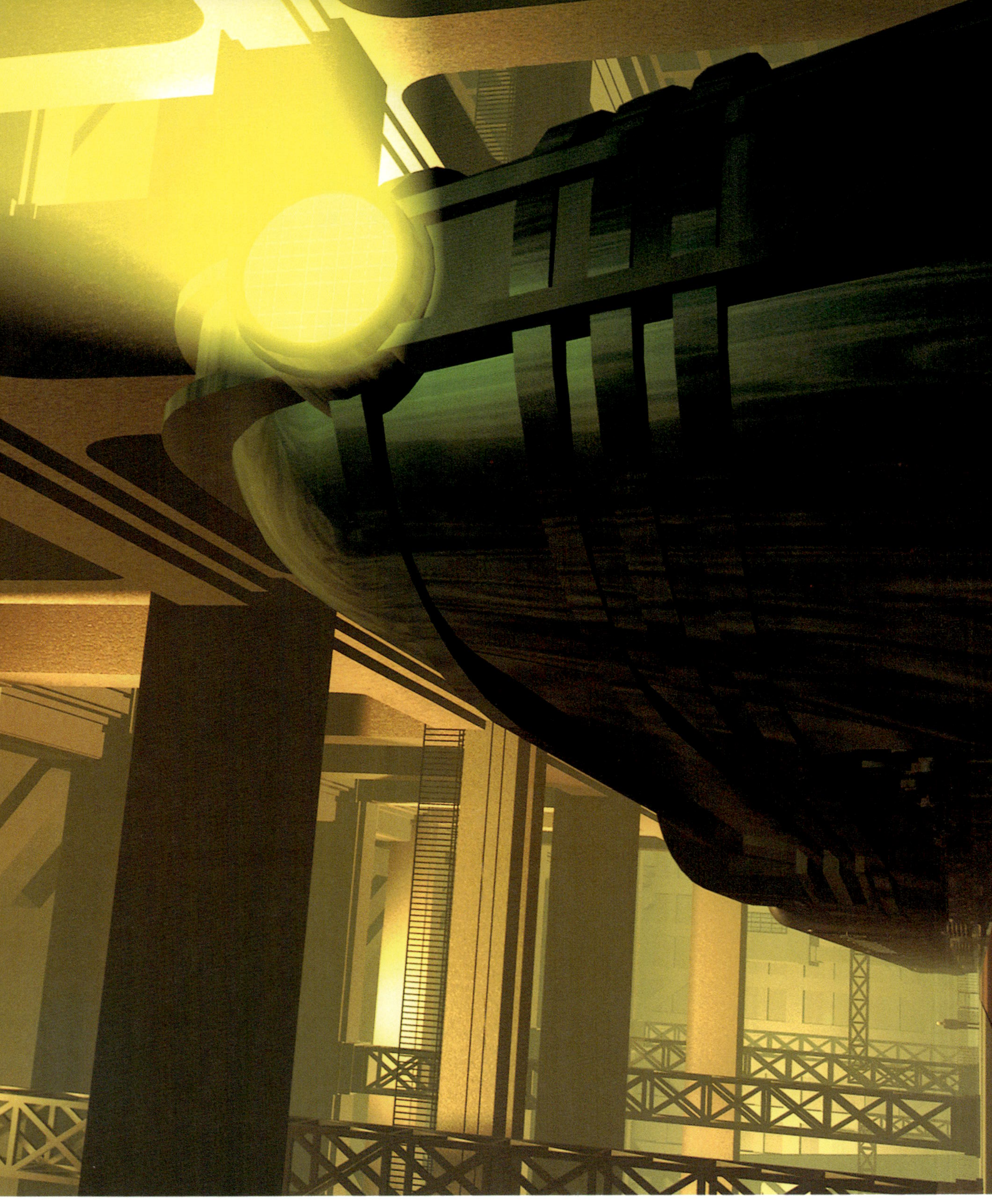

Build, mass-produce, stockpile
The smelting furnace: a plan for starting over
An era of information and natural resources
Intelligence agents make inquiries
Light and shadow, out of balance for all eternity
Documentation has been compiled
Expectations prop up a realm of facts
Needs of the new Empire
Those slow to escape will be detained

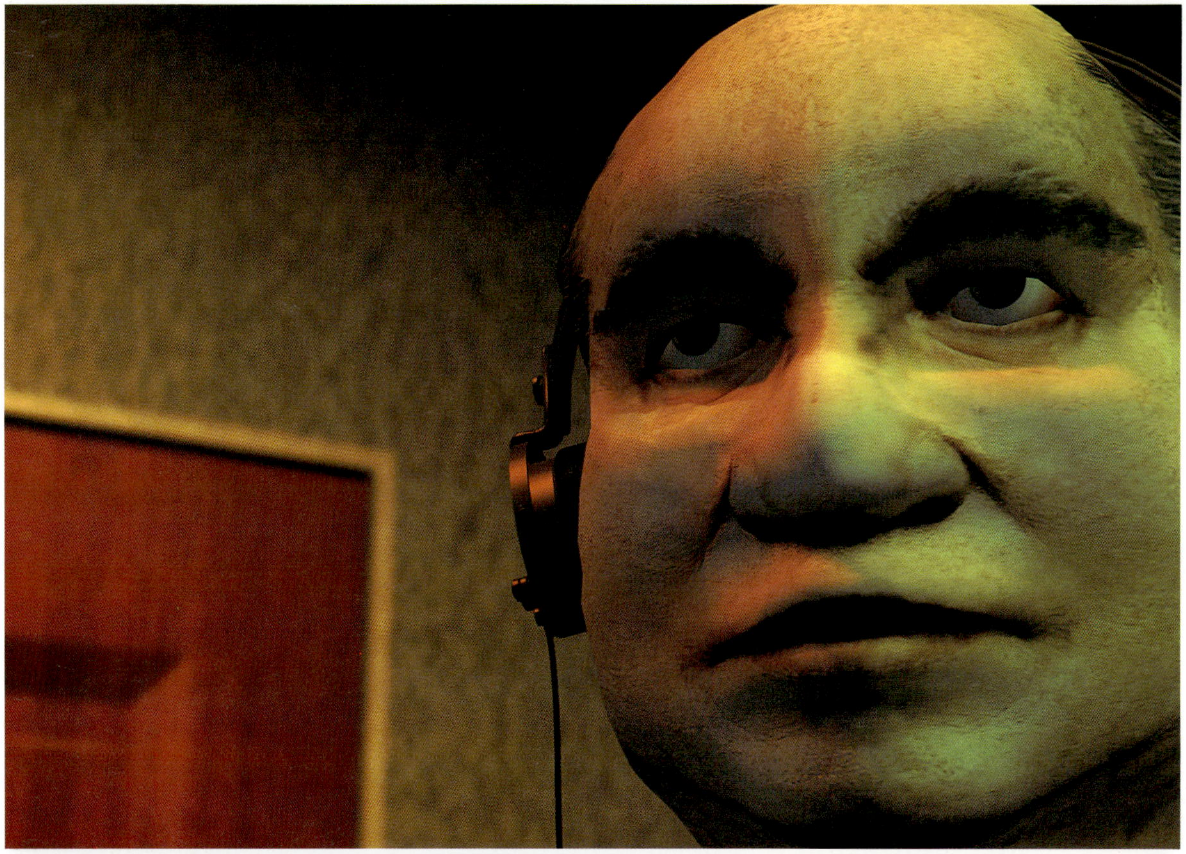

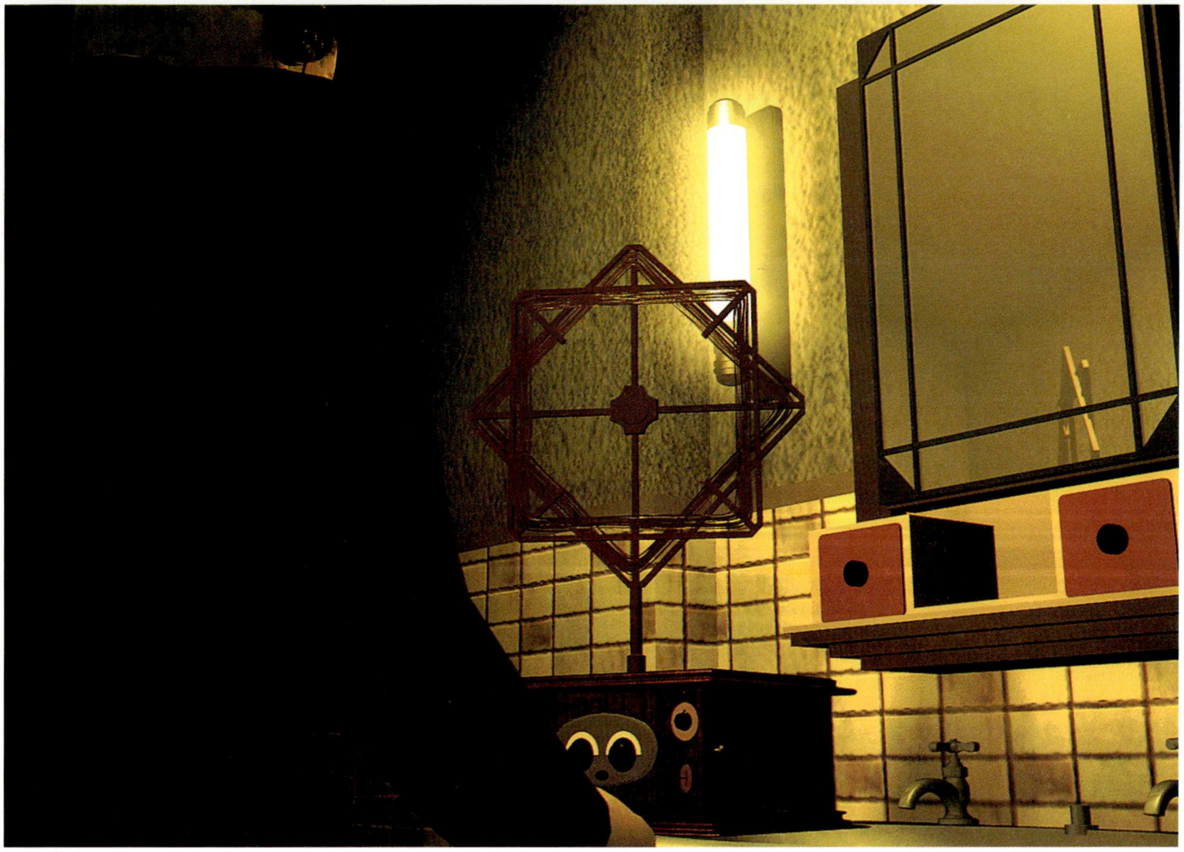

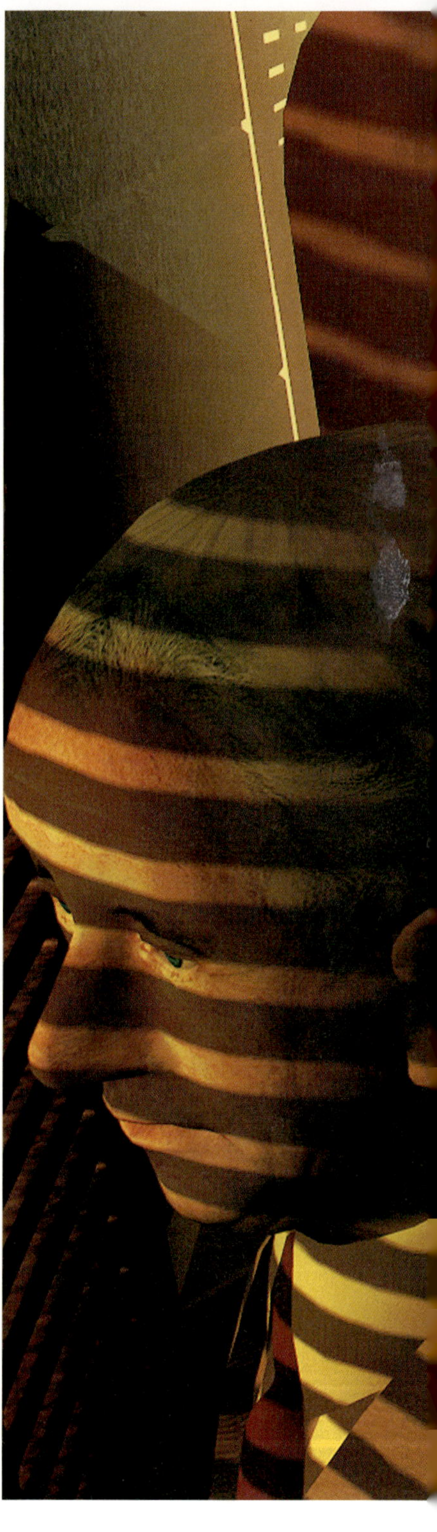

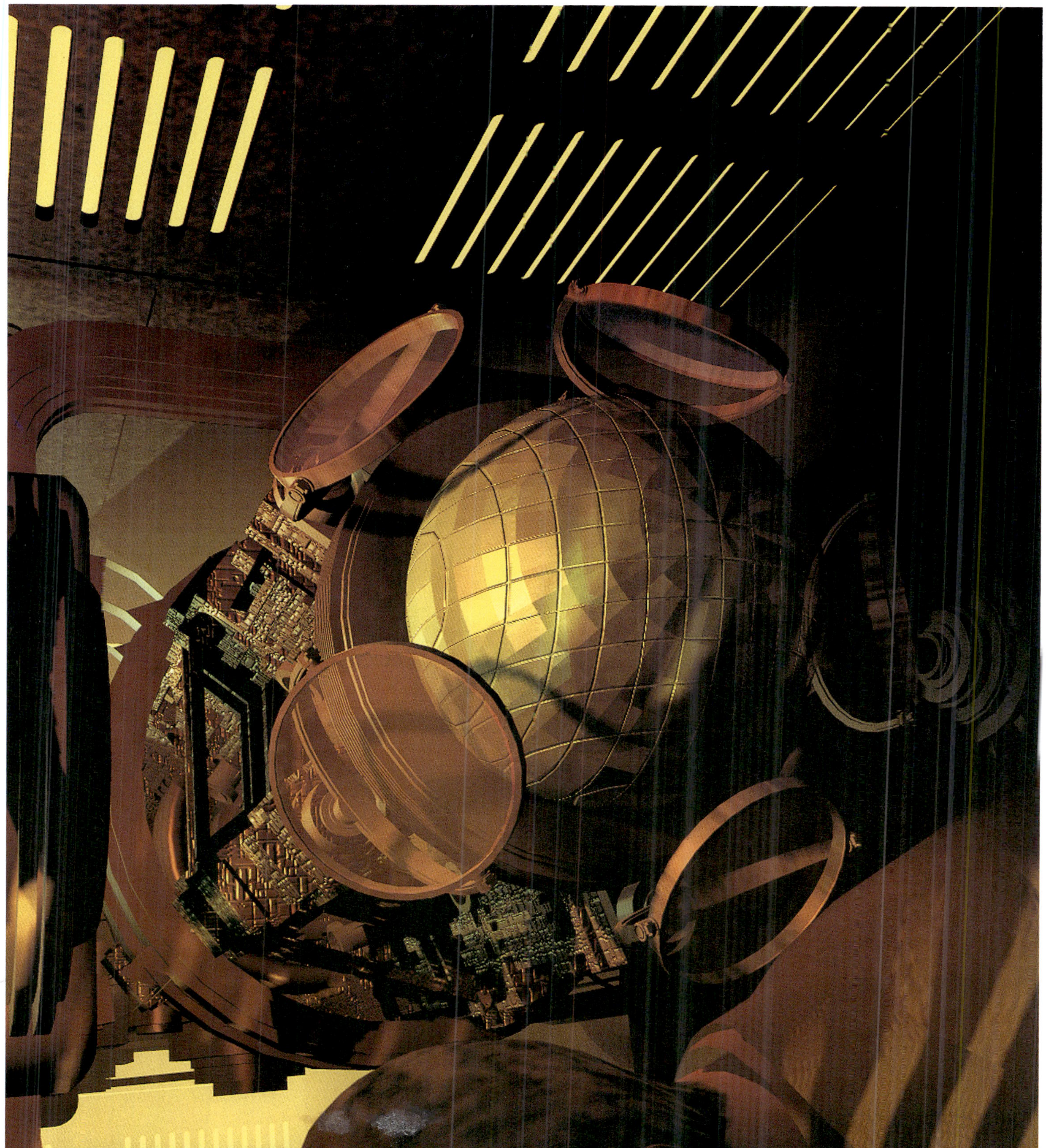

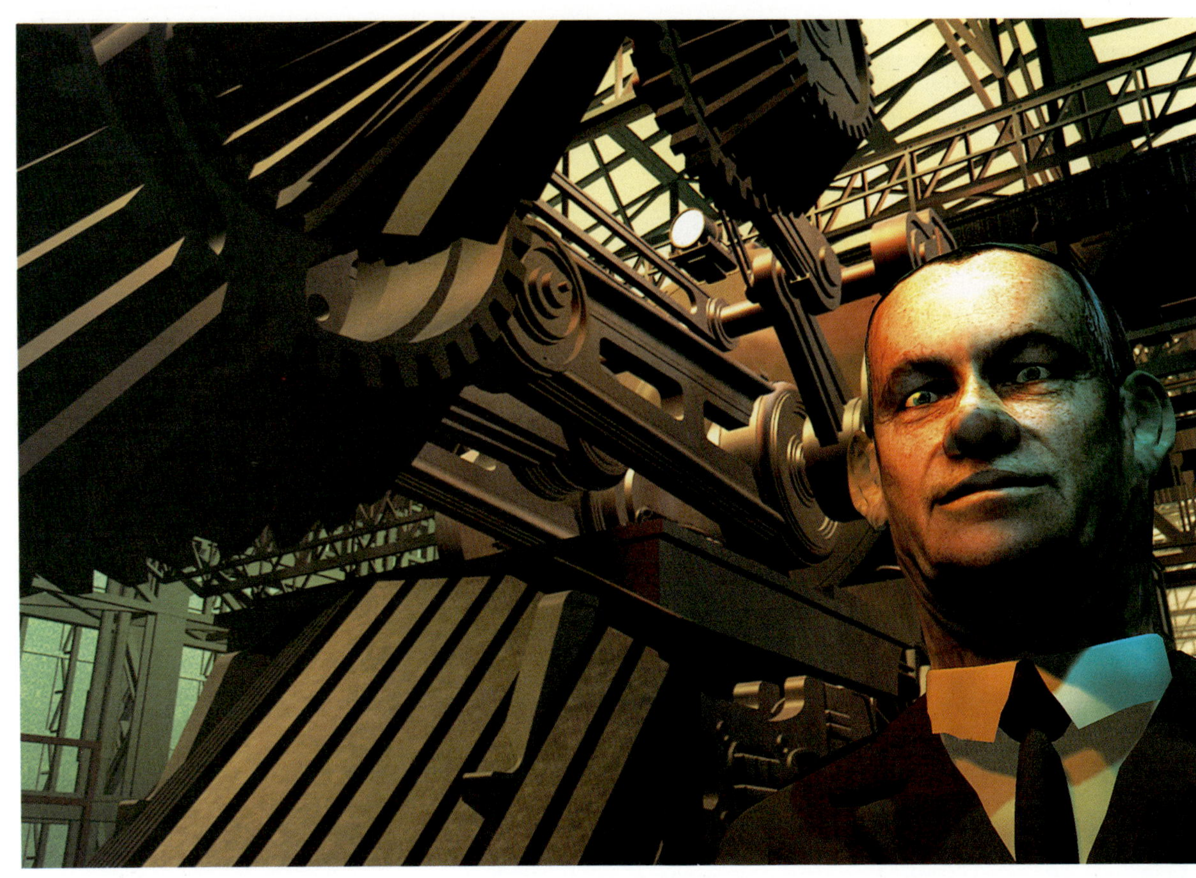

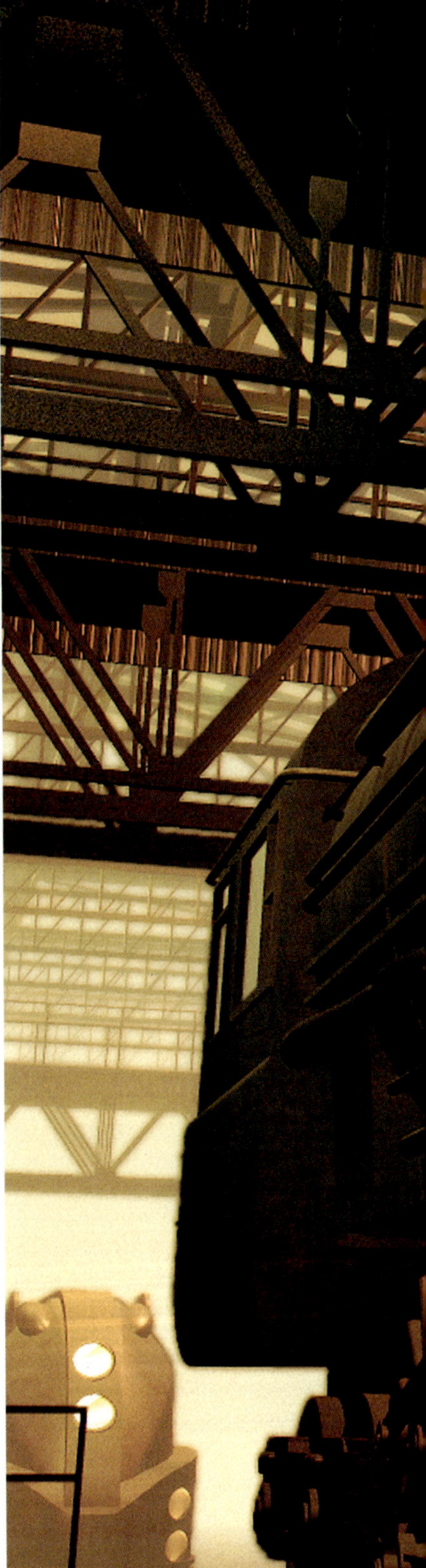

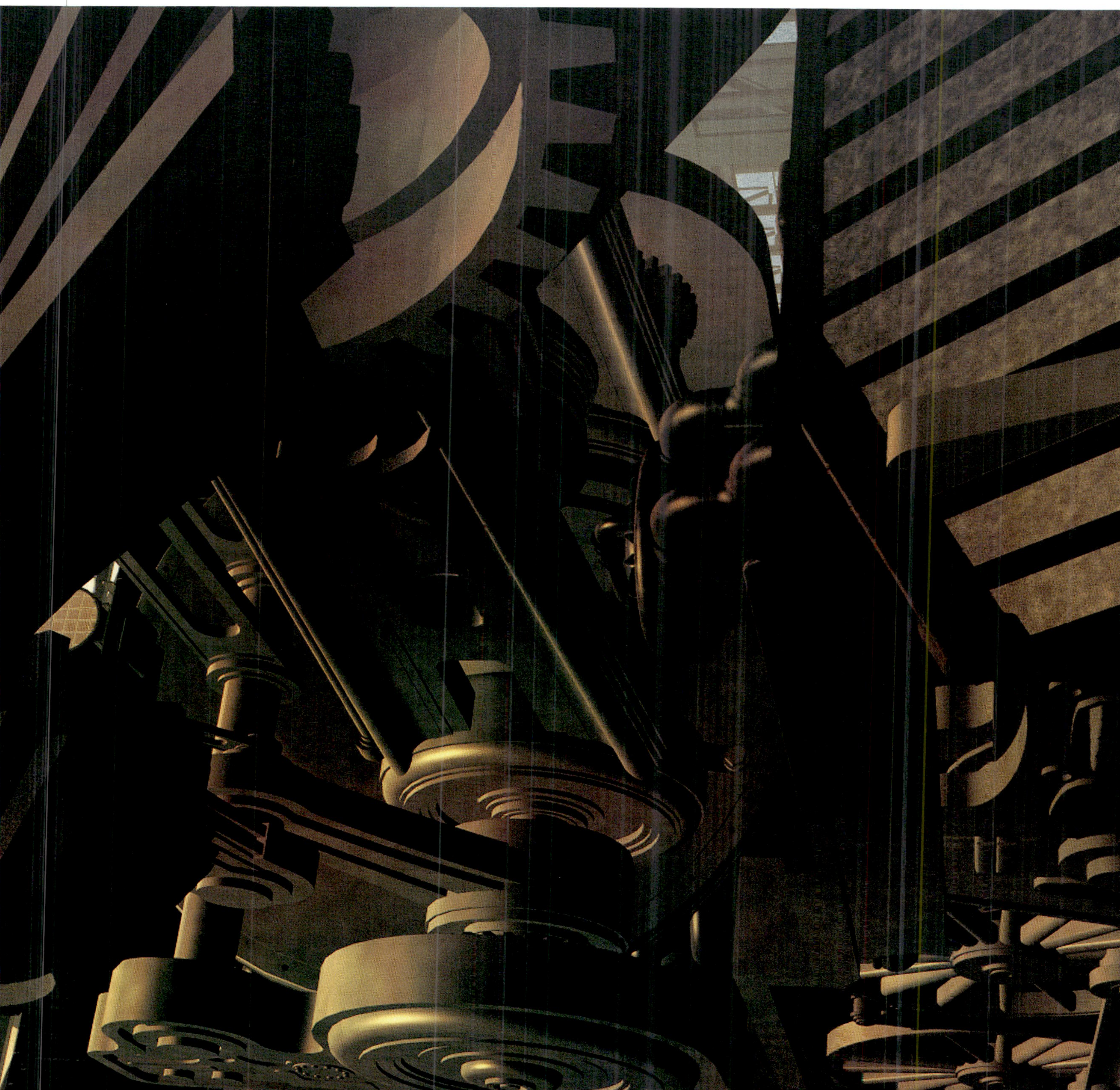

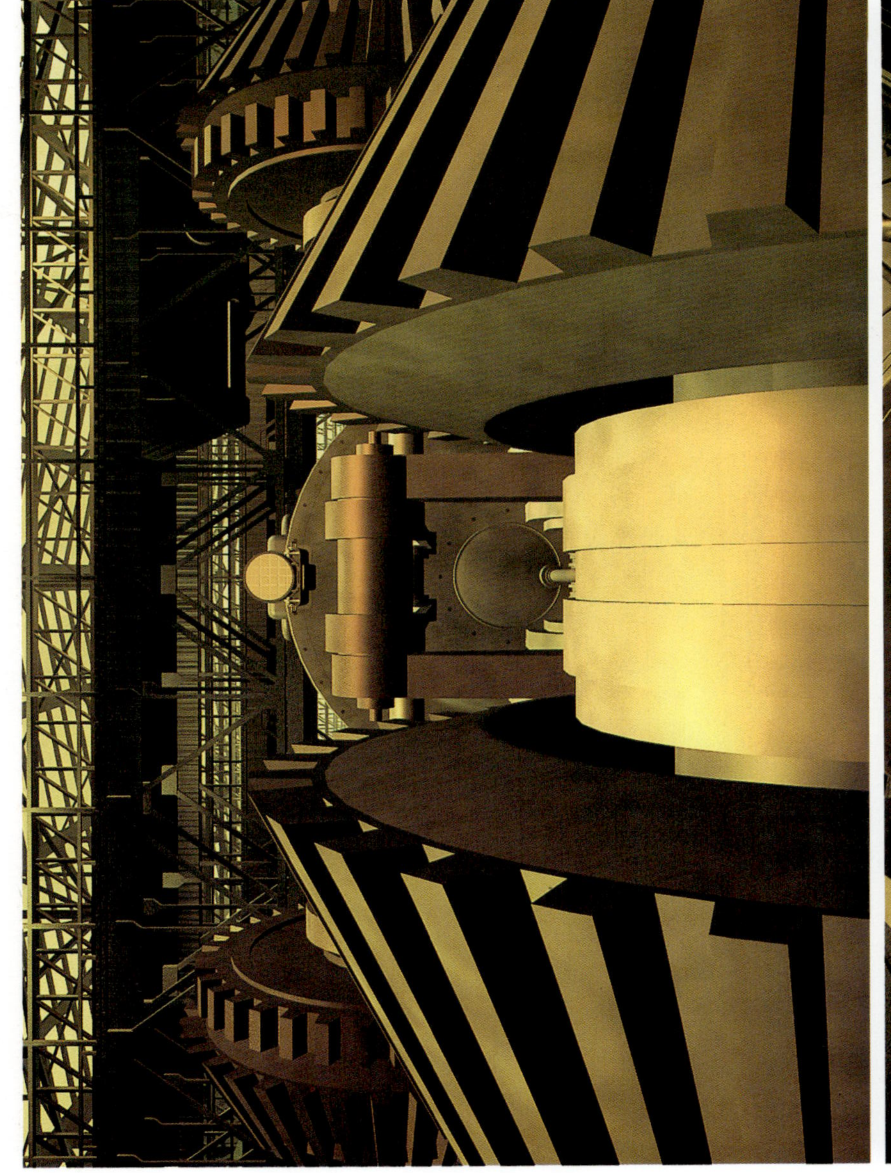

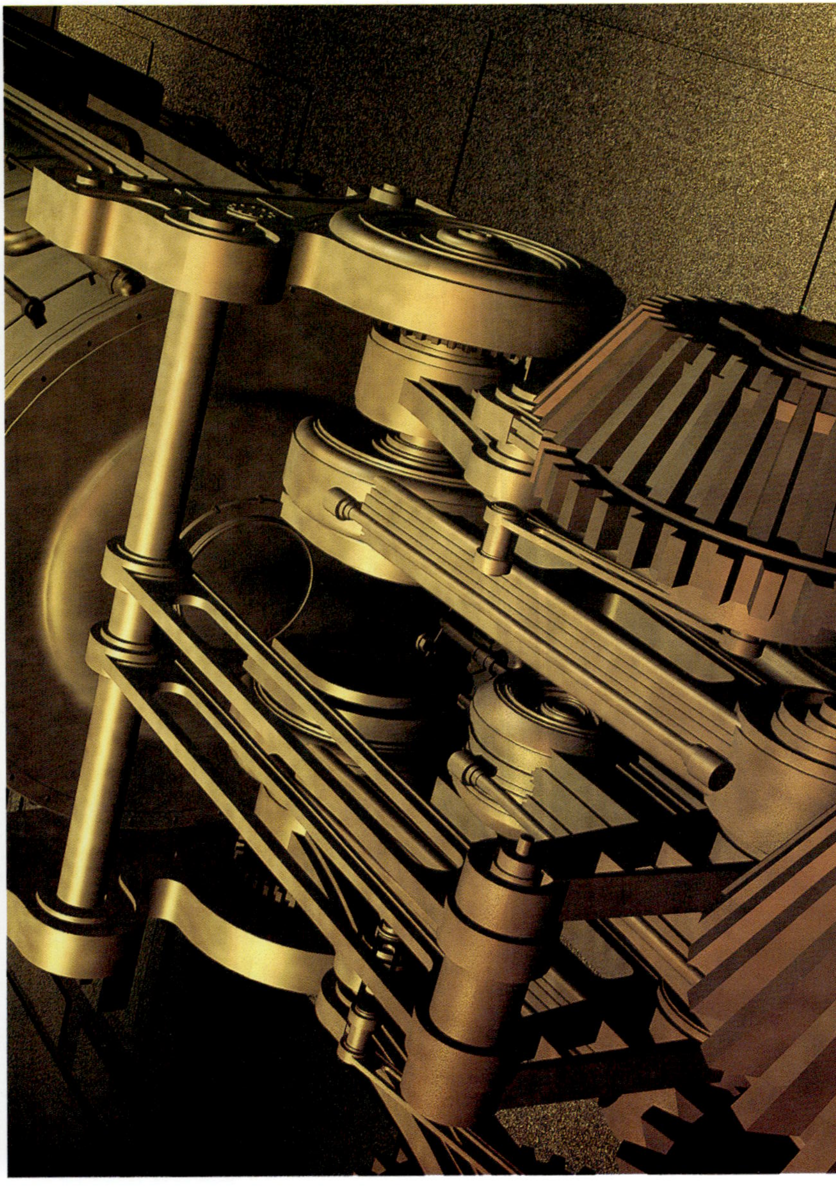

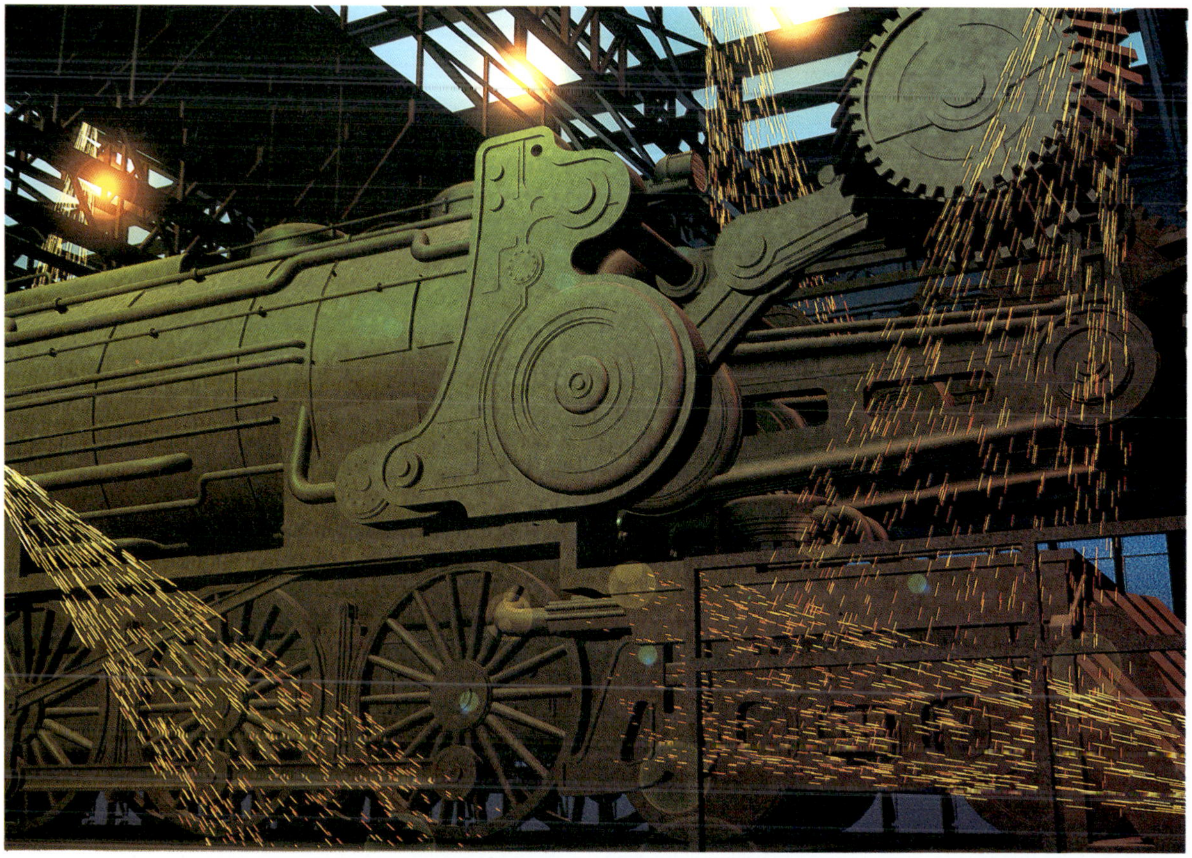

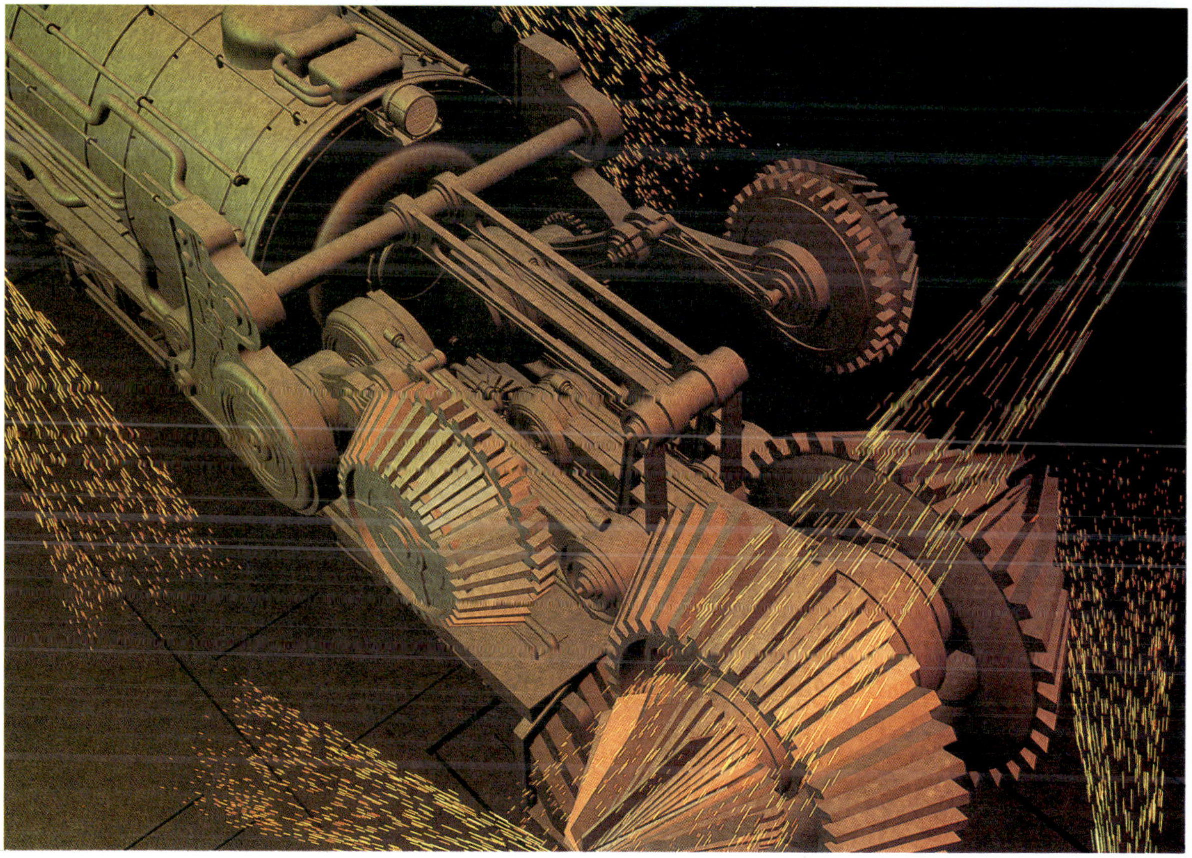

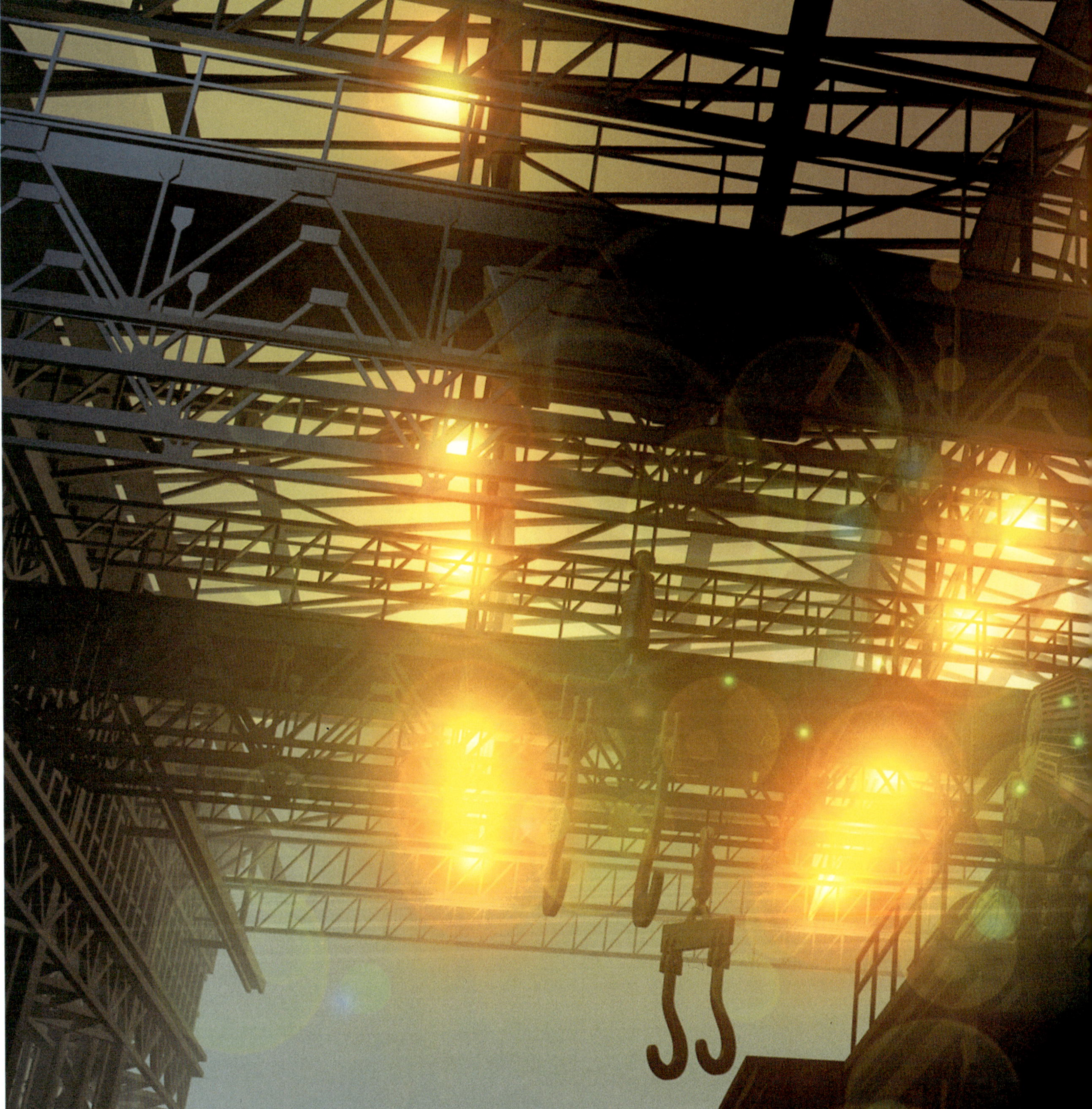

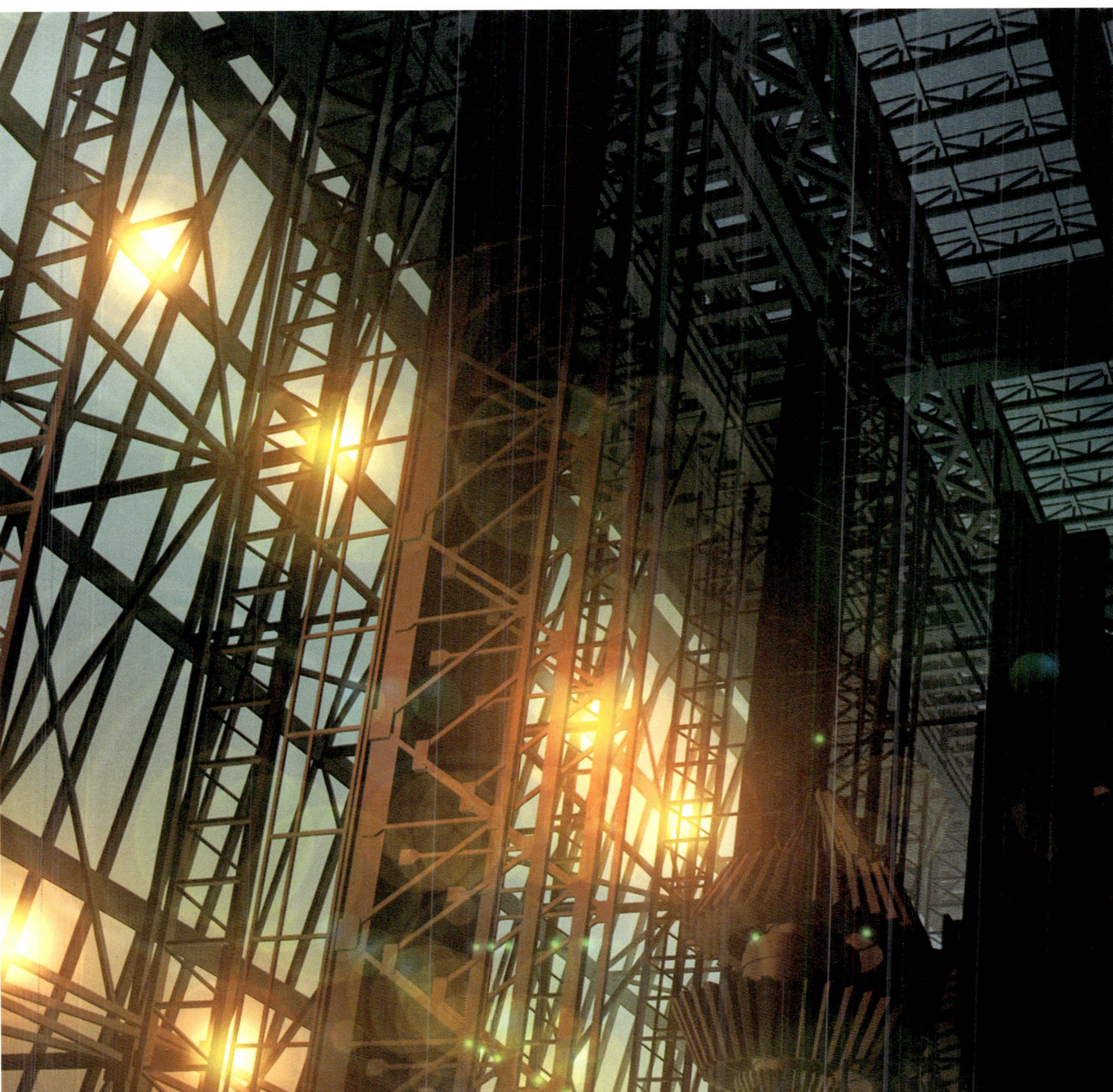

Years 5 and 6 of the Imperial Age

Build, mass-produce, stockpile

Orlovsky's policy of military expansion. Supposition of an eventual war with the Republic. Army engineers called up. Military railway built. Construction materials transported. Arms are mass-produced. Slowslop's in command. The Nova Express hurtles down the tracks.

The smelting furnace: a plan for starting over

Thomas's development of an excavator, an armored car equipped with drills. Muted sound of metal on metal, explosions reverberate from the walls of a dimly lit arms factory. Sparks fly from welding torches. Out of the smelting furnace flows a stream of molten iron.

An era of information and natural resources

An area within the empire to which entrance is restricted. Repair work on the mine tunnel is complete. An outcropping of solid rock. Discovery of a colossal meteor. Extraction of a previously unknown substance. Resource without limits. An endless supply of energy.

Intelligence agents make inquiries

Hausmann checks the Observatory. Lush foliage. Still Observatory. In the darkness floats a reflecting telescope. Pale green shadows are cast on the light collecting mirror. The concept of an unknown celestial body. Horselover breaks off contact with his associates.

Light and shadow, out of balance for all eternity

At the Museum, George and Charles carry on with the experiments. Development of the Version II Sensorama is complete. Dissonant noise, subject's body vibrates. Laws of waves and frequencies. Sensorama transformed from a healing to a brainwashing machine.

Documentation has been compiled

Clinical medicine and pharmacology. John and Constantine, now at the Imperial Army Hospital, immediately agree to George's proposal. Full participation in the radiation tests. Horselover issues detailed instructions. Five scientists surround Sensorama.

Expectations prop up a realm of facts

Radio transmissions. A mammoth revolving antenna. The voice of the undercover agent Gondarev. Secret reports on the progress of excavations, on events leading to initial shipments, on transport and inspection procedures. From his lofty office Onegin responds.

Needs of the new Empire

Imperial Intelligence has the Republic covered. Incarceration and interrogation. Truth serum and Sensorama. Isolation and torture. Chemical confession, mechanical mindbending. Memory control, electromagnetic learning experience. Submit or disintegrate.

Those slow to escape will be detained

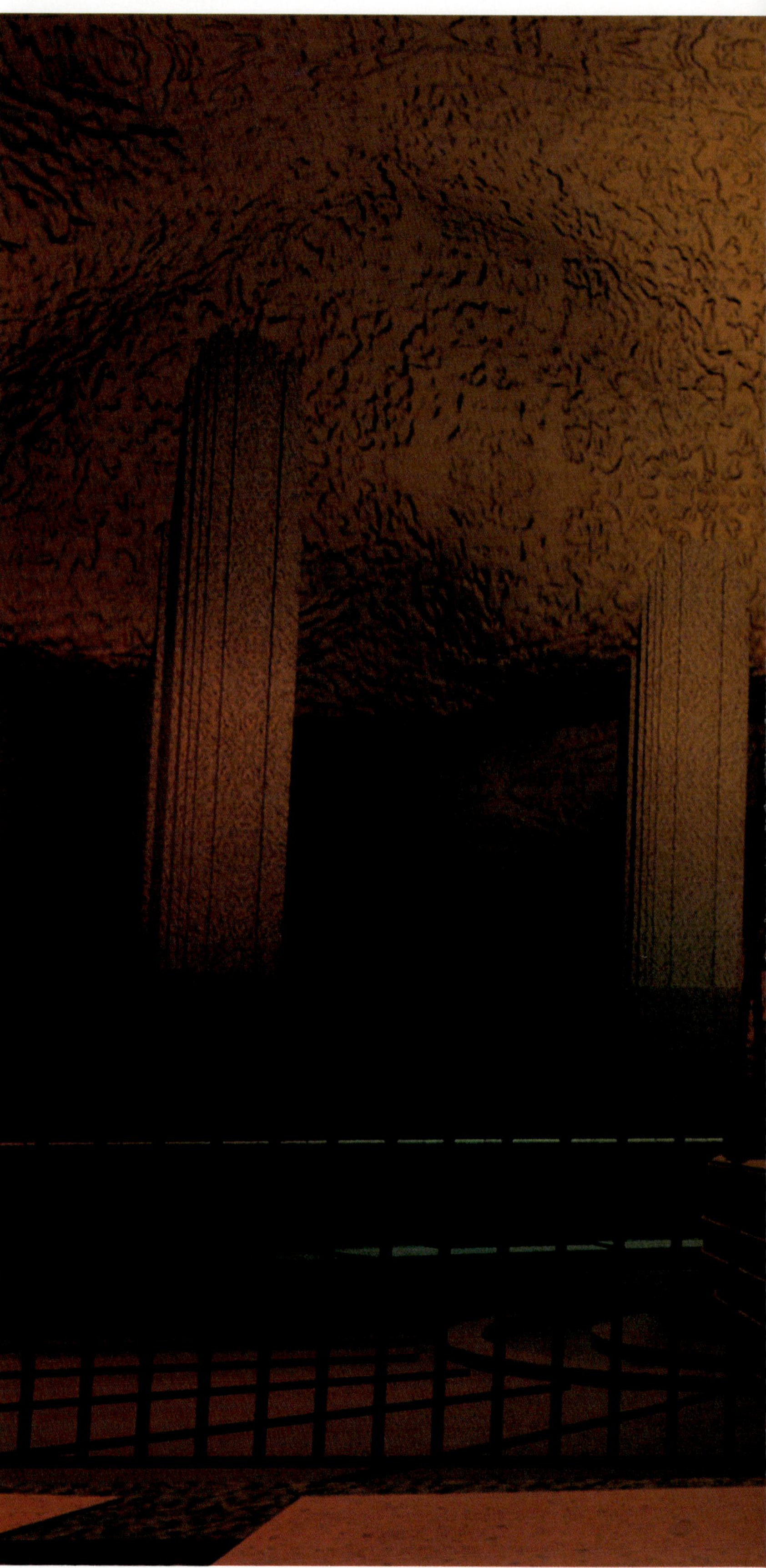

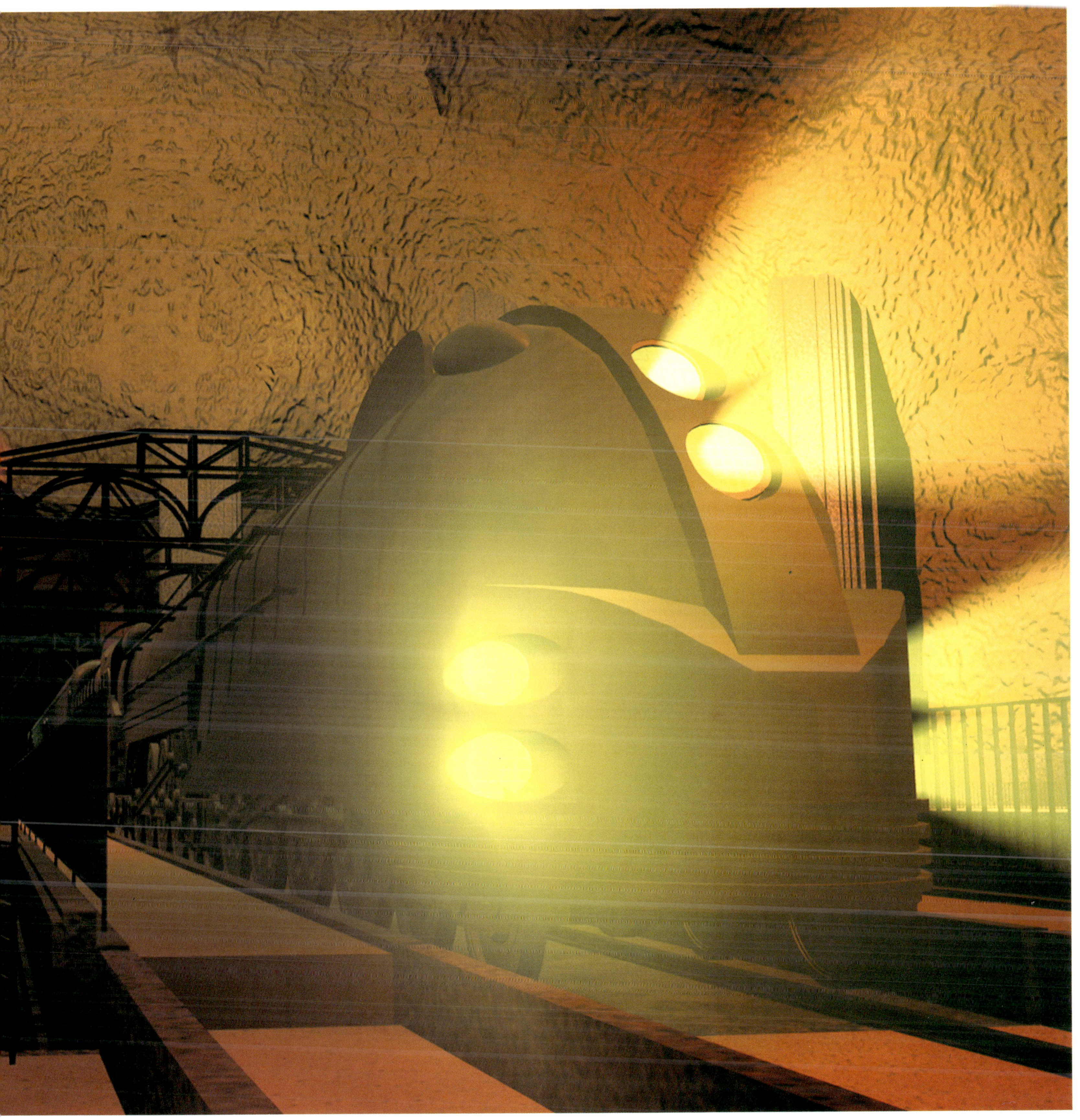

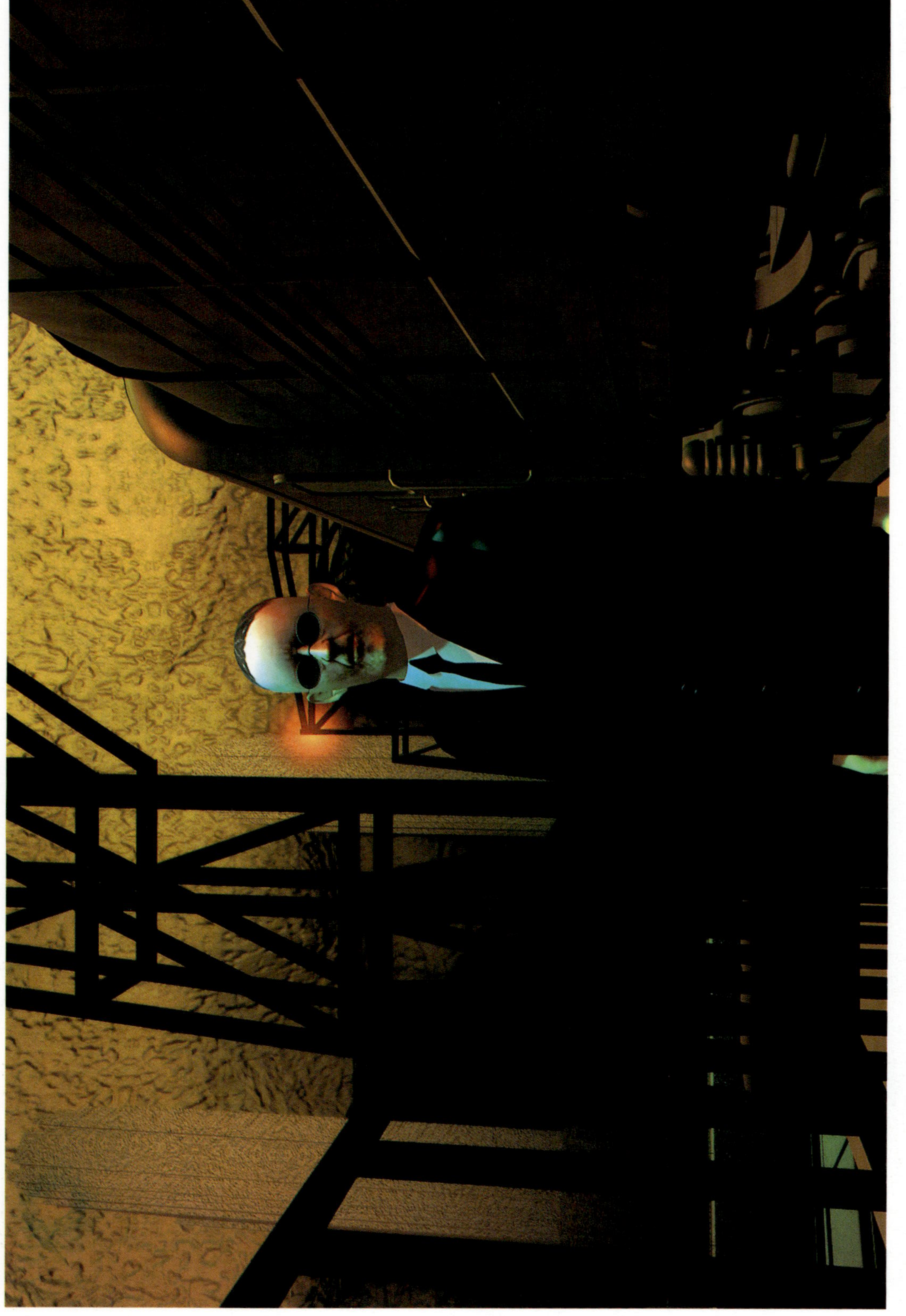

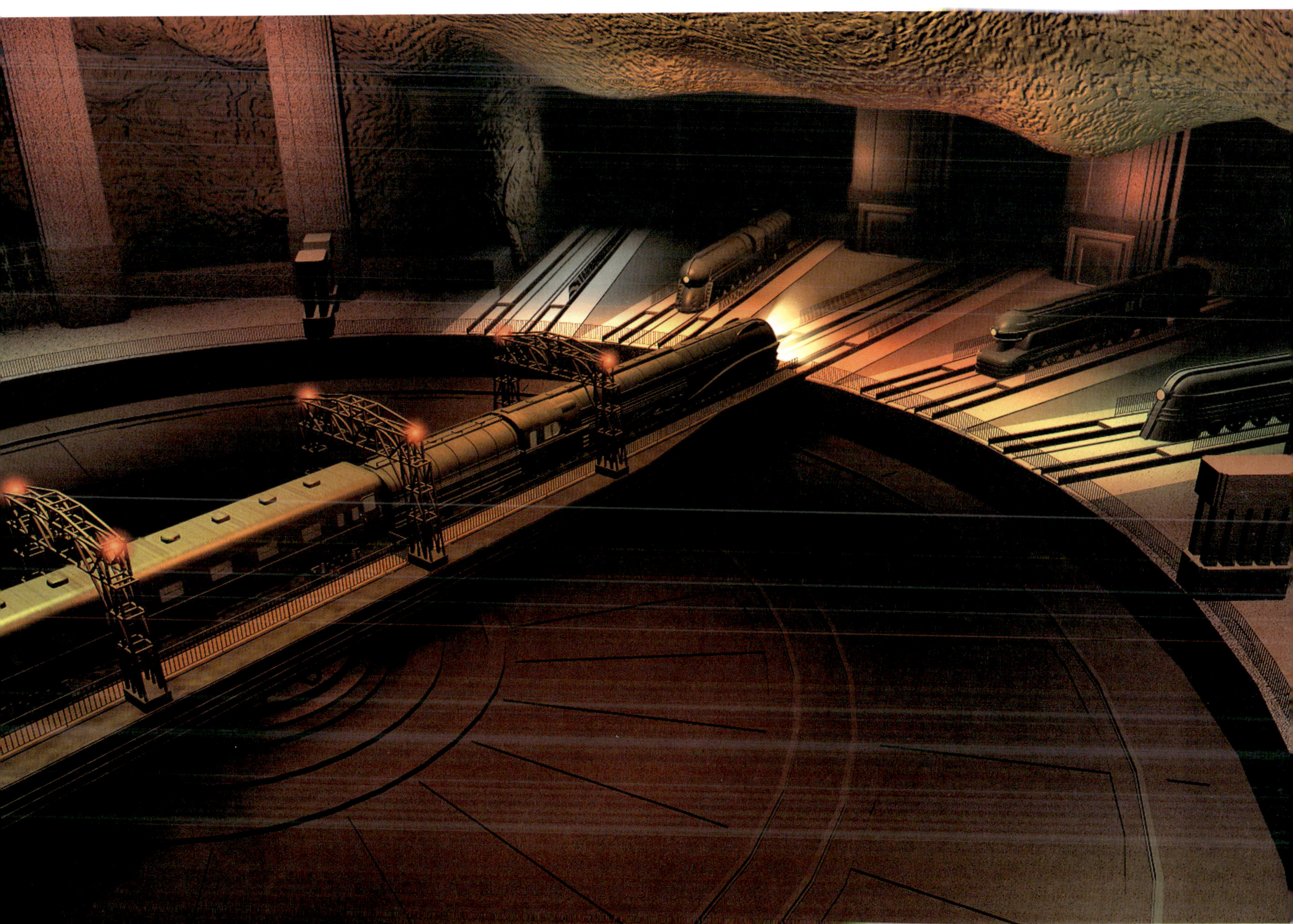

Conversation between George Tessera and Charles Reif in the Radiation Research Laboratory at the Imperial Museum

— After the last experiment Horselover said this to me. "George," he said, "the stage of data collection is over. It's time to move on to the next objective."
— I was beginning to wonder about that. From an academic point of view there seemed absolutely no reason to conduct further experiments. The Sensorama had already achieved the initial objective of inducing virtual optical perceptions.
— Quite so.
— Time, then, for data analysis and the erection of a theoretical frame, is it?
— I really don't know what Horselover's thinking.
— ....
— He's asked me to develop a Version II Sensorama.
— ....
— I'm not sure, but he doesn't seem to consider it just a therapeutic device.
— Oh...?
— The present Sensorama is a machine that uses electromagnetic waves both to create artificial optical images and to collect fragments of memory.
— And that's not enough?
— Horselover says it isn't.
— ....
— The problematic issue is the duration of electromagnetic radiation. In order to establish a stronger influence upon subjects, we need a more powerful energy source.
— ....
— Horselover has proposed we use the meteorites and John and Constantine have agreed to cooperate. We're counting on your help, too.
— ....

(13 April, Year 5 of the Imperial Age)

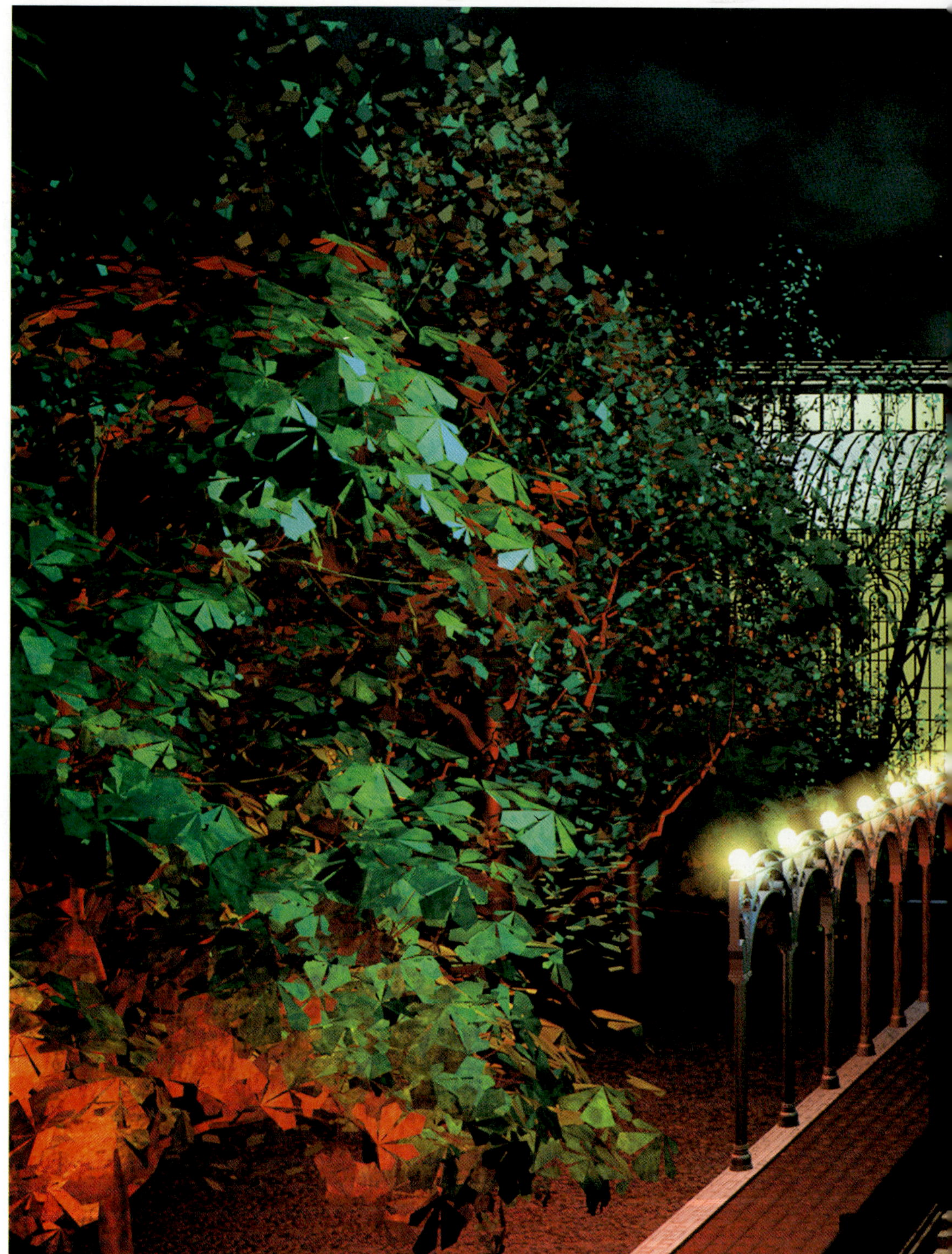

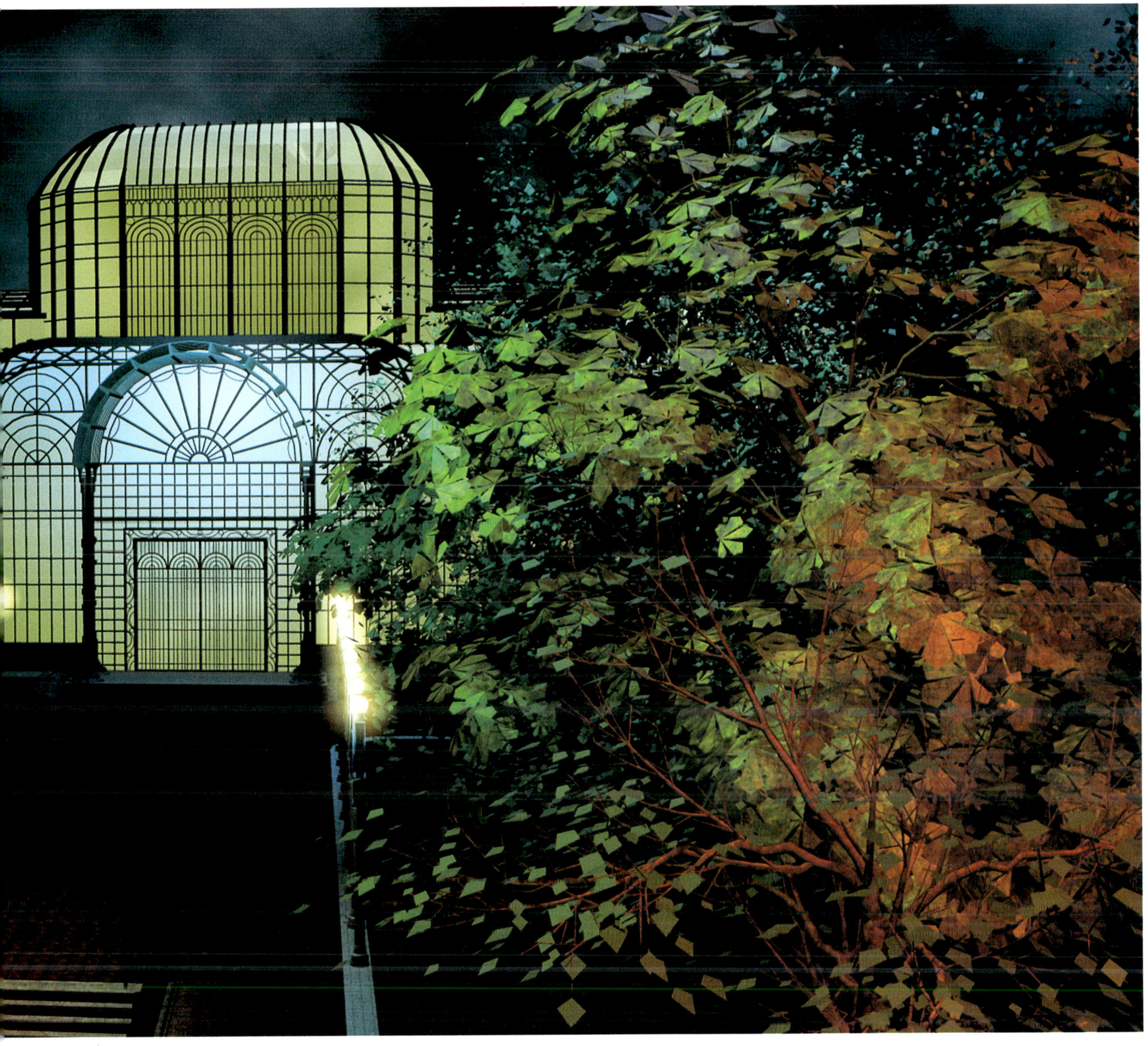

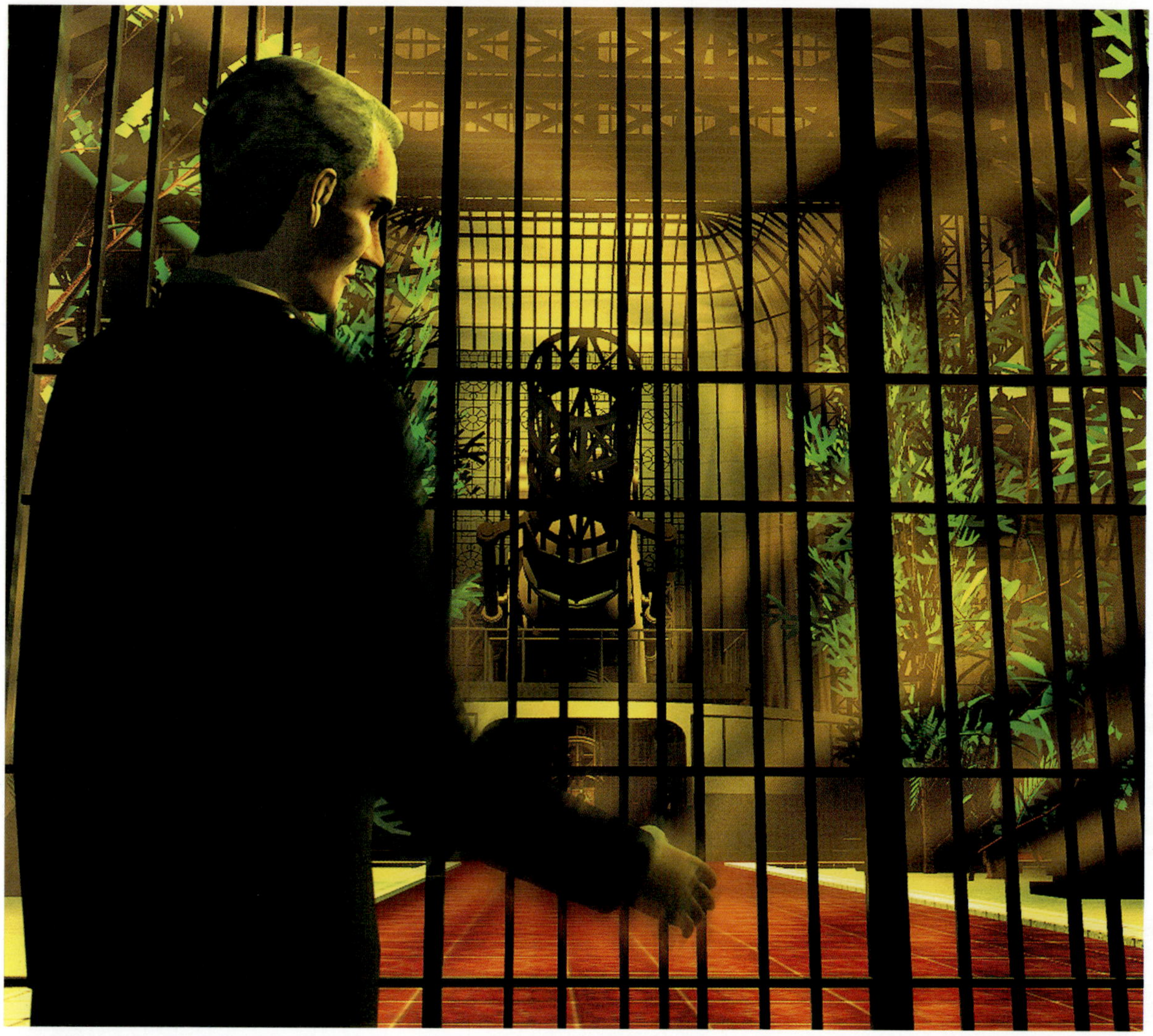

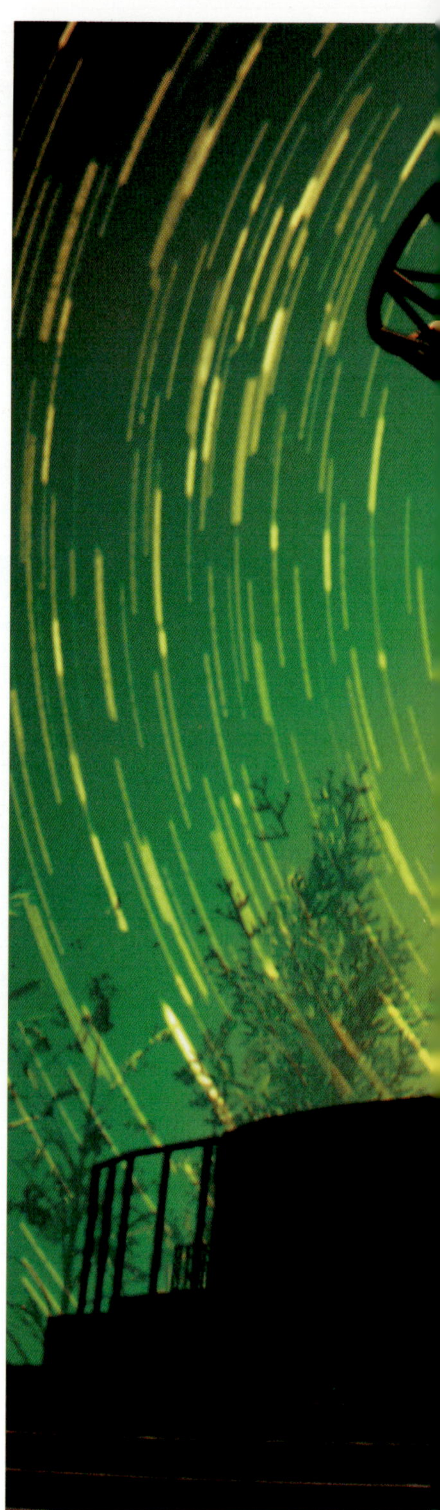

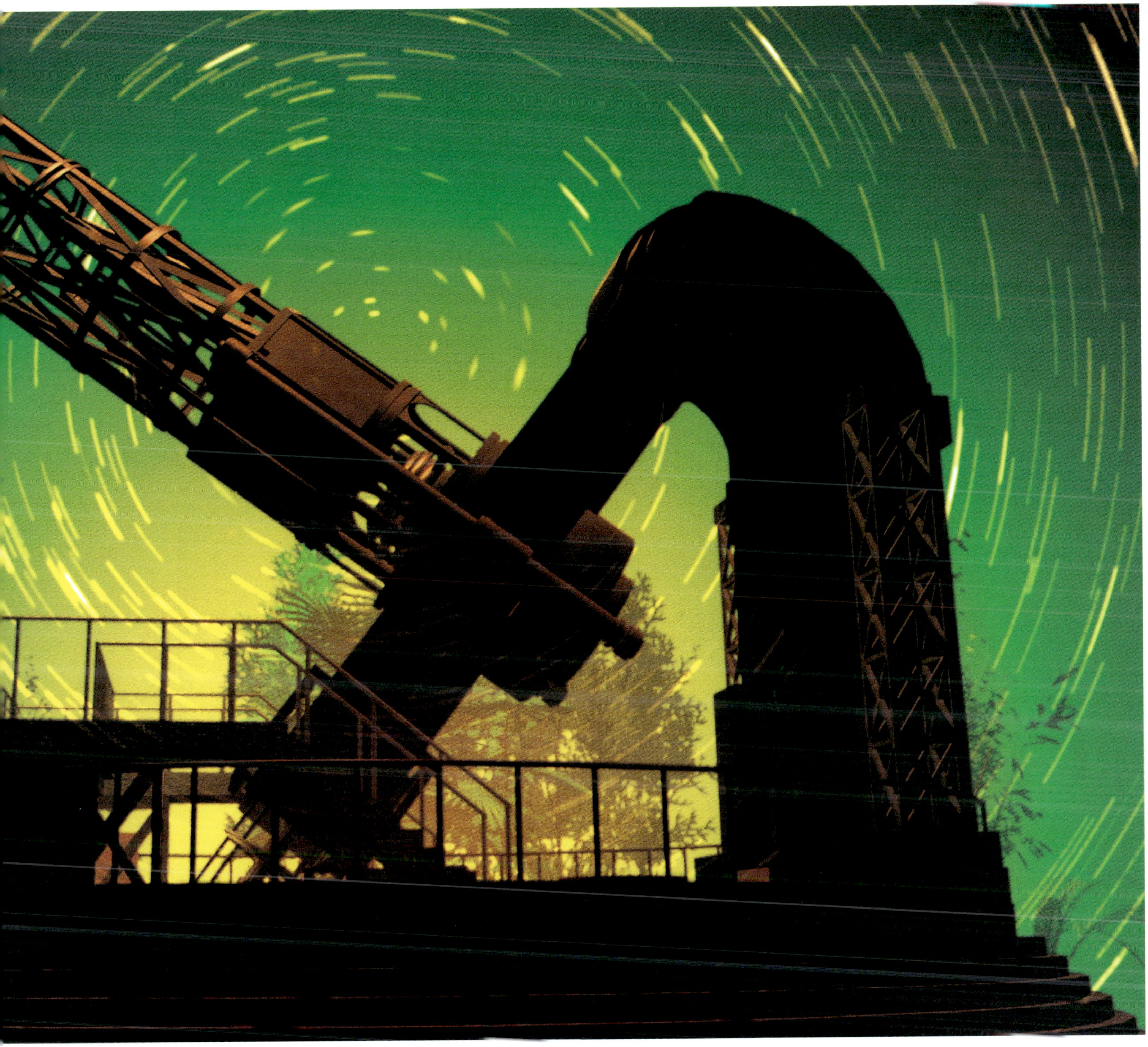

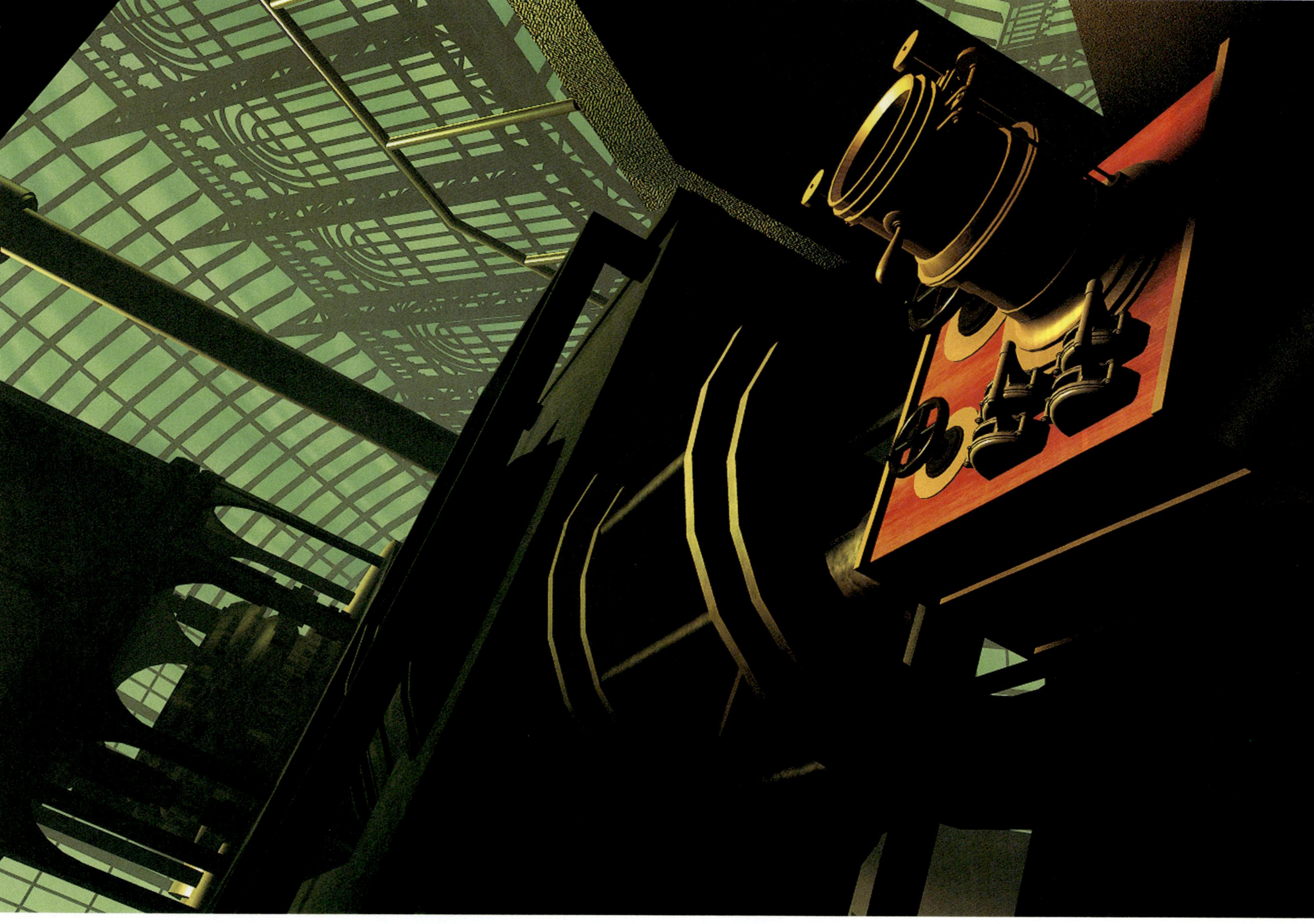

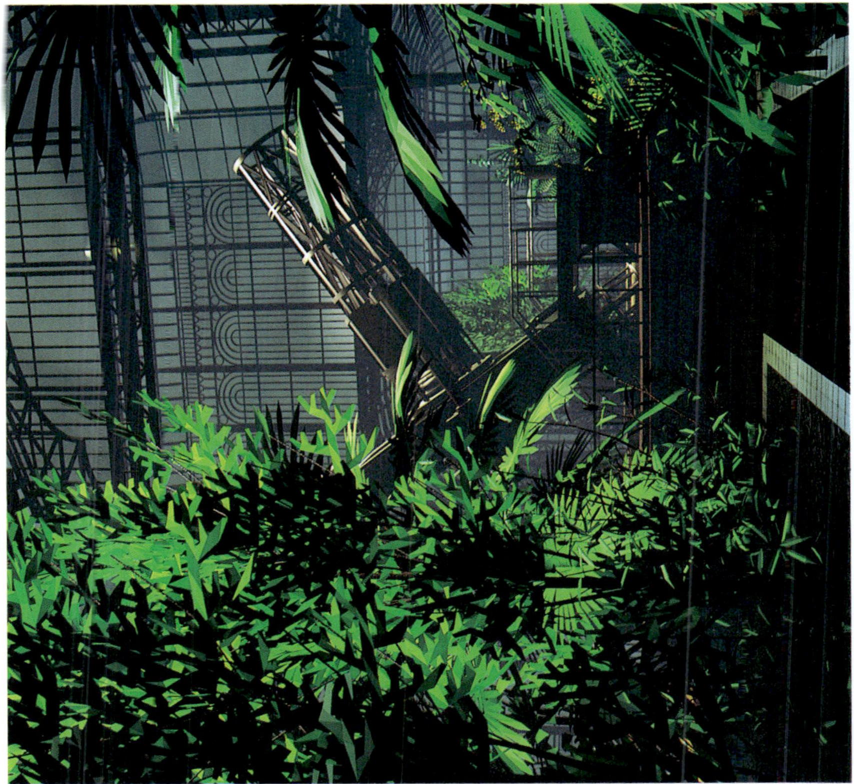

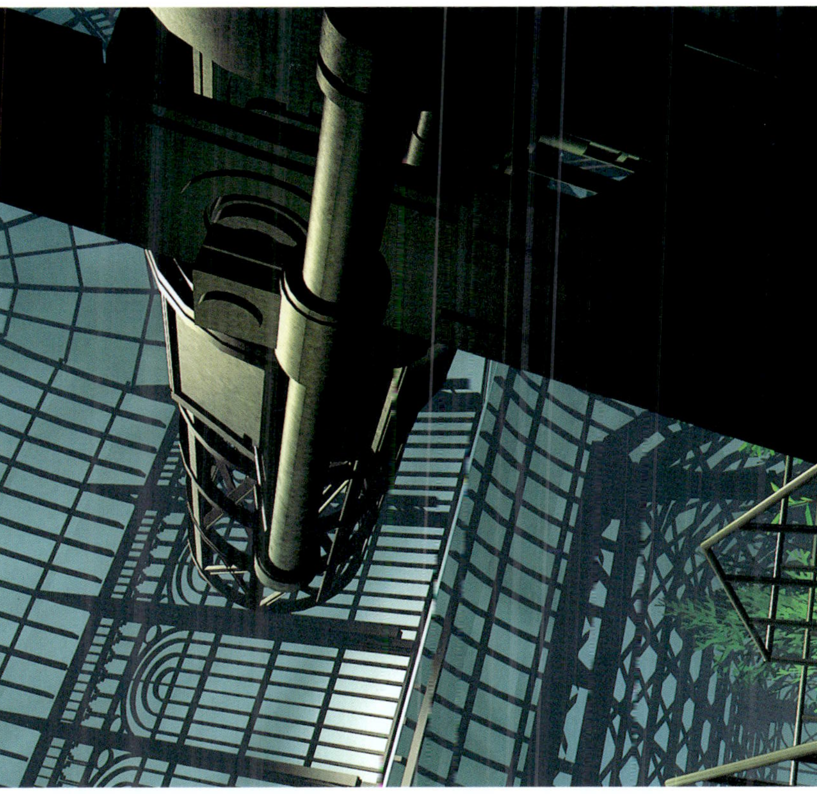

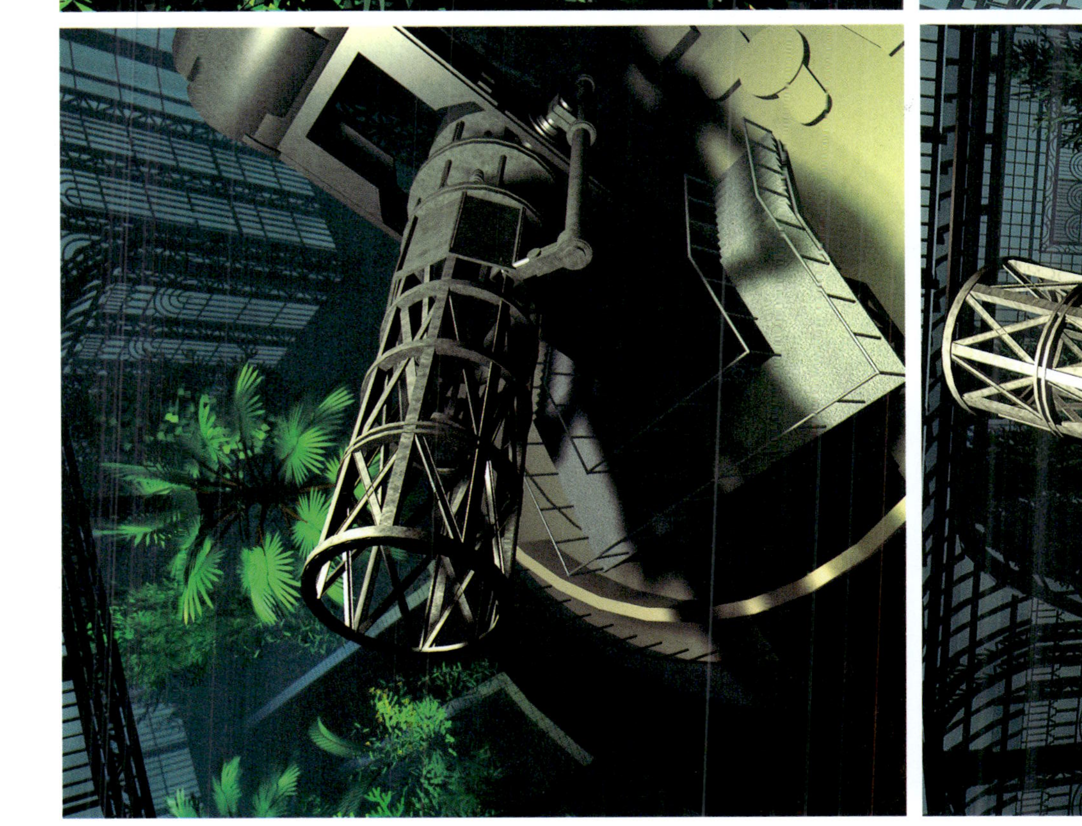

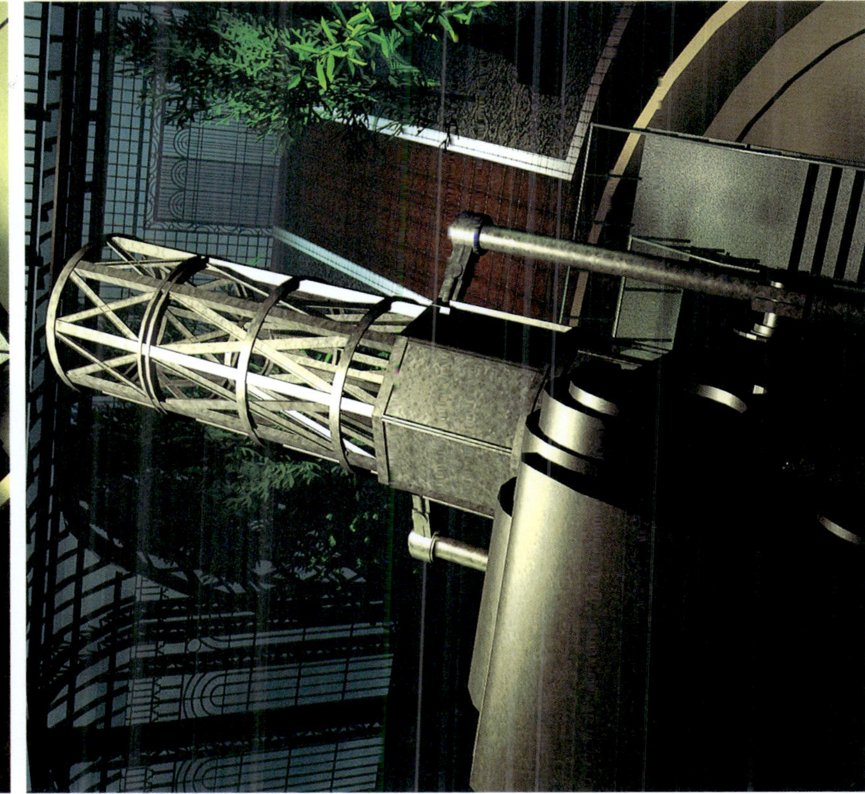

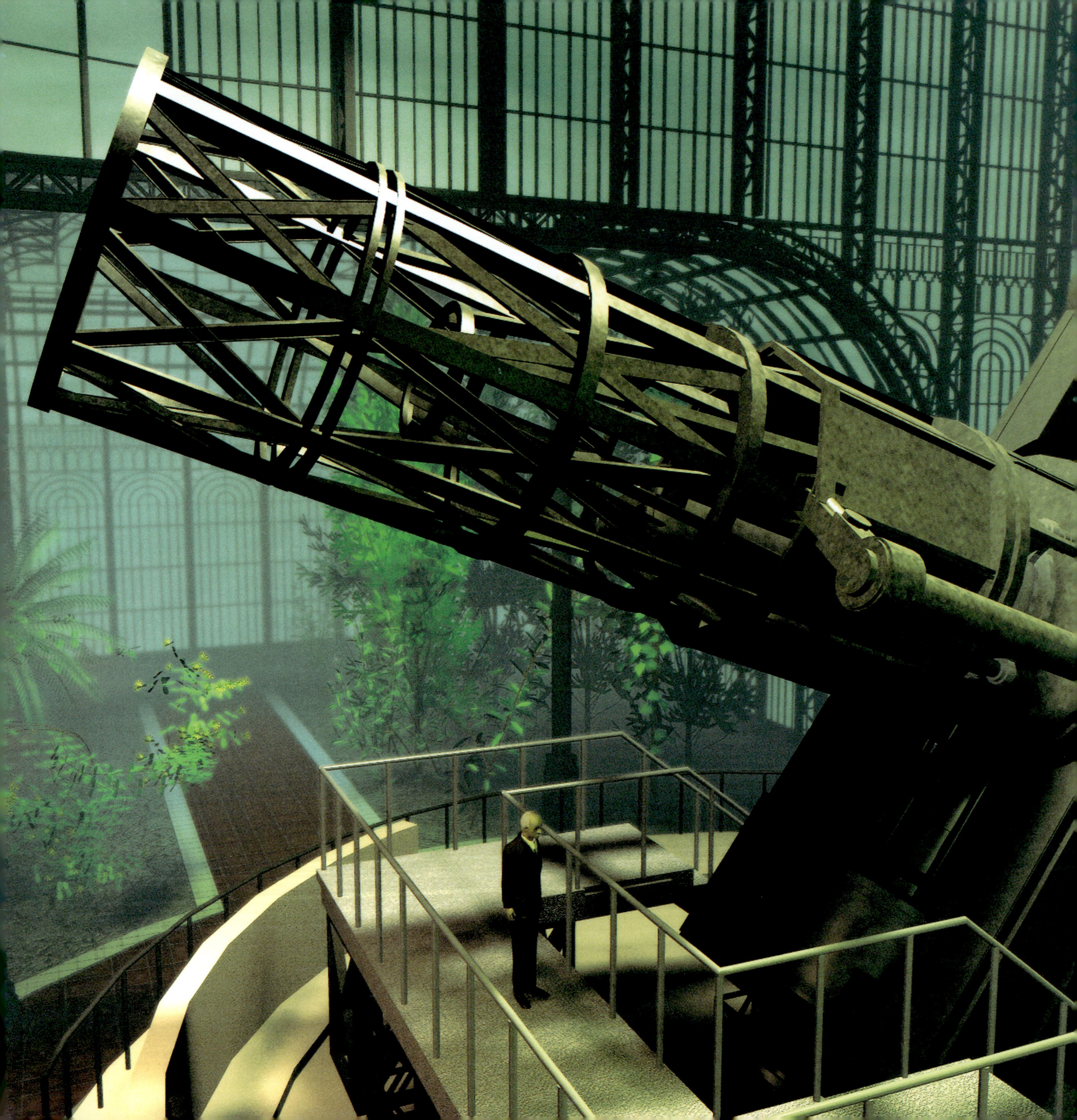

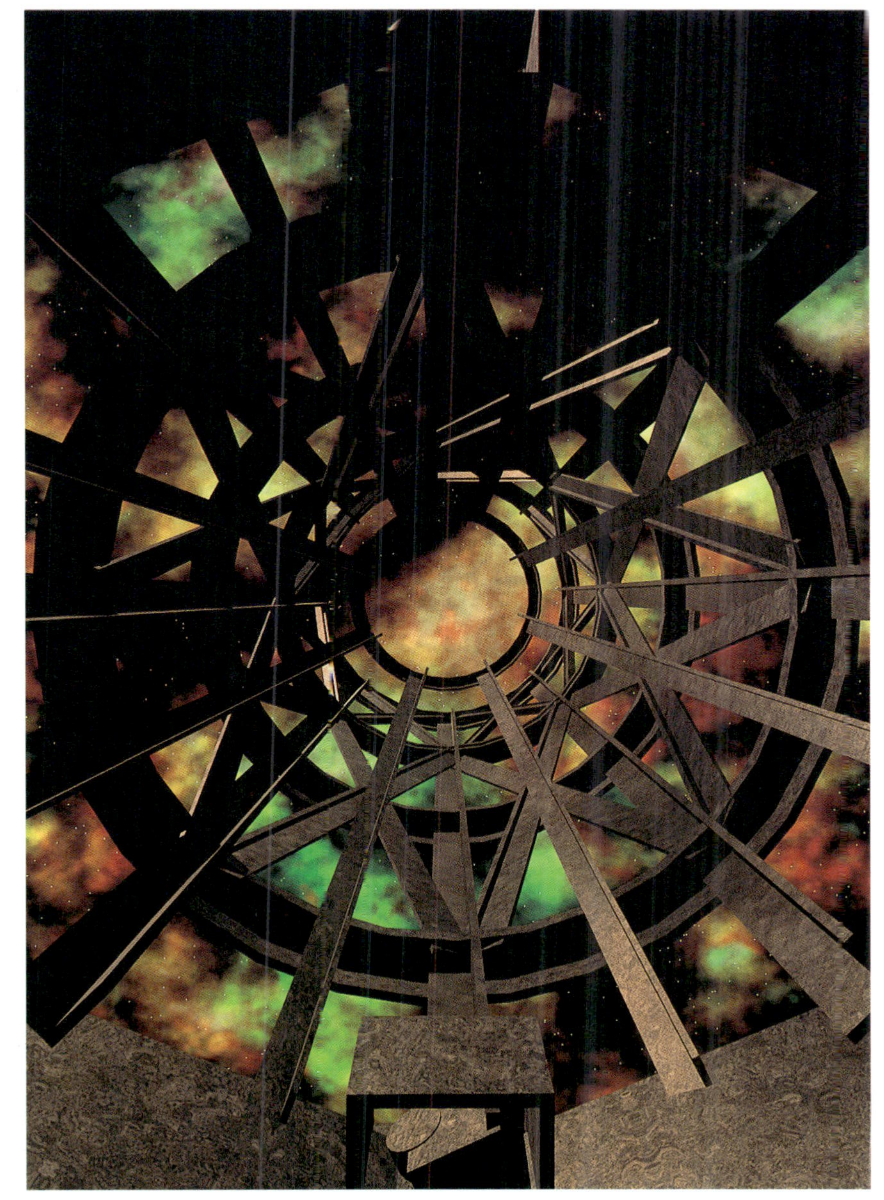

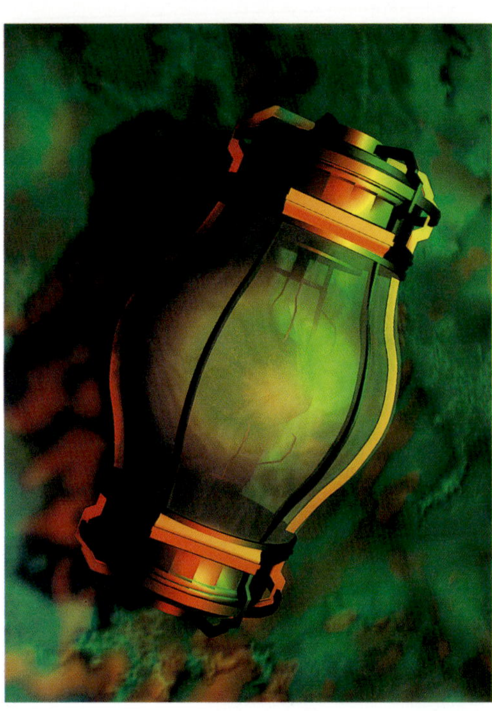

18 May, Year 5 of the Imperial Age

Excavation work has begun in the restricted area. Red laterite soil prevails in the region. A tendency to subsidence is hampering progress. Still have no idea of the quantity of meteorites. Work on the mine tunnel is behind schedule.

28 May

Received a report that excavation has uncovered an extensive rock outcropping and went to see for myself. Bedrock of mountainous appearance but was unable to estimate its extent. Texture and pigmentation correspond closely with meteorite samples. I'm waiting for the results of analysis by George Tessera.

12 June

The excavator that I've had Thomas Reich working on is finished. By the evidence of it Thomas is a master engineer.

If we can mass-produce arms that employ this ultimate energy source, our army will become the strongest military organization in the world.

15 June

Test results on the bedrock have arrived. According to the report it's a meteorite that struck the earth no less than 500 years ago. Mineral composition closely corresponds with that of the more recent samples.

The report says that "Identical composition with a meteorite that fell in the vicinity 500 years ago is too improbable to believe." But this isn't the time for arguing probabilities. The fact is there lies buried there a resource of immense military importance, the application of which has been entrusted to me. If I control both energy resource and weapons, the Revolution is not just a dream.

(From the diary of Slowslop)

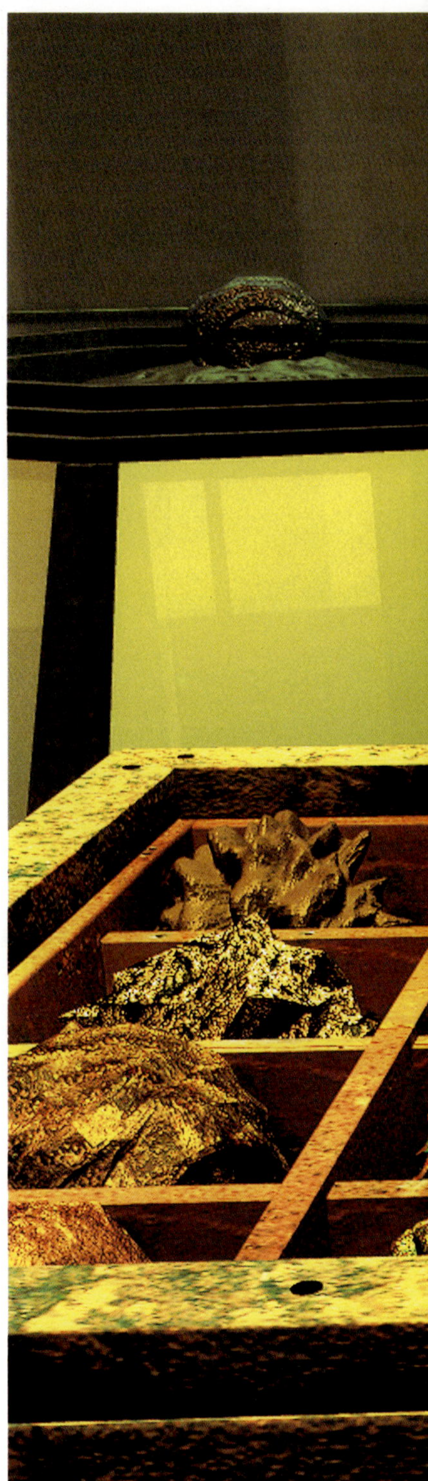

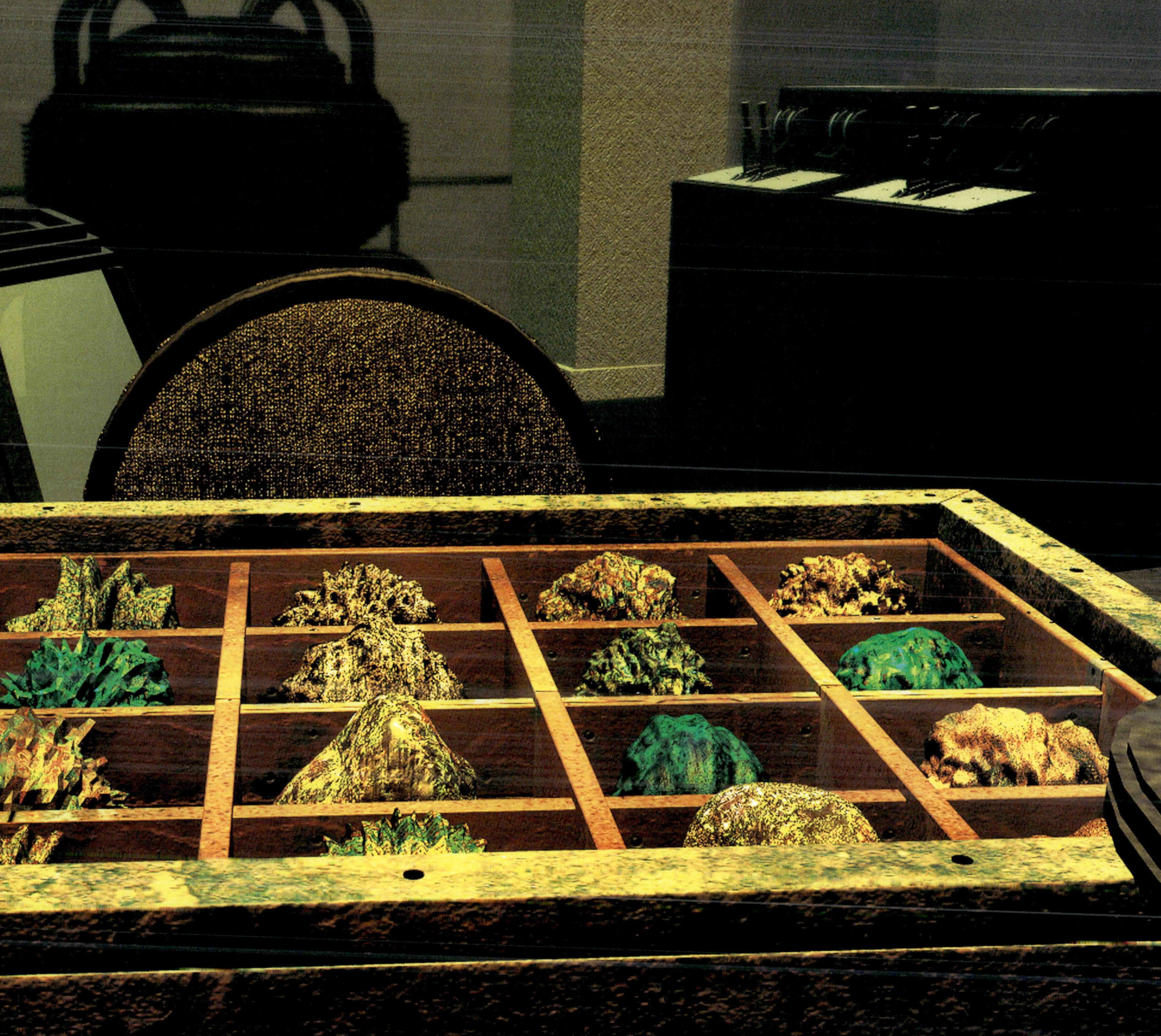

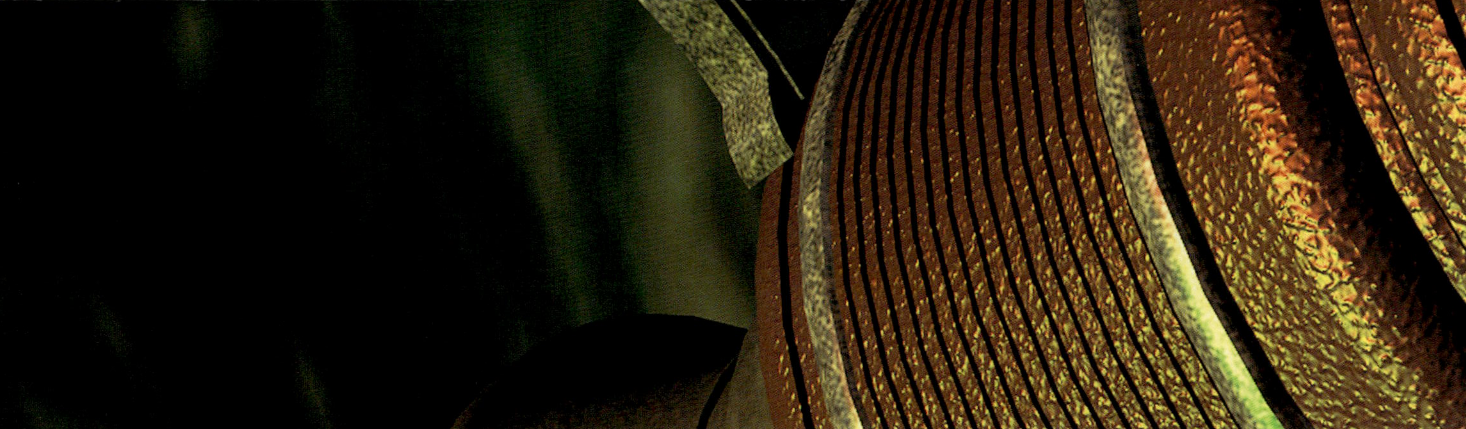

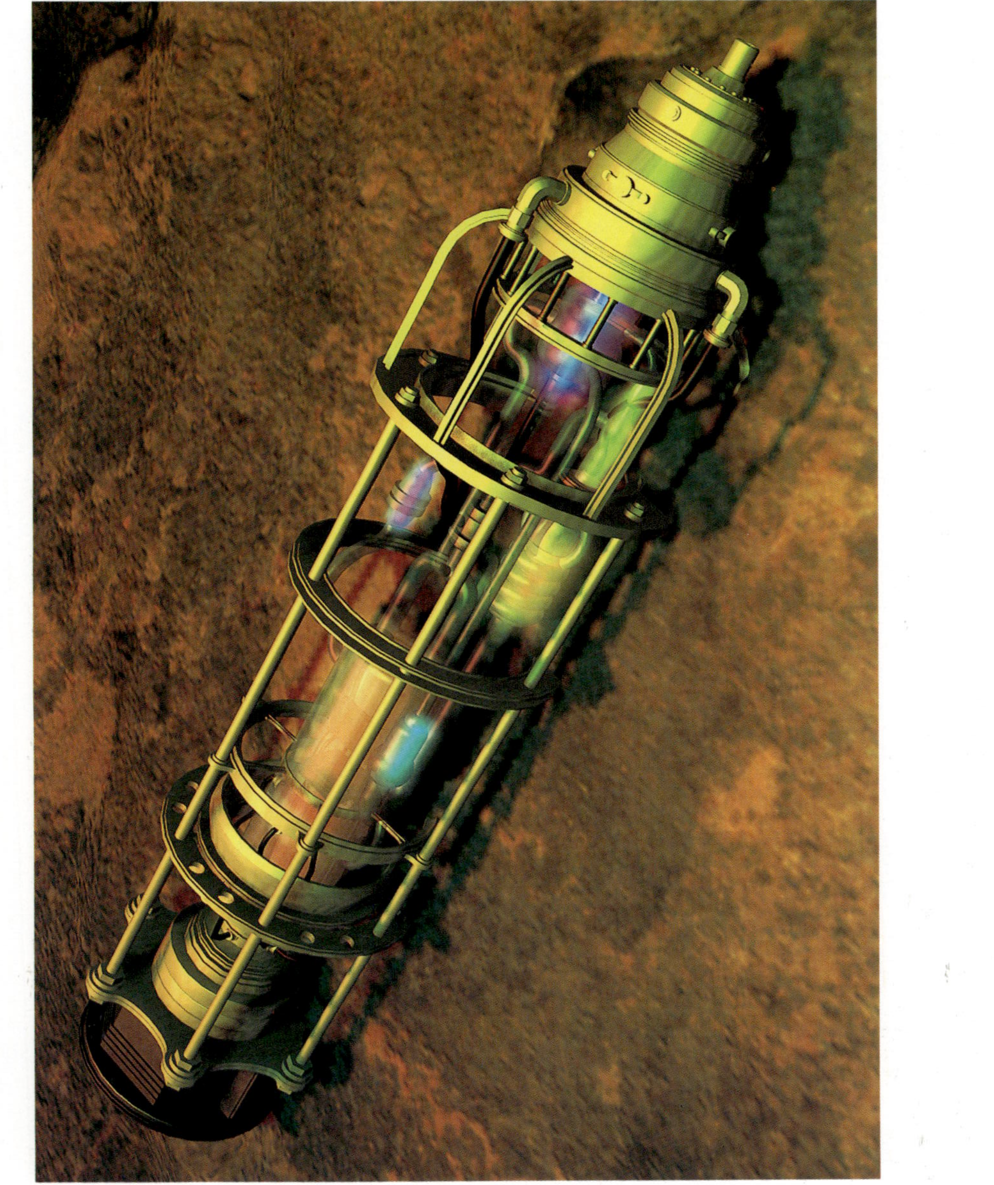

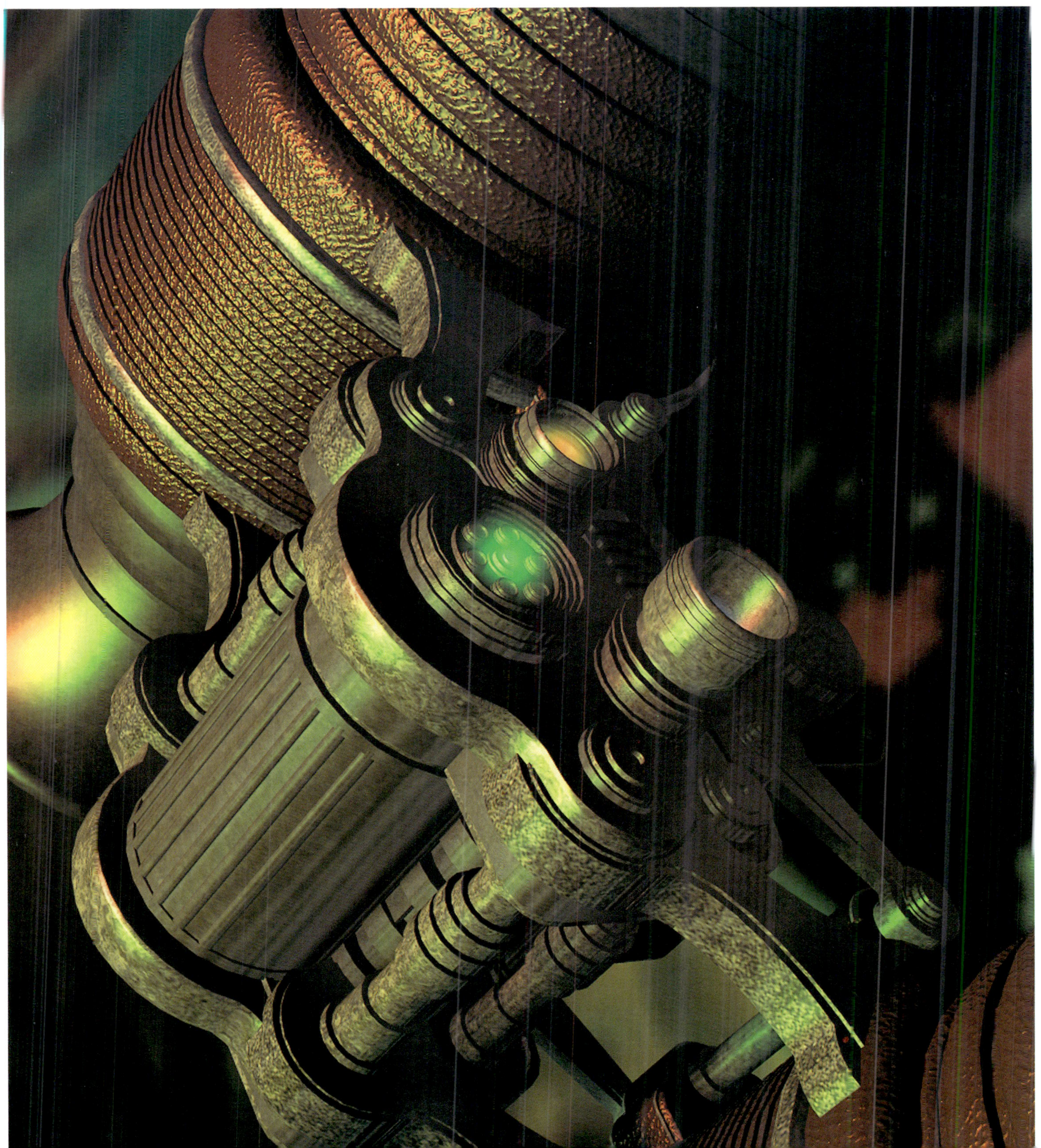

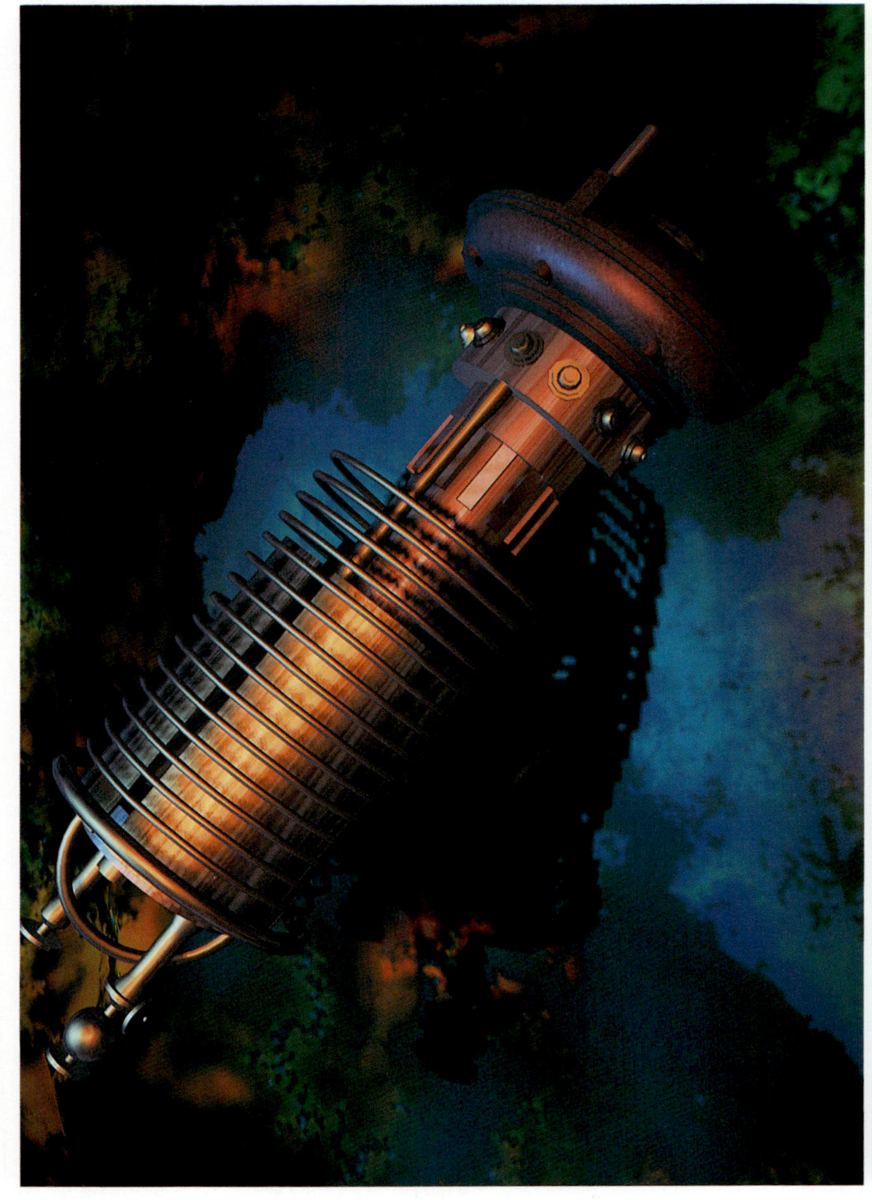

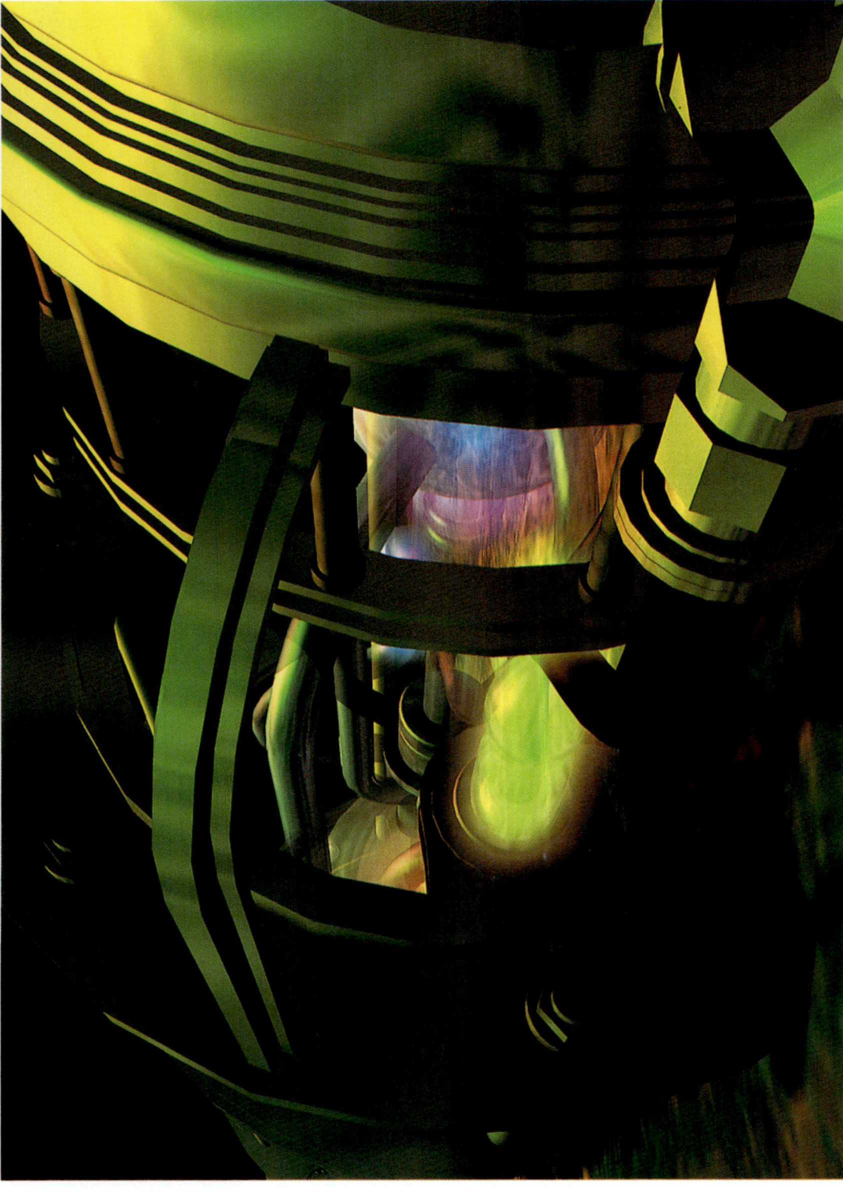

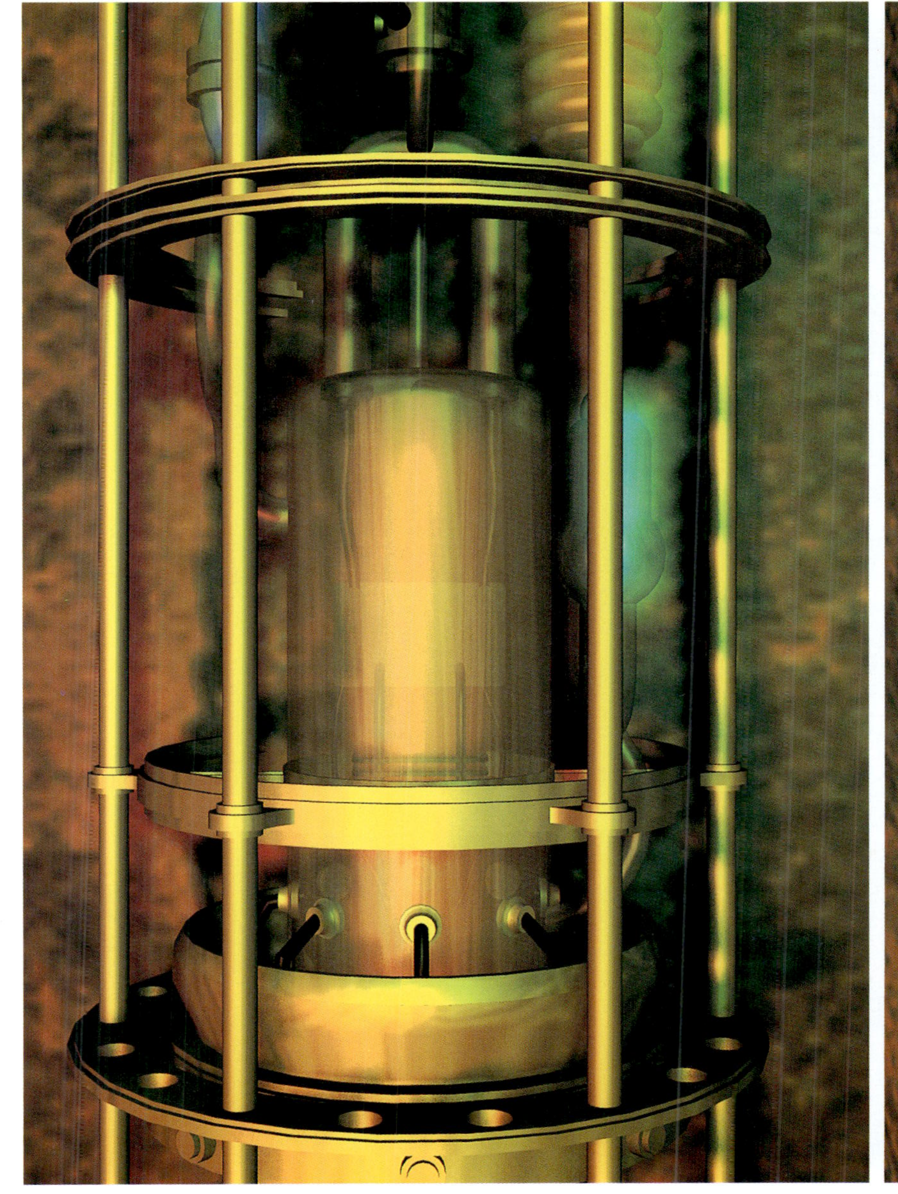

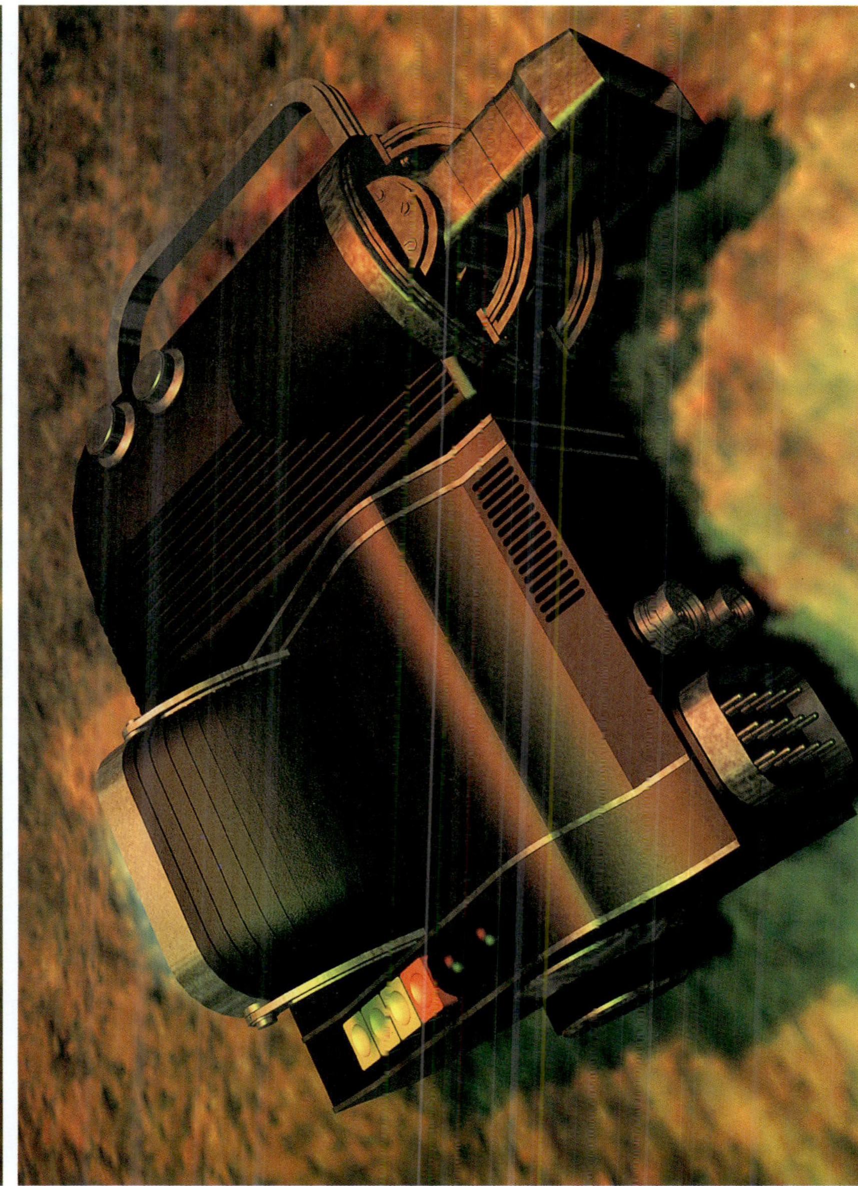

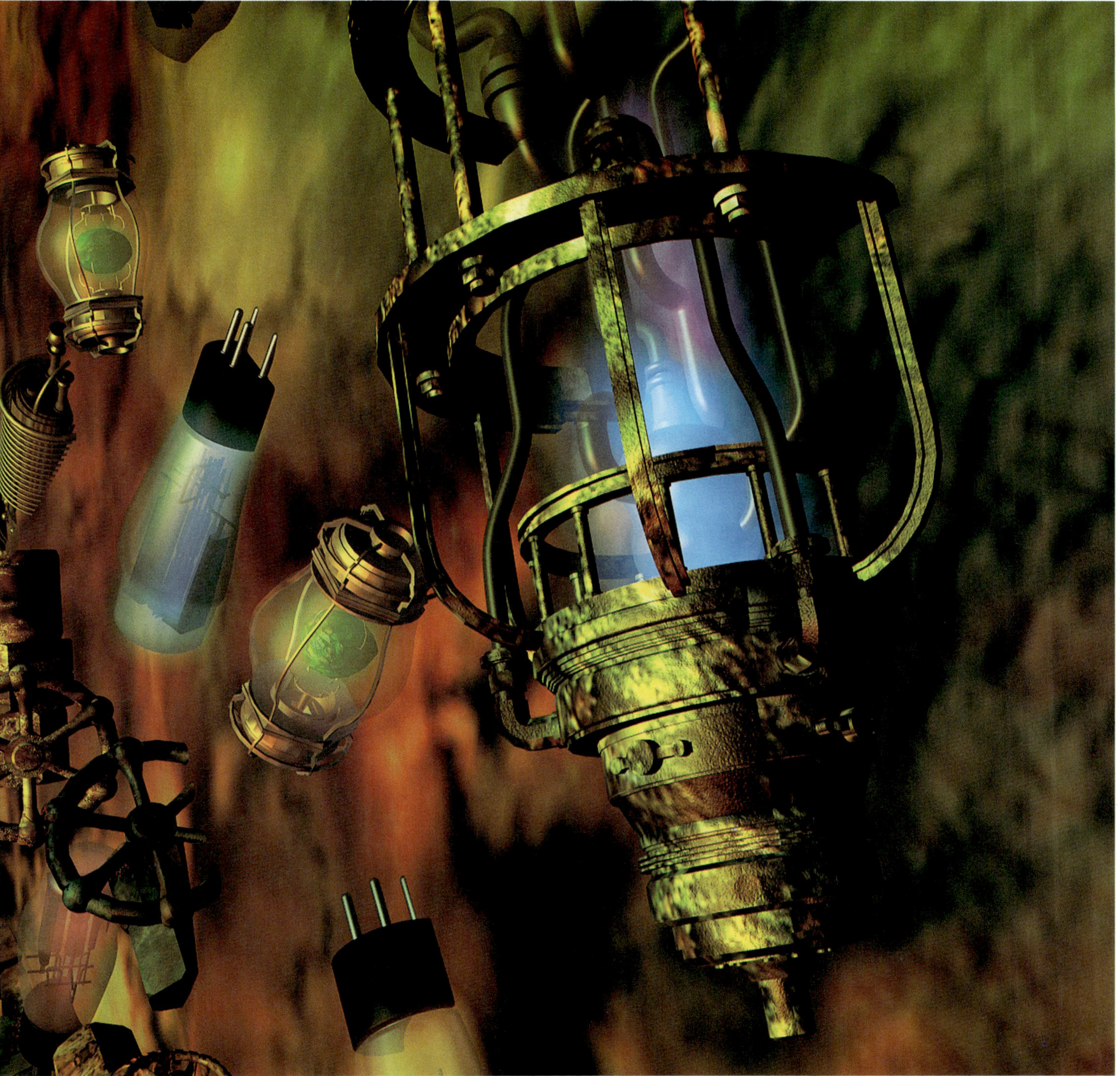

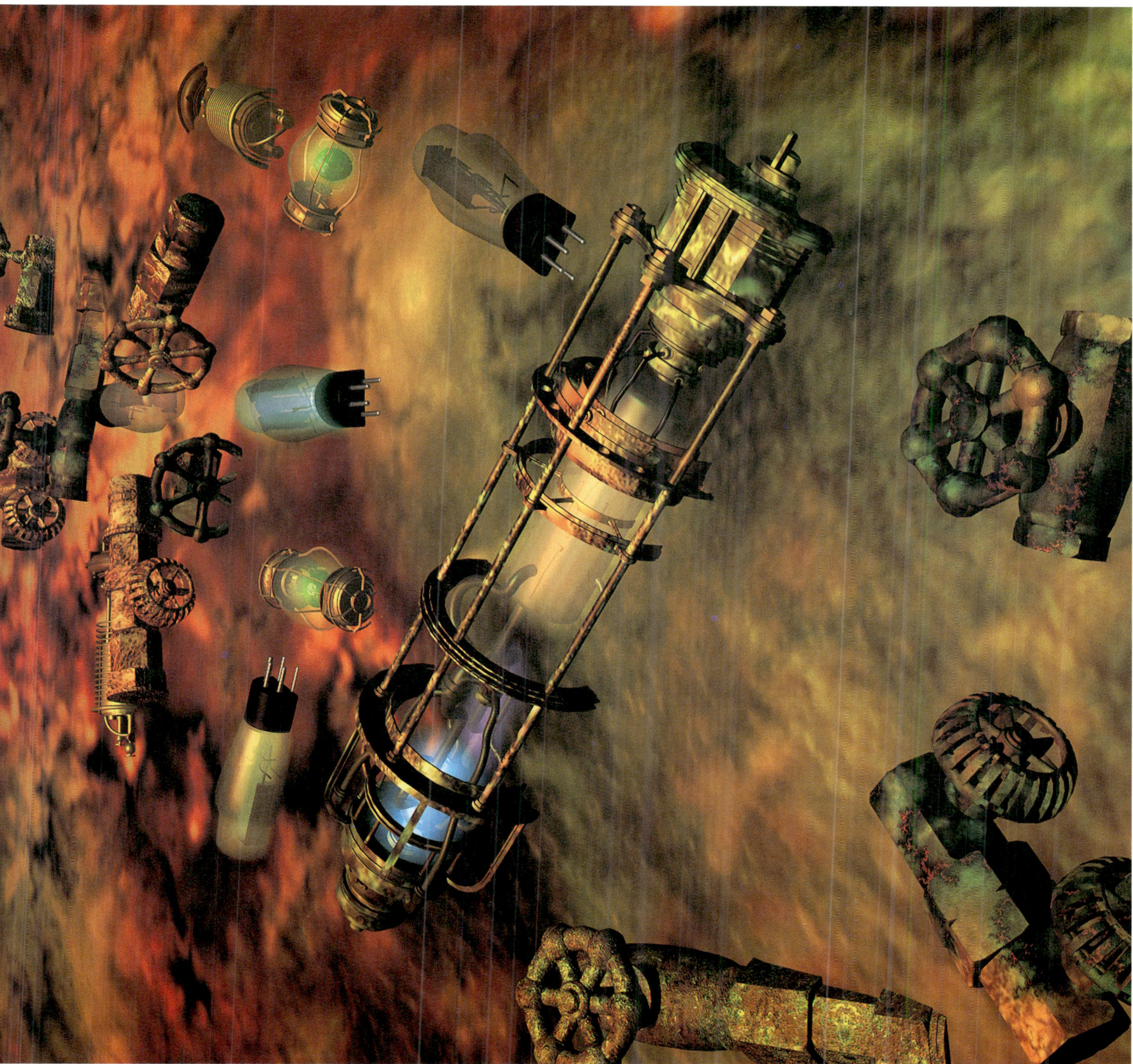

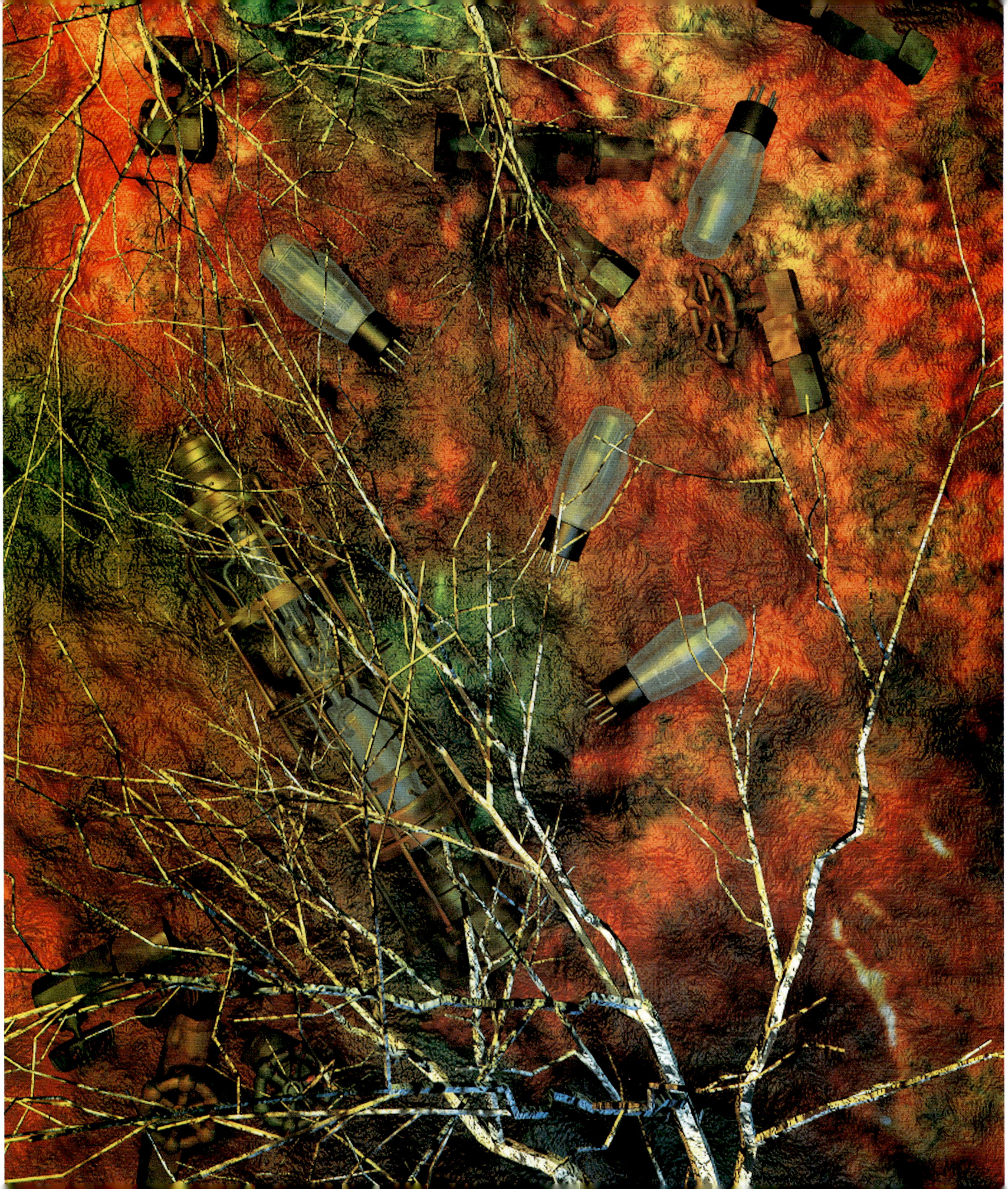

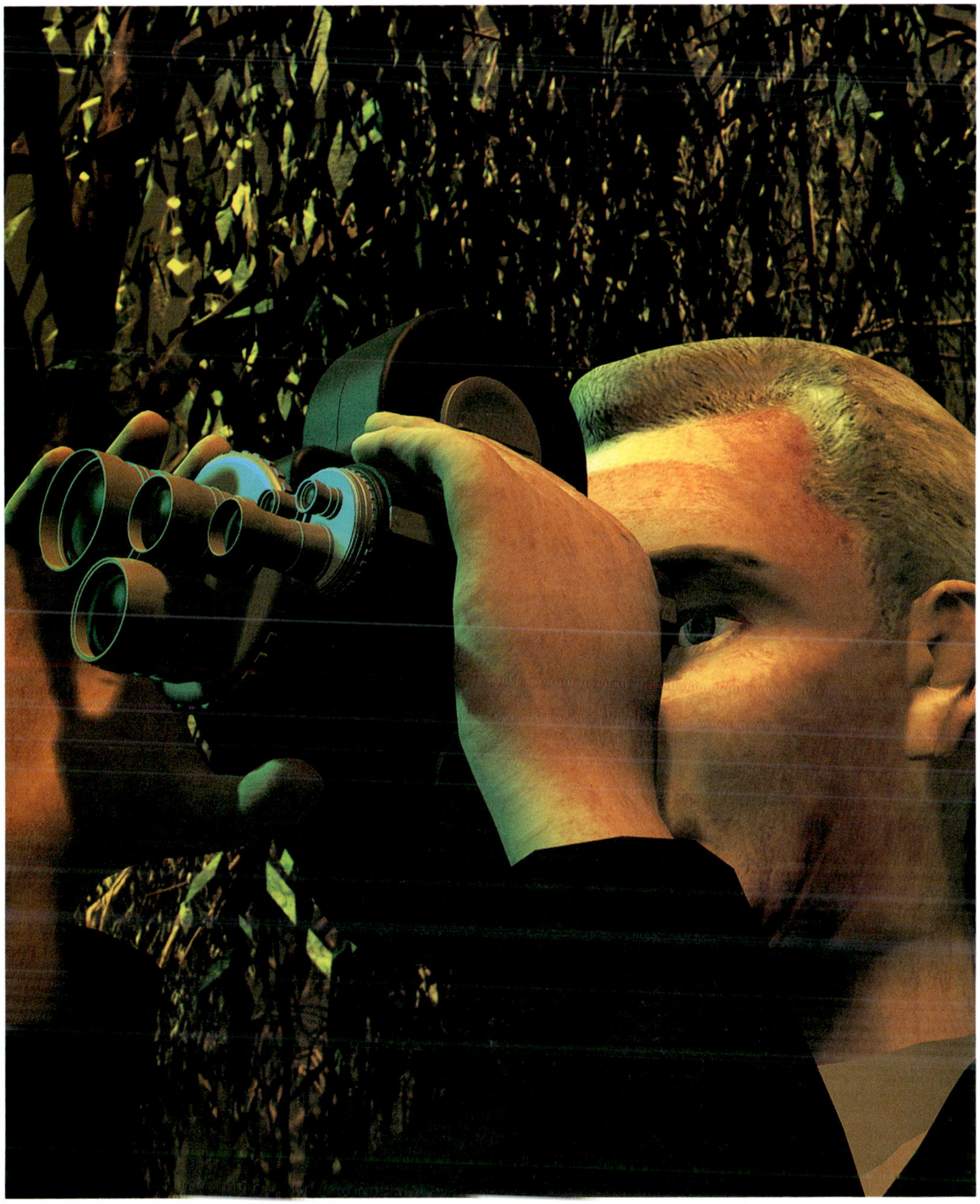

Conversation at Army Intelligence Headquarters between Intelligence Operative Second Class Hausmann and Supreme Commander Slowslop.

— Any new developments concerning Horselover and his scientists?
— No, sir. Horselover's whereabouts are still unknown. I've set a surveillance team on the Observatory as well, but no report yet of a sighting.
— And the Sensorama experiments?
— Just as before, radiation experiments are carried on at regular intervals in a laboratory at the back of the Museum. We've put taps on every terminal of their communications network. Horselover's instructions are transmitted in writing.
— They have any contact with Thomas?
— He's made phone calls. Of course we listen in, but the conversations all have to do with development of the excavator...nothing of special importance.
— How far have their experiments carried them?
— They've completed the Version II machine. In appearance it's hardly changed at all, the one big difference compared with Version I being the noise it makes. When the motor starts up at the beginning of the experiment there comes a grating noise that's almost unbearable. We have film records of all the experiments and I'll pass them on to you later.
— Is there a written report.
— I'll submit it with the film.
— Very good. Carry on with your work.
— Yes, sir.

(2 September, Year 5 of the Imperial Age)

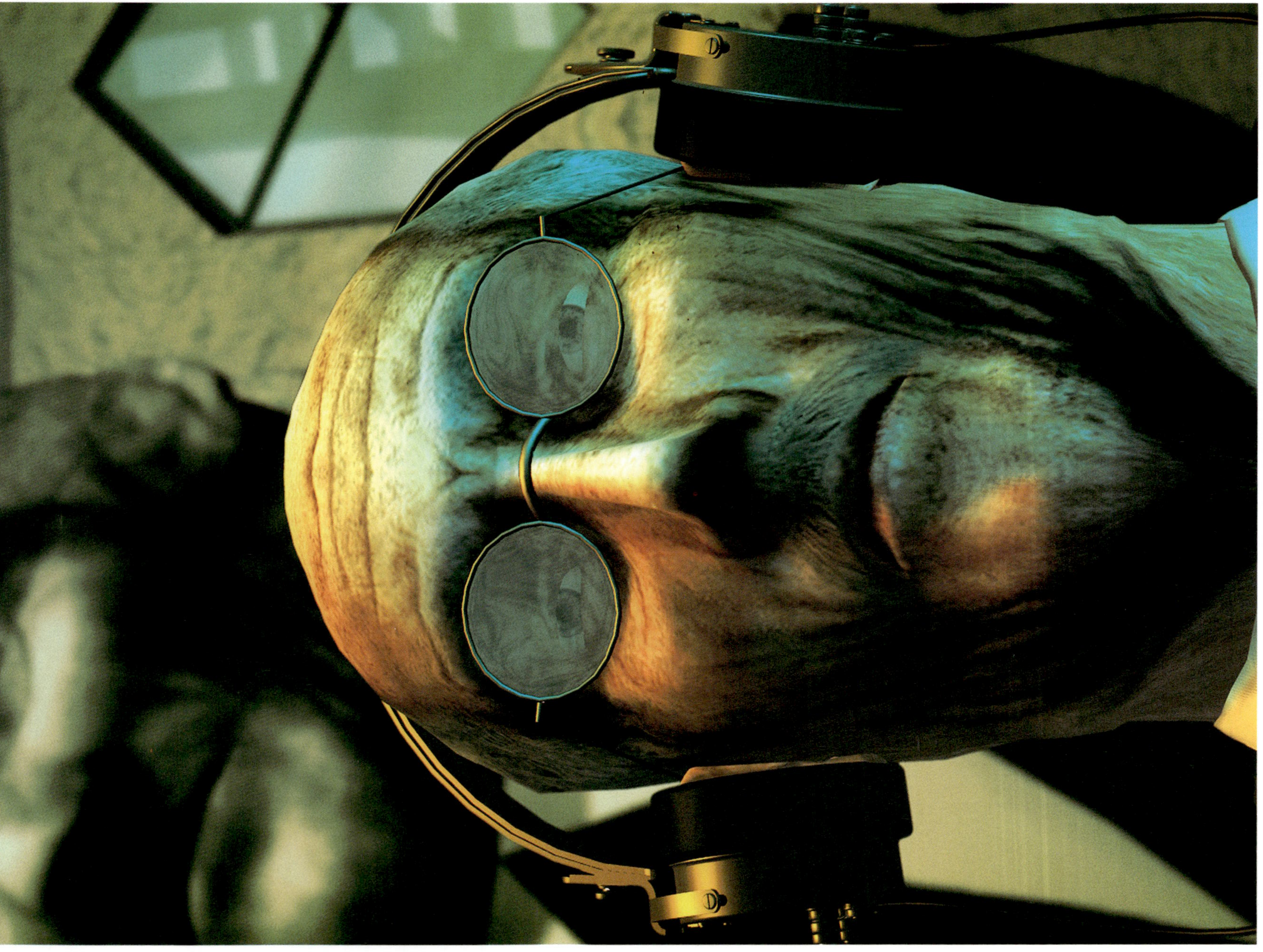

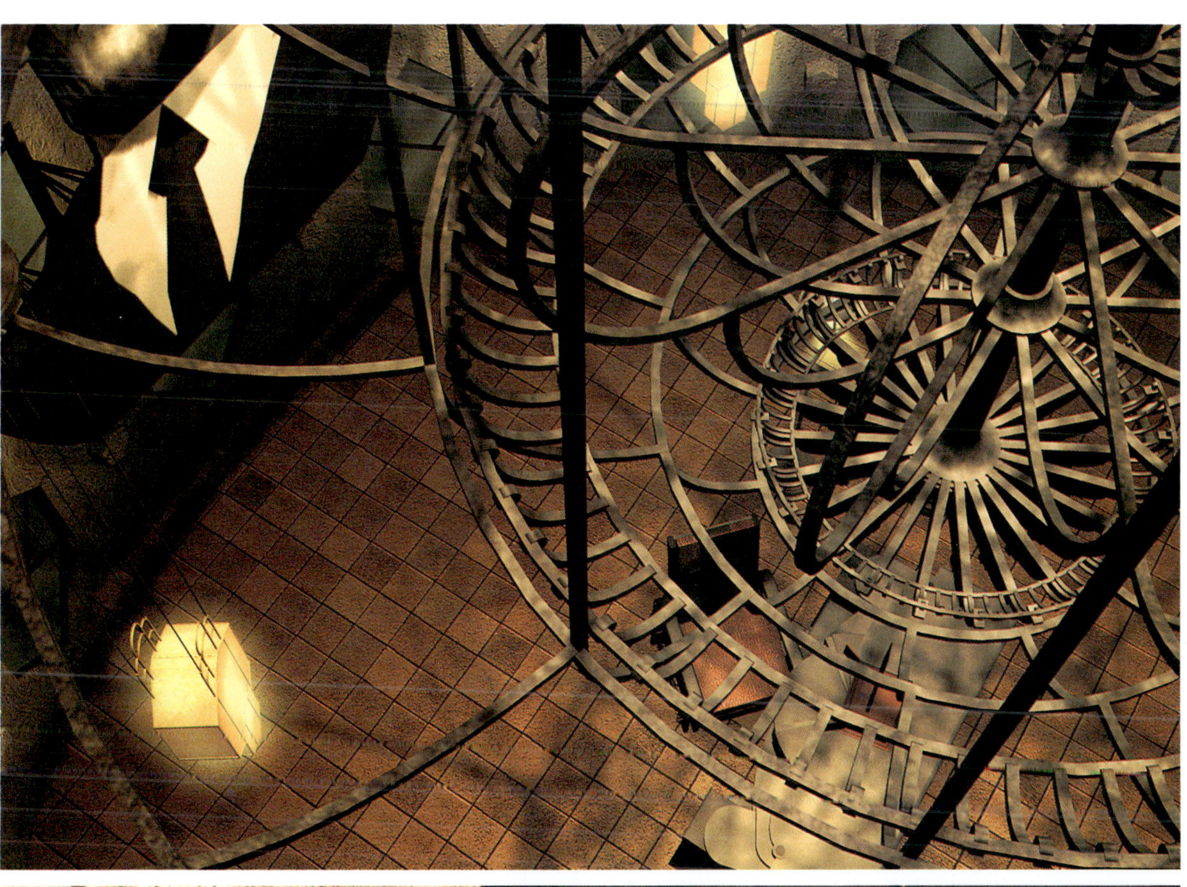

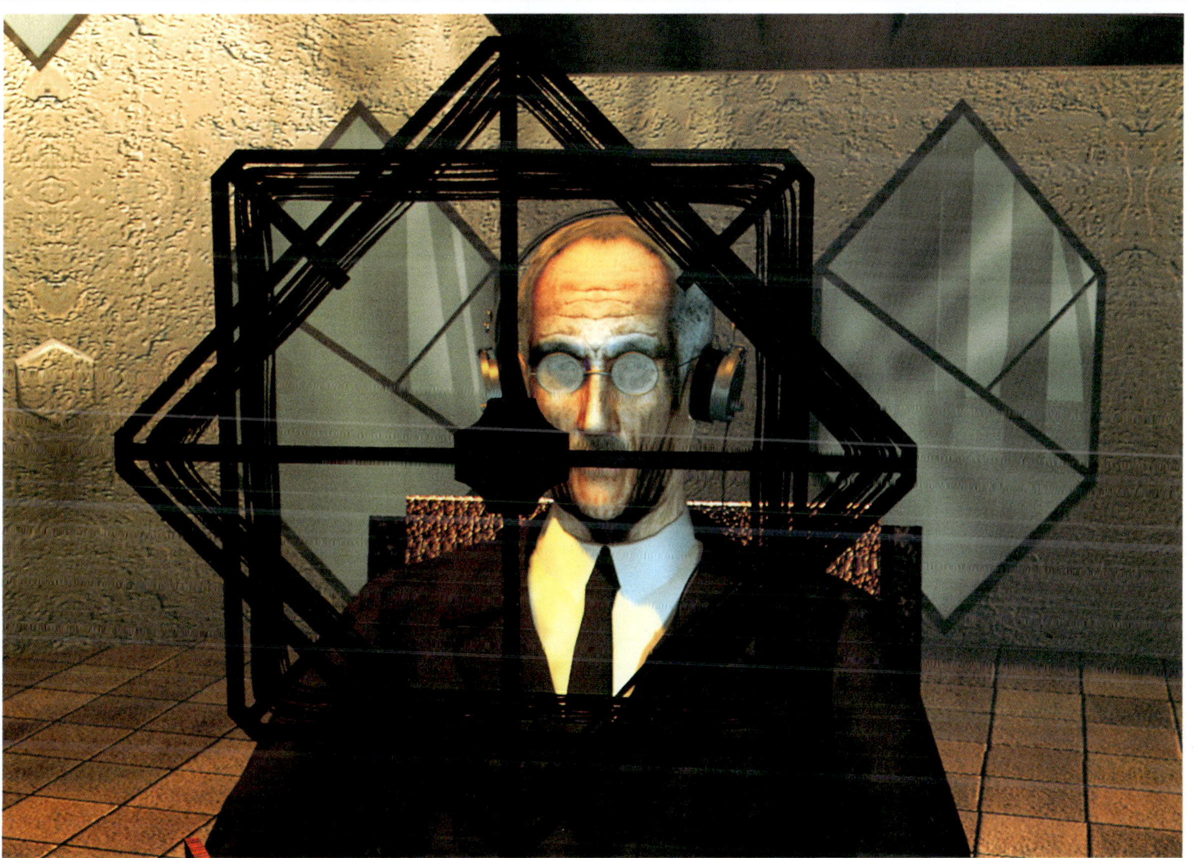

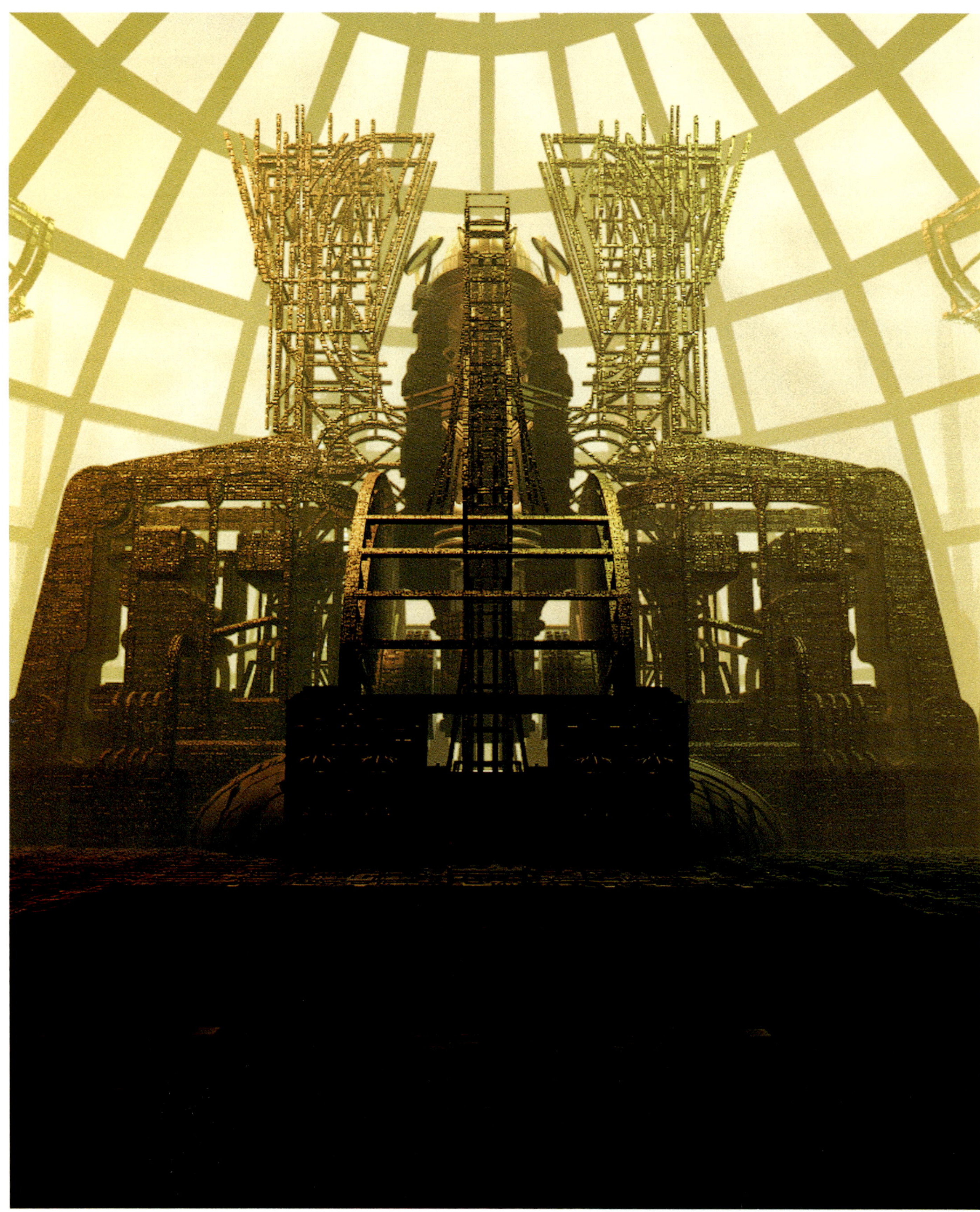

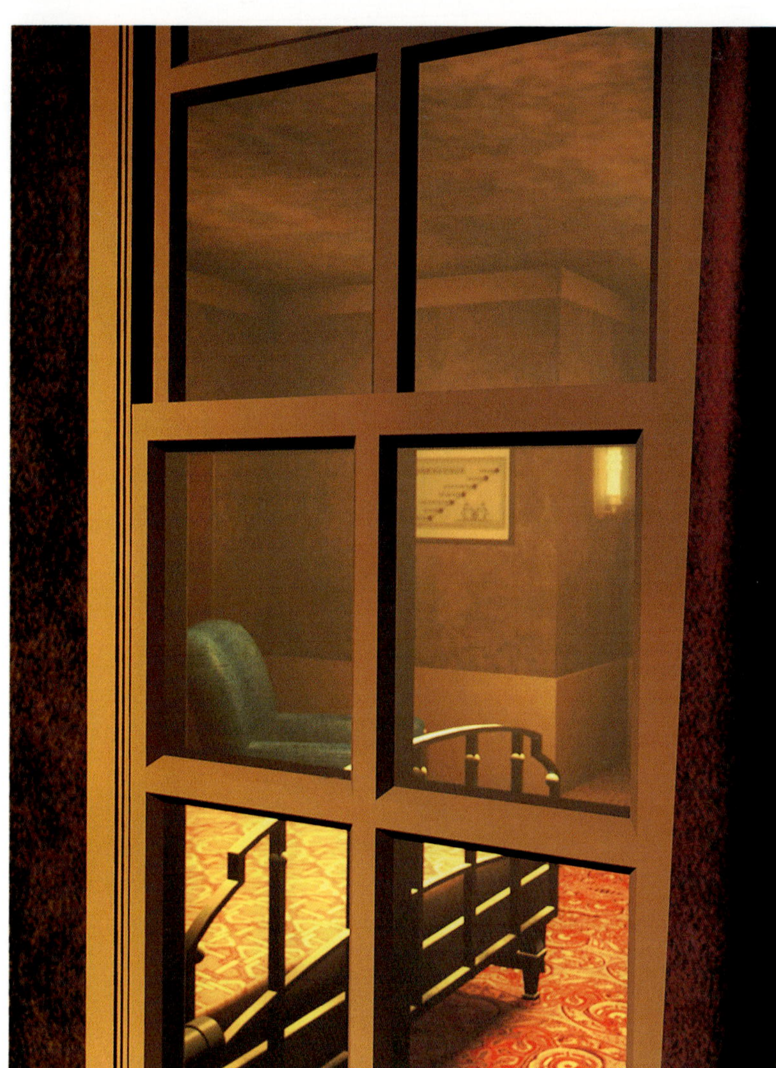

Radio conversation between the intelligence operative O. Gondarev and Party Chairman Onegin of the Socialist Republic.

— Gondarev, sir.
— Any chance someone's listening in?
— Not on this frequency, sir. Empire receivers can't monitor it.
— What have you to report?
— Excavation of the meteorite's begun.
— Have they completed restoration of the tunnel.
— Yes. They started using the excavator today. It's built to carry the ore it digs up through the tunnel to the Ordnance Factory.
— How is the ore stored?
— The meteorites are kept in a warehouse until they're brought to the smelting furnace. The iron and calcium are melted away leaving the special substance in nearly pure form.
— And then what?
— It's packed in containers and put aboard the Nova Express.
— What's that?
— A railway used exclusively by the Army that runs between the Ordnance Factory and Grand Central Station in West End. When the Nova arrives, it's inspected by Army officers before the containers are unloaded. The shipments are parceled out in the freight yard and transshiped to arms factories throughout the Empire.
— ....
— Up to this point everything's gone according to Orlovsky's plan, but there's one thing he's overlooked. On his own initiative Slowslop has kept back a good half of the meteoritic rock.
— How interesting.
— ....
— Let me think this out. I'll get back to you.
— Yes, sir.

(14 January, Year 6 of the Imperial Age)

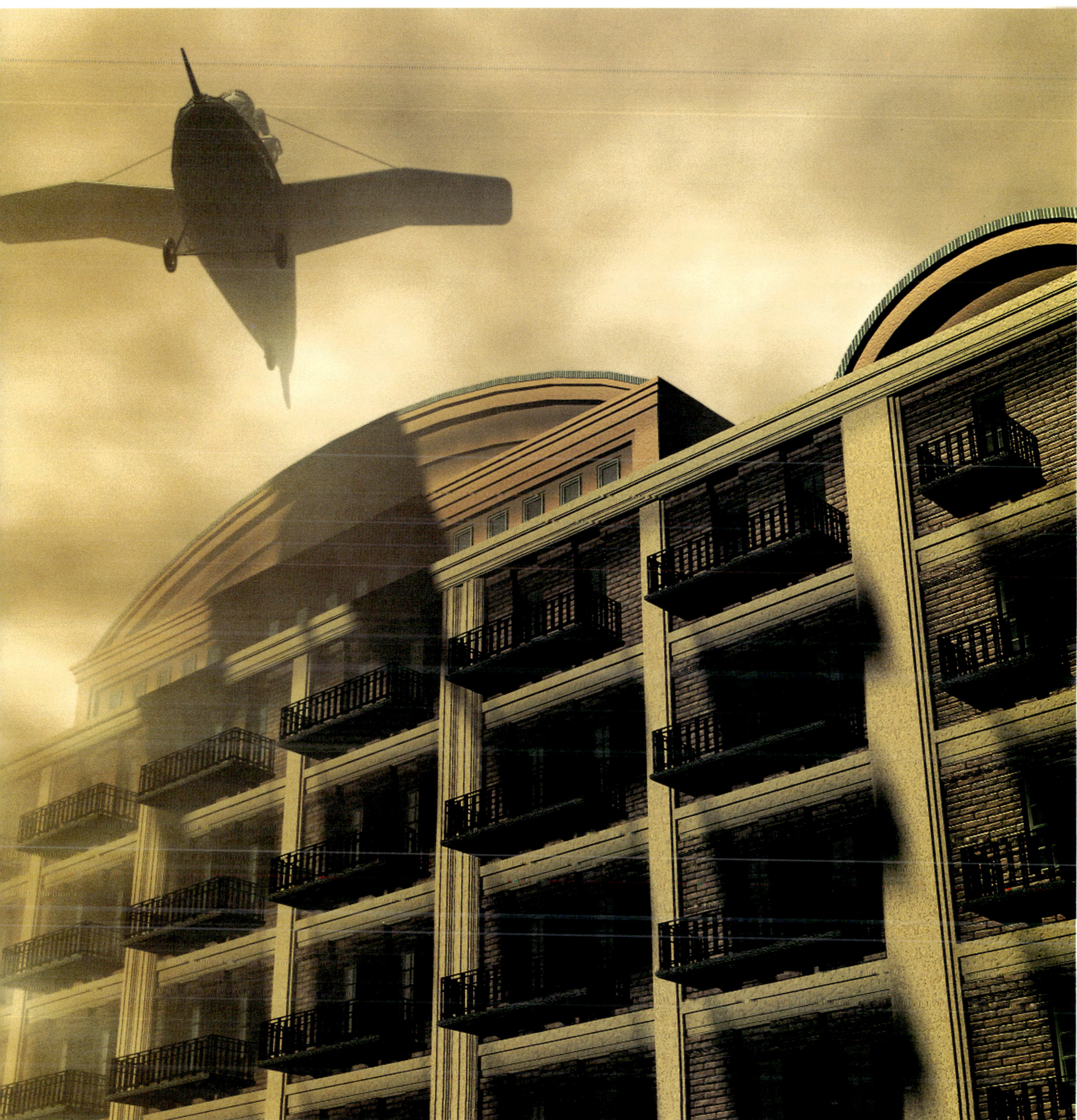

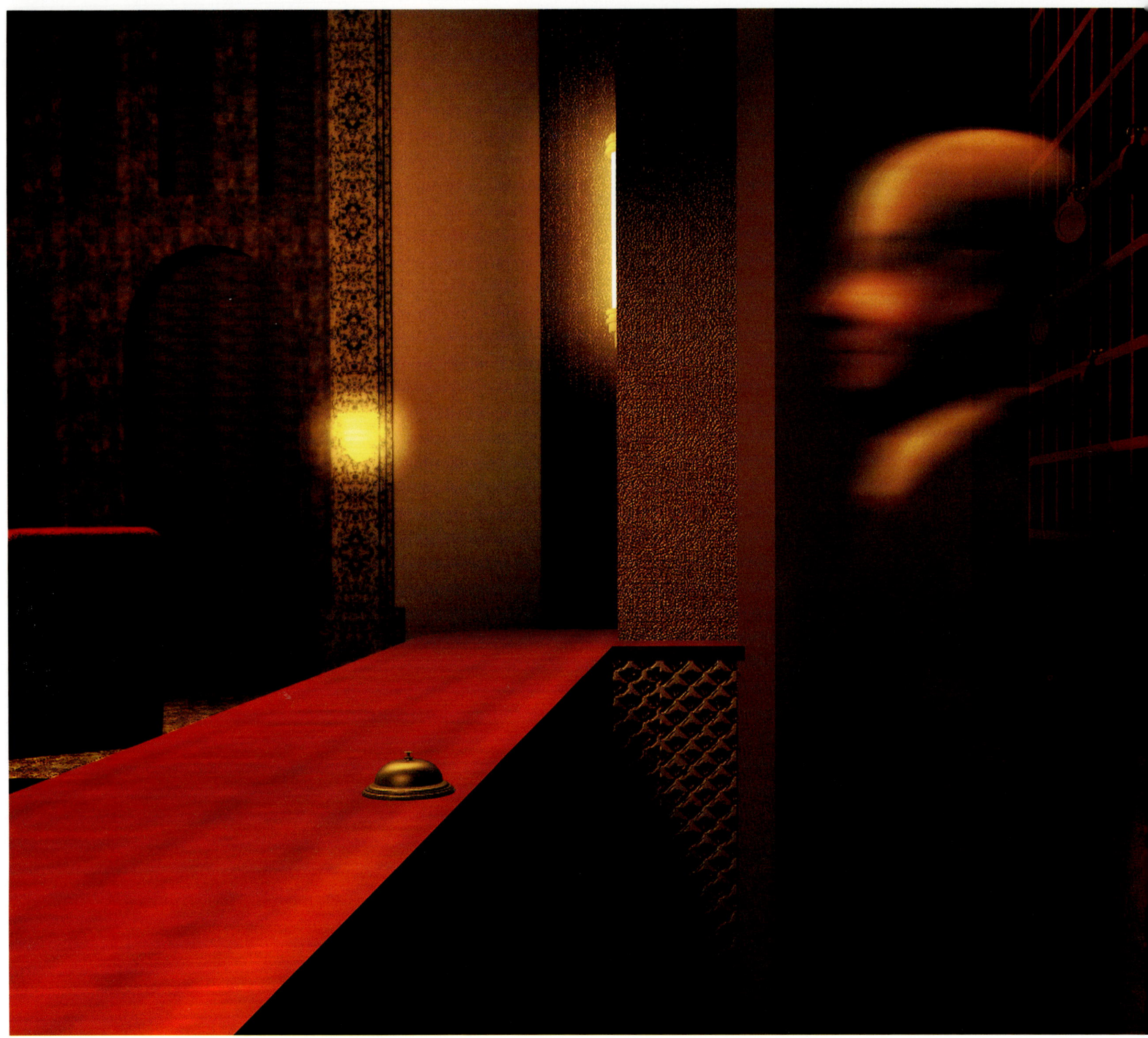

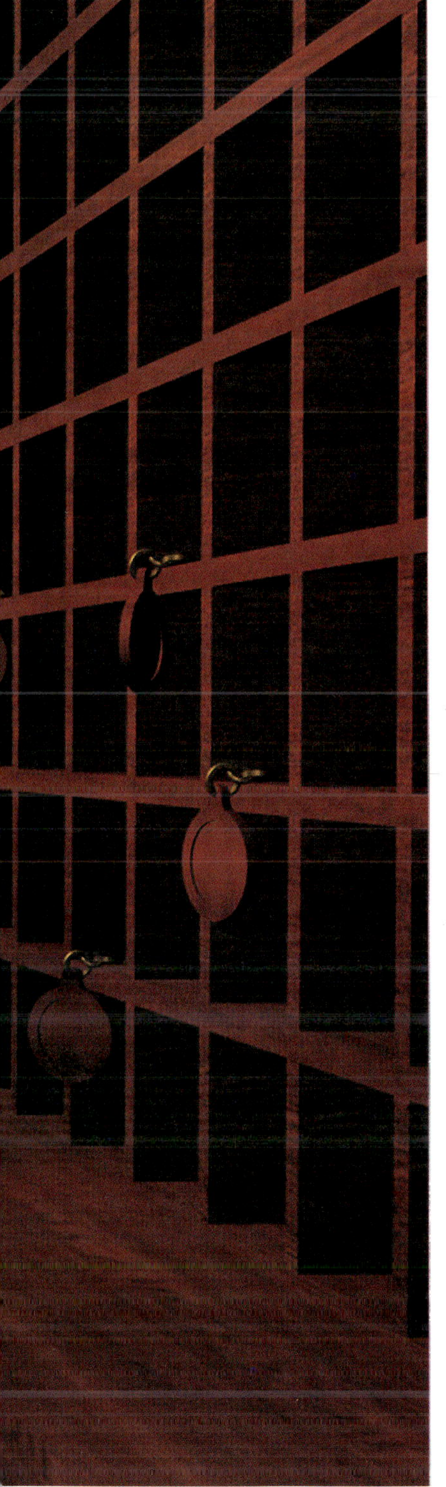

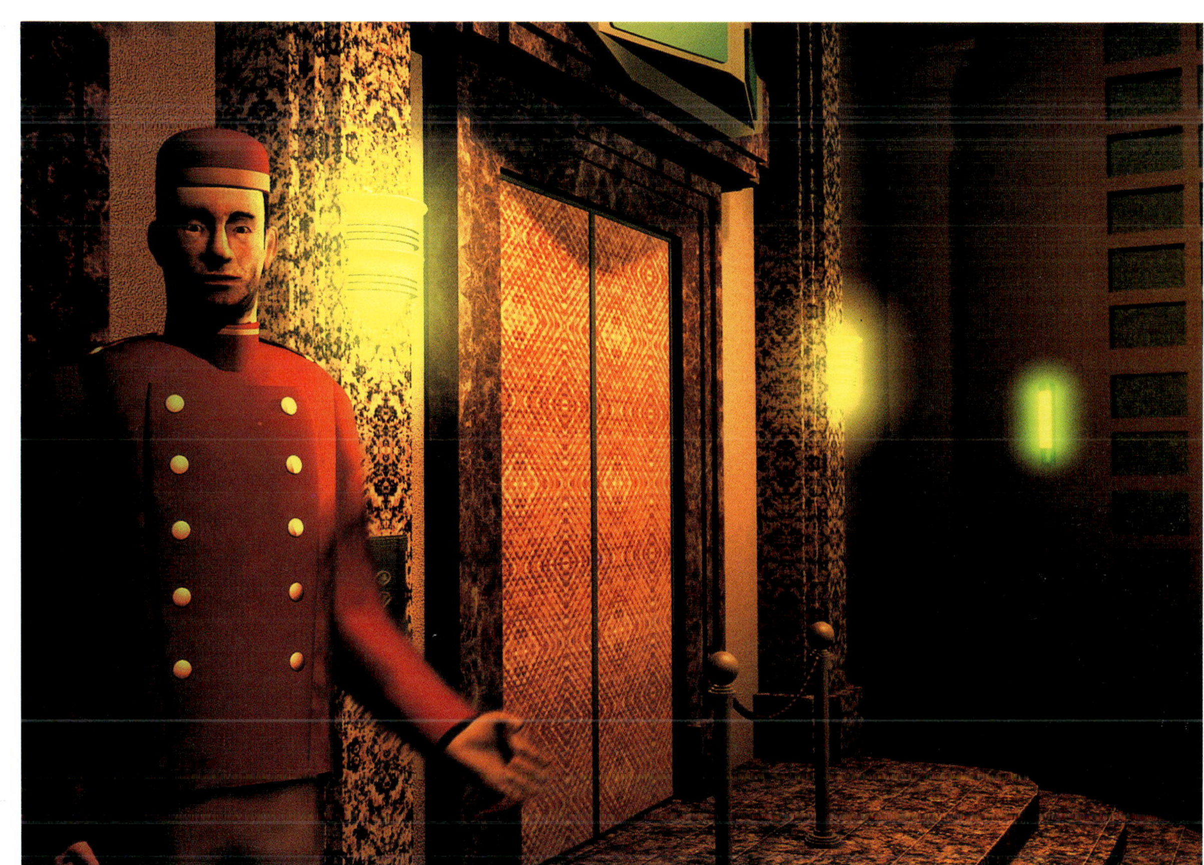

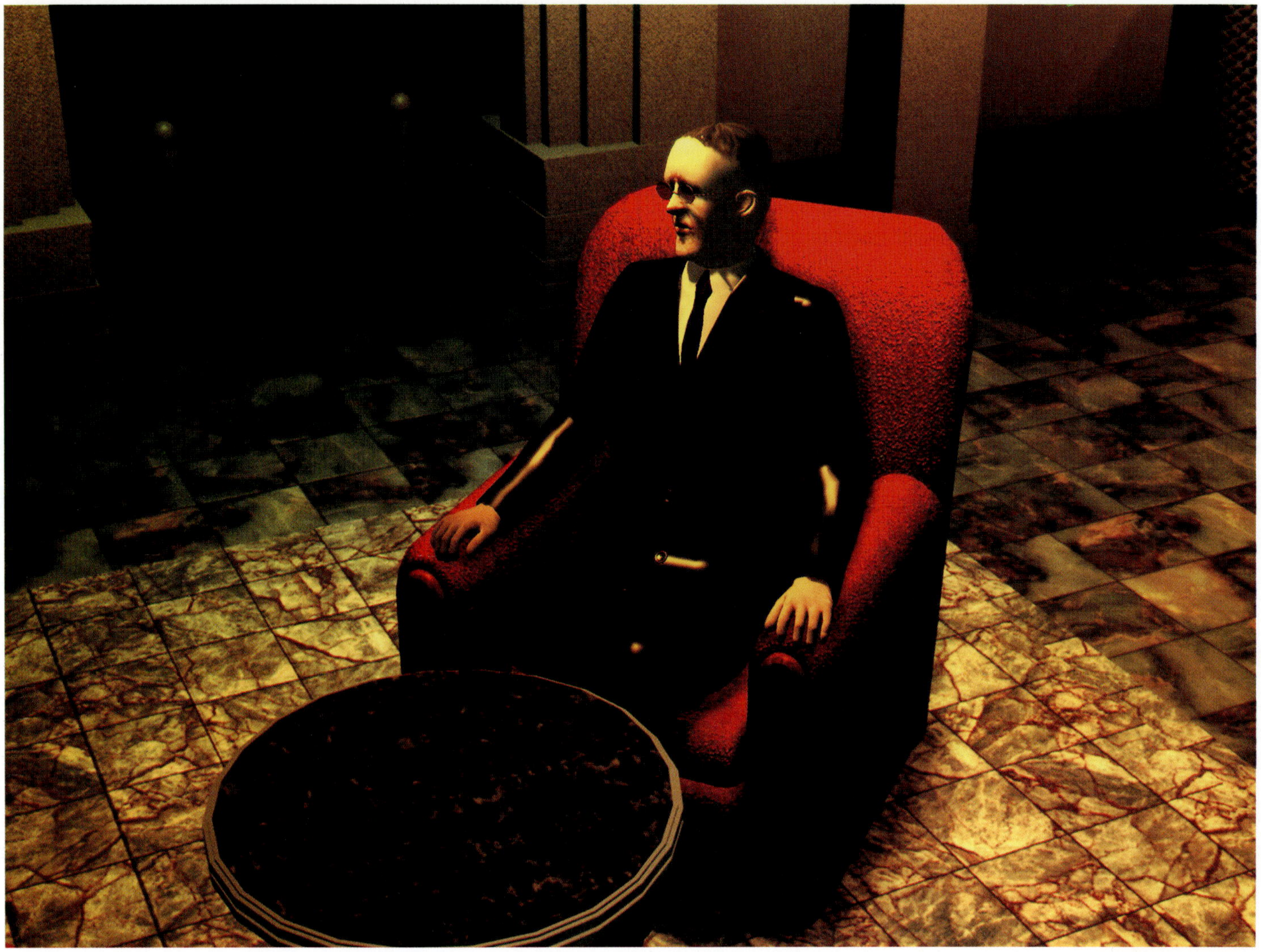

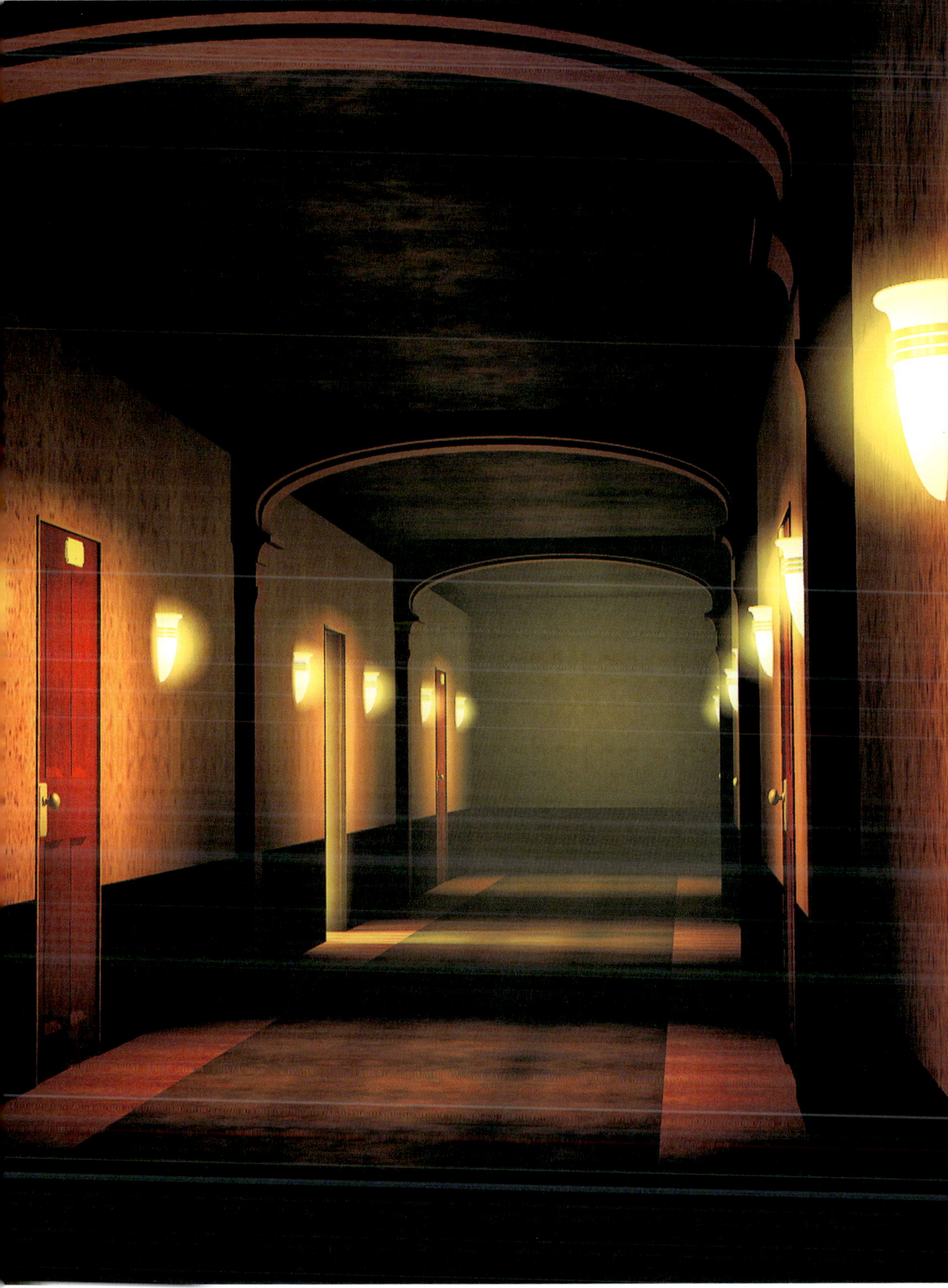

Conversation between Orlovsky and Slowslop, who has been called to the dictator's office.

— What is it you wish to know, My Lord?
— About the Sensorama.
— Have you read my report?
— I glanced over it. Improved performance, I see.
— To be utterly frank with you, there are numerous aspects of the scientist's activities that I find incomprehensible.
— They're working for the Empire, think of it that way. The scientists themselves aren't aware of it, of course.
— I fail to understand.
— The Sensorama is a brainwashing device.
— ....
— I have not actually charged them with a mission, but the excellent minds of Horselover and his six scientists are working to satisfy a certain need of the Empire.
— What need is it you speak of, My Lord.
— Our policy of military expansion has resulted in a radical increase in the Empire's power. For this reason we should assume that the Socialist Republic has introduced agents into our national infrastructure.
— Force them to confess and then purge them, is it?
— No need.
— ....
— As soon as the Sensorama is perfected we'll give them all an education.
— ....
— And not only the Republic. There are reactionary elements plotting revolution here in the Empire itself.
— ....
— Eventually, I'll decree that every citizen of the Empire must undergo a Sensorama baptism.
— ....
— Just Horselover and Charles will do. Pick the right moment and put them in custody. Get everything ready.
— Yes, My Lord.

(16 October, Year 6 of the Imperial Age)

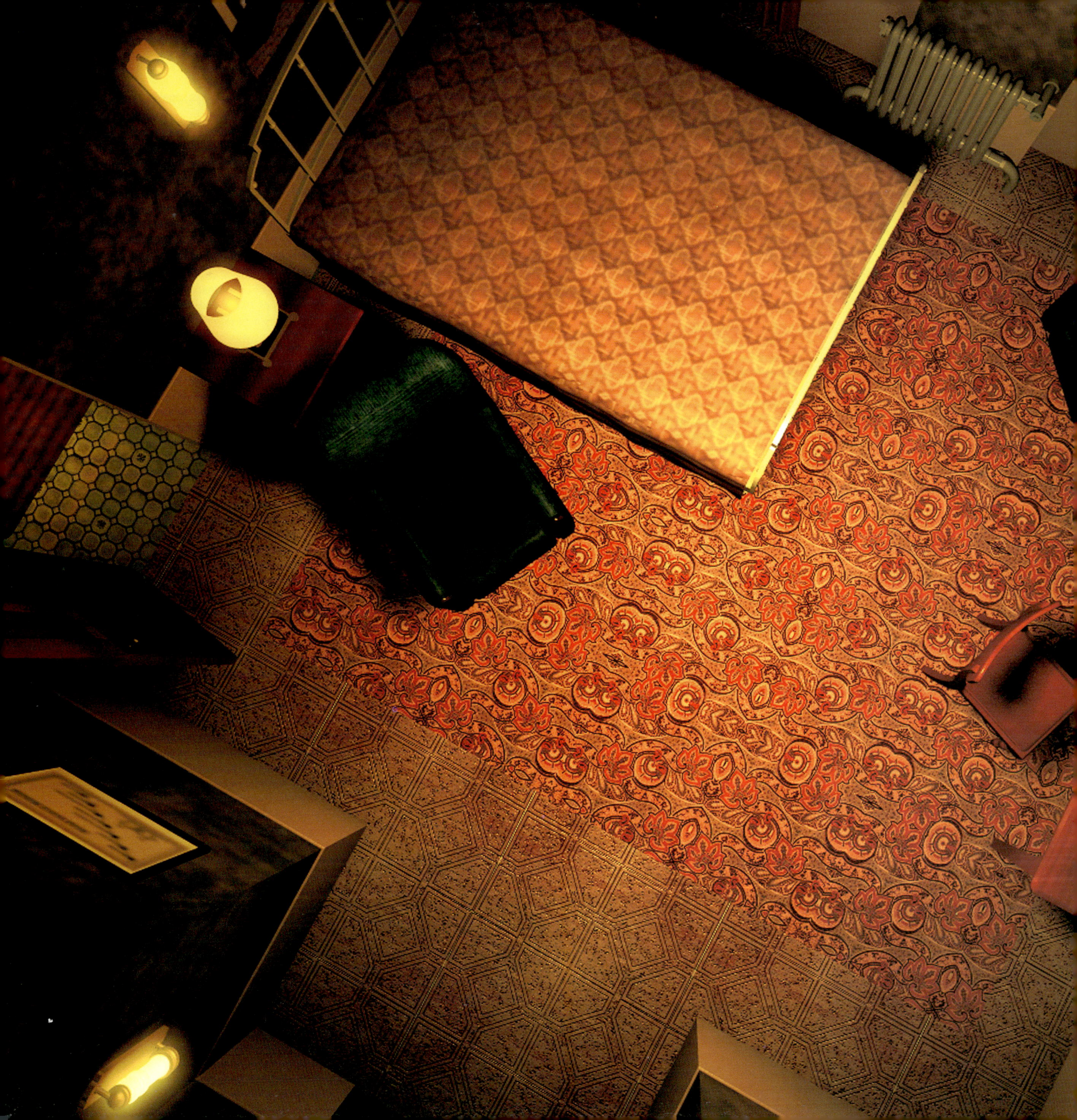

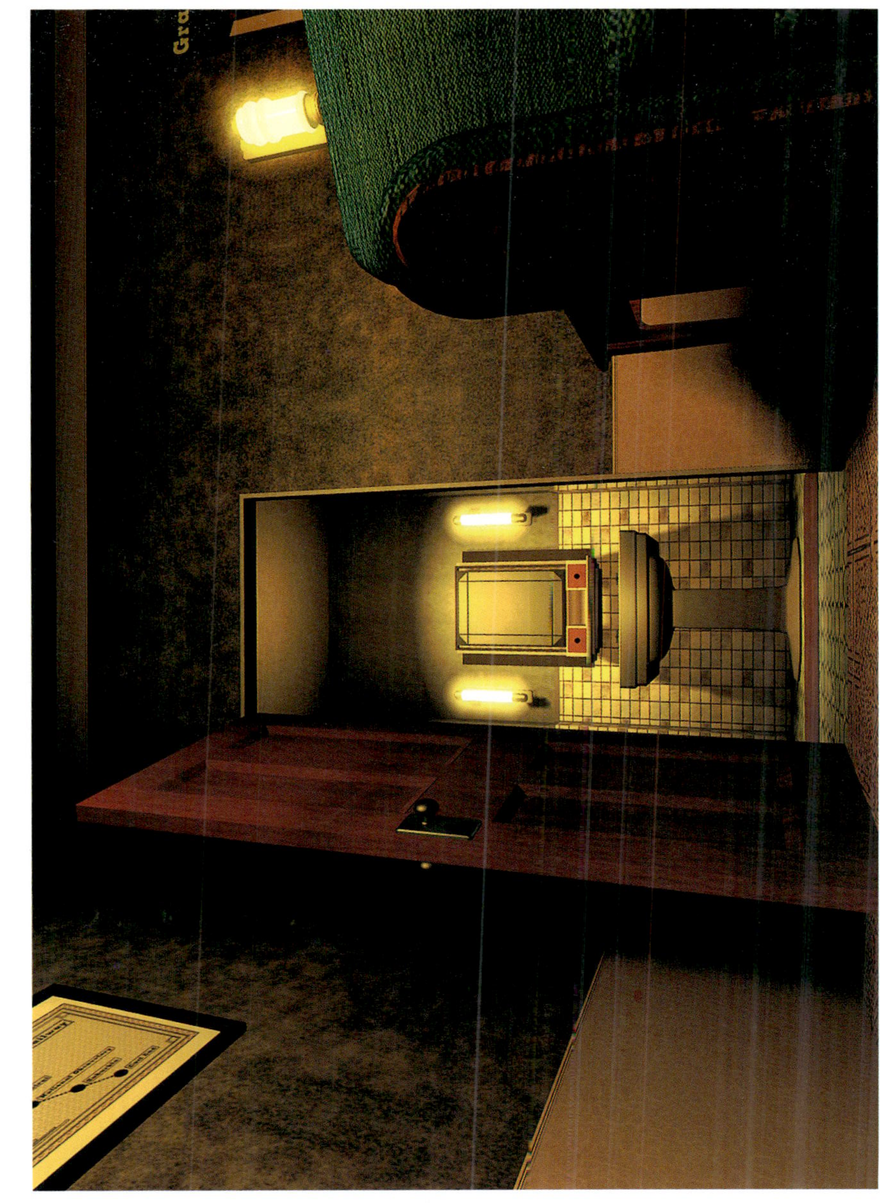

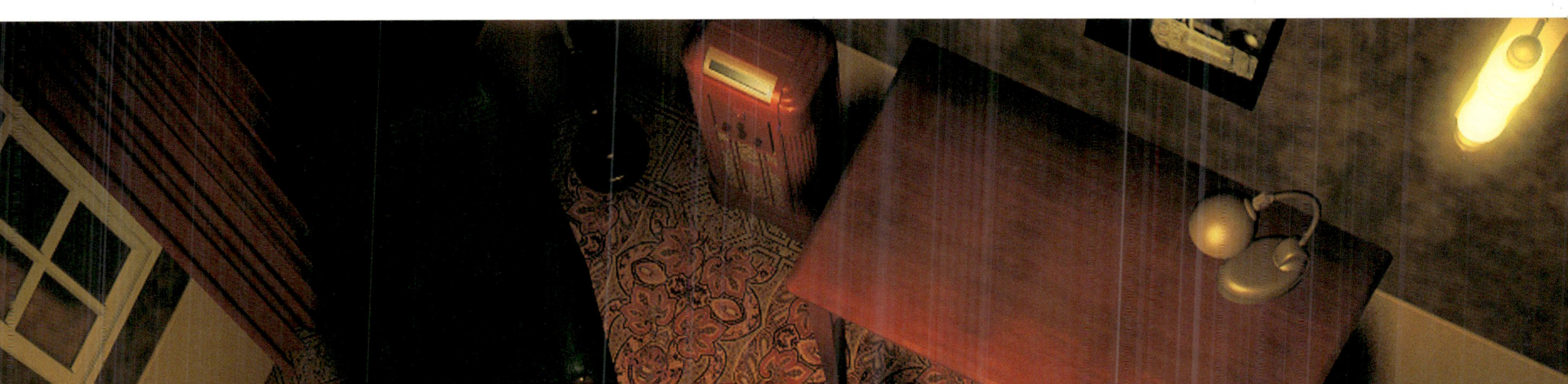

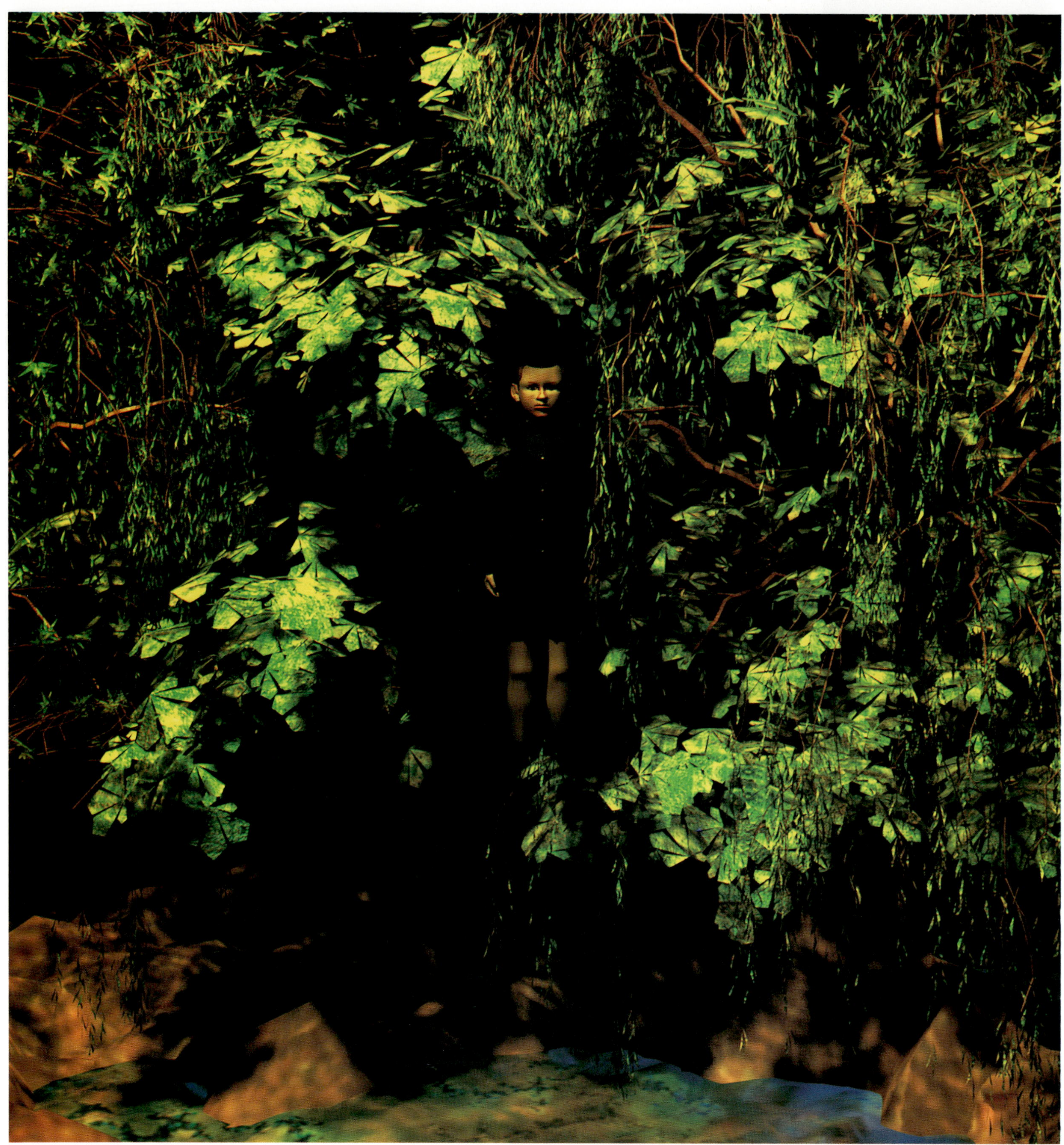

Cool decisions and cold judgements
Interrogation, cross-examination, torture
Twelve victims
Version II: an experiment in group study
Ore and the boy
Mission given
Fate transmitted
The planets and their satellites still revolve
Time without space cannot exist

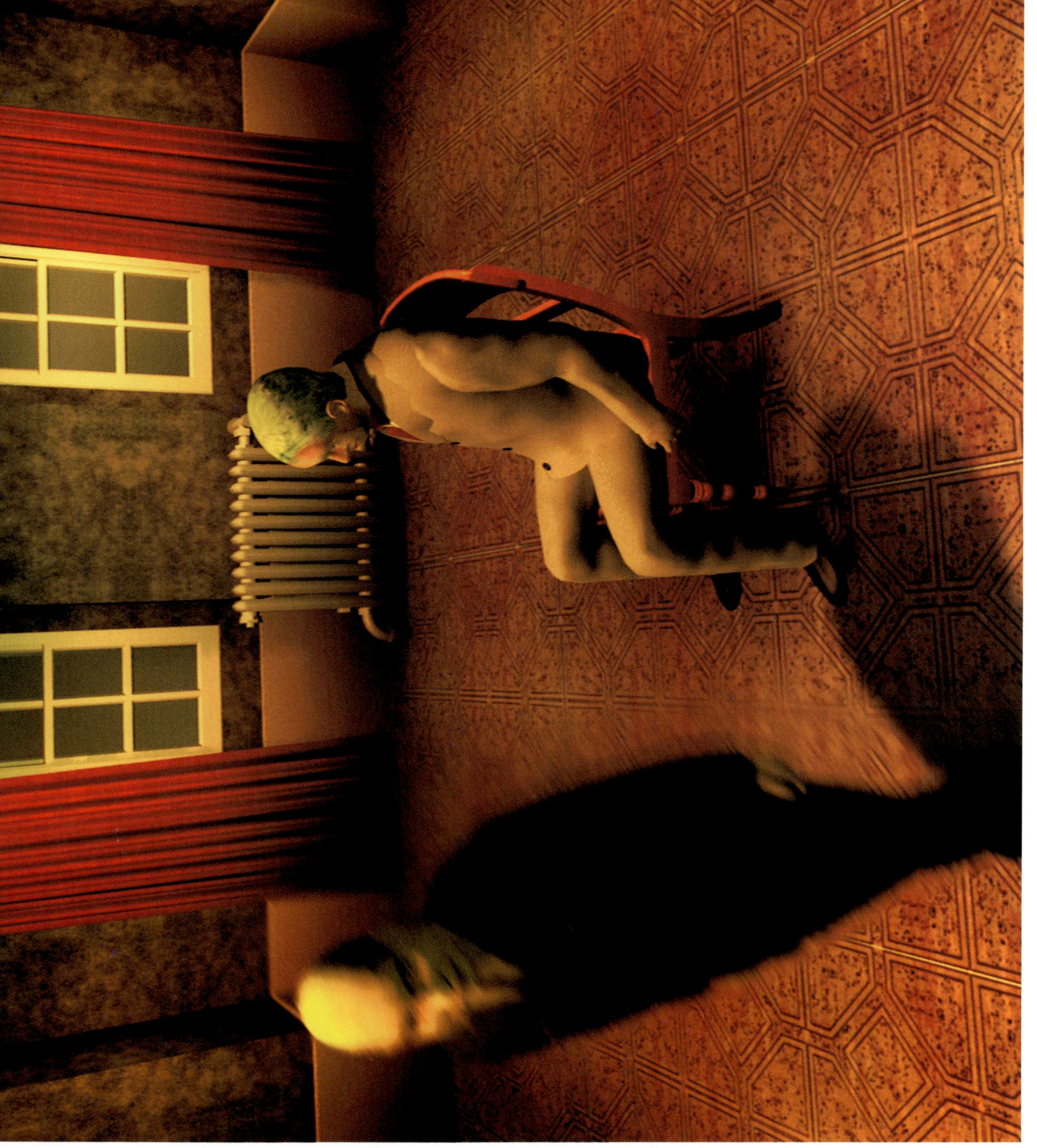

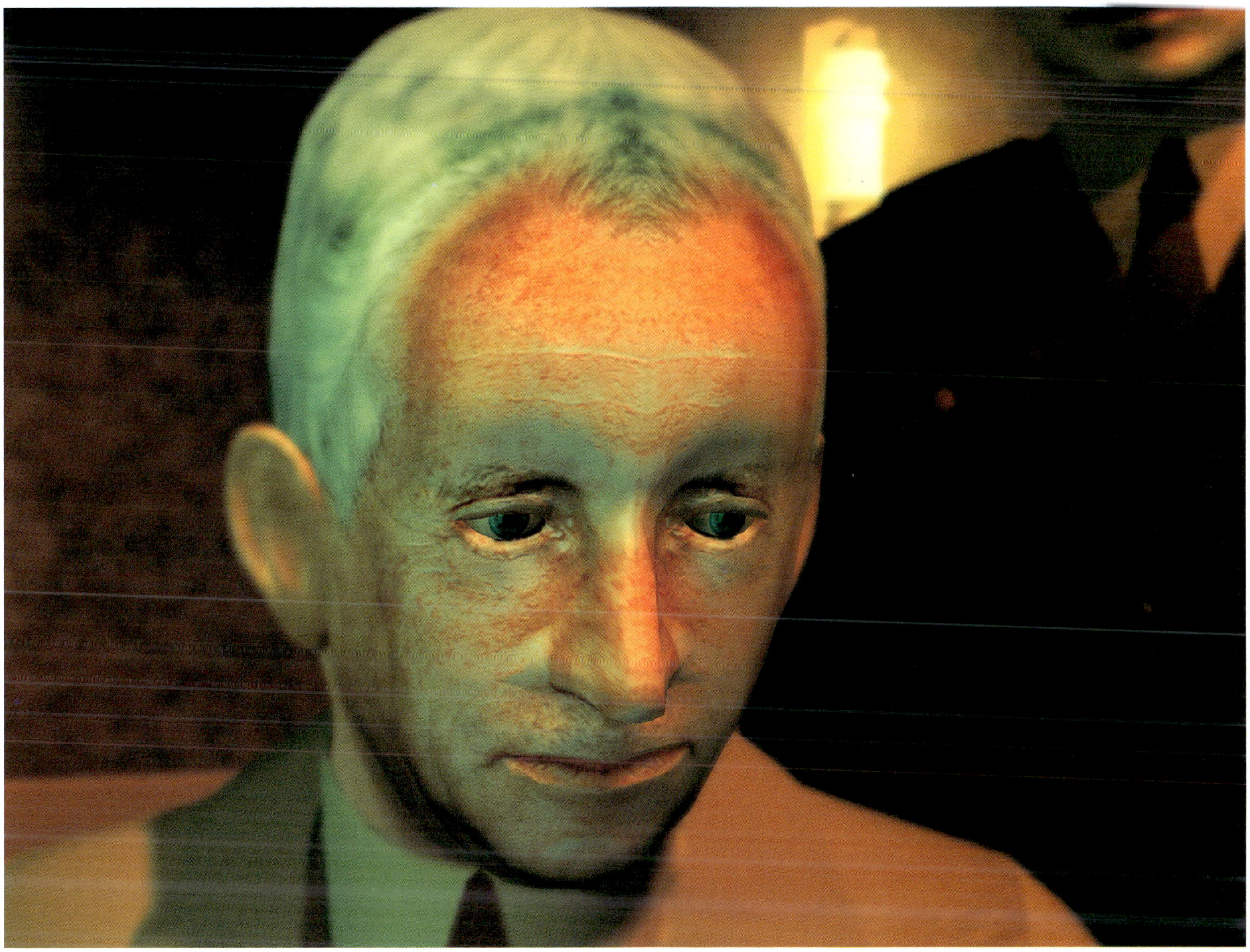

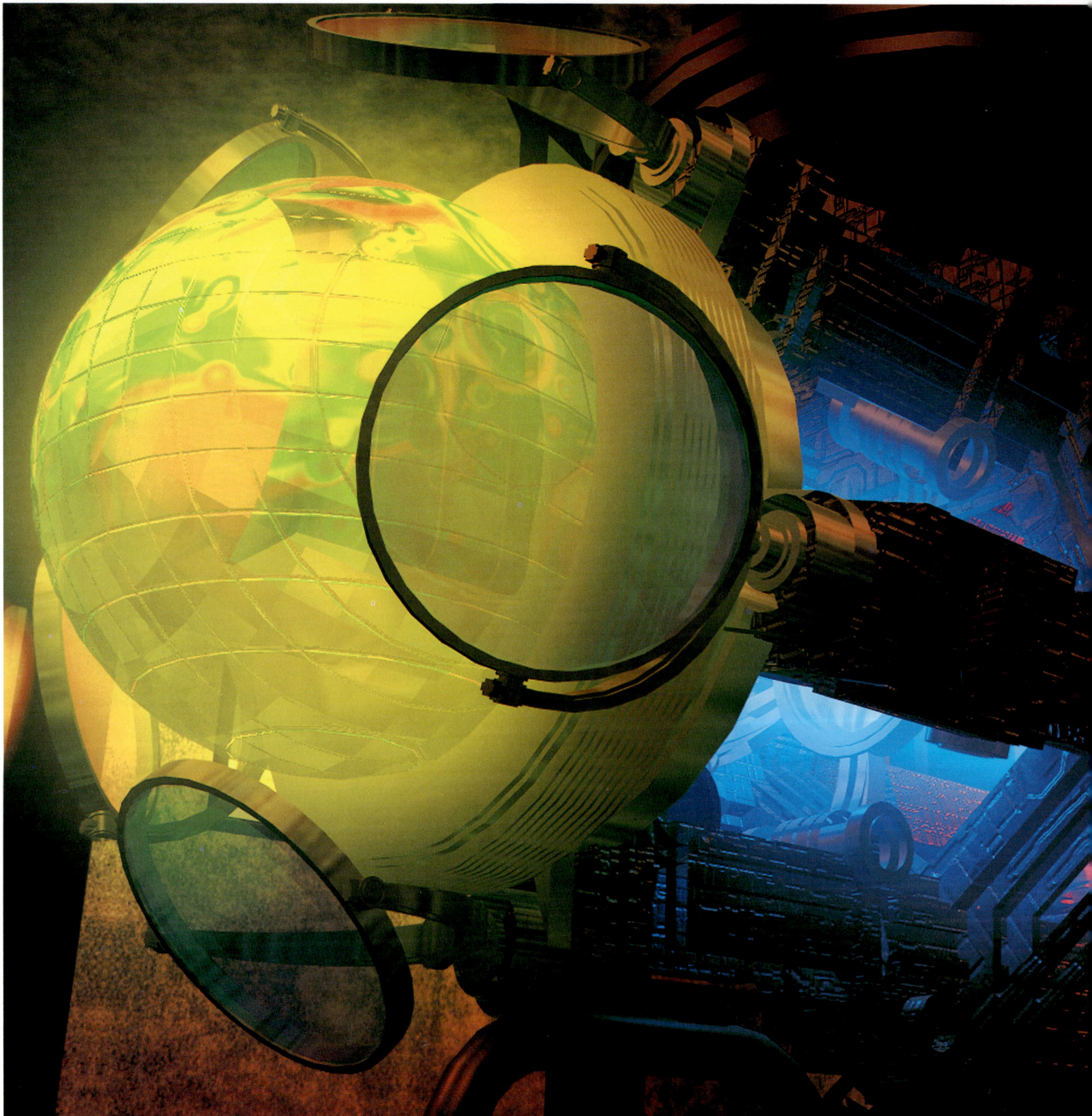

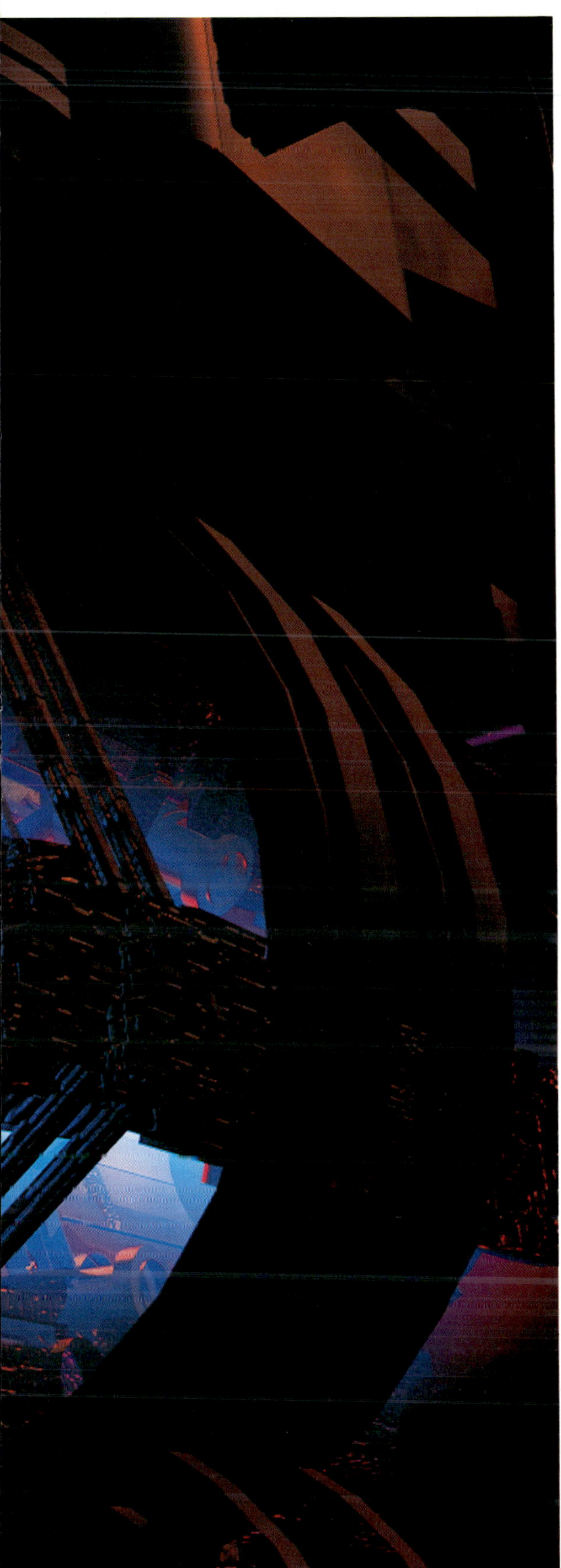

Years 7 and 8 of the Imperial Age

Cool decisions and cold judgements

The Imperial Guards place Charles in custody. Stripped of light and language, put in solitary confinement. Slander and insult. Bruises and lacerations. In the last extremity everything is relinquished. In equal measure is permanent pain bestowed on mind and body.

Interrogation, cross-examination, torture

Persuasion and exaction. Penitence and appeasement. Assent to the Empire's demands. Release of Charles. Version II: a remodeled Sensorama. Birth of a brainwashing machine. Orlovsky's will, or Imperial necessity, extends to experimentation on human subjects.

Twelve victims

Radiation tests in Room 306. The subjects are twelve convicts, delivered under guard by Hausmann. The full program carried out. Repeated shudders, then the moment of blackout. Brainwashing and consequent madness are the order of the day for Sensorama II.

Version II: an experiment in group study

Following electromagnetic wave radiation, muscle tissue convulses, control of the limbs is lost. In the fundus of the eye are artificial images. Cells split, optic nerve abrades. Incessant reverberation of dissonance. Memory flows away, lost, replaced, or transplanted.

Ore and the boy

A boy is admitted to the Imperial Army Hospital. Unconscious, perhaps in a coma. Constantine diagnoses and prescribes. Body temperature falls. Yet the pulse remains normal. Astounding pharmacological immunity. But he flees in the night, he vanishes.

Mission given

Hausmann adjusts the frequency. Intercepts a radio conversation. The voices of Gondarev and Onegin rise above the crackle of static. A report, or simply a betrayal of secrets. Both commander of the Imperial Guards and Republican operative. Plots and stratagems.

Fate transmitted

Onegin stands in the Command Tower of the Republic. Letter from Horselover, a scientist of the Empire. With approach of the comet, extinction of the Republic. The end is near. The sudden instant of unavoidable destruction. A single alternative is put forward.

The planets and their satellites still revolve

Scientists in the Observatory measure the focal distance. Analyze triangulated observations. Calibrate the comet cluster's speed of approach. Collision with the nucleus is a dead certainty. Meteors shower down on the Empire, on the Republic. Little time remains.

Time witout space cannot exist

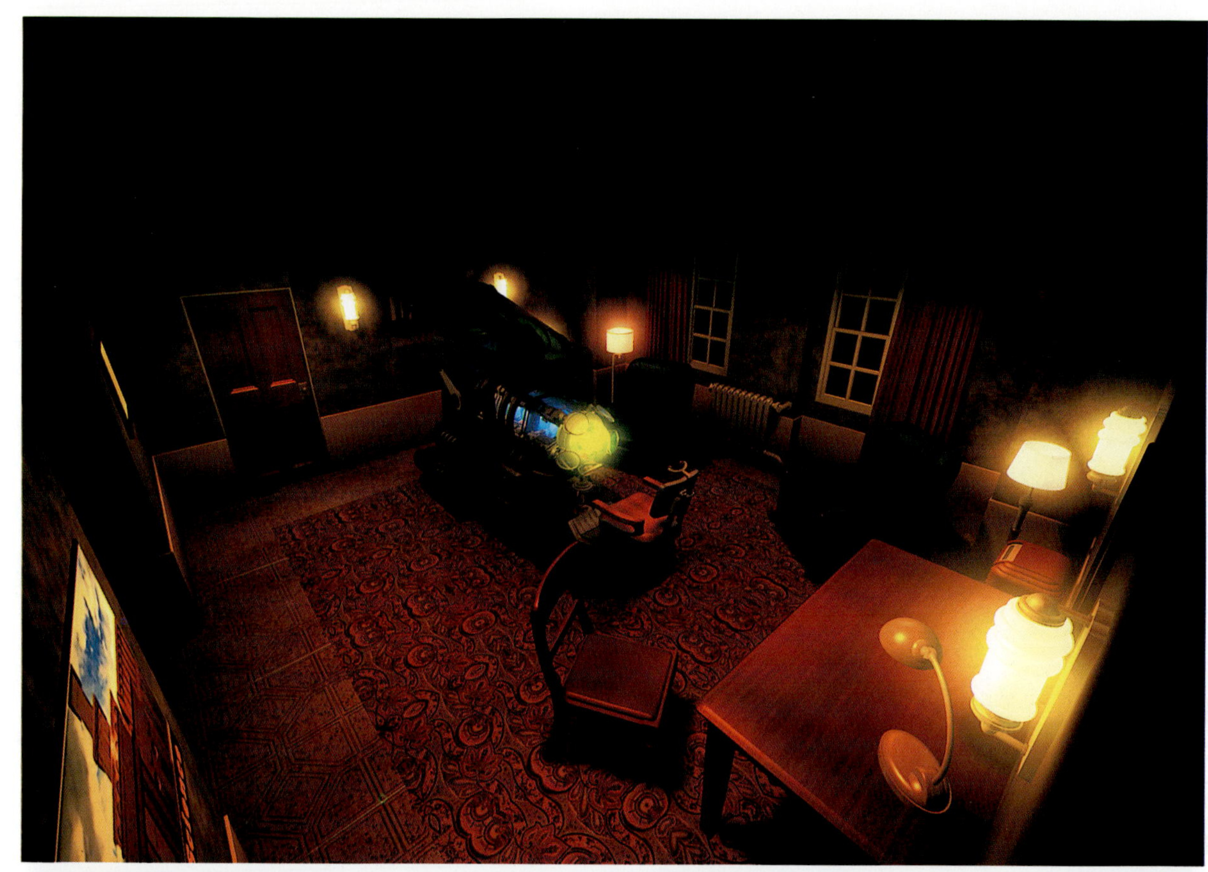

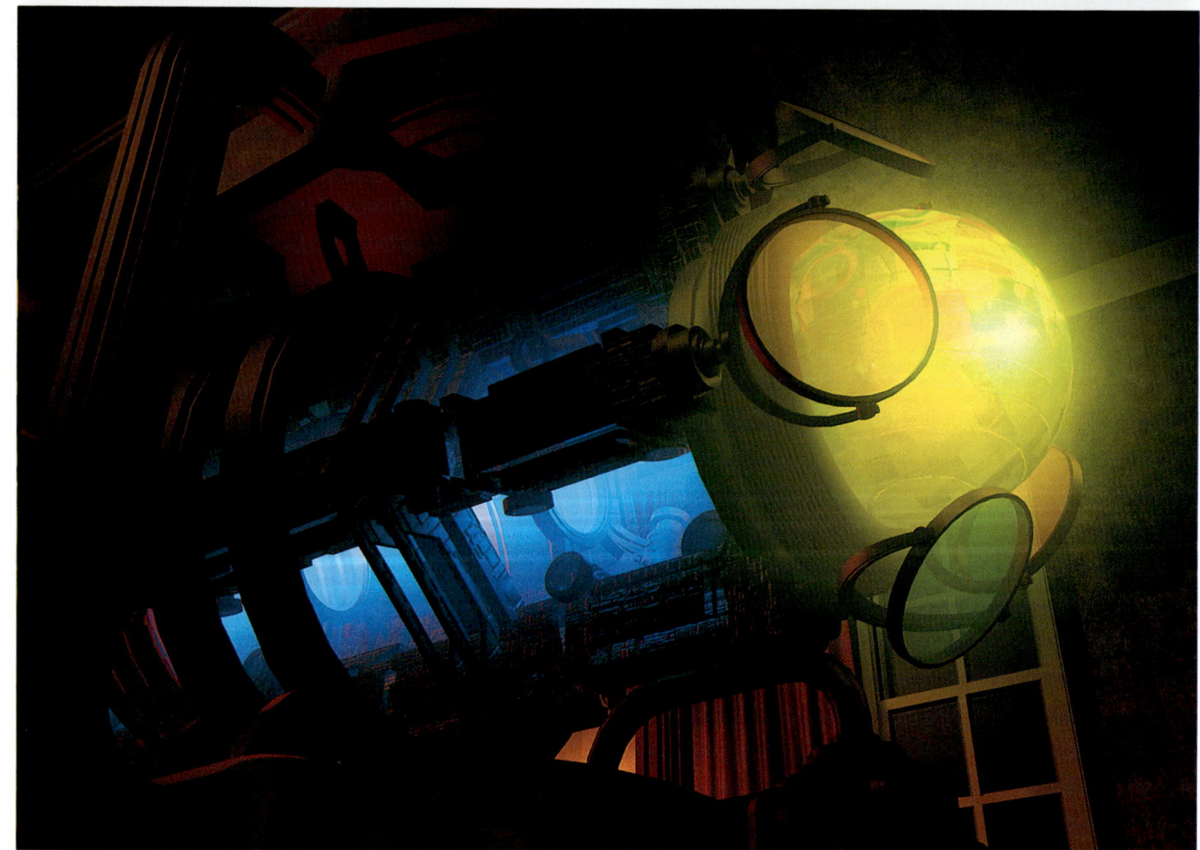

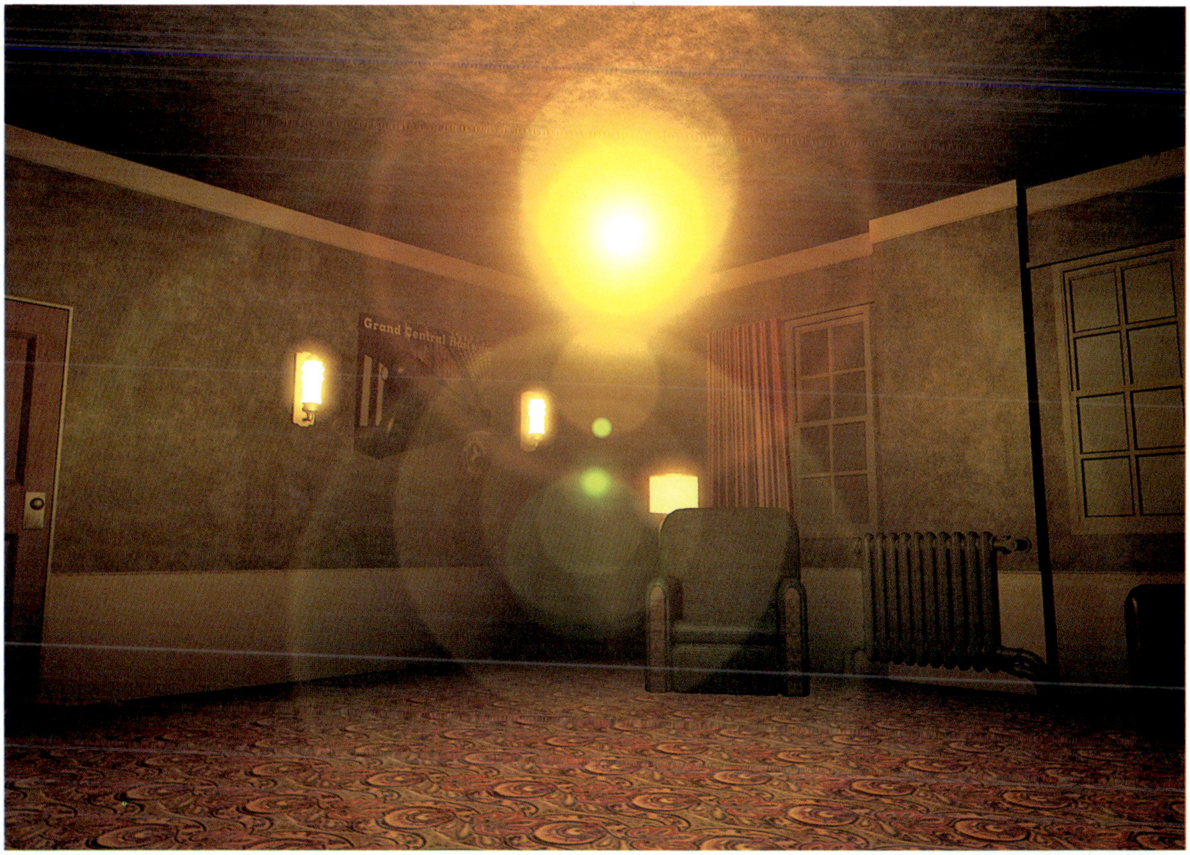

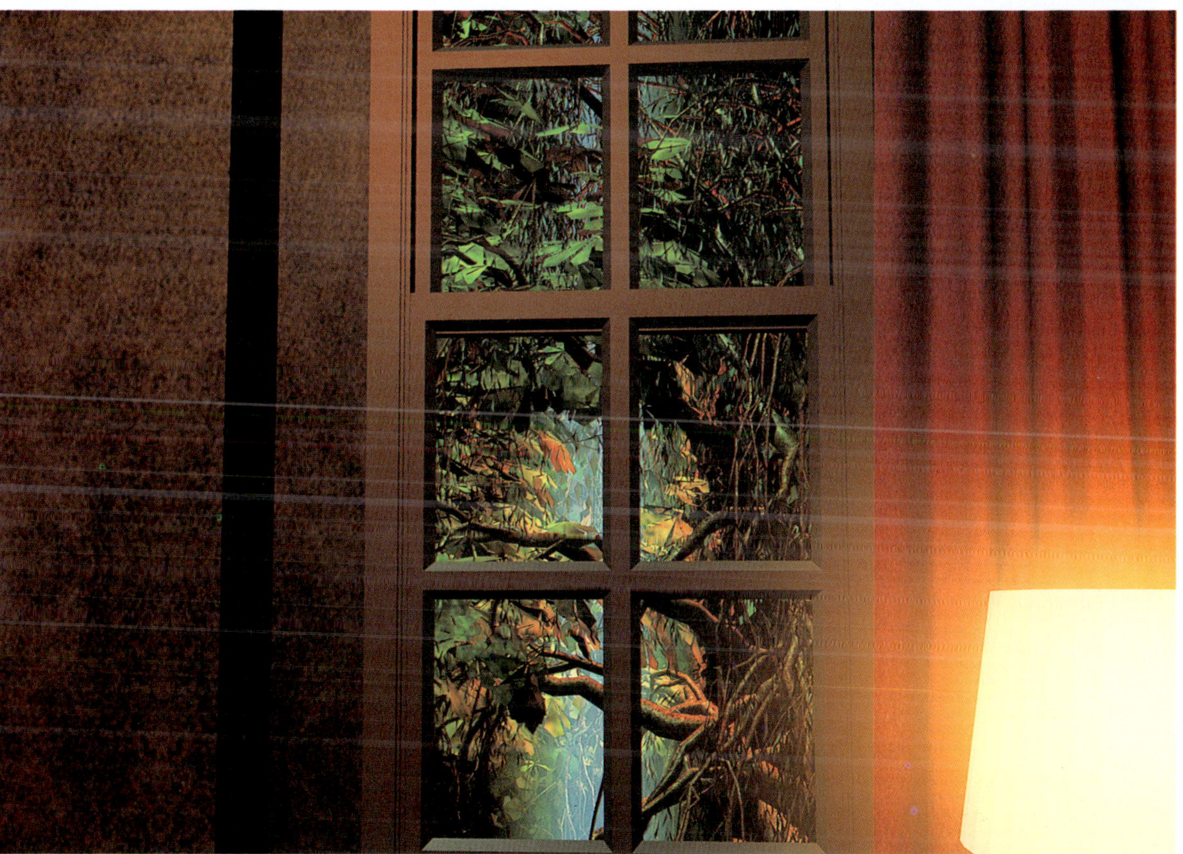

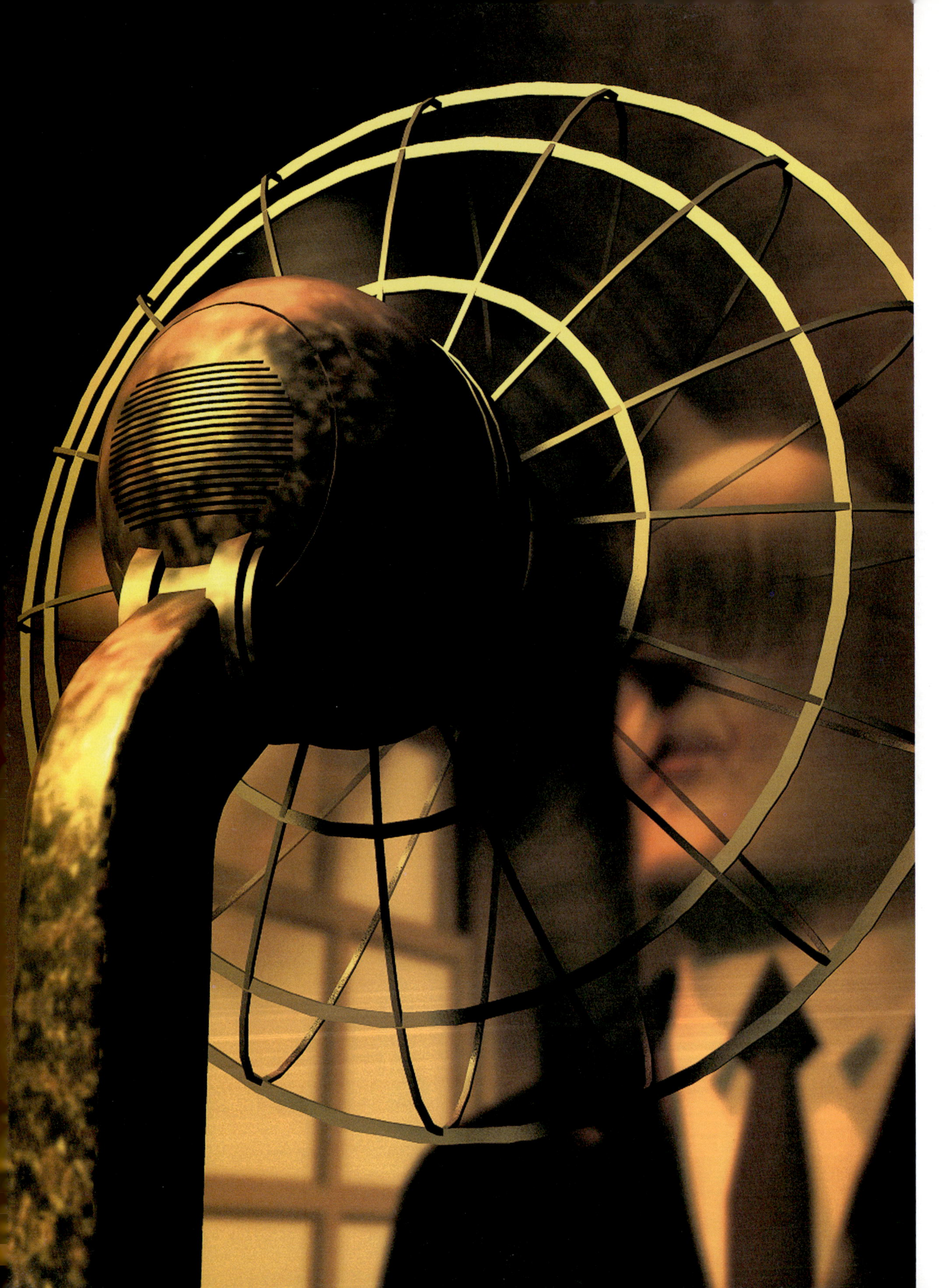

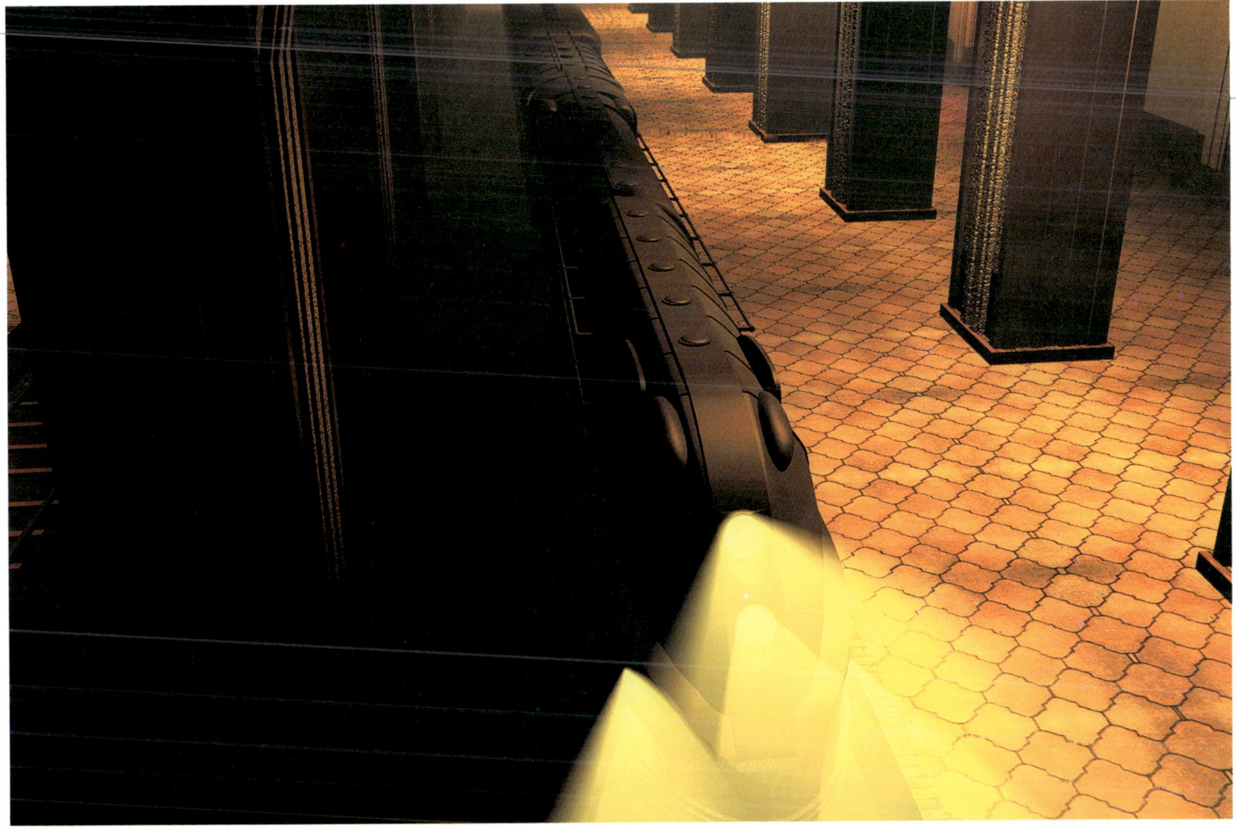

19 September, Year 7 of the Imperial Age

Picked up Charles and took him to the Hotel. Brought in the Version II Sensorama. He's locked up and on starvation rations. Haven't resorted to the rough stuff, yet. By just breaking off all means of communication we've caused considerable psychological damage.

25 September

Heard from Hausmann. Still no sign of Horselover. Lost track of Wilhelm and the others, too.

4 October

Took John MacNaughton and Constantine Wallace into custody at the Imperial Hospital. Interrogation begins tomorrow.

5 October

Began examination of John and Constantine. All I did this first day was take statements. The real work begins day after tomorrow.

7 October

John and Constantine have had nothing to do with the radiation experiments for a year now. I'm interrogating them in separate rooms, but their statements concerning the matter appear to be consistent.

(From the diary of Slowslop)

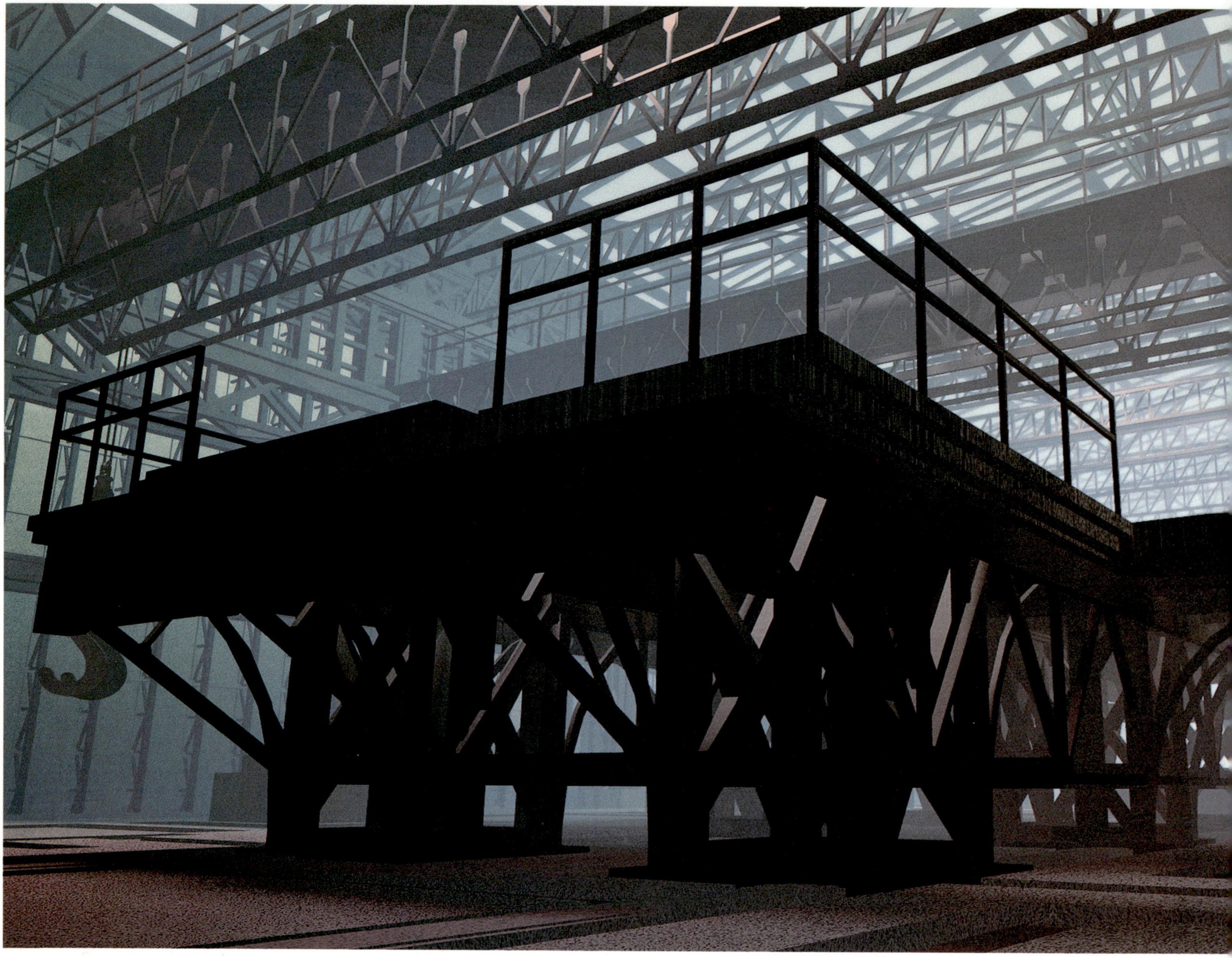

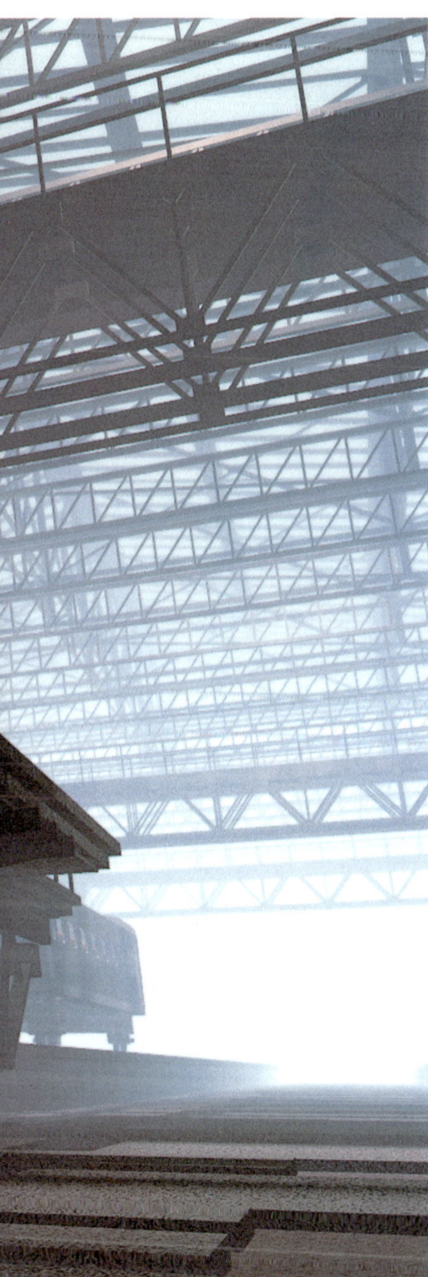

5 December, Year 7 of the Imperial Age

Released John and Constantine. Of course I'll continue to keep track of their movements. We have intelligence agents in the Army Hospital.

19 December

It's been three months since we placed Charles in confinement. Interrogation began today. His mental derangement makes it impossible to take a statement.

20 December

Second day of Charles's interrogation. Gathered six hours of testimony. We'd allowed him a meal and sleep and he's settled down. I asked him to cooperate with the Imperial Army. In the end he agreed. Tomorrow he'll begin work on modifications we need done. When everything's ready we'll start on our education experiments.

(From the diary of Slowslop)

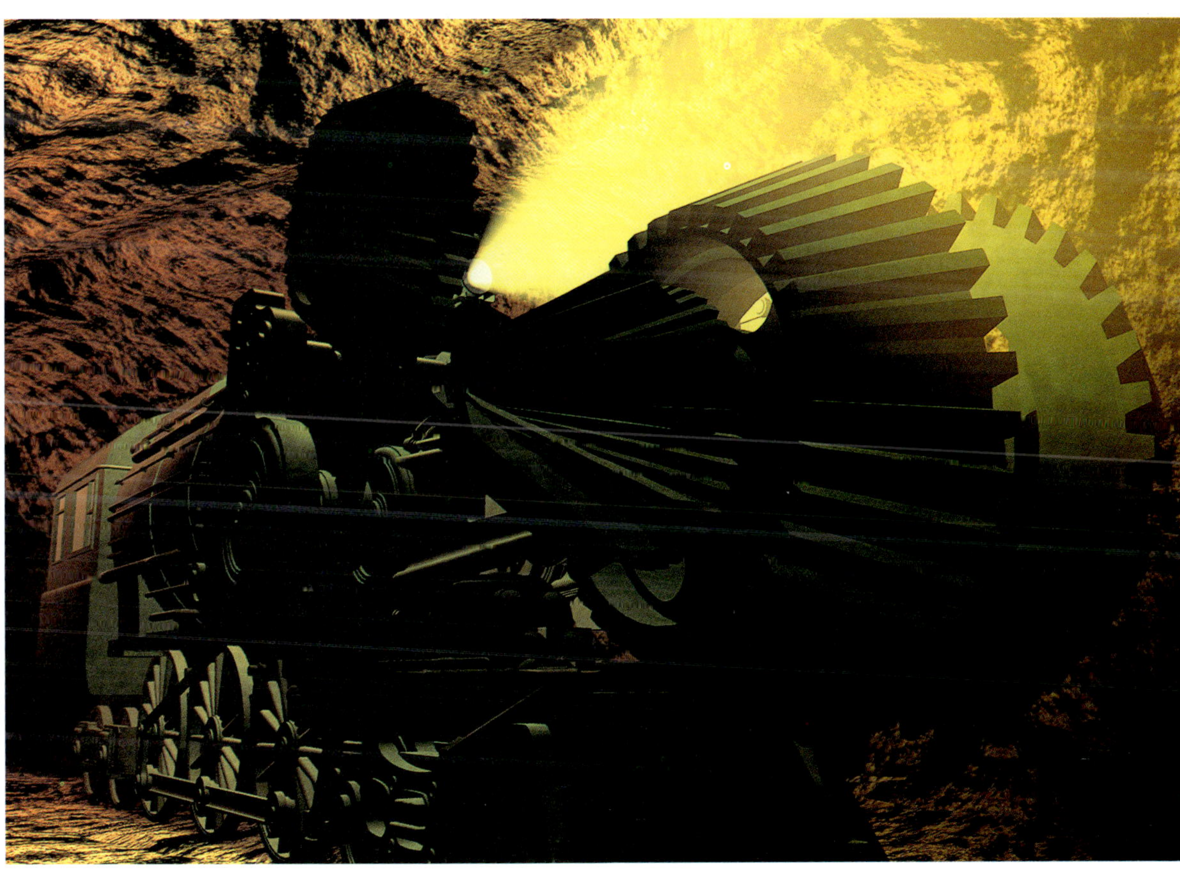

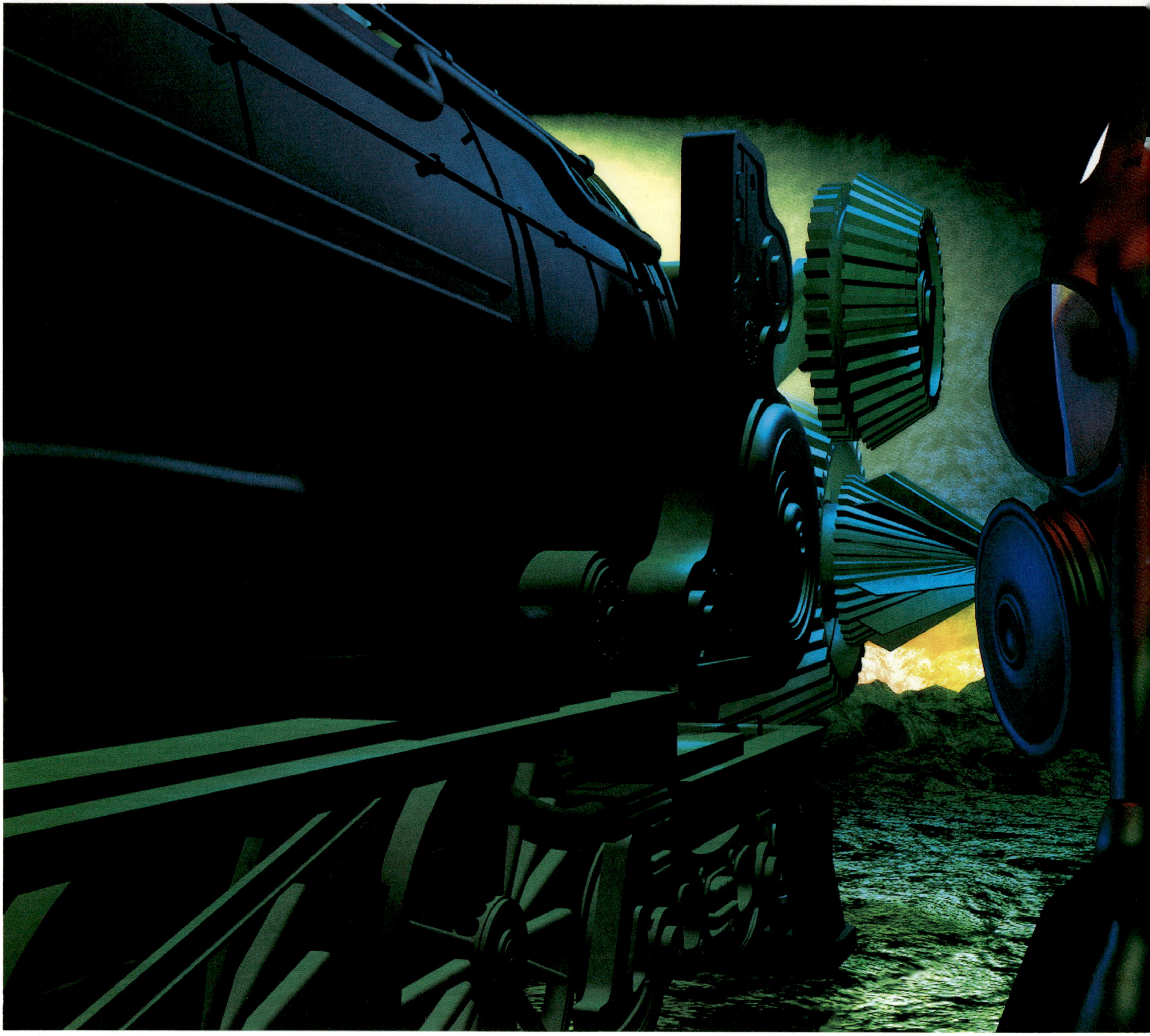

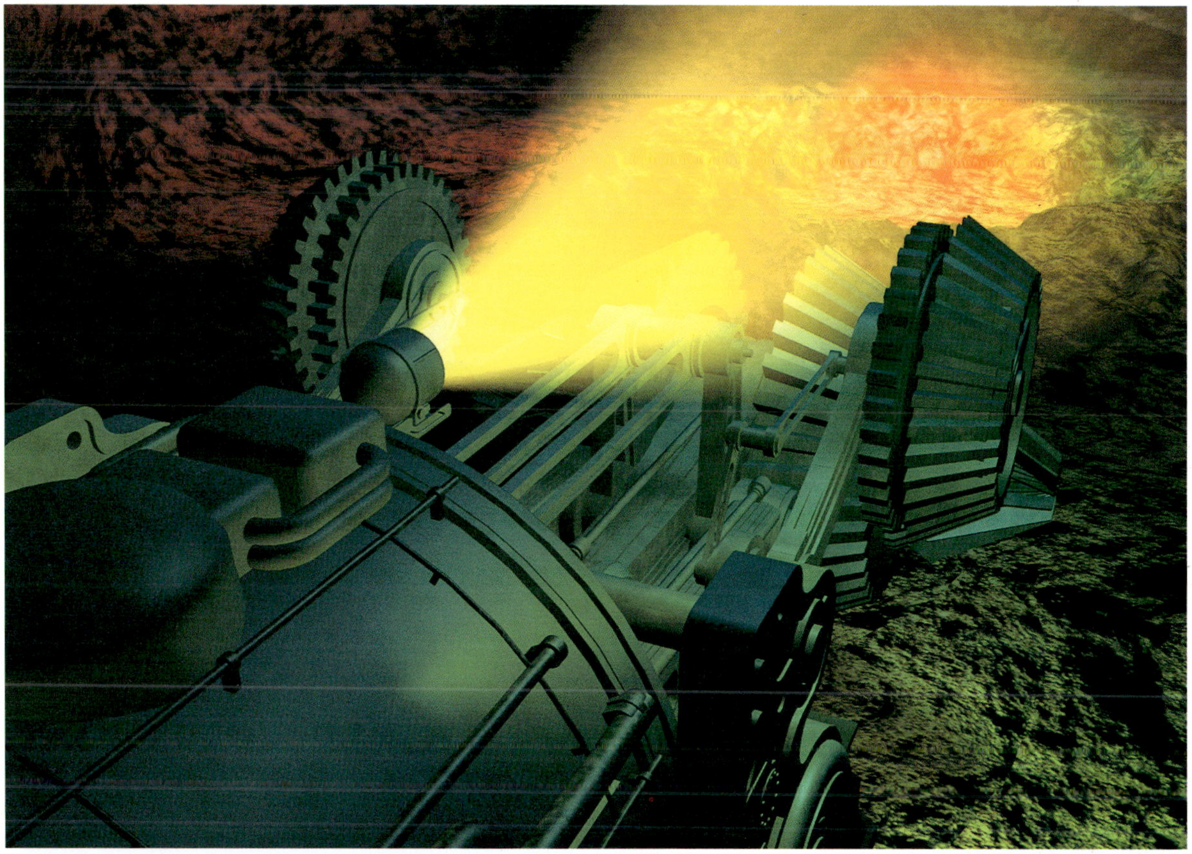

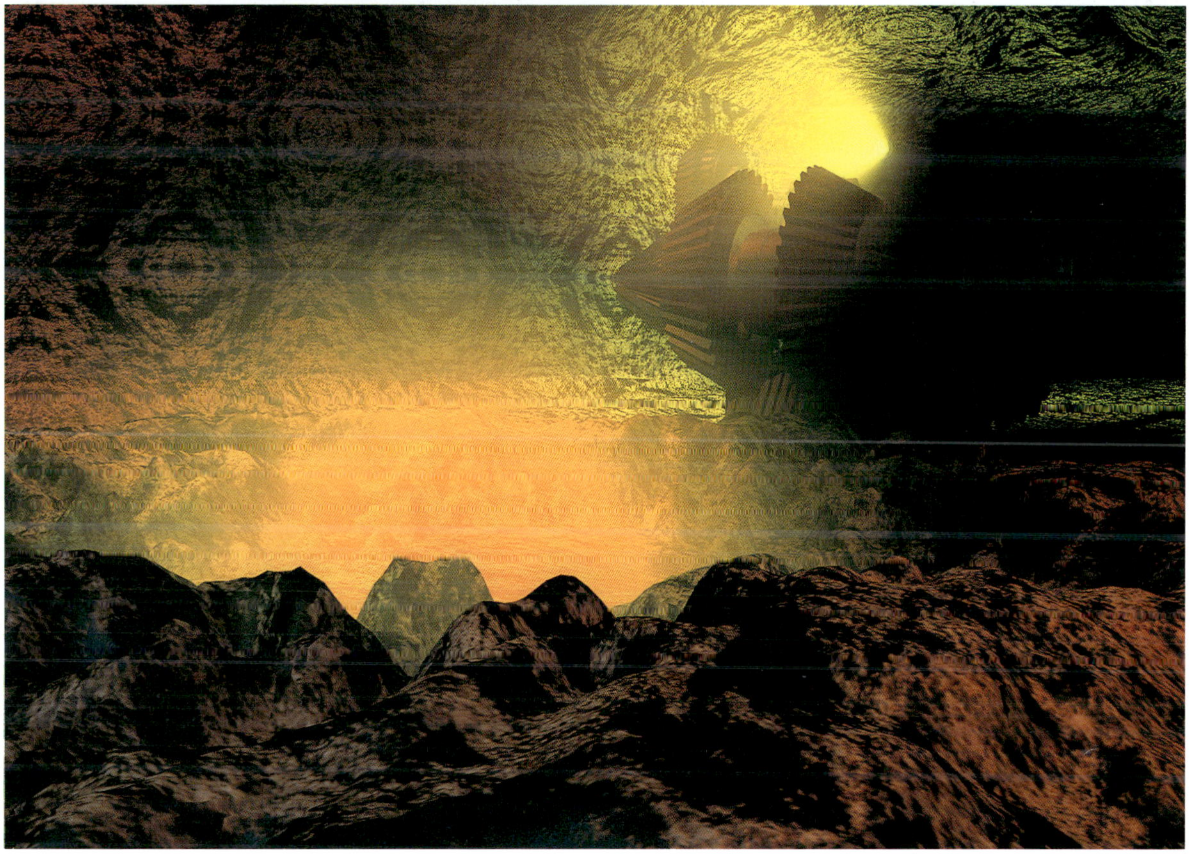

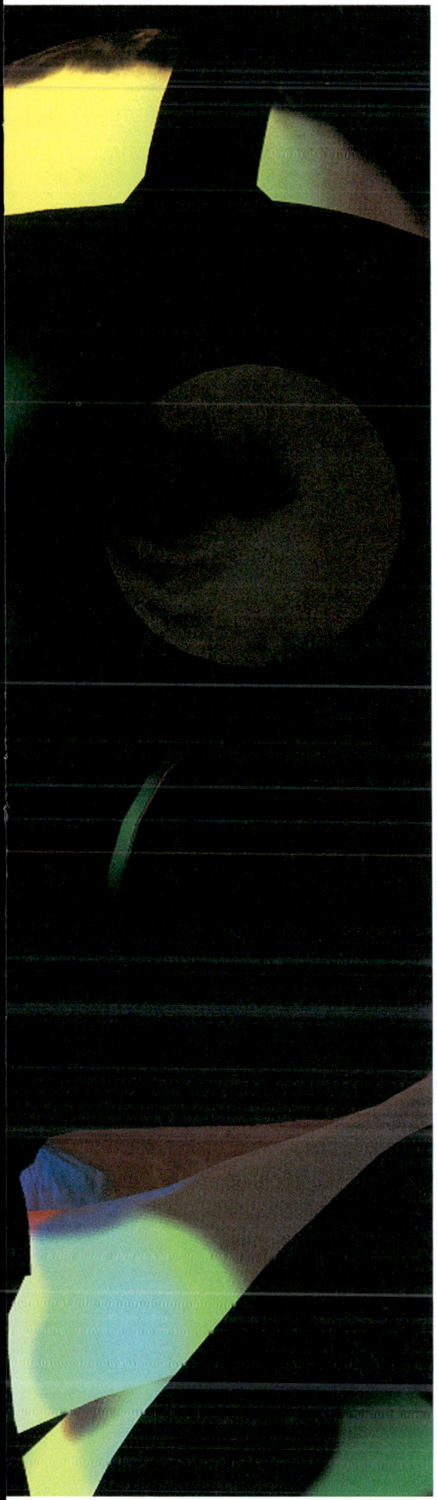

7 March, Year 8 of the Imperial Age

My Dear Professor Horselover,

I am at present being kept under physical restraint. The place of my confinement is West End Hotel. To all appearances it's maintained as a proper hotel, but it takes in no ordinary guests. They all have connections with the Imperial Army. The fact is it's Army Intelligence Headquarters.

Sad to say, what you have long feared has come to pass.

For some three months I was kept locked up in a narrow cell on the third floor. Being wrapped away alone in the dark for so long took a terrible toll on my nerves, and my will to resist was stripped away.

I have now completed modifications to Version II and have built in an education program specified by the Army. I am well aware of the gravity of what I have done and have a fairly clear idea of what will ensue upon success of the experiments.

The education regime results not only in the brainwashed subject's loss of memory, but also dissolution of the very faculty of reason. The mere expansion of this one among the several functions of the Sensorama has made it into a brainwashing machine, while meteorite power has given it unlimited potential. No doubt Orlovsky is aware of what he has created.

I am under constant observation here in Room 302, but under the guise of performing calculations I have managed to pen this letter. As things stand I have not even the liberty to take my own life.

I do hope that you may find it in your heart to forgive me for what I have done.

I pray that this letter will find its way into your hands.

Your humble servant,
Charles Reif

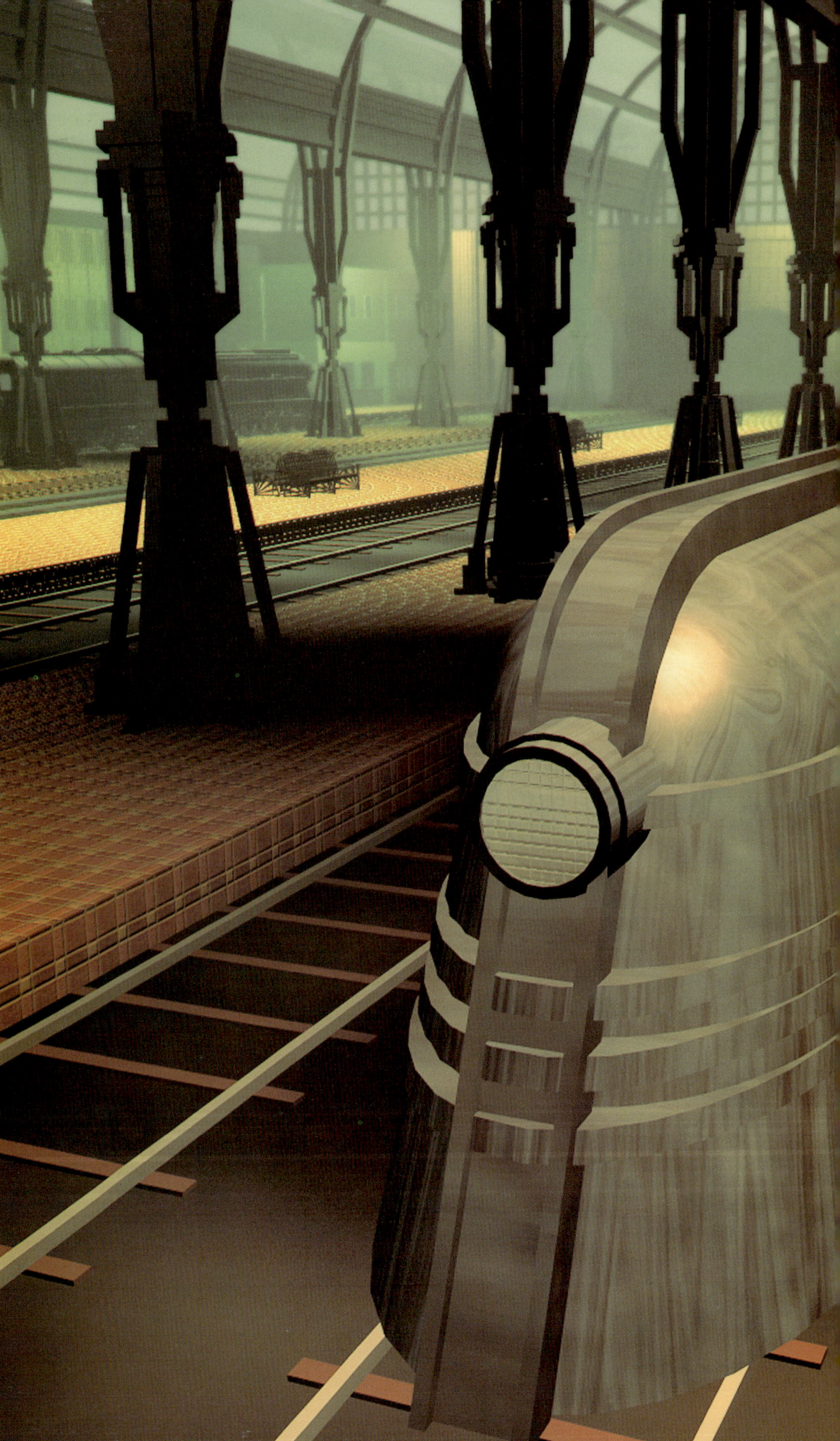

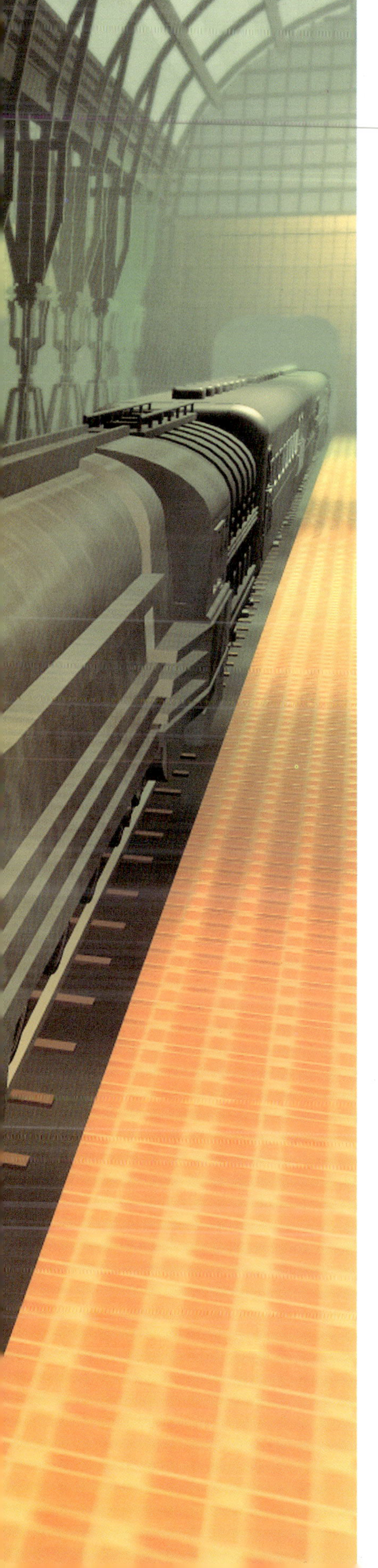

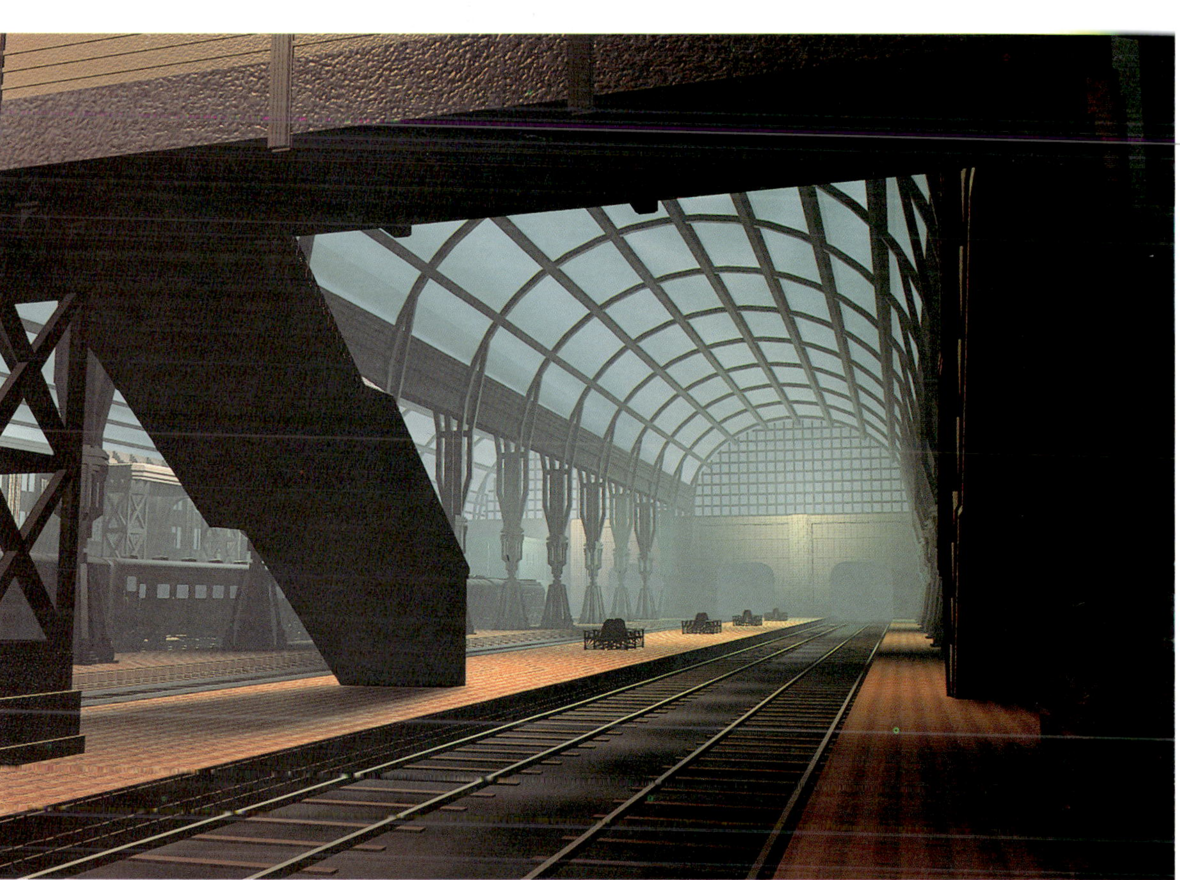

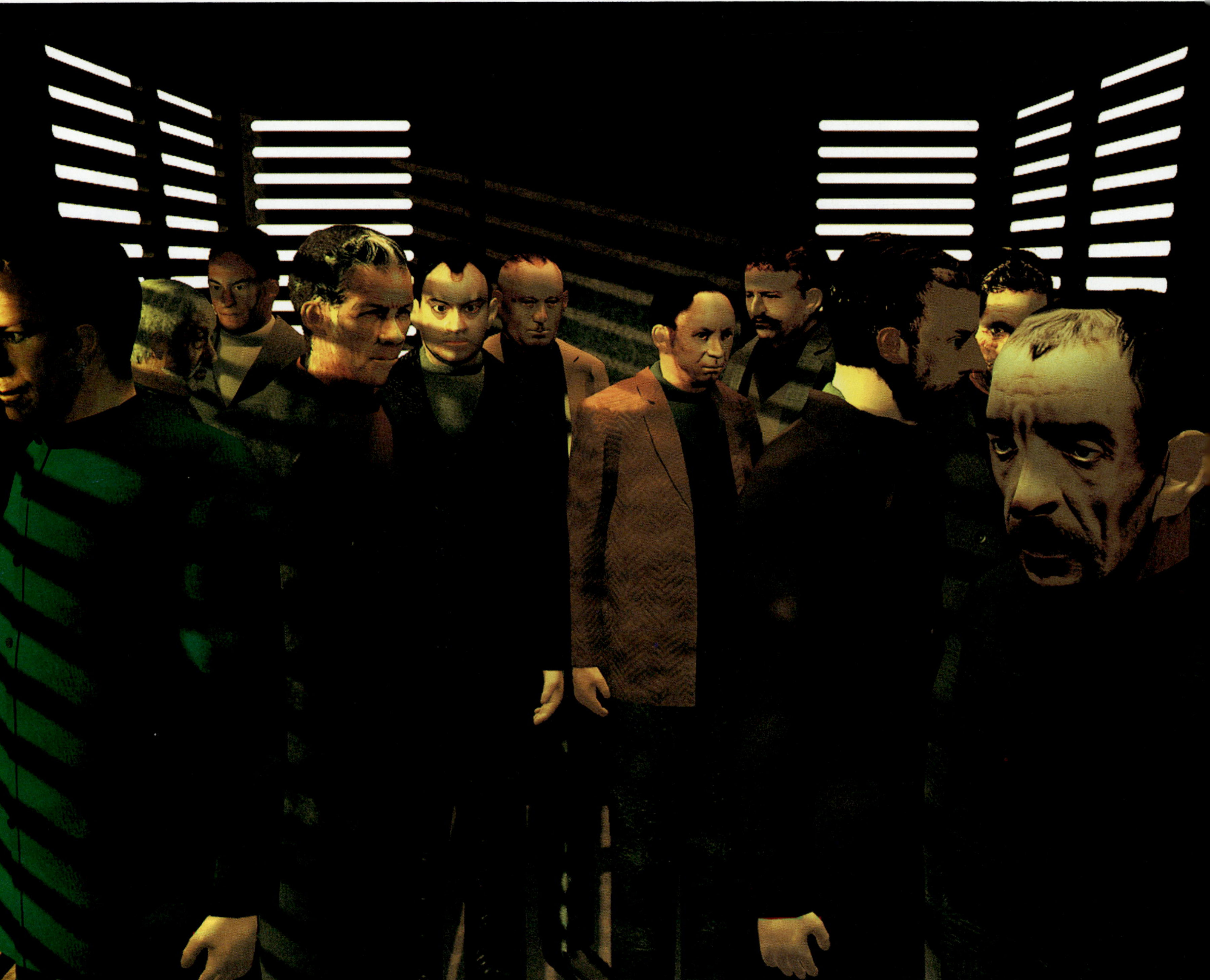

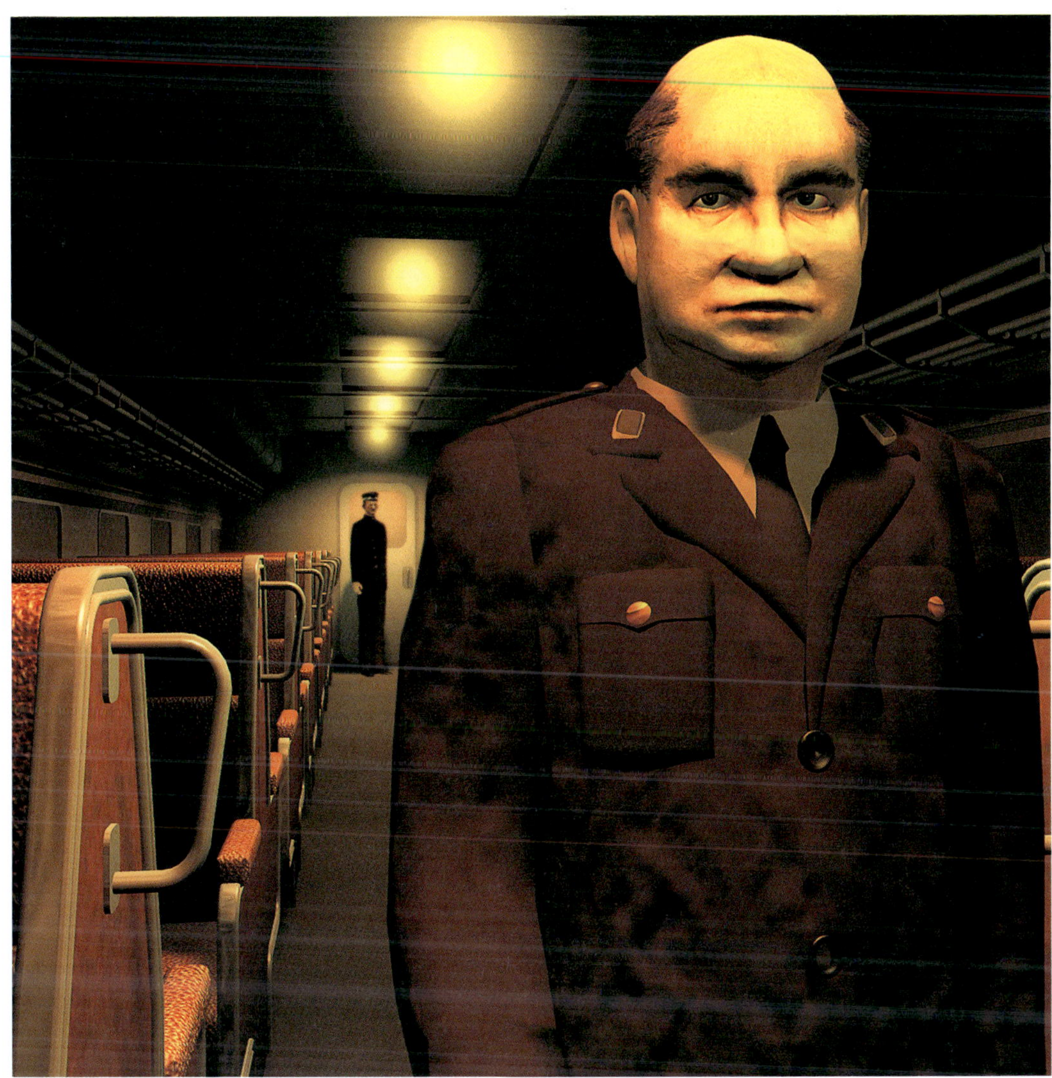

4 November, Year 8 of the Imperial Age

Per orders from Slowslop I transported under guard twelve prisoners held at Grand Central Penitentiary. All are to be used as test subjects for radiation experiments using the Version II Sensorama. All twelve are serving sentences for thought crimes. I am curious to see what change in attitude is worked by the brainwashing, and for purposes of comparison have had a film record made during the trip to Army Intelligence Headquarters in West End.

The radiation experiments began in the afternoon in Room 306. Charles adjusted the machine and set it in operation. Each testee was subjected to some two hours of electromagnetic radiation and then a further hour of examination. Results were judged on the spot and adjustments made for the person's next stint of radiation education. The supervising officer of the experiment is Captain Gondarev of the Imperial Guards. Five or six men from Army Intelligence have been posted there for security.

9 November

Results are not good. The attitude of the thought criminals shows no improvement. If the experiment doesn't have the expected effect the convicts can't be released. Electromagnetic radiation is being administered repeatedly.

24 November

The convicts' physical strength is weakening. Psychologically, they are at the end of their ropes. There seems little point in continuing the experiment. One can only conclude that the notion of mechanical brainwashing is an impossibility.

30 November

Slowslop has ordered a halt to the project. The thought criminals, their attitudes unimproved but their politics eradicated, are to be released into the civilian population. An order has been issued for a replacement crew of convicts and the brainwashing experiments in room 306 will continue. Tomorrow I go to the penitentiary to pick up the next batch of victims.

(From the diary of Hausmann)

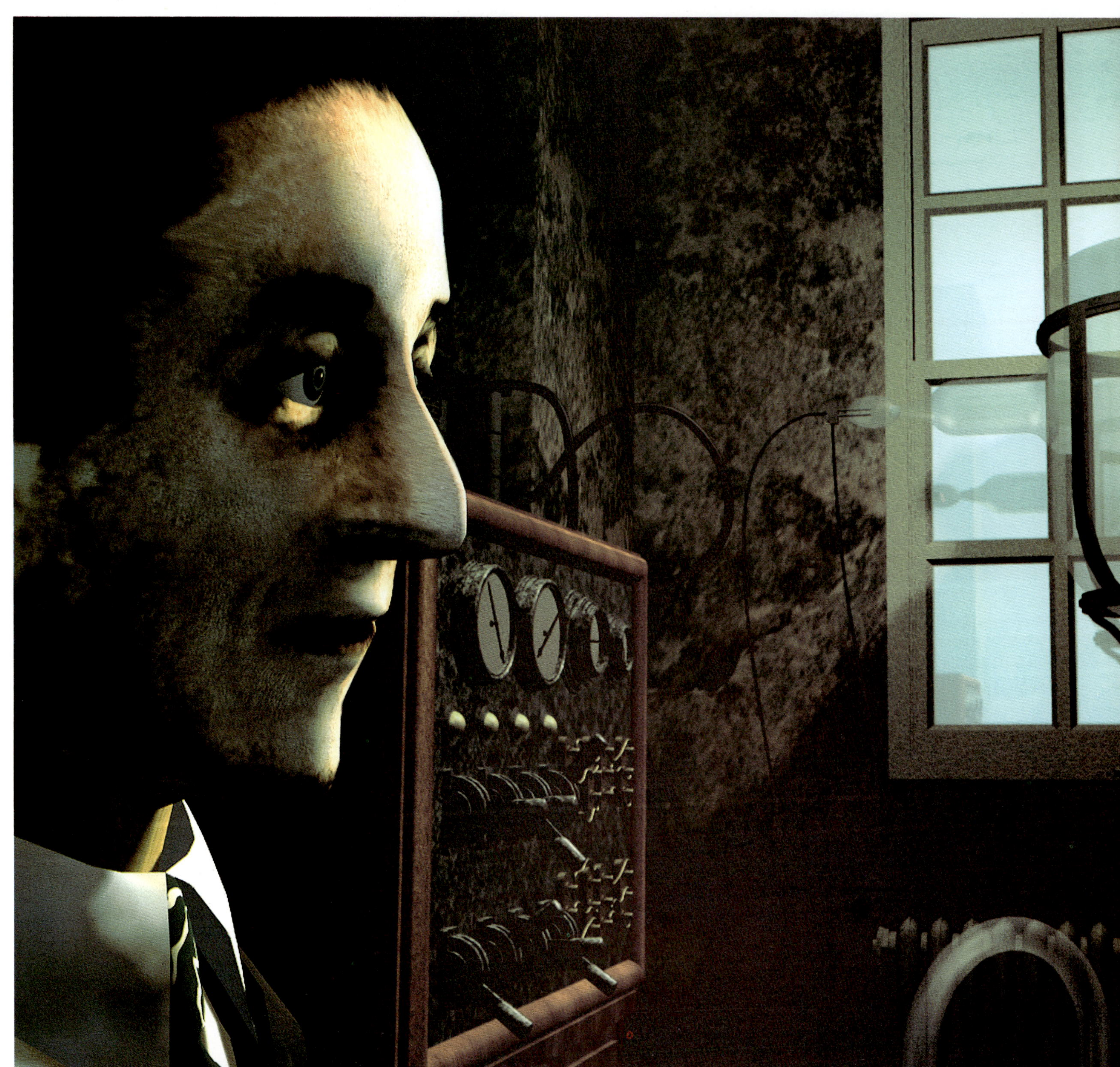

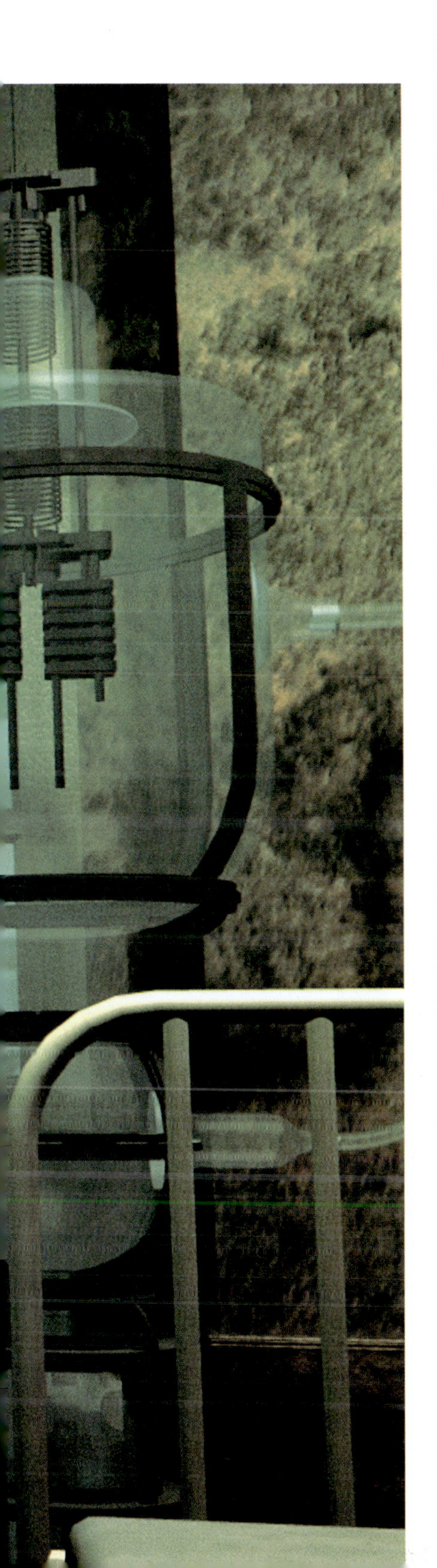

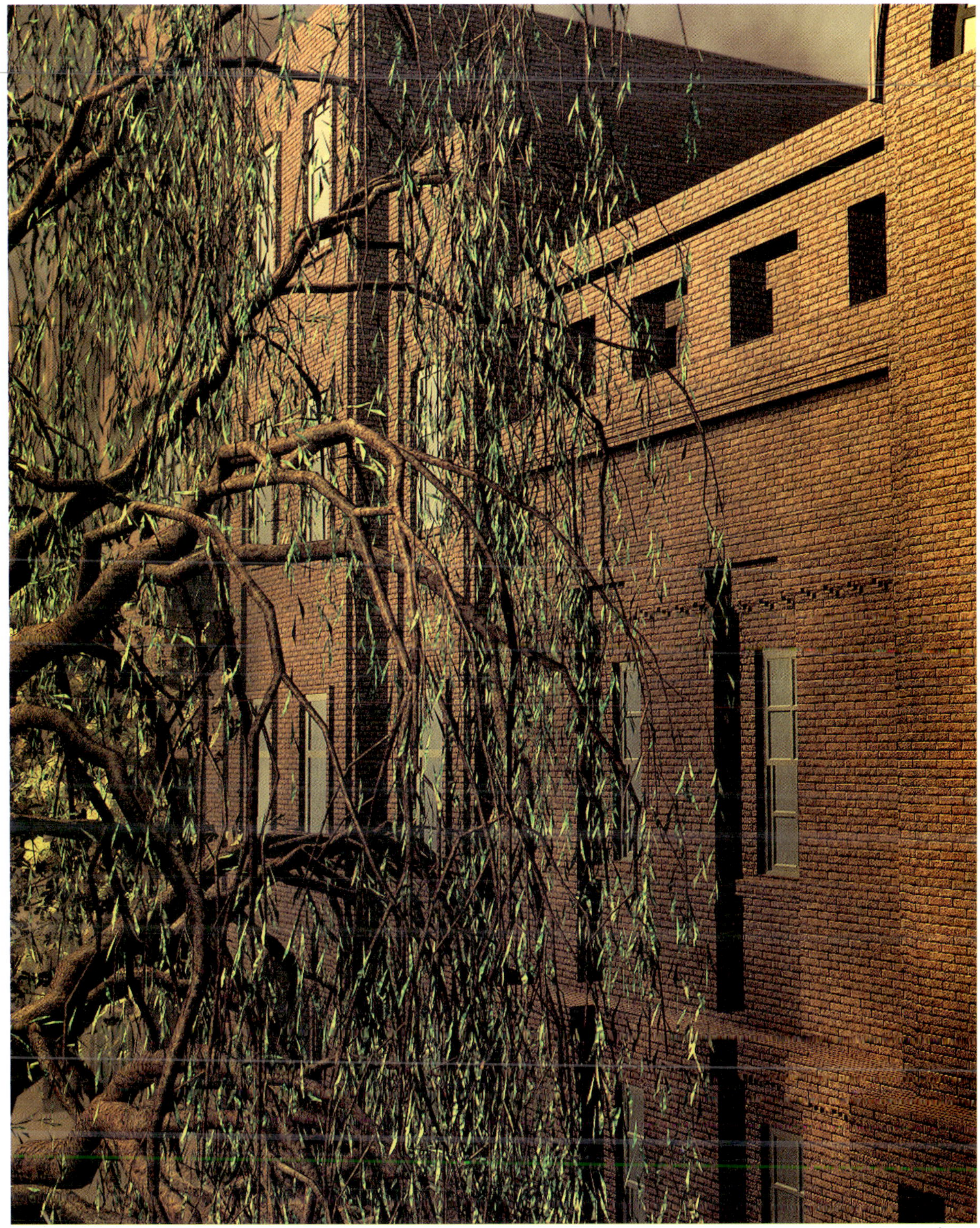

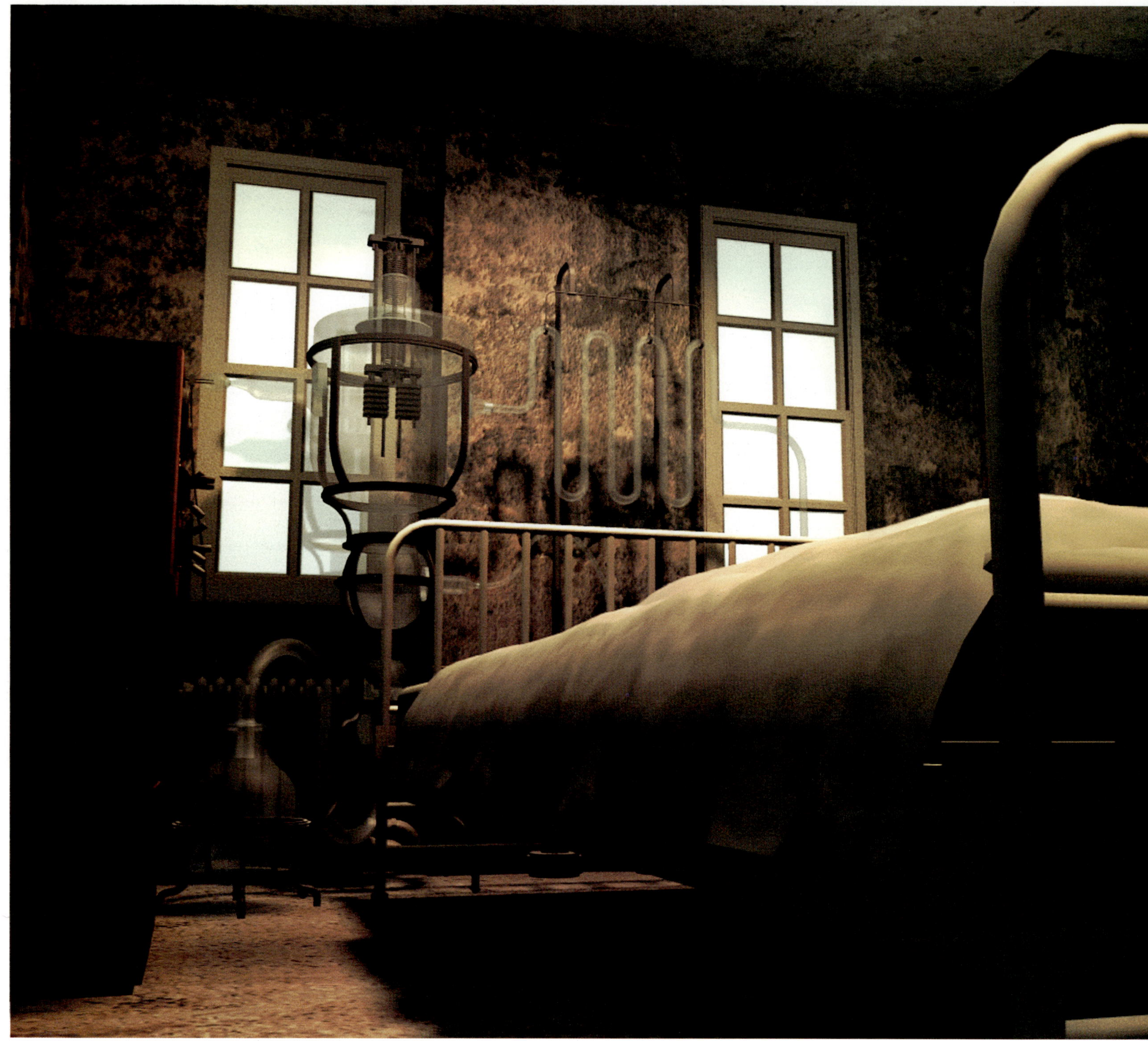

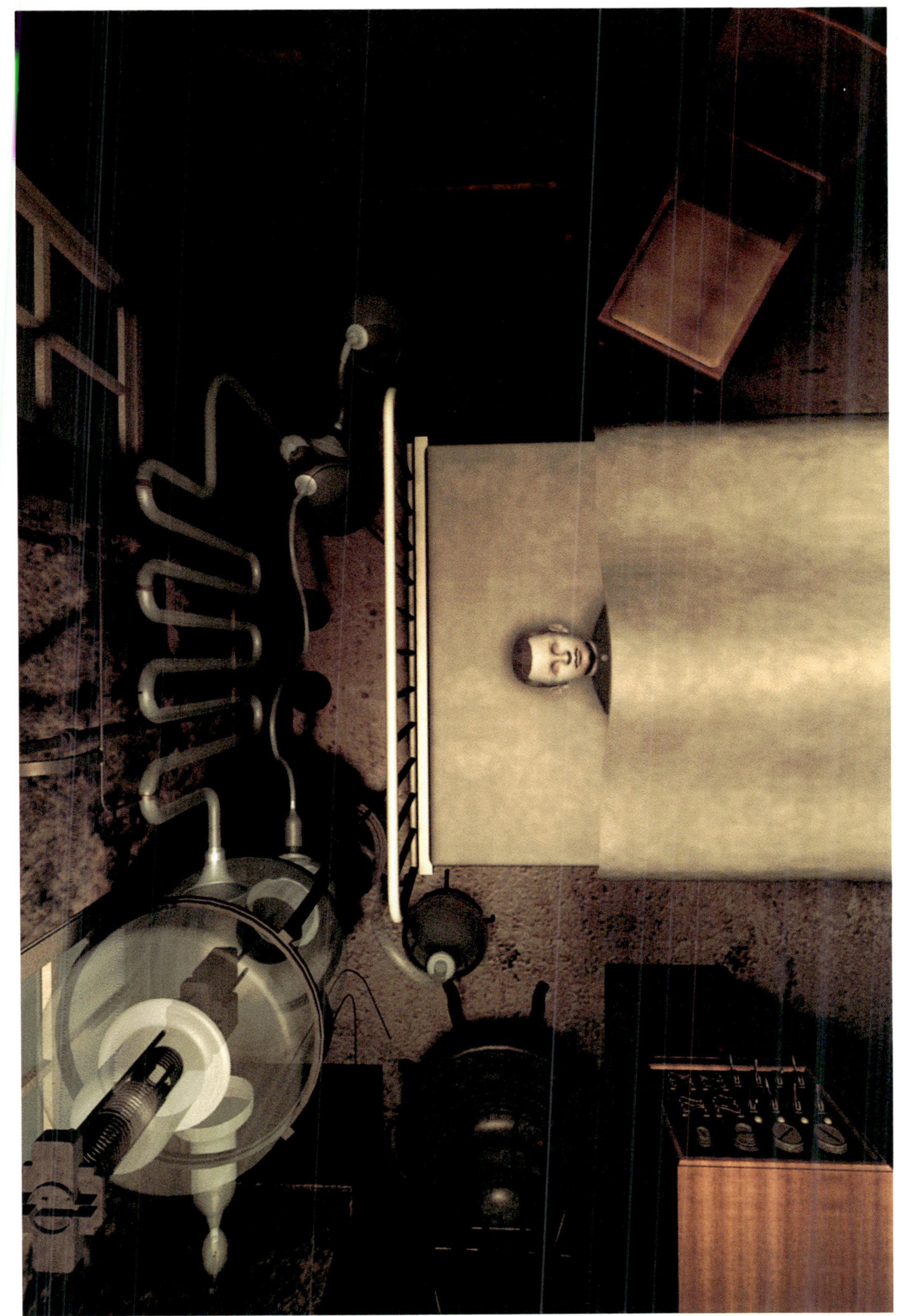

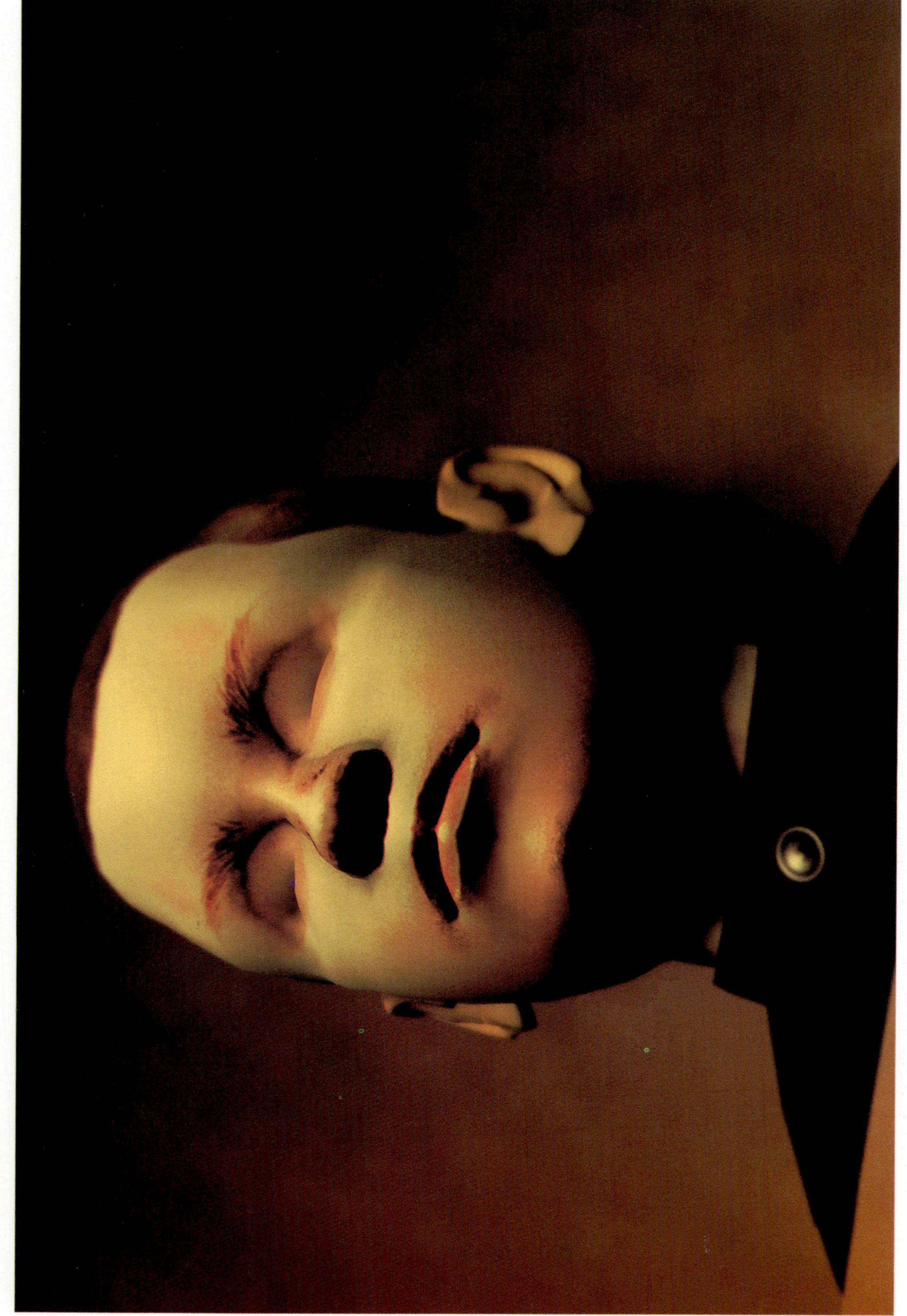

2 December, Year 8 of the Imperial Age

Sometime after midnight a boy was carried into the Hospital. The ambulance crew said he had collapsed in the restricted area.

His body temperature, blood pressure, and pulse are all normal, but he does not reply to my questions. He does not speak at all.

I discern no antagonistic impulse in him and so do not construe this as a willful exercise of silence or denial. His staring eyes and dreamy expression suggest to me that he is suffering temporary aphasia due to a psychic shock.

At any rate, a detailed examination will have to be put off until tomorrow. We have no idea who he is, so there's nothing we can do but await the results of an examination. As he collapsed in the restricted area it is likely that the Army will begin an investigation if he remains silent (or aphasic). For the boy's sake I hope that can be avoided. An Army investigation always includes torture.

3 December

At dawn the boy's temperature and blood pressure began to drop and he fell into a coma. Surprisingly, his pulse remains constant. I gave him oxygen and injected a stimulant, but it produced no change. I have no inkling of the cause and can only keep a watchful eye on his condition.

5 December

His pulse remains steady, but body temperature and blood pressure continue to trace a downward curve. If things continue this way he won't last another day.

9 December

He's still 'hibernating.' A week has gone by since he went into the coma. As always his heartbeat remains strong, but body temperature hovers at 85 degrees. His condition is by no means normal.

There is no point in administering drugs. His body shows no response to them. John and I tried a range of chemical therapies but none was effective.

11 December

The boy has vanished. He was not in his bed when I looked in early this morning. The Army Hospital maintains 24-hour surveillance, so assuming that he awoke in the night there is no way that he might have gone out alone.

I put in an inquiry to the Army, but they have no record of his being taken into custody. And, after all, this is the Army's hospital: what reason should they have for spiriting a patient away? This whole affair is an absolute mystery to me.

(From the clinical records of Dr. Constantine Wallace)

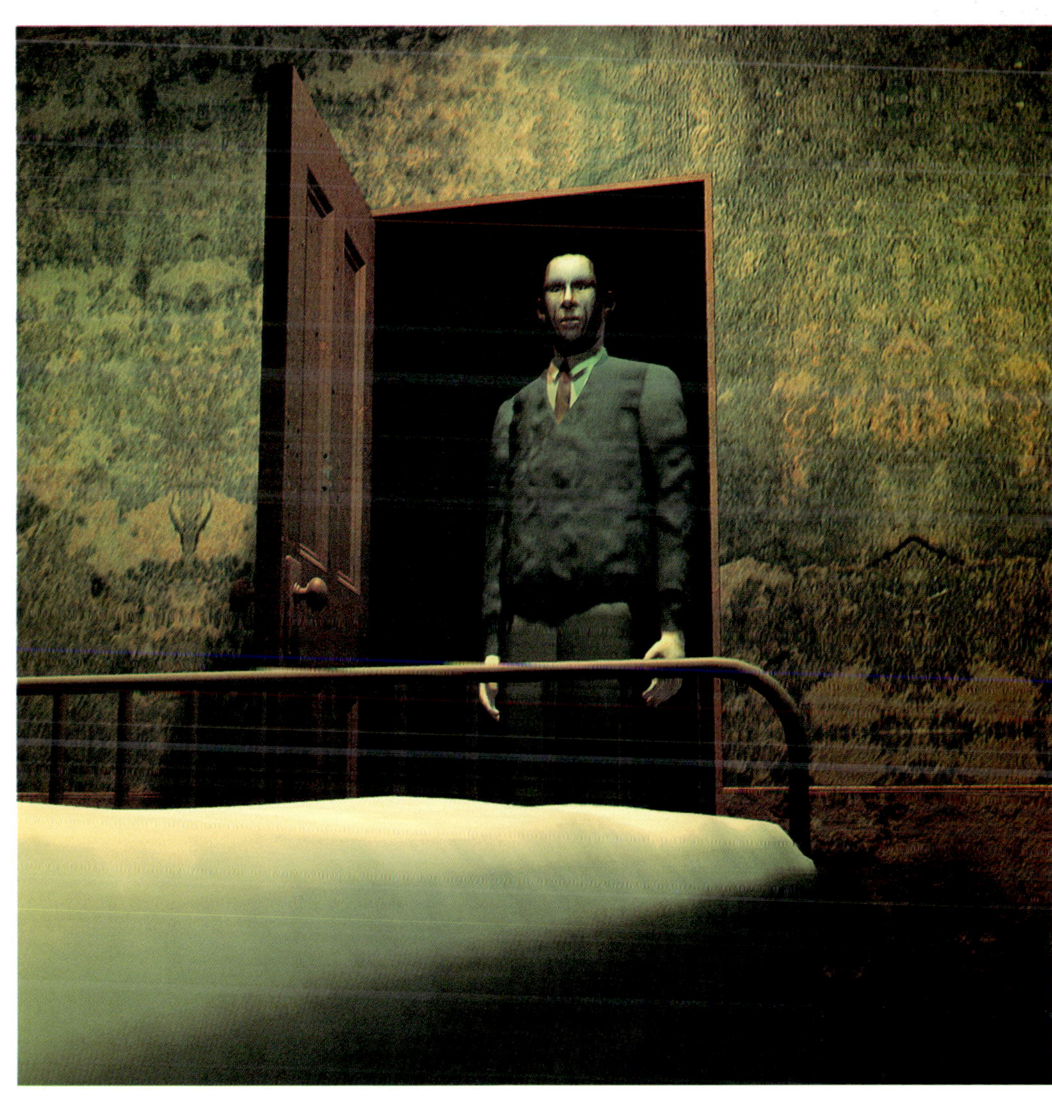

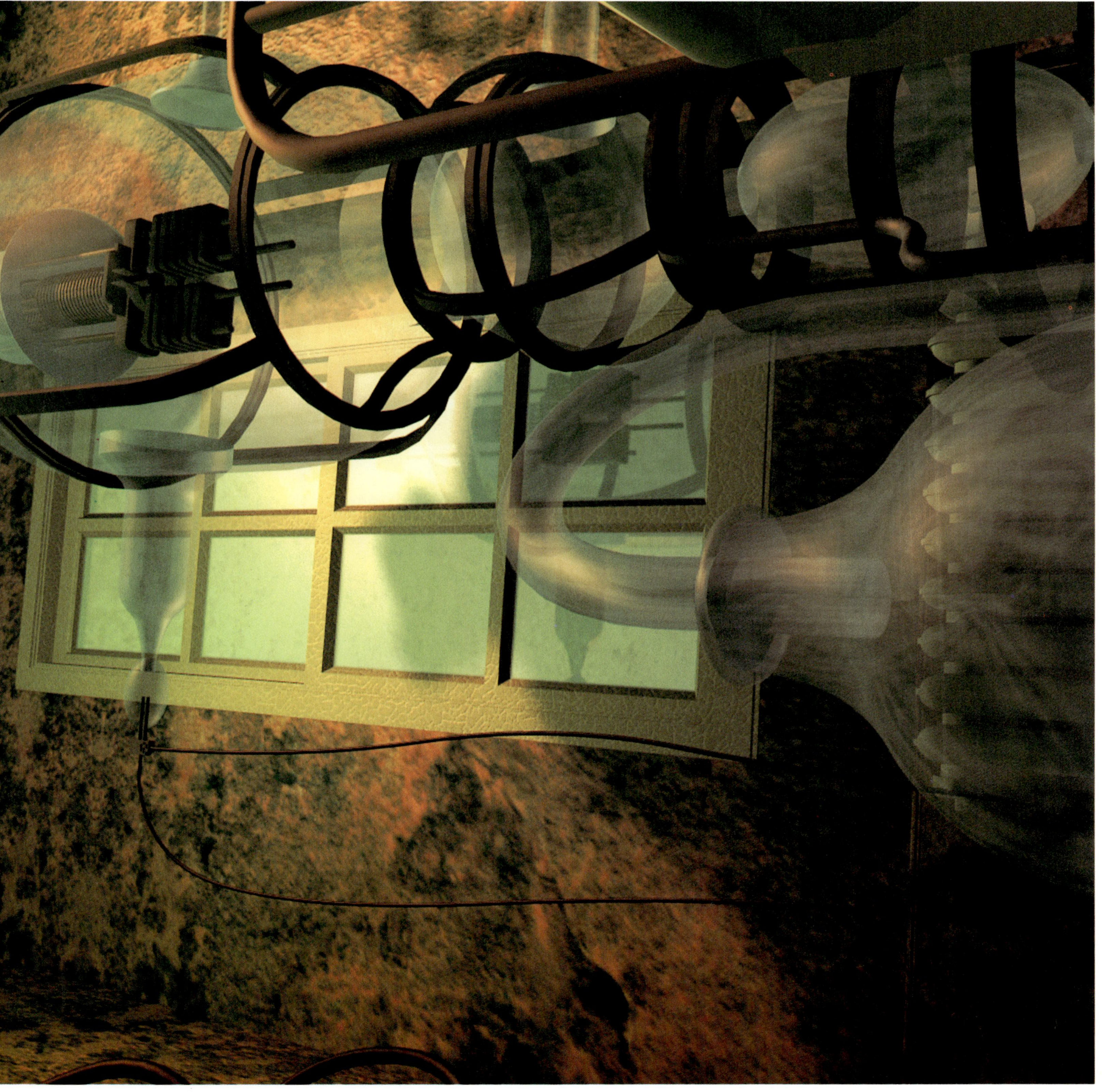

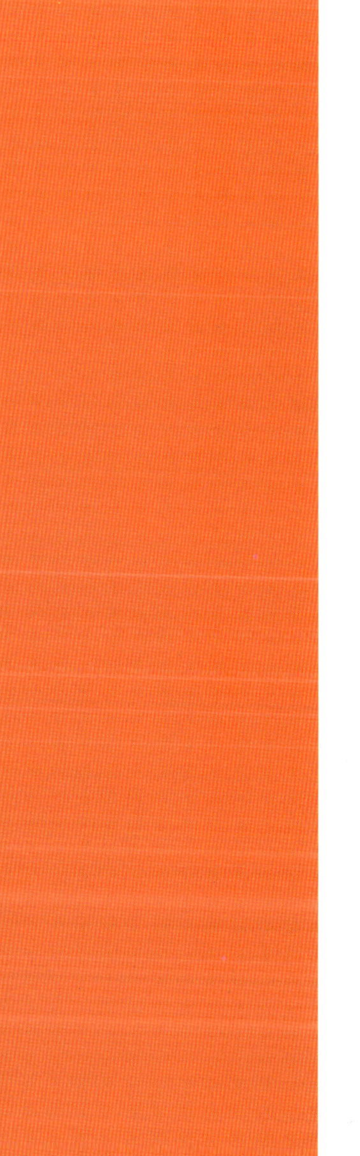

Those slow to escape are executed
The opened door
Woods, water, machines
Rusty iron bridge
They who know too much are dealt with
The great and glorious cycle
Consciousness or coma
Primal premonition
The inexorable approach of the comet cluster

Those slow to escape are executed

Room 306 of the former West End Hotel. Gondarev's education in pain begins on Sensorama II. The machine starts up. Radiation, countless electromagnetic waves. Memory falls away, never to be recalled. Consciousness is now lost, never will it be restored.

The opened door

Repeated experiments performed on human subjects. Transported convicts. Criminals are made victims of radiation experiments. Detached retinae, impaired hearing. Memories lost, transposed. These are consequences of supervised study under Lord Orlovsky.

Woods, water, machines

A forest wrapped in a veil of mist. Everywhere branches of trees. Green images cast on water. Reflections of gentle light. Torpid air. An excavator half submerged. Now they all vanish without a trace. Time to surrender each its place. A contract made with space.

Rusty iron bridge

Gondarev will never return. A victim entrapped by electromagnetic waves. The corpse disposed of by Army authorities. Sensorama II is the means of implementing the Empire's Program. Supervision or practical education. Stunning success of the brainwashing machine.

They who know too much are dealt with

Hausmann's arrest is ordered by Slowslop. Memory deletion, or is it the expunging of personality. The door is now closed on Room 306. All light blocked off. Orlovsky, alongside, watches in silence, a smile hovering upon his lips. Version II starts up with a hiss and a whine.

The great and glorious cycle

From the Hotel to the Imperial Museum, the water tower, and then on to the Observatory and Army Ordnance Factory. The hurtling Nova Express and the Ark. Command Tower and colossal receiver. Seven scientists, a lone boy, and Supreme Commander Slowslop.

Consciousness or coma

A ringing in the ears and migraines. A heavy lassitude settles over the skull. Parched lips. Contracted muscles. Numbed nerve ends and optic thalamus. The past is completely lost. There is no door that opens onto the future. Just a passing ship. A comet closing.

Primal premonition

Another shower of meteors rains down. The land has been burned to the color of lead. The Republic disappears in an instant. Amid the ruins of the Capital stands the empty Command Tower. On the top floor, mindlessly, the mammoth antenna spins on, round and round.

The inexorable approach of the comet cluster

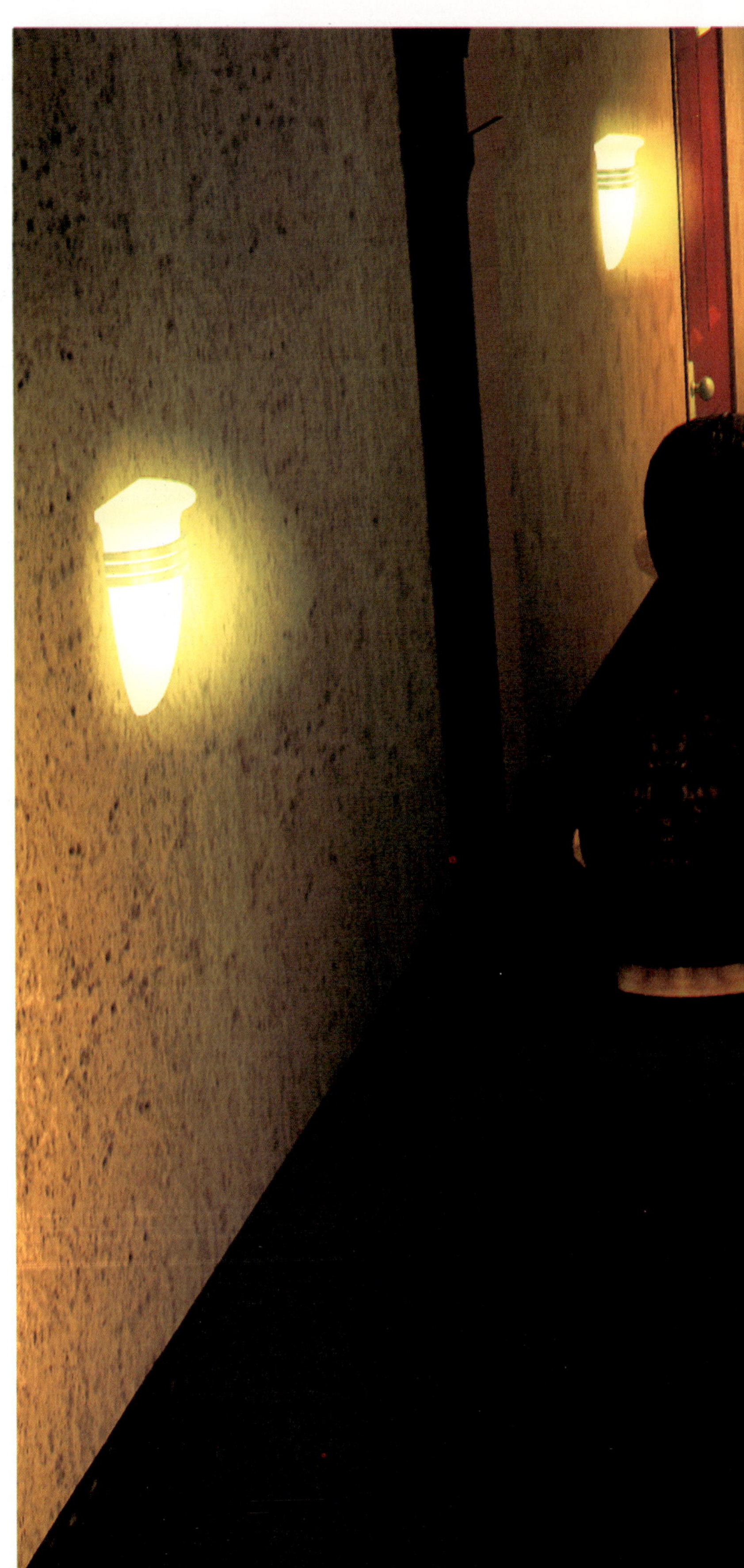

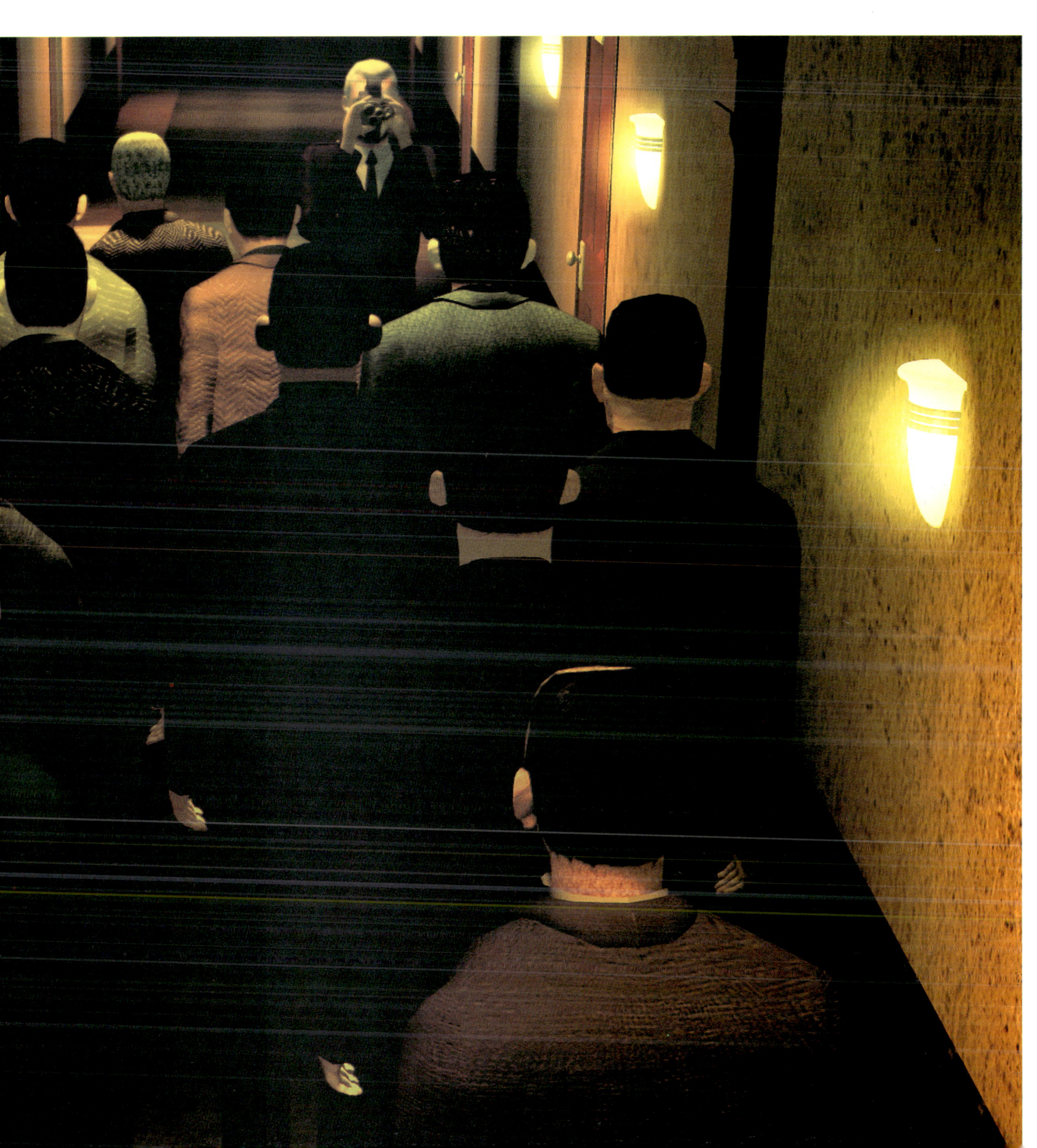

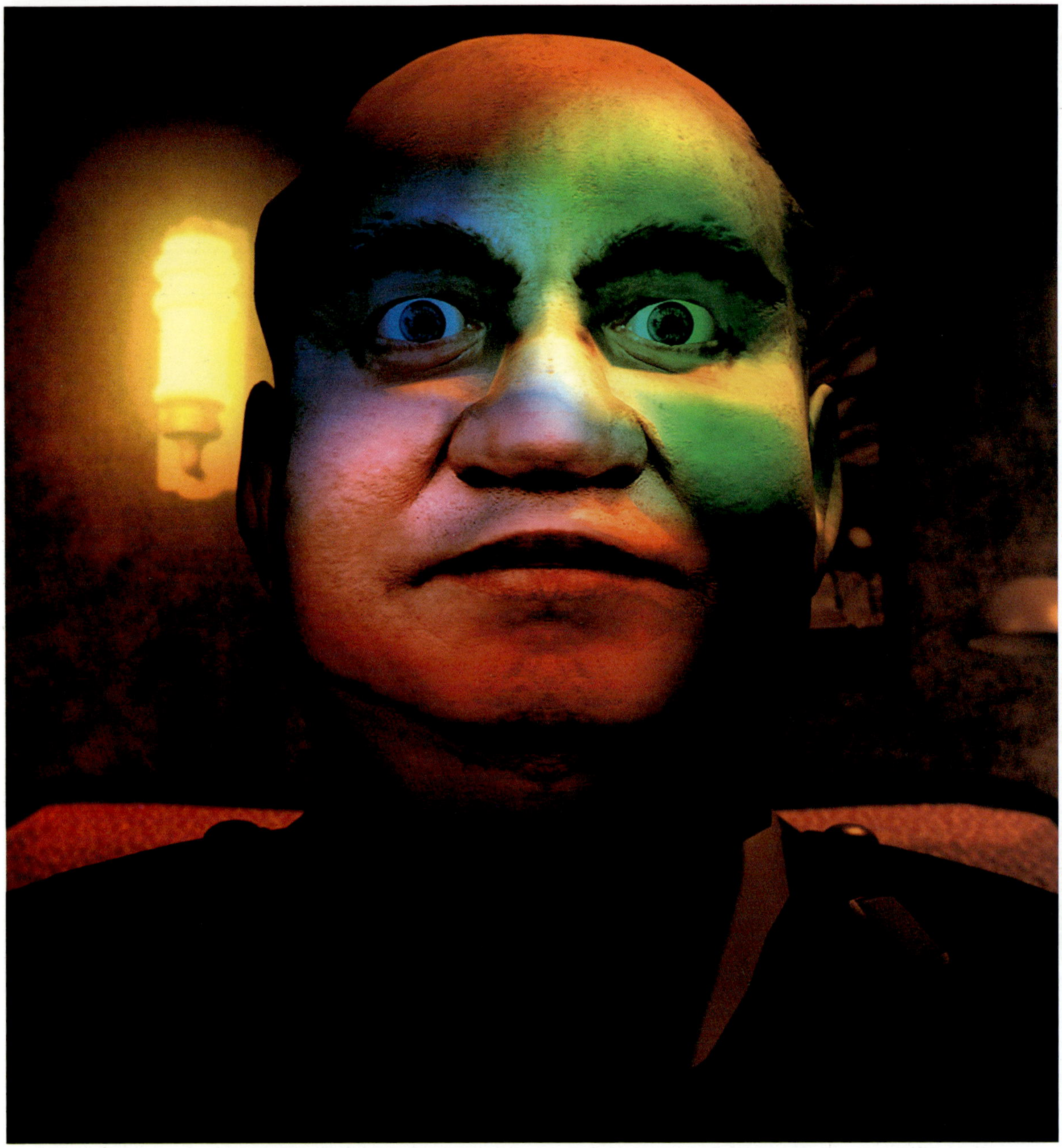

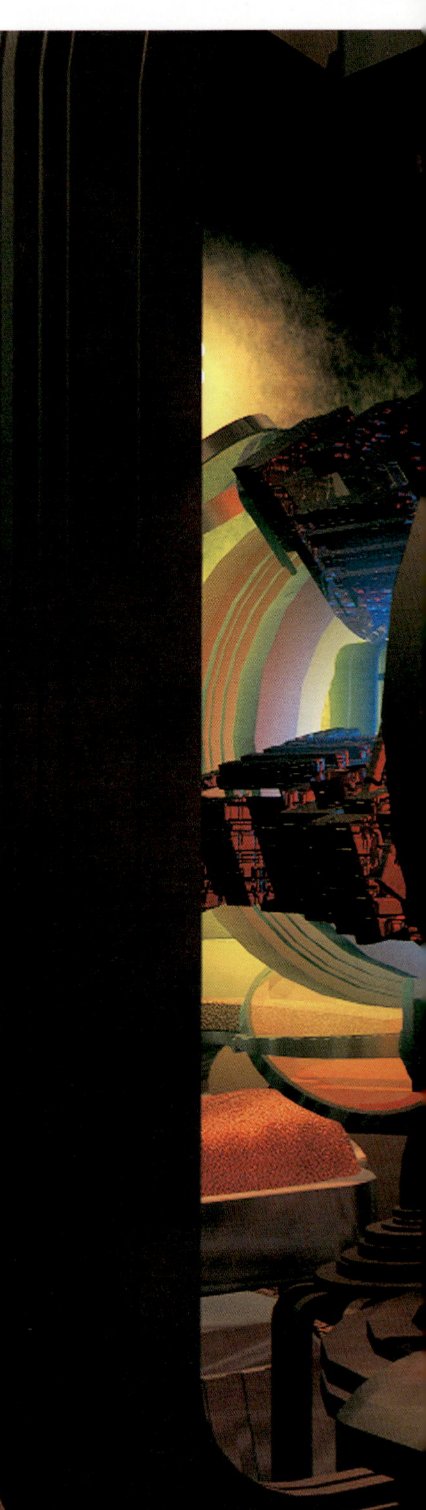

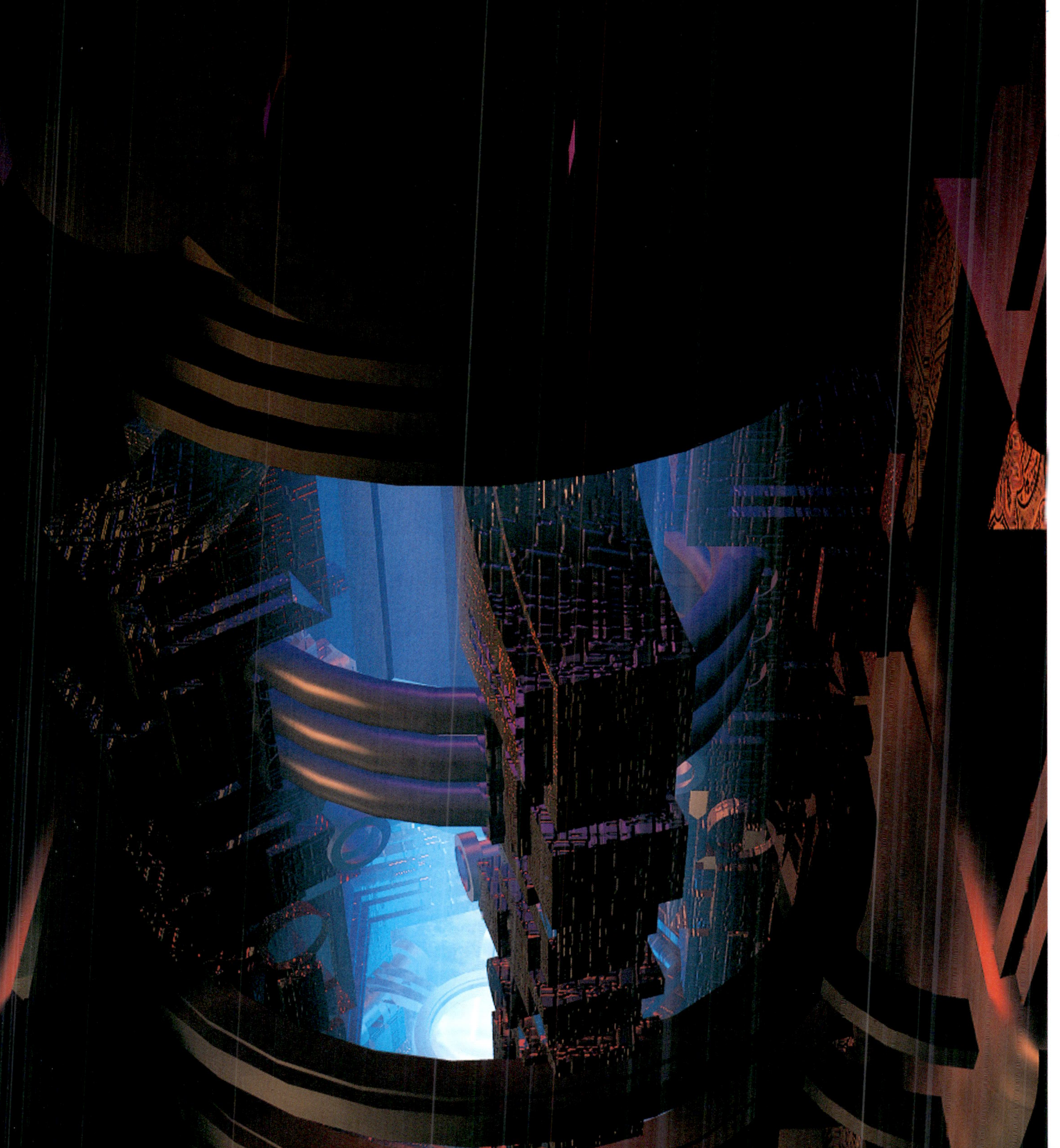

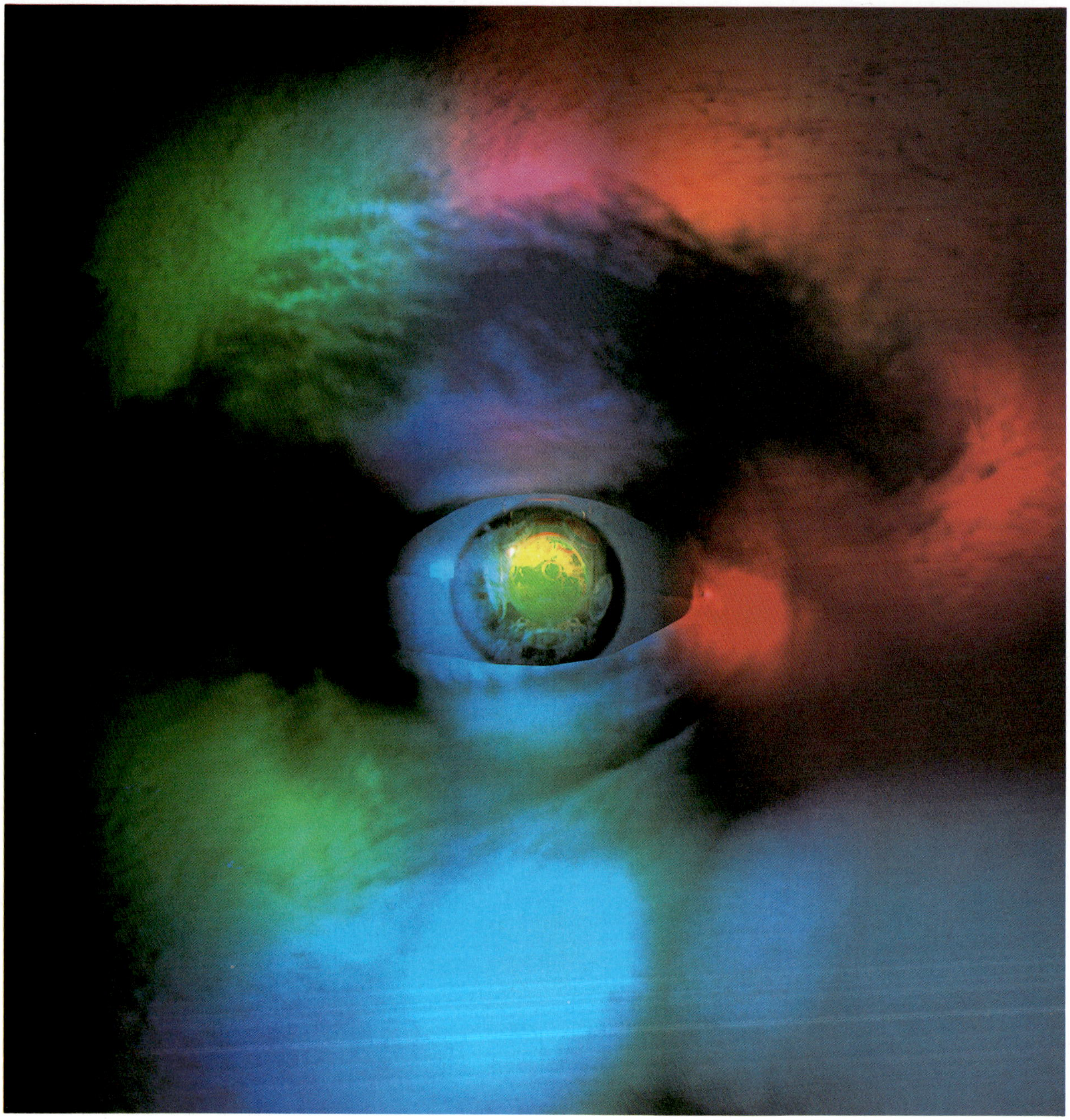

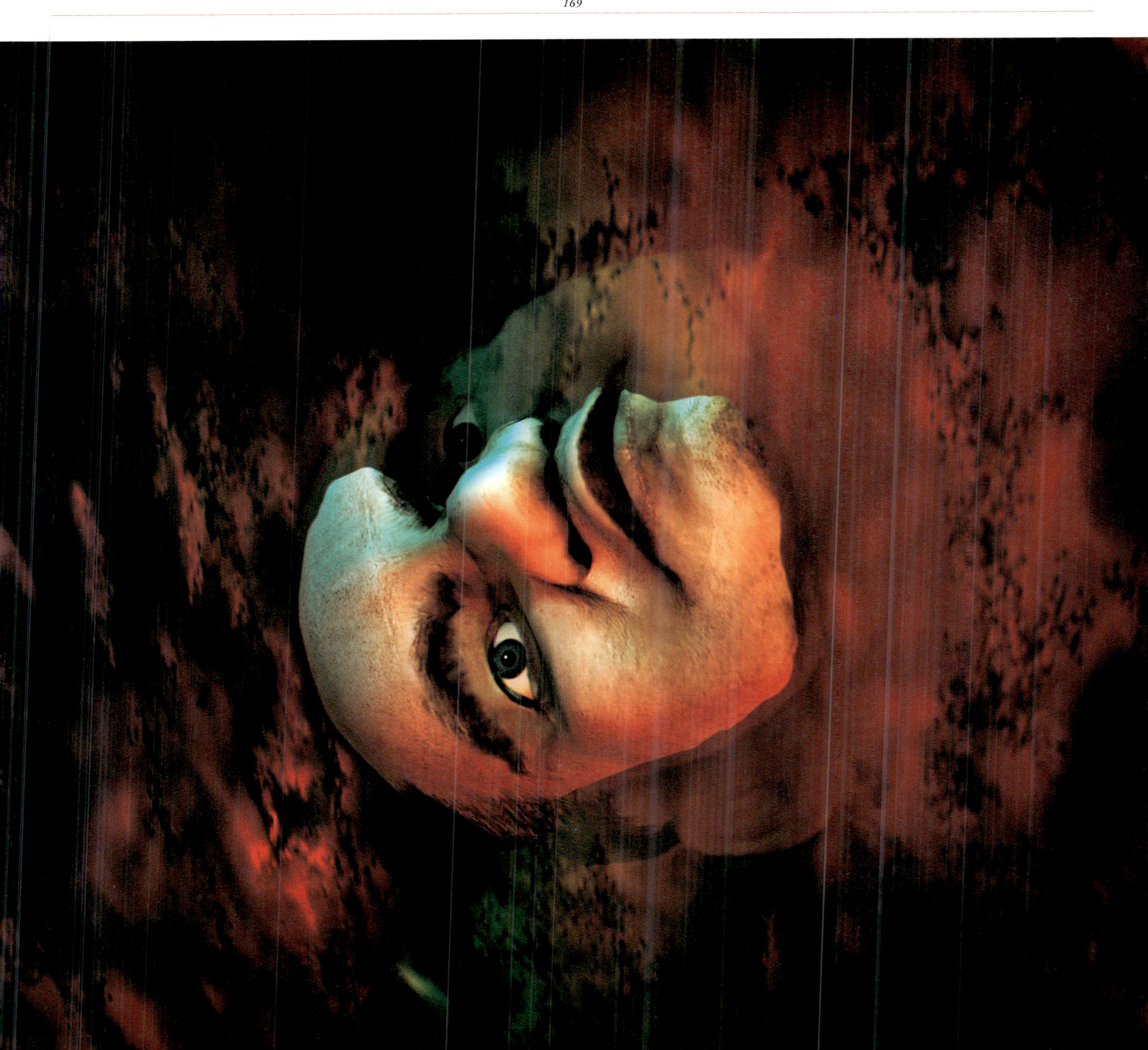

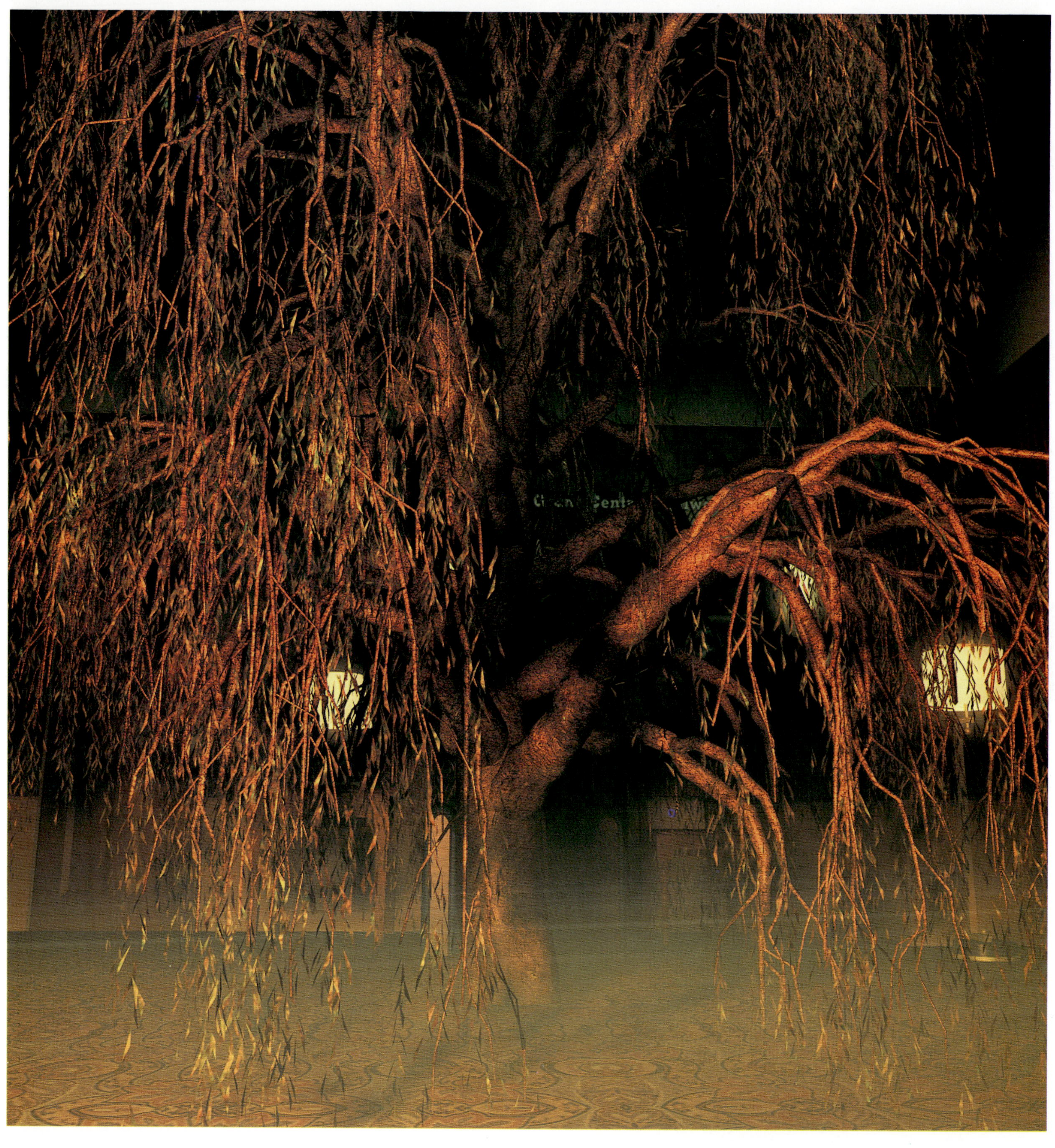

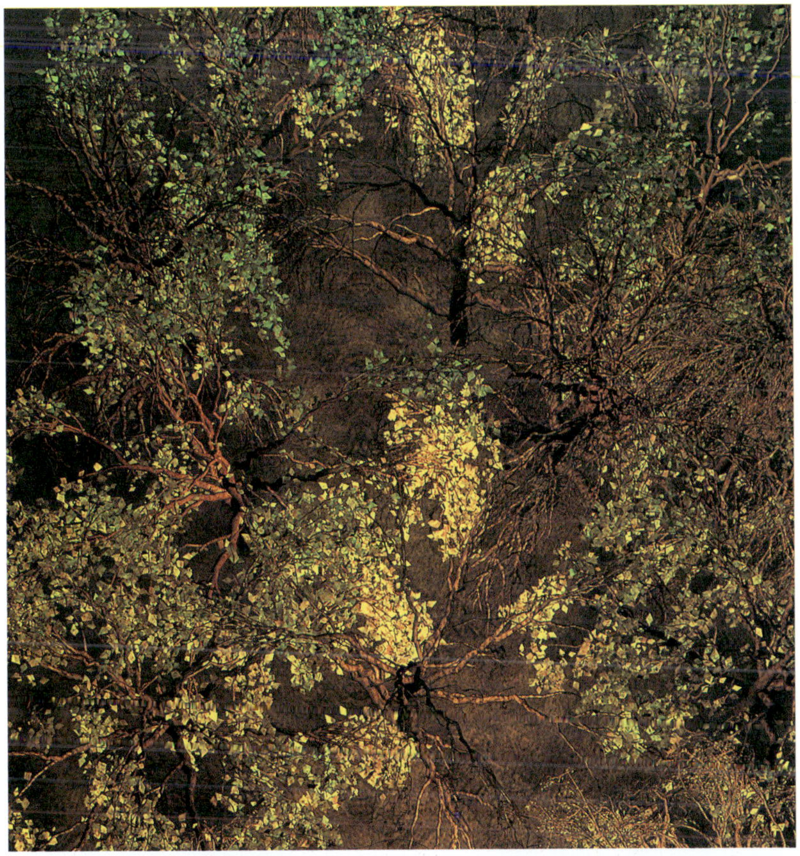

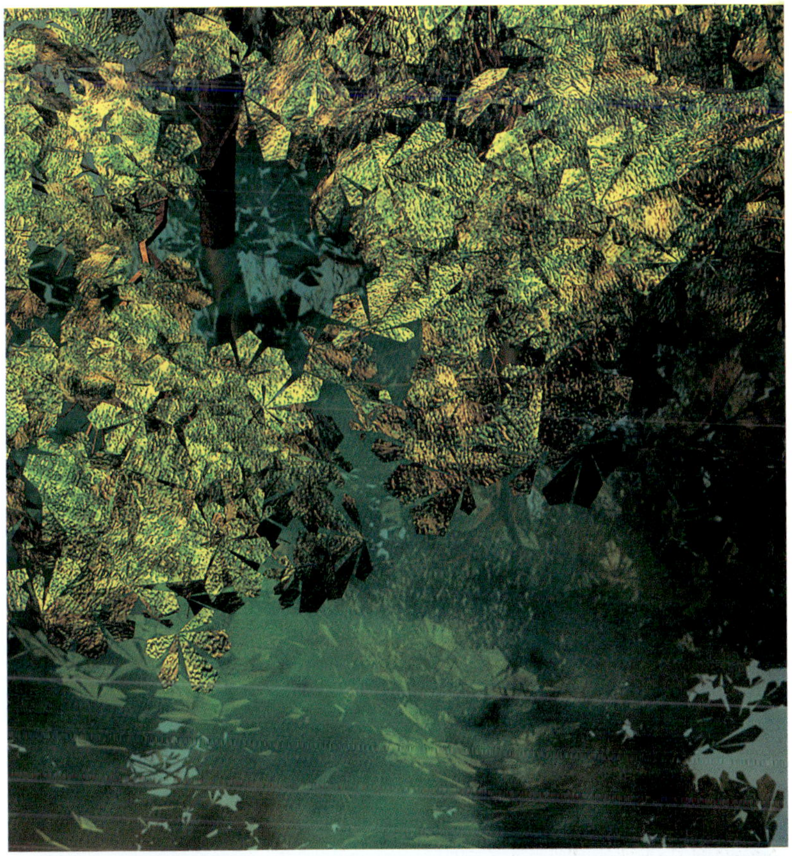

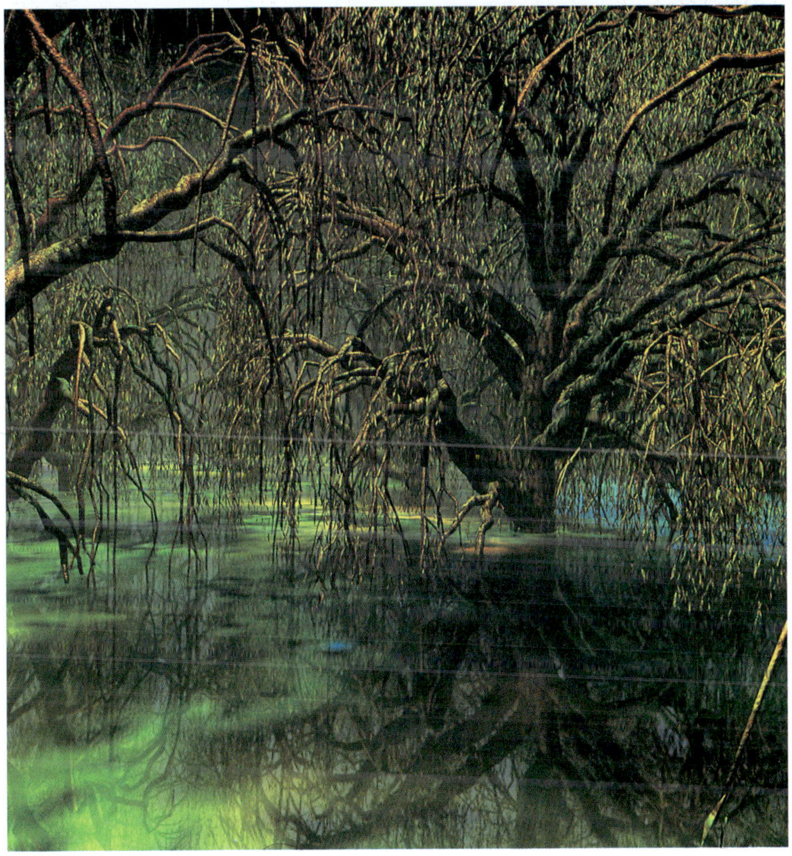

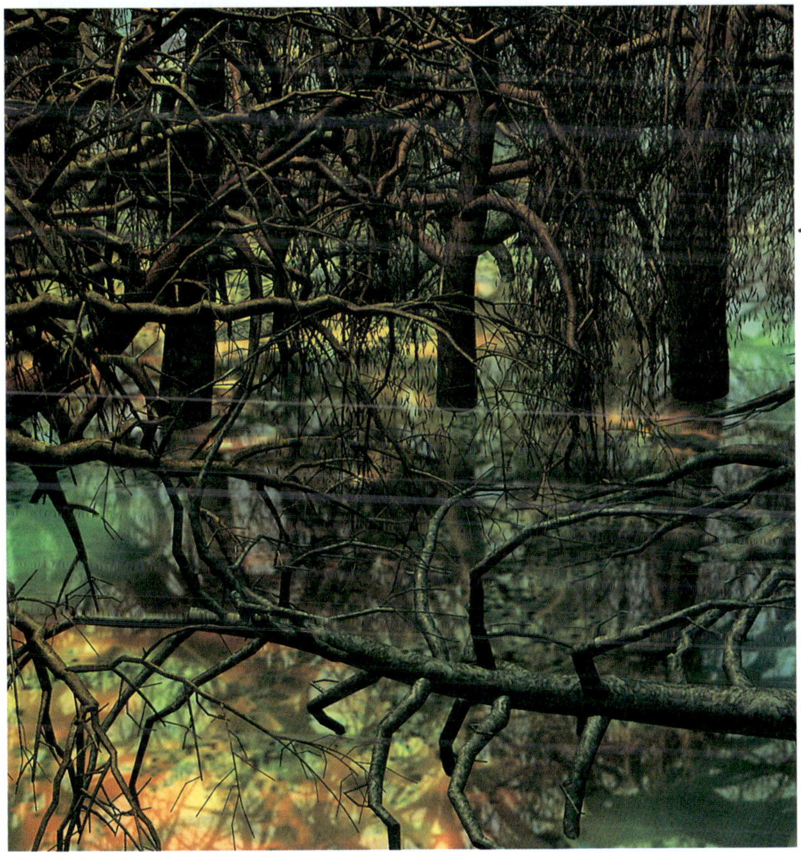

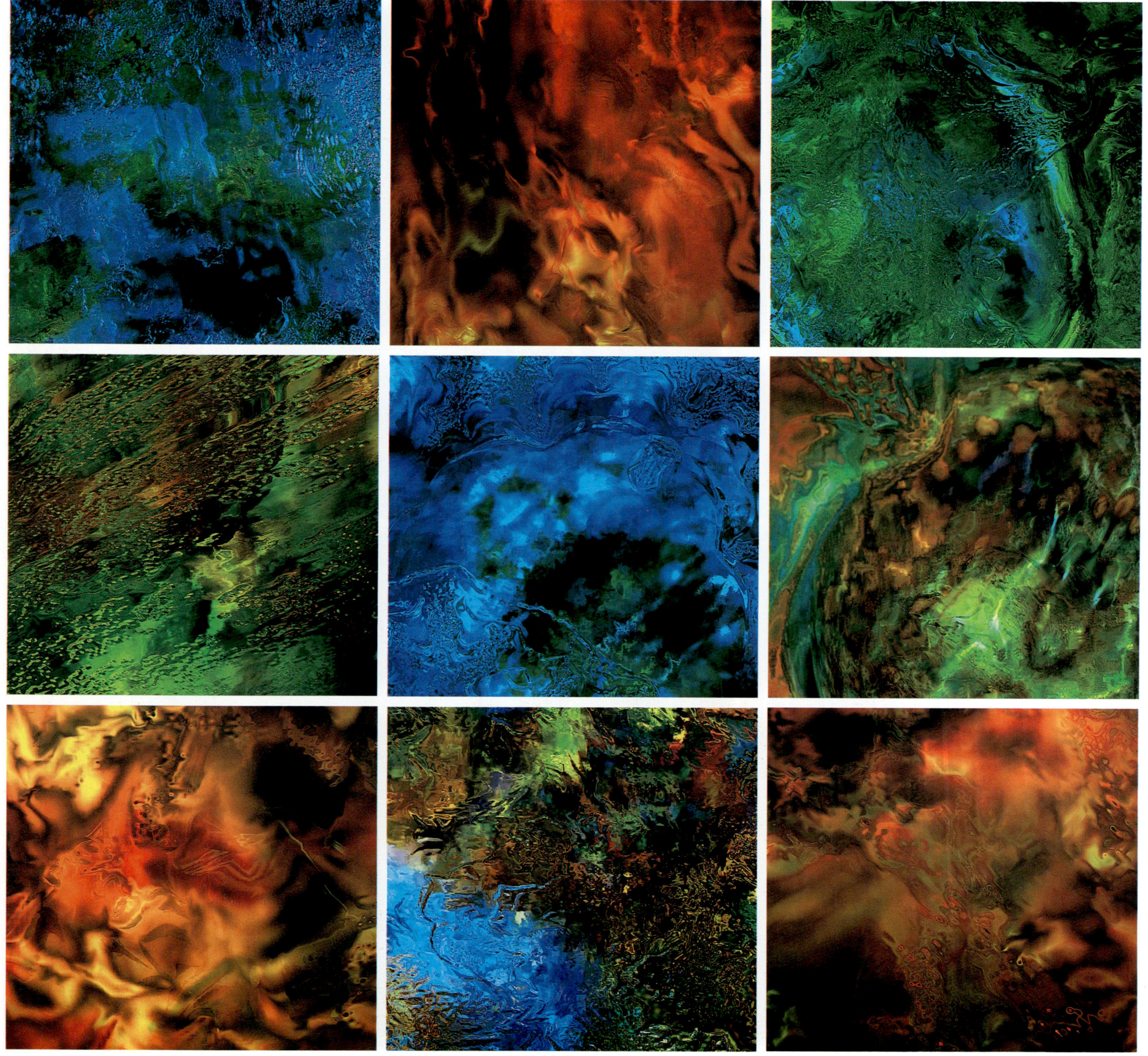

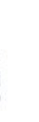

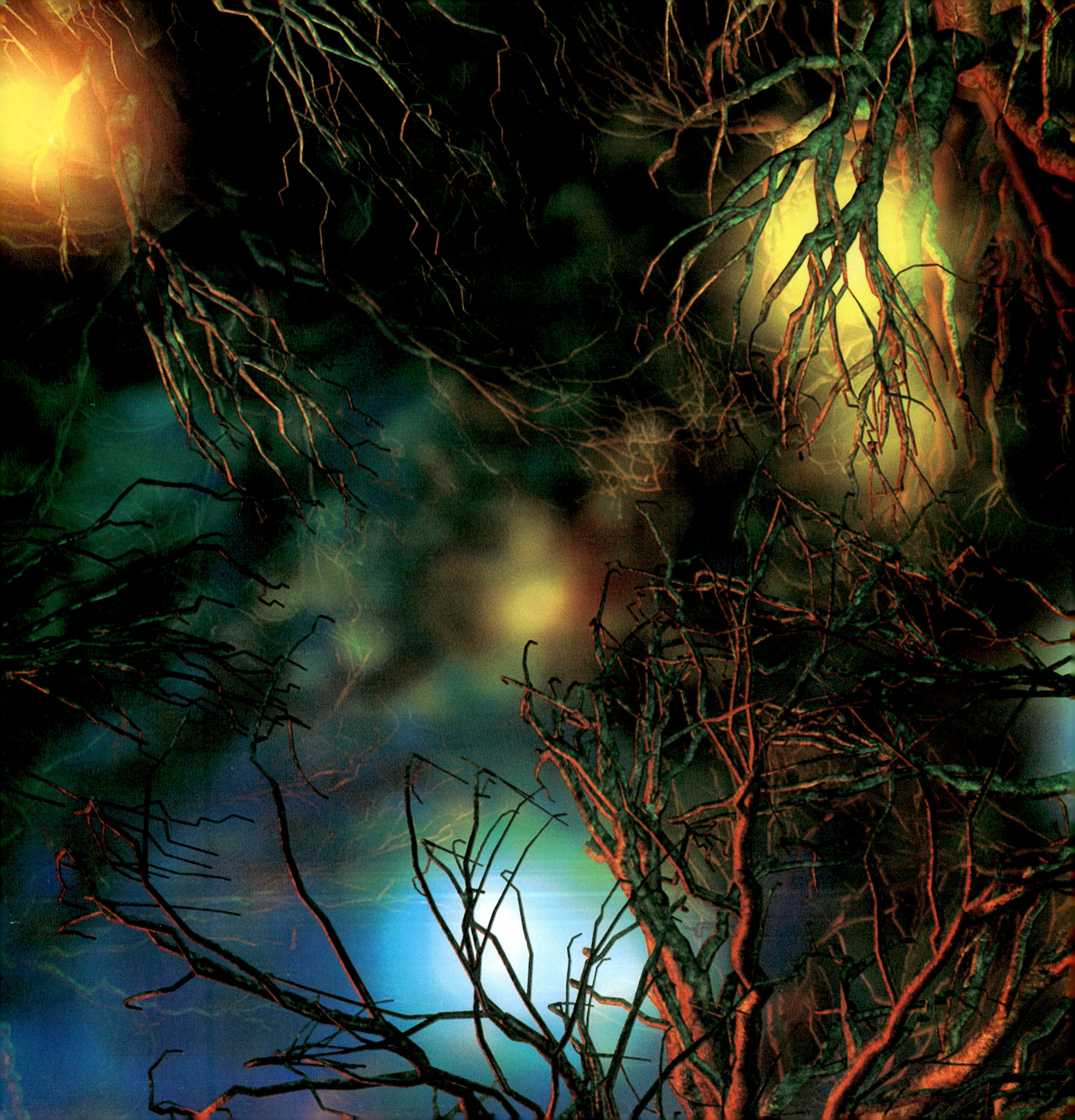

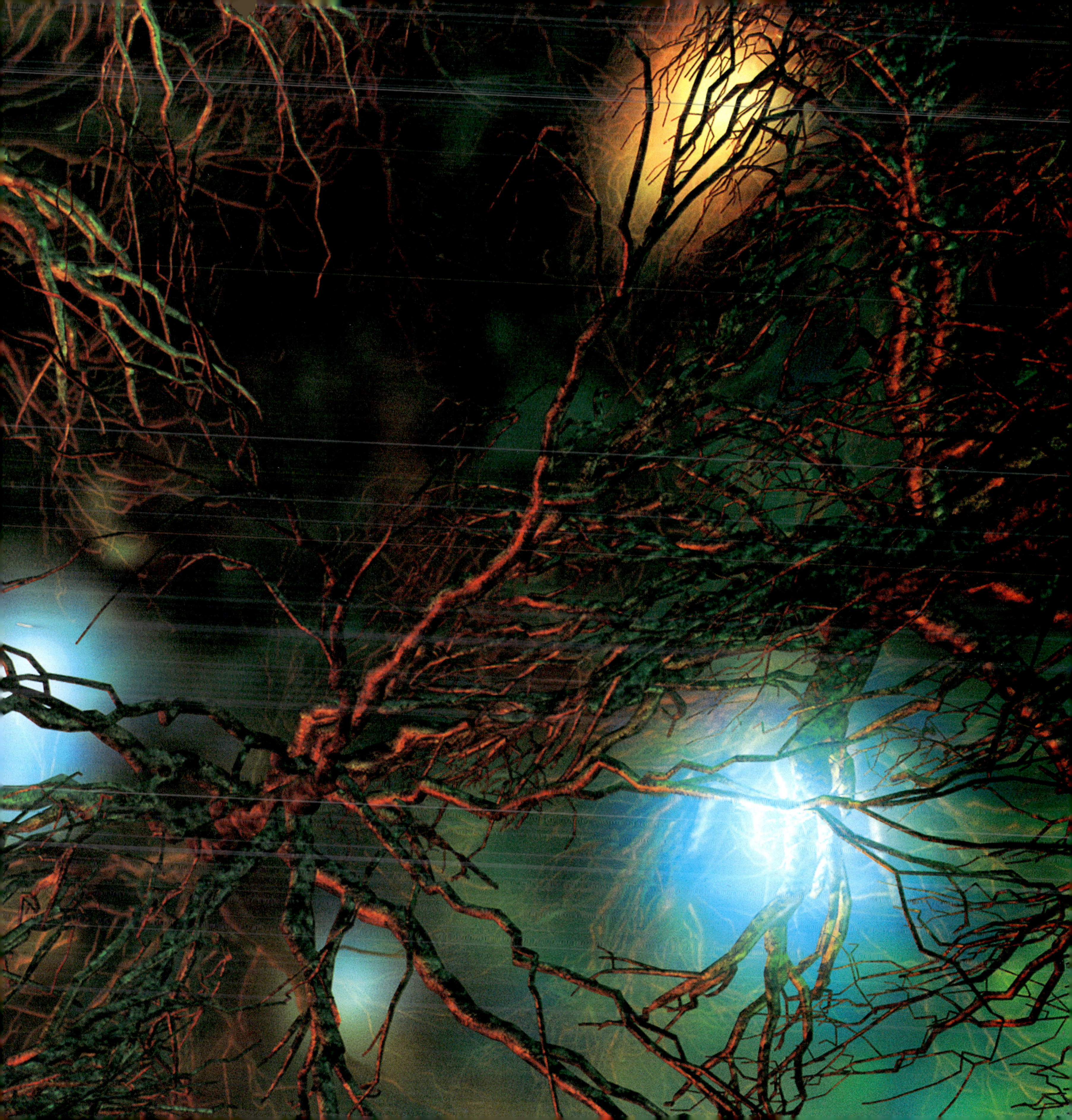

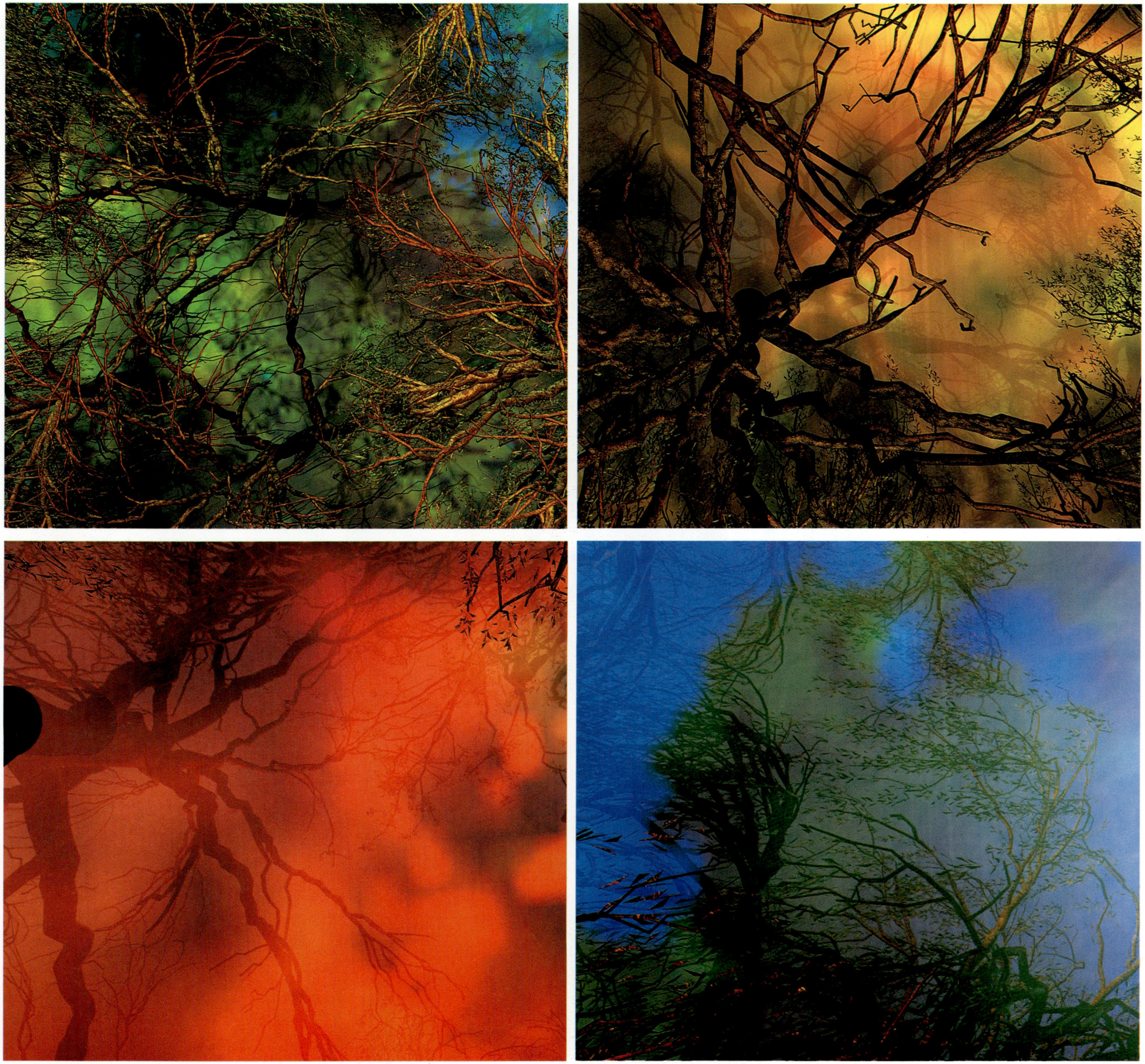

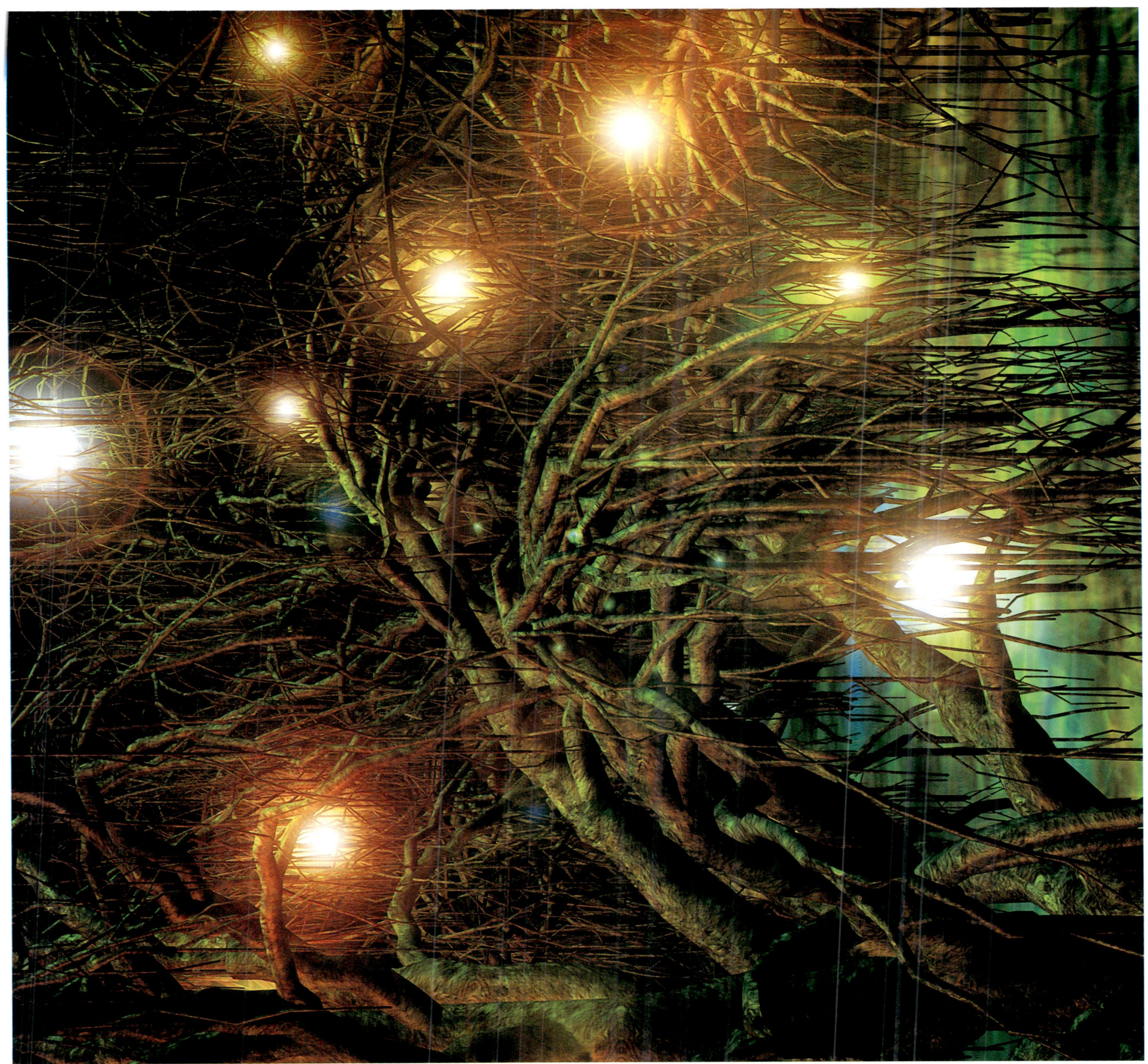

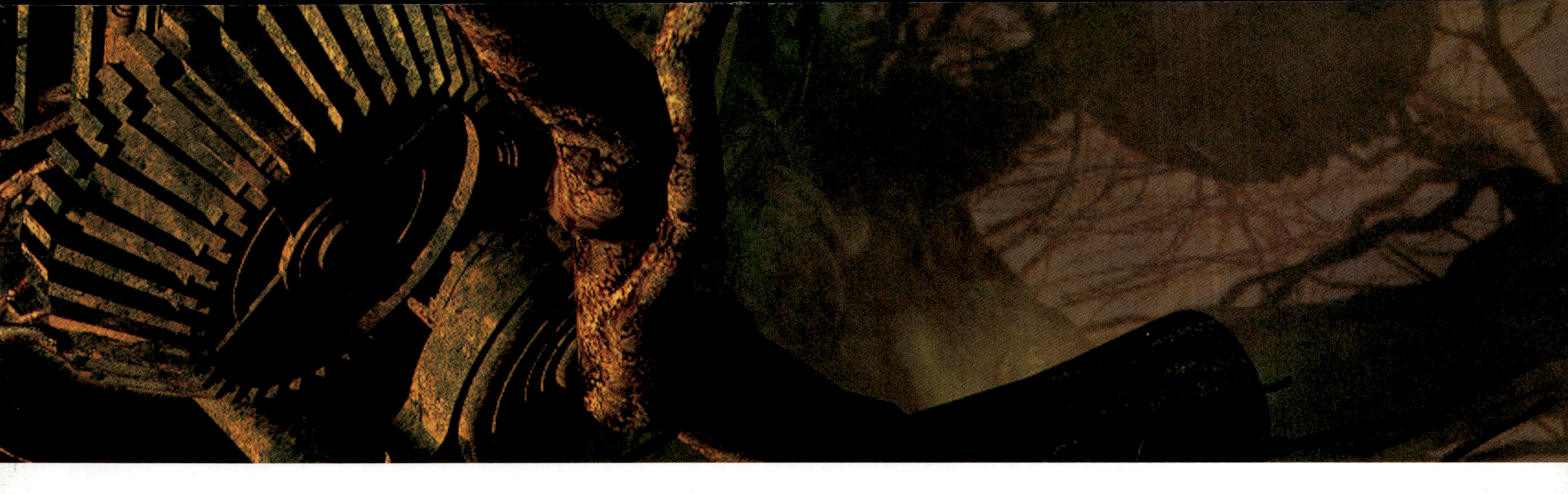

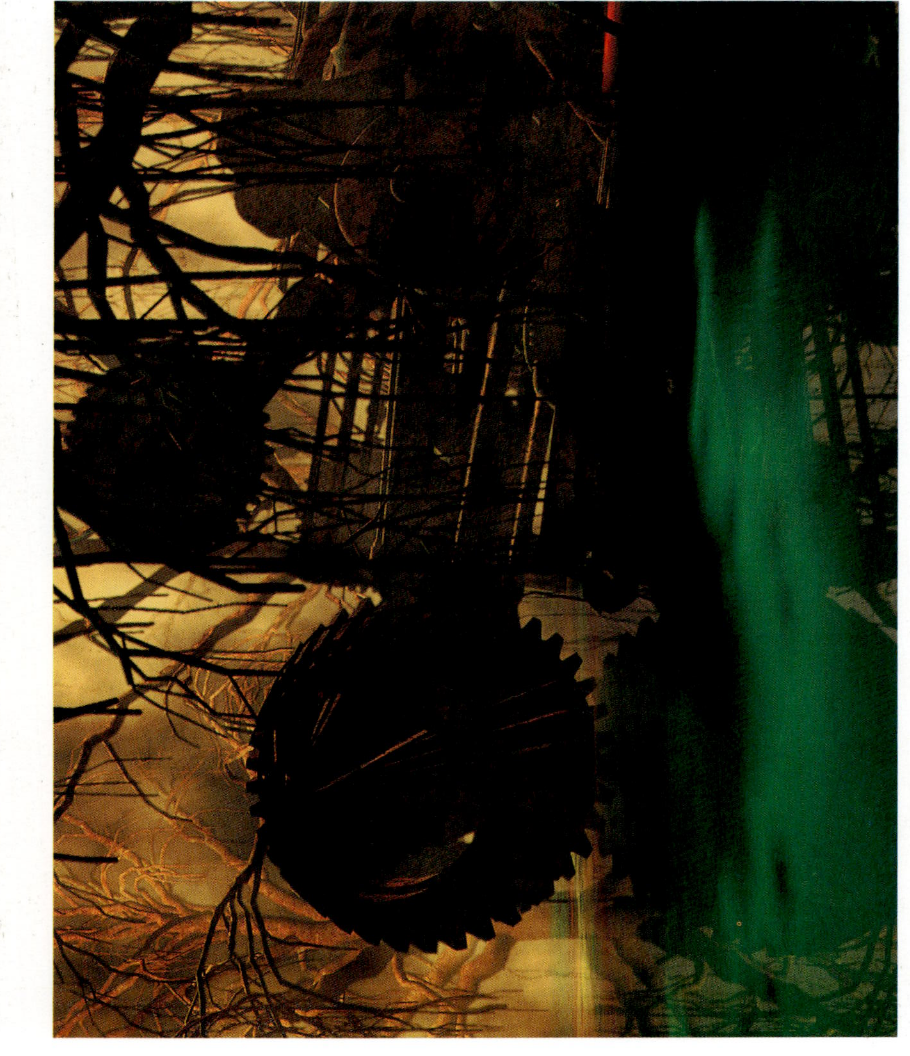

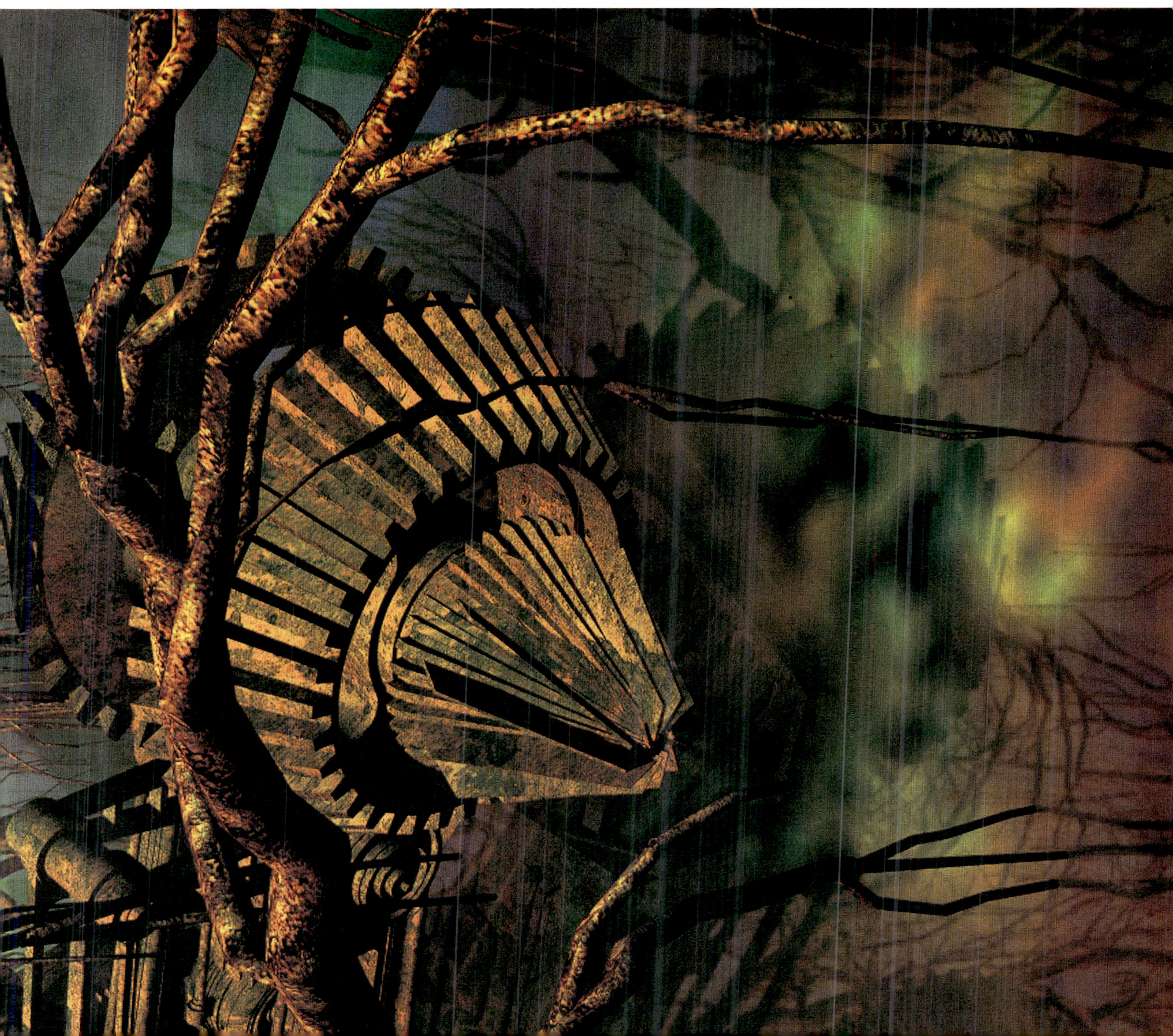

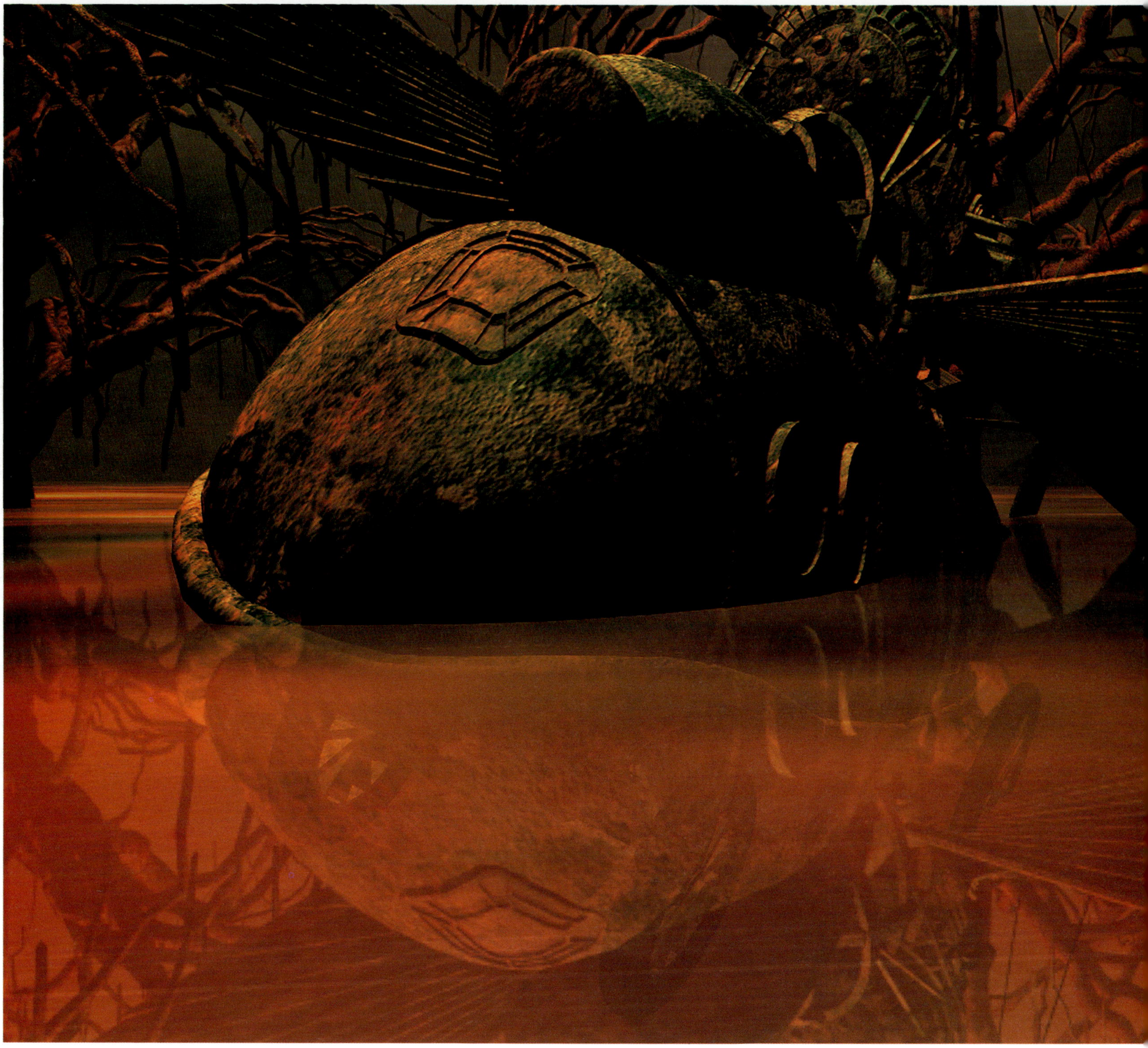

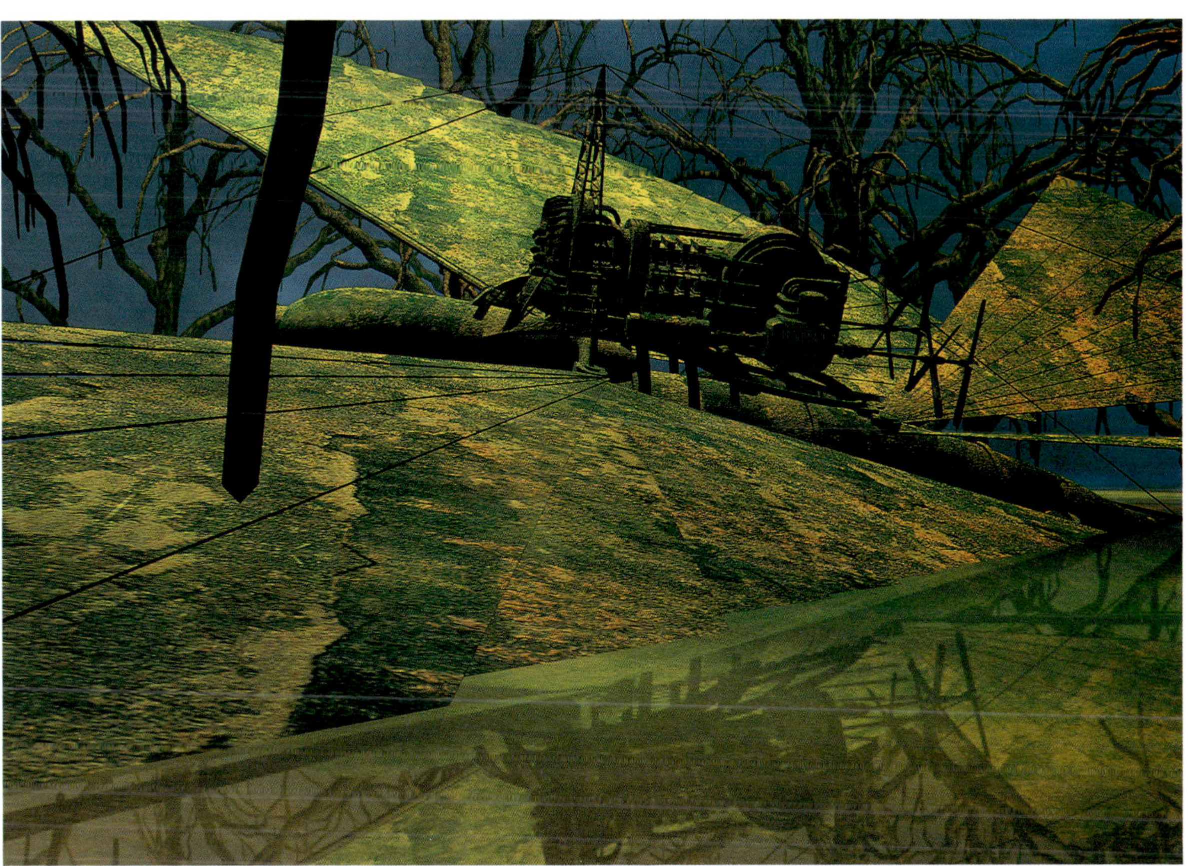

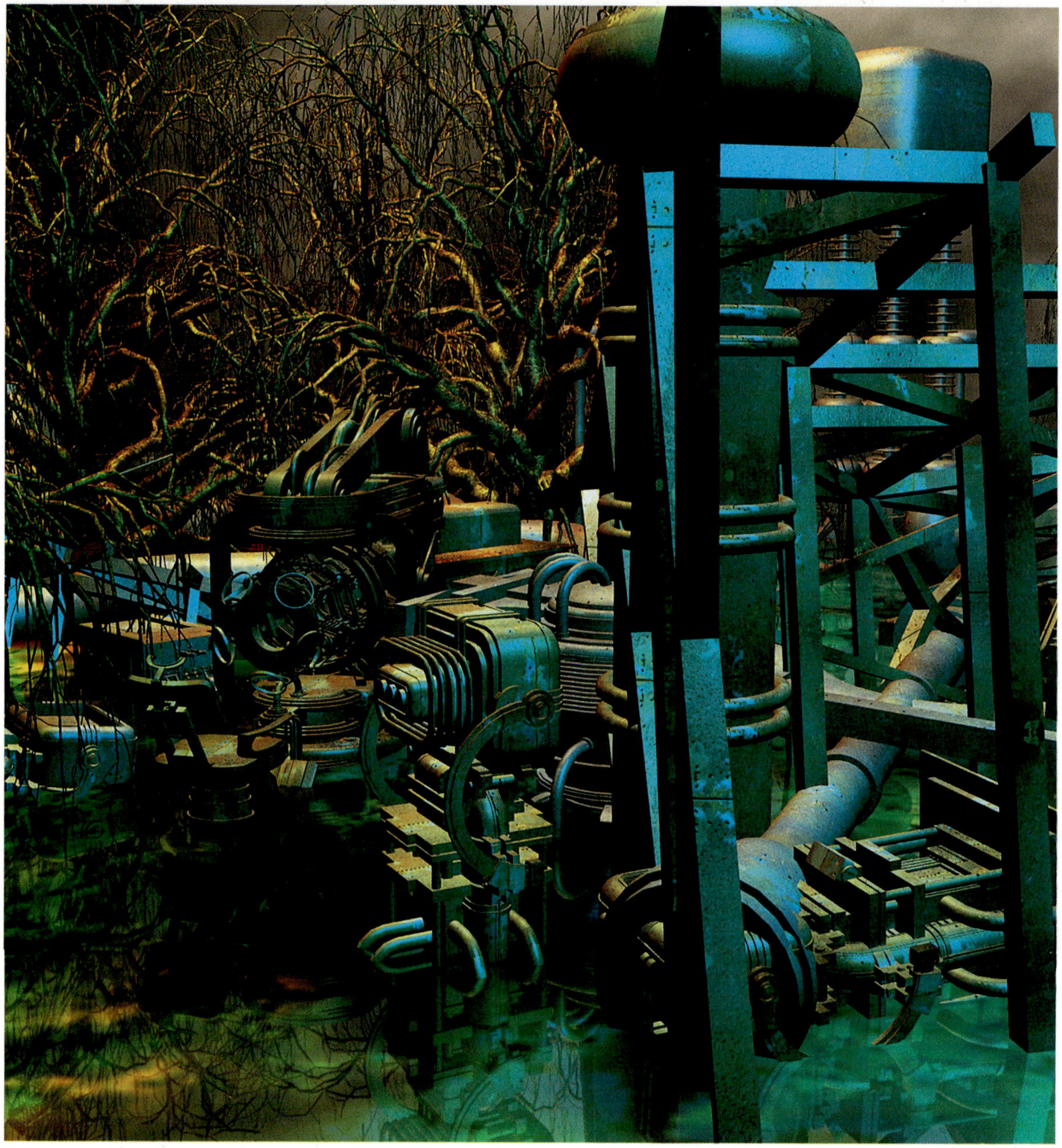

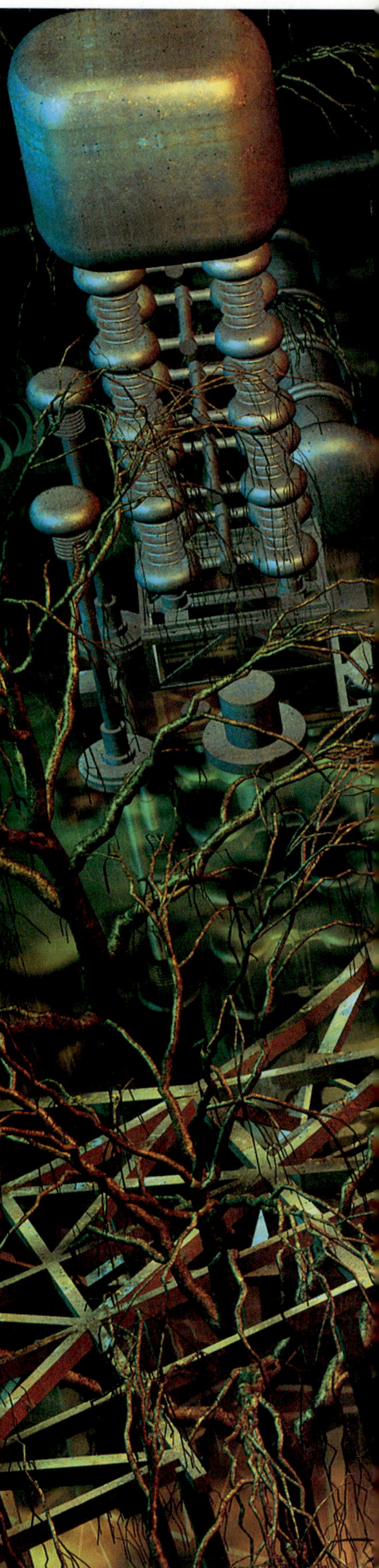

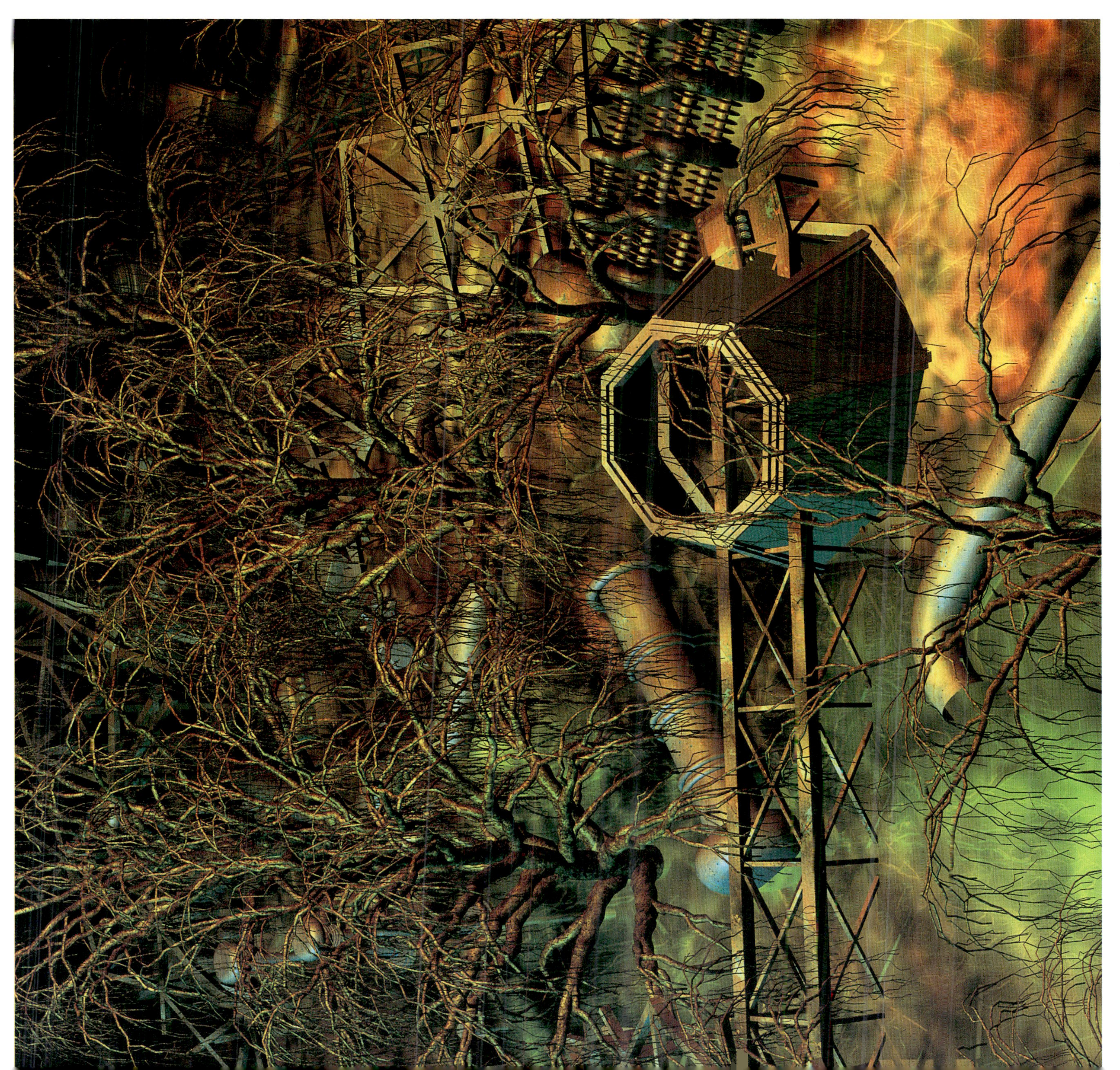

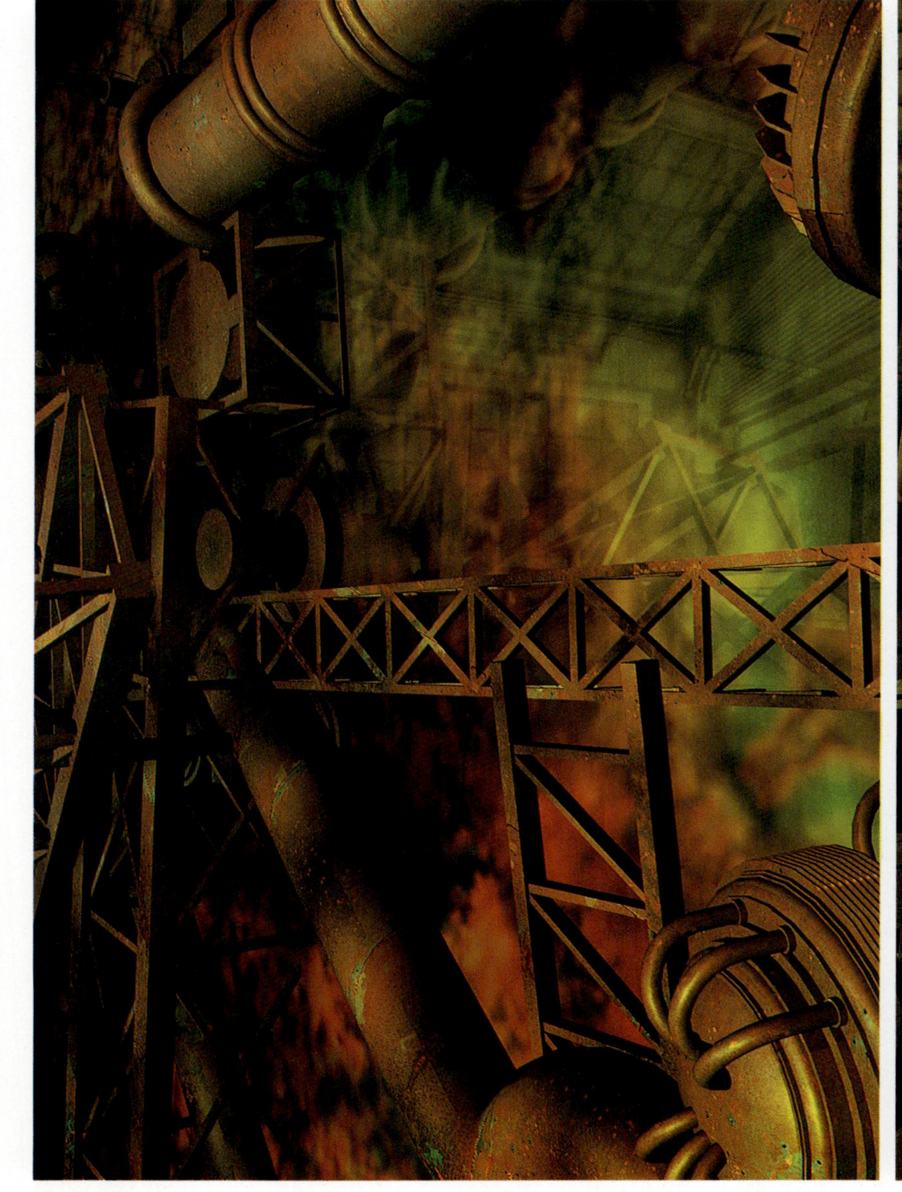

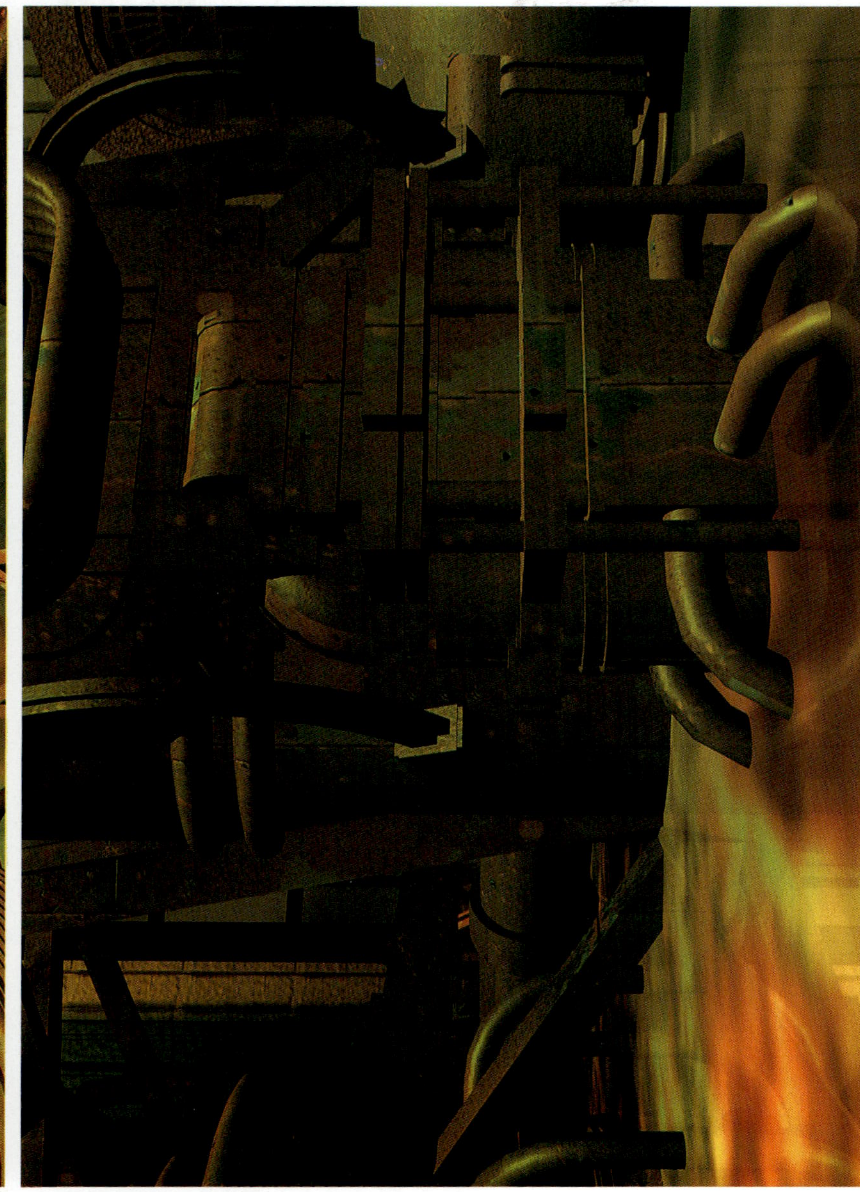

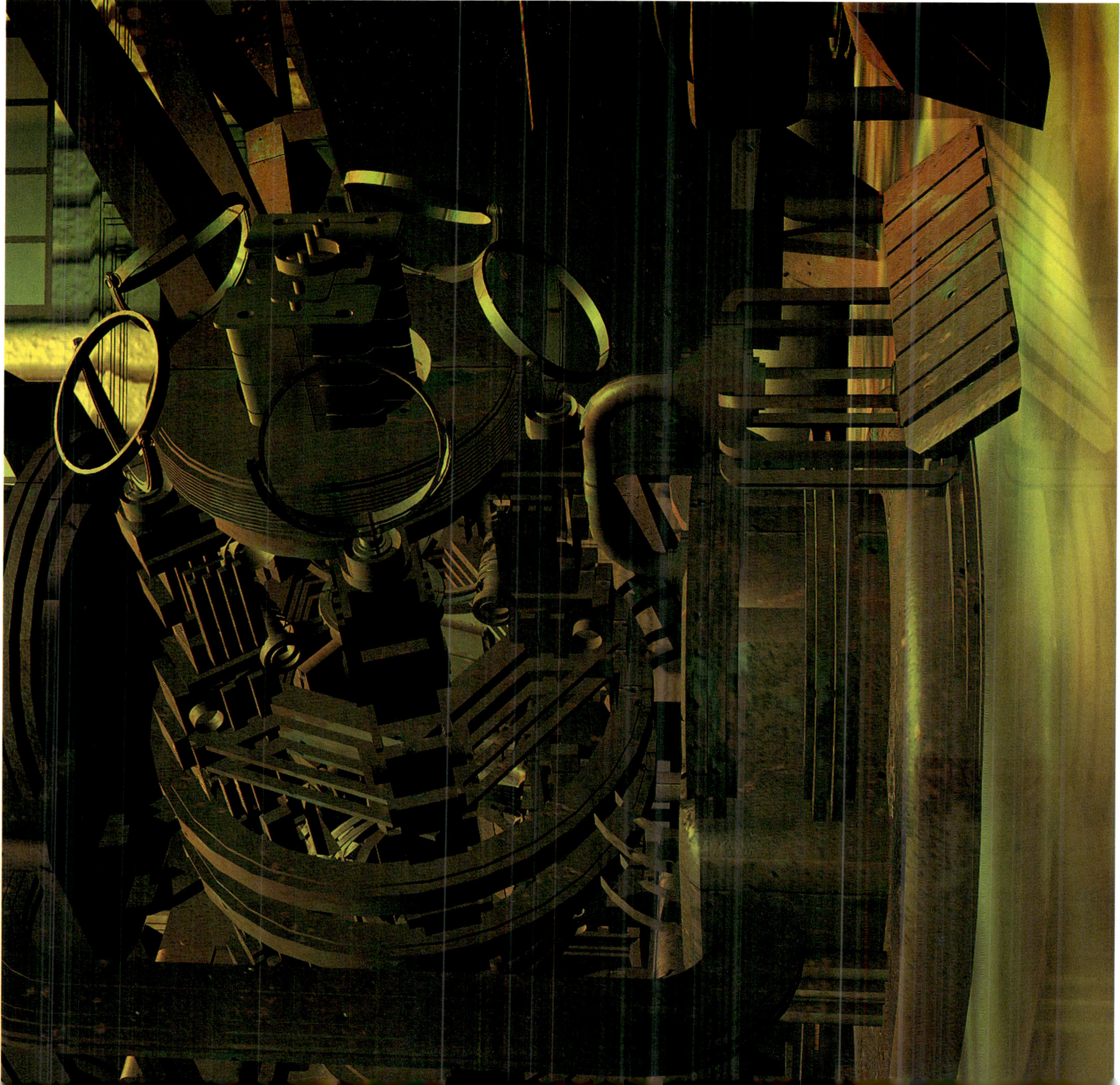

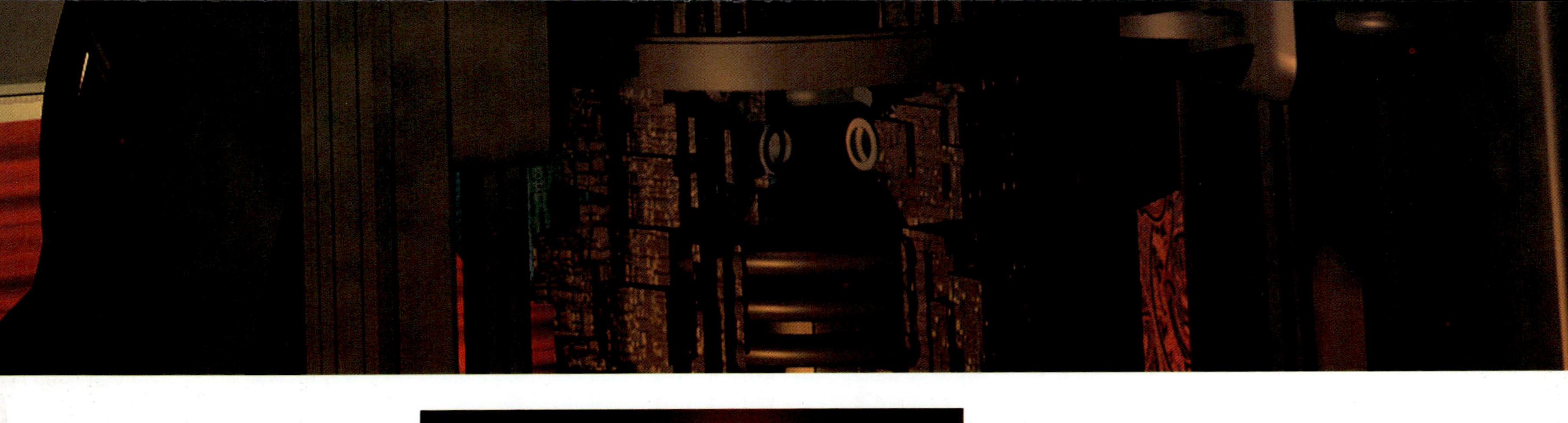

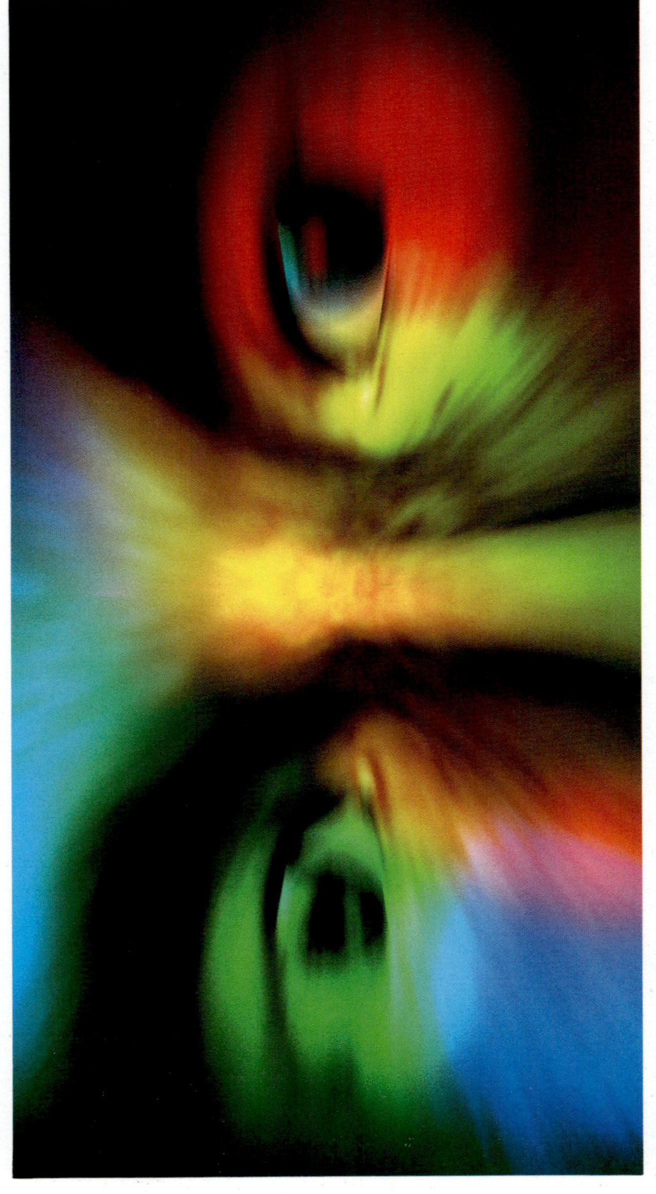

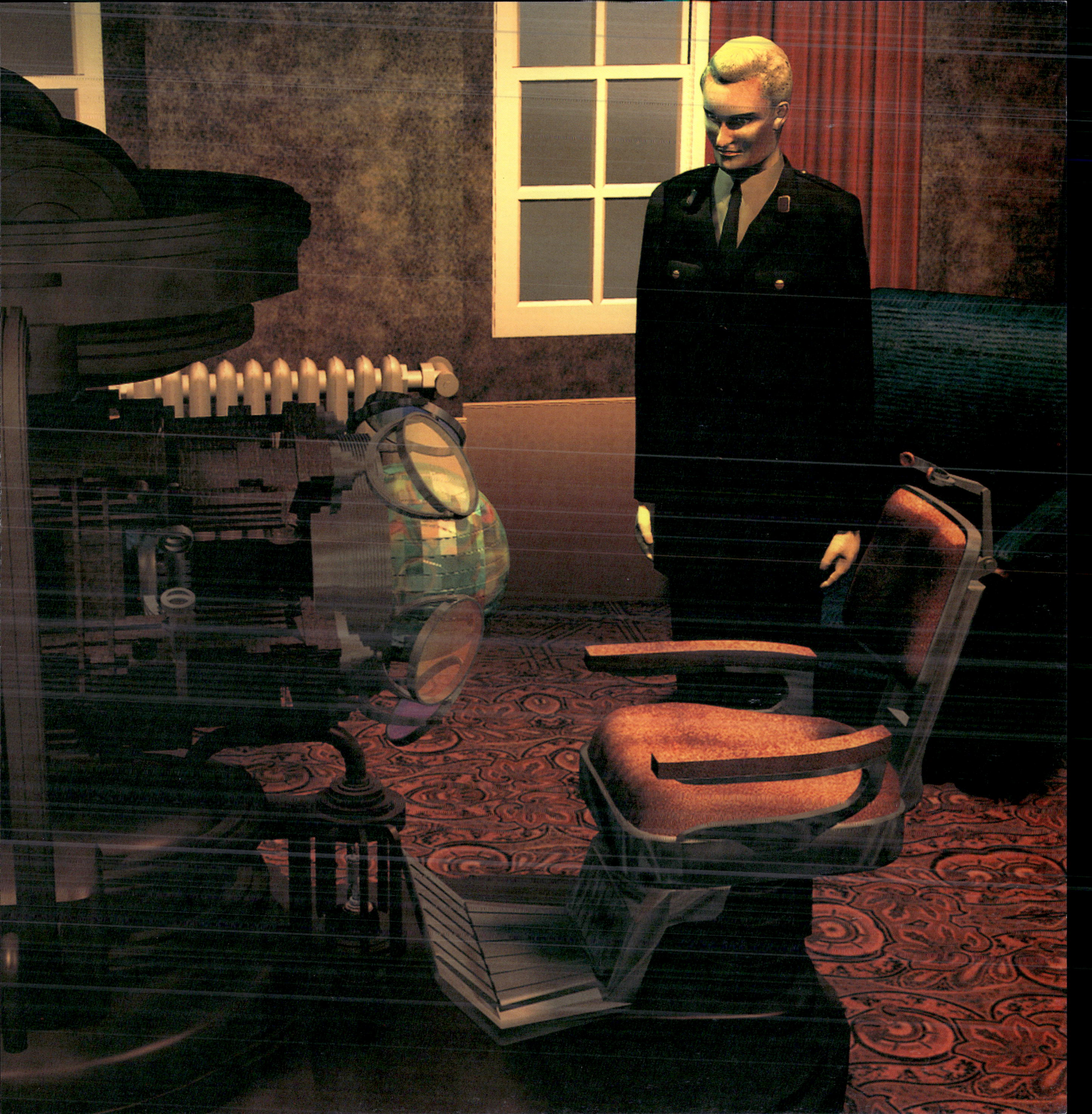

7 January, Year 9 of the Imperial Age

What has Army Intelligence done to Charles? The Version II Sensorama was almost finished. We'd reached the point where further experiment was meaningless.

The neural and the circulatory—the two gates to the human brain. Version II is a machine that attempts ingress through the neural gate, but even intense electromagnetic radiation has not achieved satisfactory results. There is a danger of its impairing the autonomic nervous system beyond the possibility of recuperation.

What does the Imperial Army want Charles to do? At this point I can't say, but I must prepare myself for the worst.

8 January

The Version I Sensorama was a device for eliciting fragments of memory. Images that the testees considered artificially induced were, in fact, vivifications of images they had actually experienced but which lay dormant in each individual's subconscious. In every case the apparatus relied on images preserved in the mind of the individual.

At the time we completed Version I we were examining applications in the realm of psychiatric medicine, that is, its possible use as a therapeutic device.

We weren't happy, though, with the results. Version II was an electromagnetic radiation device designed along significantly more progressive lines. Quite the opposite of Version I, which was intended for the extraction of memories, Version II was designed to implant factitious memories.

The human subject, counterpoised against the machine, is pressed to absorb an artificial optical image that has been previously prepared for him. But implantation of this artificial memory is entirely dependent upon the native susceptibility of the testee.

He has two choices. He may either accept a cooked-up story as fact or he can warp his mind in the effort of denying it. Either way he loses. We should never have attempted development of this machine.

(From the diary of Horselover)

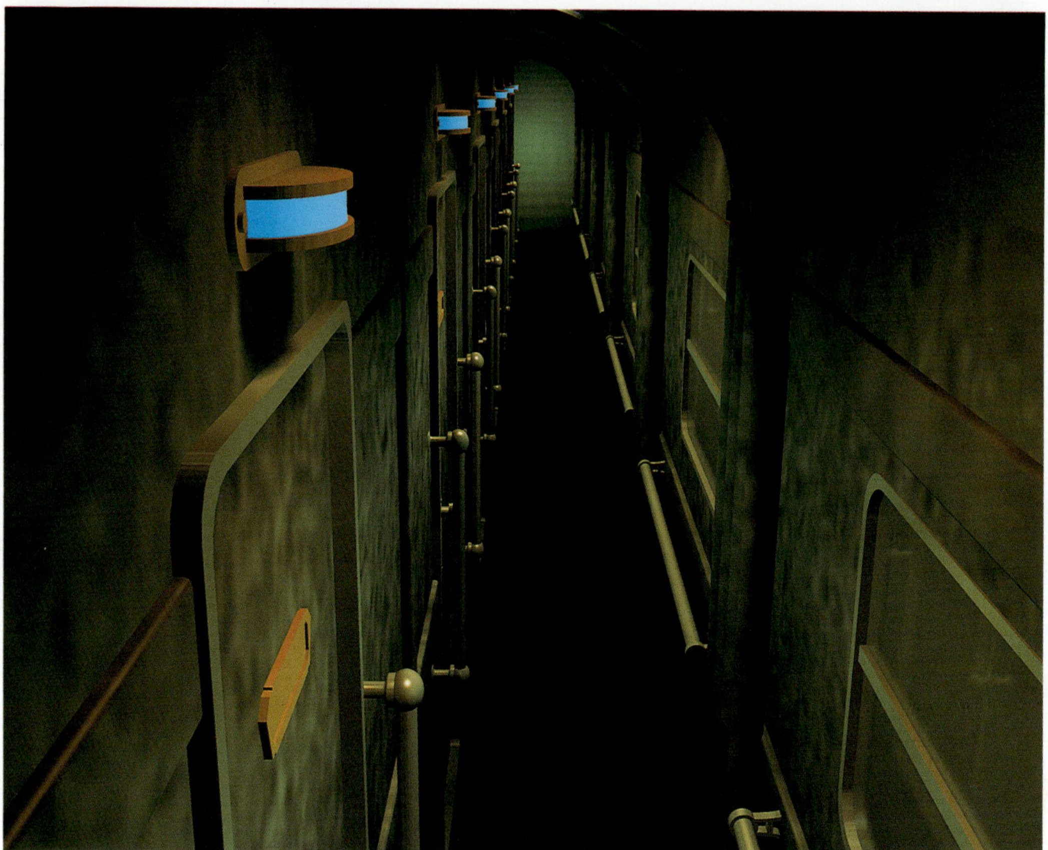

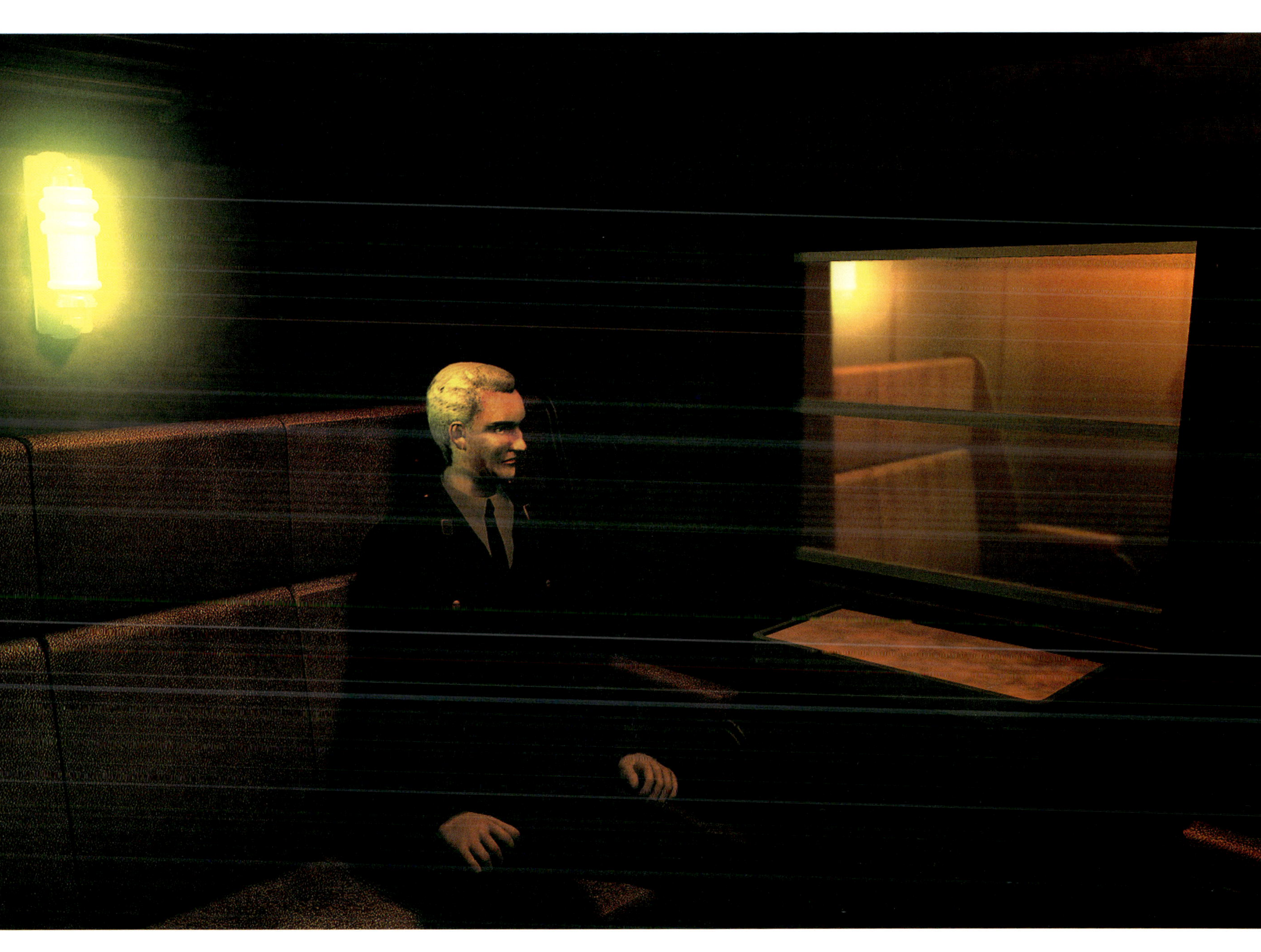

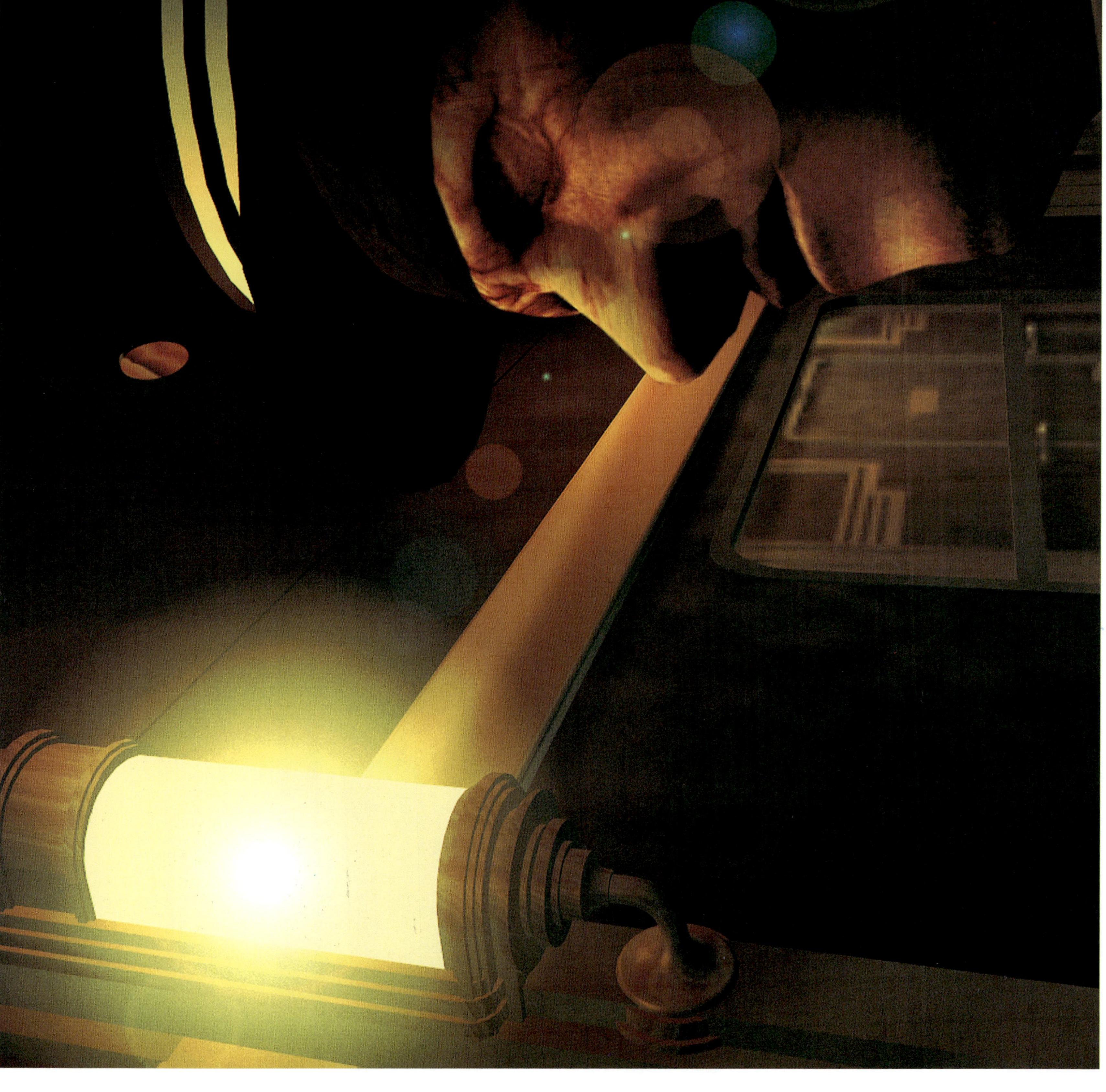

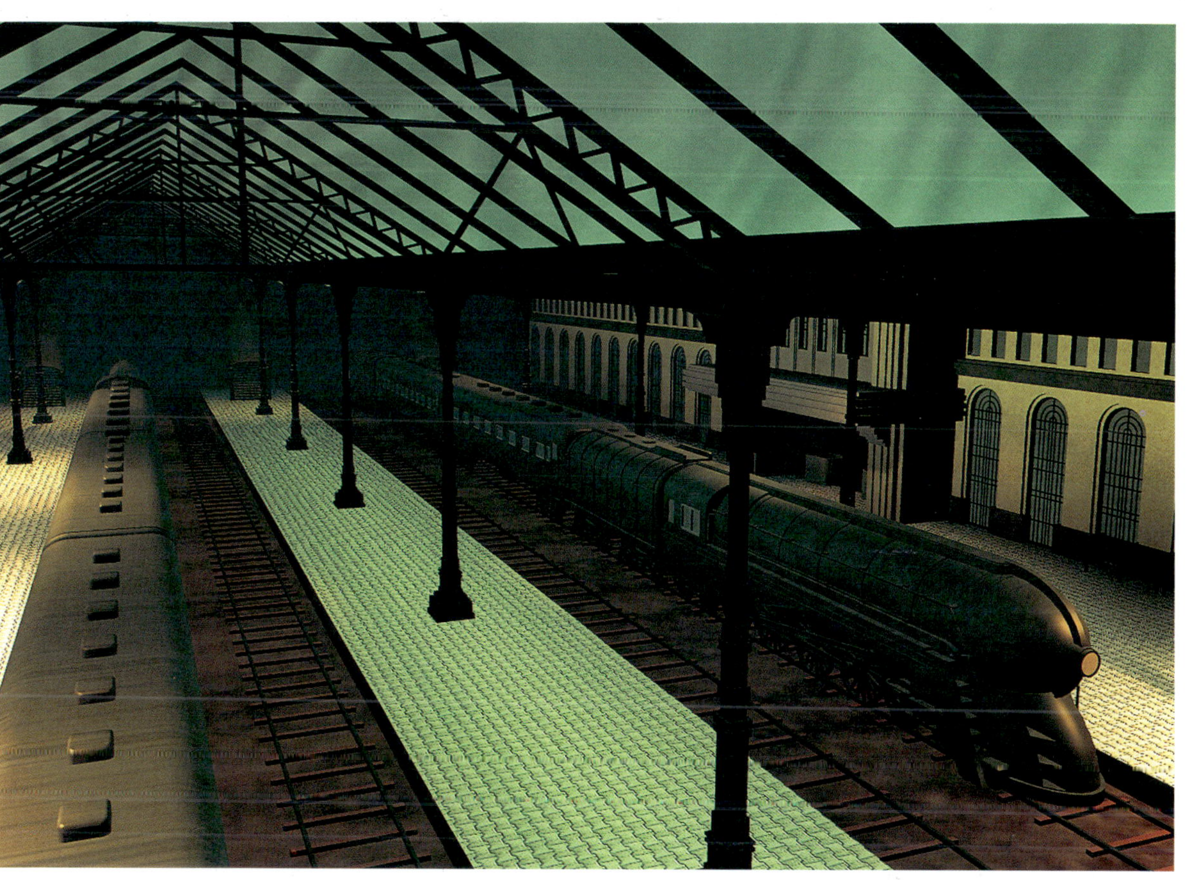

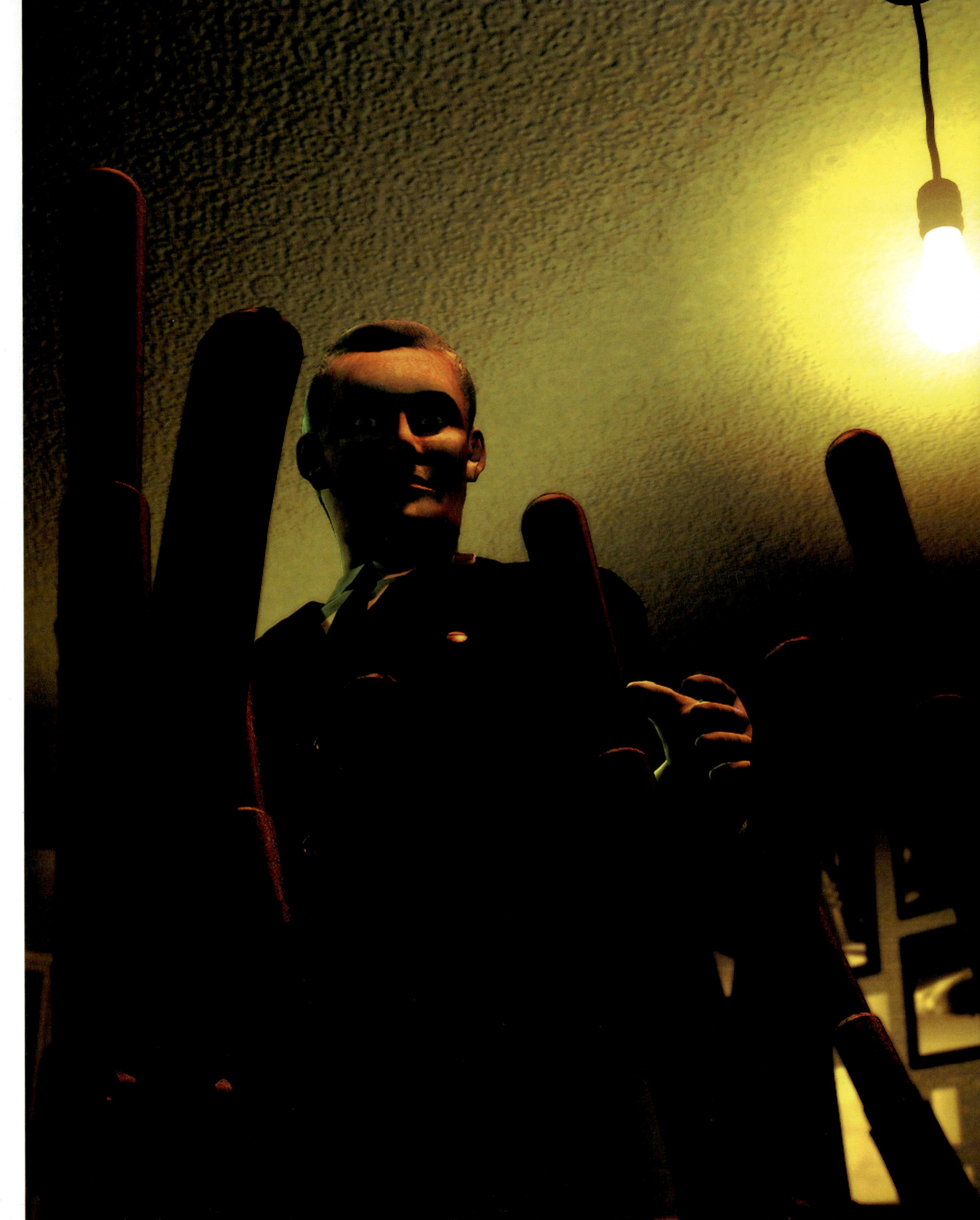

9 September, Year 10 of the Imperial Age

Charles has evaded his guards and escaped. Of course his recapture is only a matter of time. It is absolutely important that we protect the secrecy of the information he carries, and Intelligence has put every man it can spare in the field. Slowslop has concluded that we have no further need of Charles.

27 September

Gondarev has had his memory deleted by Sensorama. His nervous system was damaged and he killed himself. When he was taken away by the Secret Police after treatment in Room 306 there wasn't a spark of emotion in his face. His eyes were like two knotholes in a board. Everyone who goes into that room comes out looking like a remote-controlled doll.

3 November

We still have no leads to the whereabouts of Horselover. I've done all in my power. I used every resource of Army Intelligence's information network... and still not a single clue.

In the rolls of the former Academy of Science he's listed as a professor of Astronomy, but every detail in his file has been concocted. He isn't even on the rolls of the Imperial Observatory, which is given as his present place of employment.

And that letter of his we confiscated, the handwriting experts say it was actually written by Horselover's colleague George.

Assuming Horselover doesn't really exist, why should George create this deception? Have the scientists taken measures to deal with Army Intelligence? Were their reports on the Sensorama based from the very beginning on the assumption that Intelligence would be monitoring them? And what does the letter Charles wrote to Horselover from Headquarters mean?

I simply can't make sense of it.

(From the diary of Hausmann)

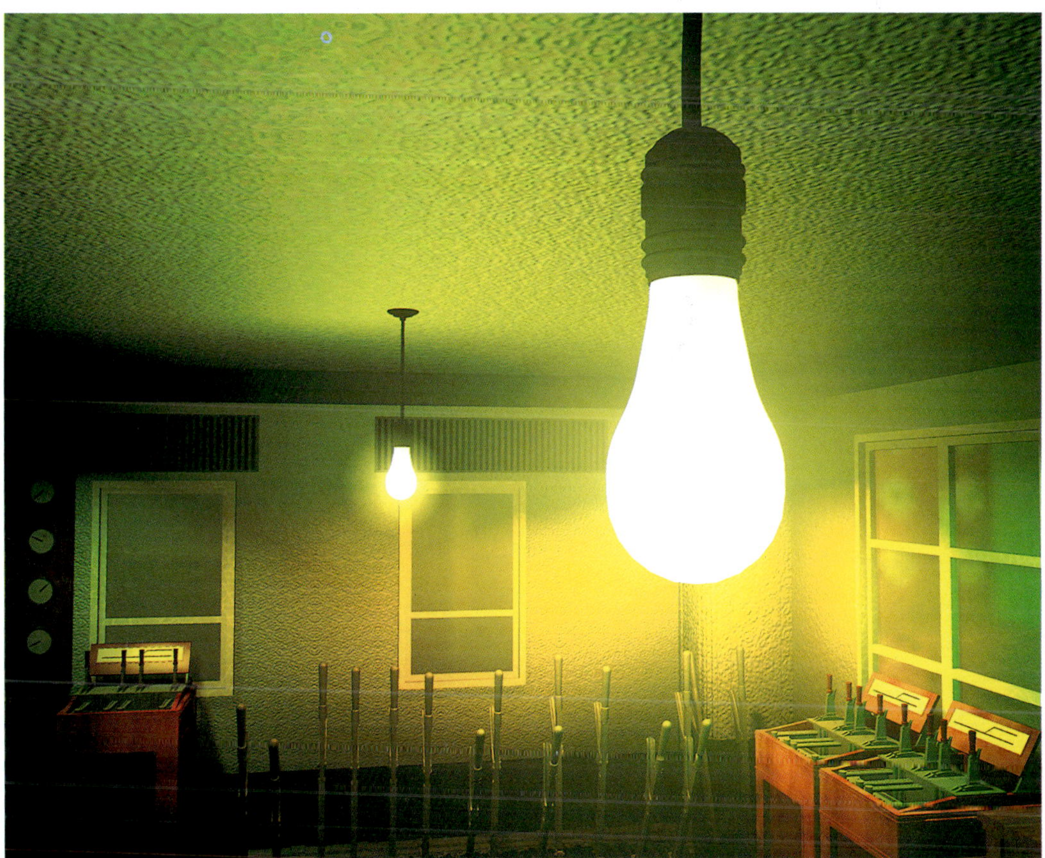

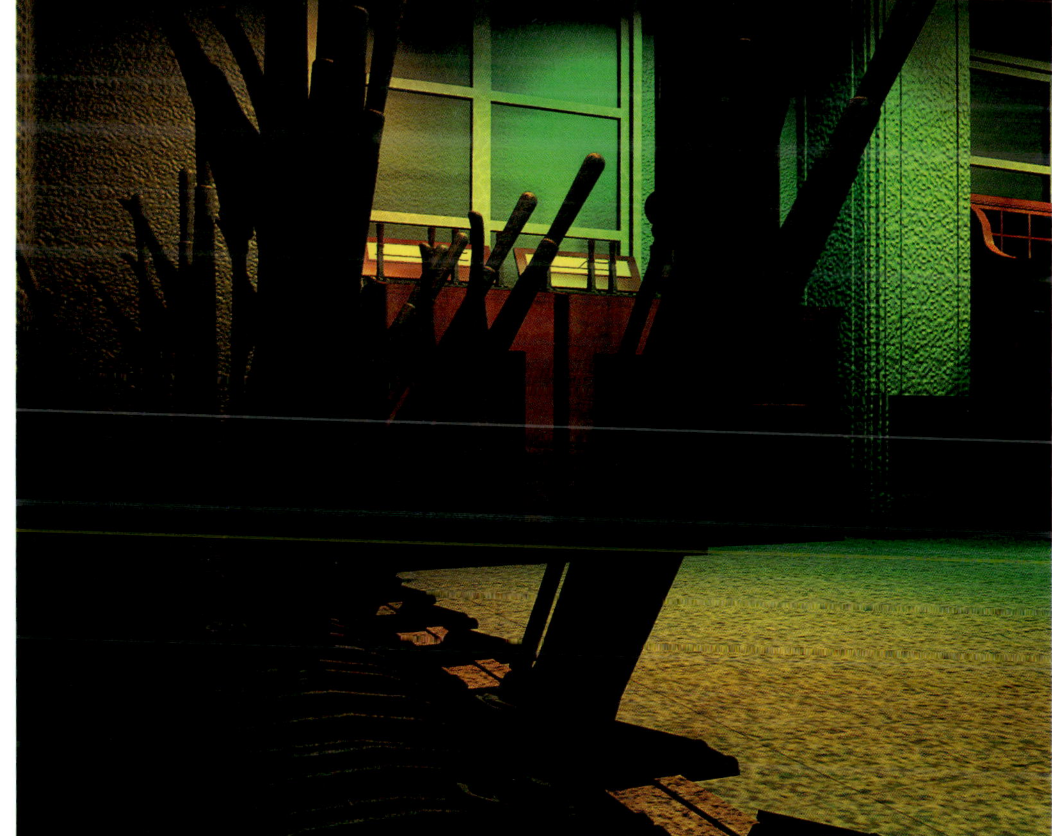

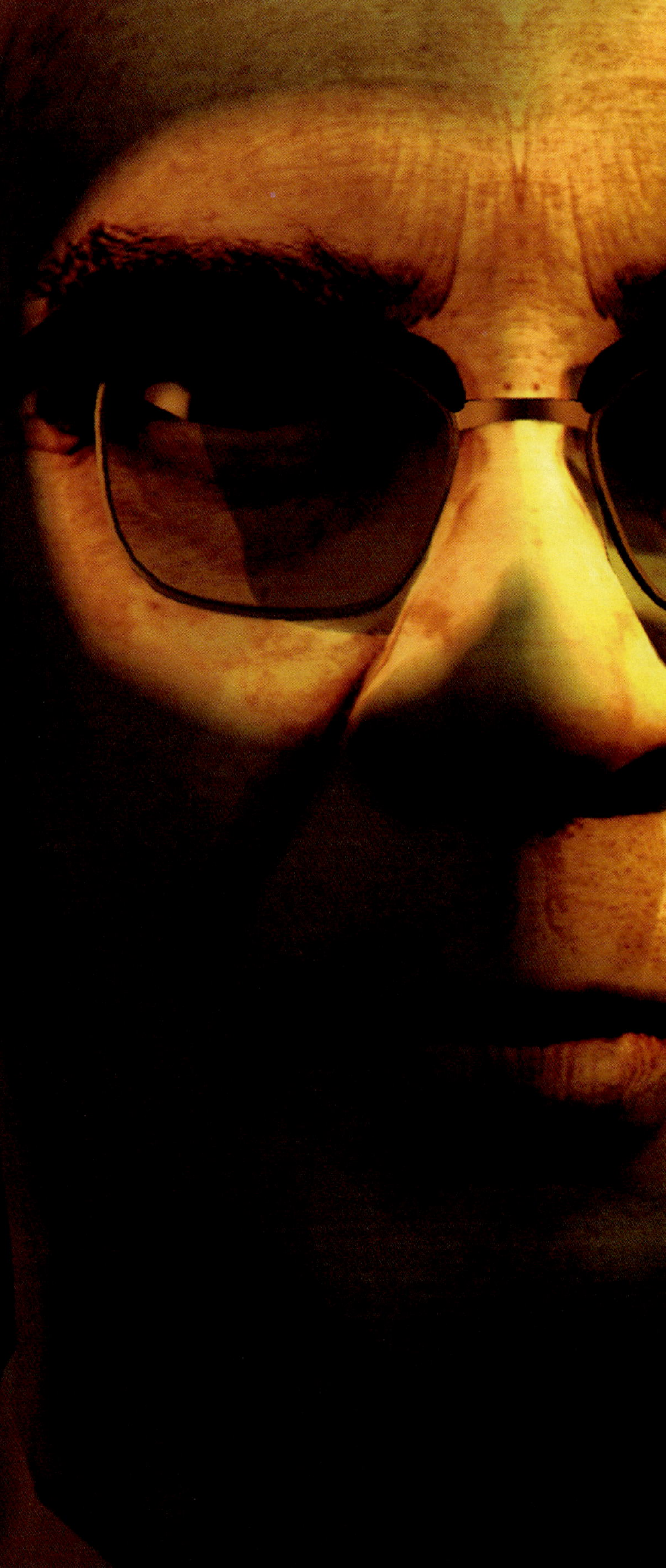

16 December, Year 11 of the Imperial Age

Lieutenant Hausmann,

Sensorama is not a weapon of destruction.

Some ten years ago we began experiments on the Beam Machine at the national research facility–it was then known as the Academy of Science. The Beam Machine was a type of hallucination-inducing machine that extracted certain images lying dormant in the subconscious. It was a therapeutic appliance intended for the treatment of psychological disorders. At the time we thought it would prove effective in the treatment of such conditions as amnesia.

But then along came the revolution, the establishment of Orlovsky's Empire, and the closing of the Academy. The Beam Machine project was thus brought to a halt.

It was Charles's idea to resume the research. He gathered our colleagues at the Imperial Museum and started doing experiments. We rechristened the machine 'Sensorama' and regularly conducted experiments there at the Museum. It was around then that you were first dispatched to the Museum by Army Intelligence.

Realizing that our activities were now being monitored, we came to a decision. The new Empire's policy of prosperity through military strength would inevitably result in war. If the Empire engaged the Socialist Republic in an all-out war, human civilization would come to an end. As long as the dictator Orlovsky remained in power there could be no future for any of us.

Using the Sensorama we embarked on research into hypnosis. We attempted to induce the memory of specific items of information through the action of electromagnetic waves. Hypnosis *per se* is not an unusual technique. Moreover, there is no need to use the Sensorama when comparable results can be achieved with the human voice. However, by using the Sensorama a signal could be transmitted directly to the brain. Decisive results could be achieved without alerting a third party to the content of the hypnotic suggestion.

In the Version II Sensorama we introduced the message: "Nonviolent insurrection. Topple the Empire!" Each subject would also be primed with the 'key' that would unlock this latent suggestion.

At the same time we developed a plan for the launching of a huge airship. The airship was the key that would unlock the hypnotic message sending an unspecified number of testees into action. We would achieve, without threat of failure, a nonviolent revolution.

The problem was how large an army of testees we could build up. At that point we hit upon a bold plan. We created our putative mentor, Horselover, and with him exchanged messages–meant to be intercepted by the Empire's watchdogs–warning of the military applications of Sensorama as a brainwashing machine. There is no scientist named Horselover. The plan was carried out at my instructions.

The arrest of Charles was a development that we had anticipated. It proved impossible, employing the technologies at our disposal, to manipulate at will the mnemonic powers of human subjects. With great subtlety Charles acted out his role as the collaborator who redesigns the Version II Sensorama to serve as the Empire's brainwashing machine.

The results of radiation experiments conducted on drugged subjects are largely dependent on the psychic condition and subconscious content of the individual's mind. The convicts suffered a temporary psychic shock, but they did not lose their memories nor did they suffer damage to the nervous system. Each quietly waited for the message to be unlocked by our key.

Unfortunately, we were compelled to abandon this plan. It was not fear of the consequences; a circumstance arose that made the plan meaningless.

John MacNaughton, formerly of the Academy, is a trained astronomer. Through the intercession of an old friend, he has for the past year been observing a cluster of comets.

We are faced with the worst possible situation. According to John's calculations, roughly one year from now the nucleus of this comet cluster will collide with earth. The end draws near. There is no escape.

Using the persona of Horselover I have warned the Party Chairman of the Socialist Republic. What the Republic will do with this information is no concern of ours.

However, we do feel an obligation to be honest with the citizens of the Empire. It is for this reason that we have decided to tell you all.

We have no illusions about the consequences of appealing directly to Orlovsky. We lodge all our hopes in you. It is unlikely that you will ever see us again.

Respectfully and expectantly yours,
George Tessera

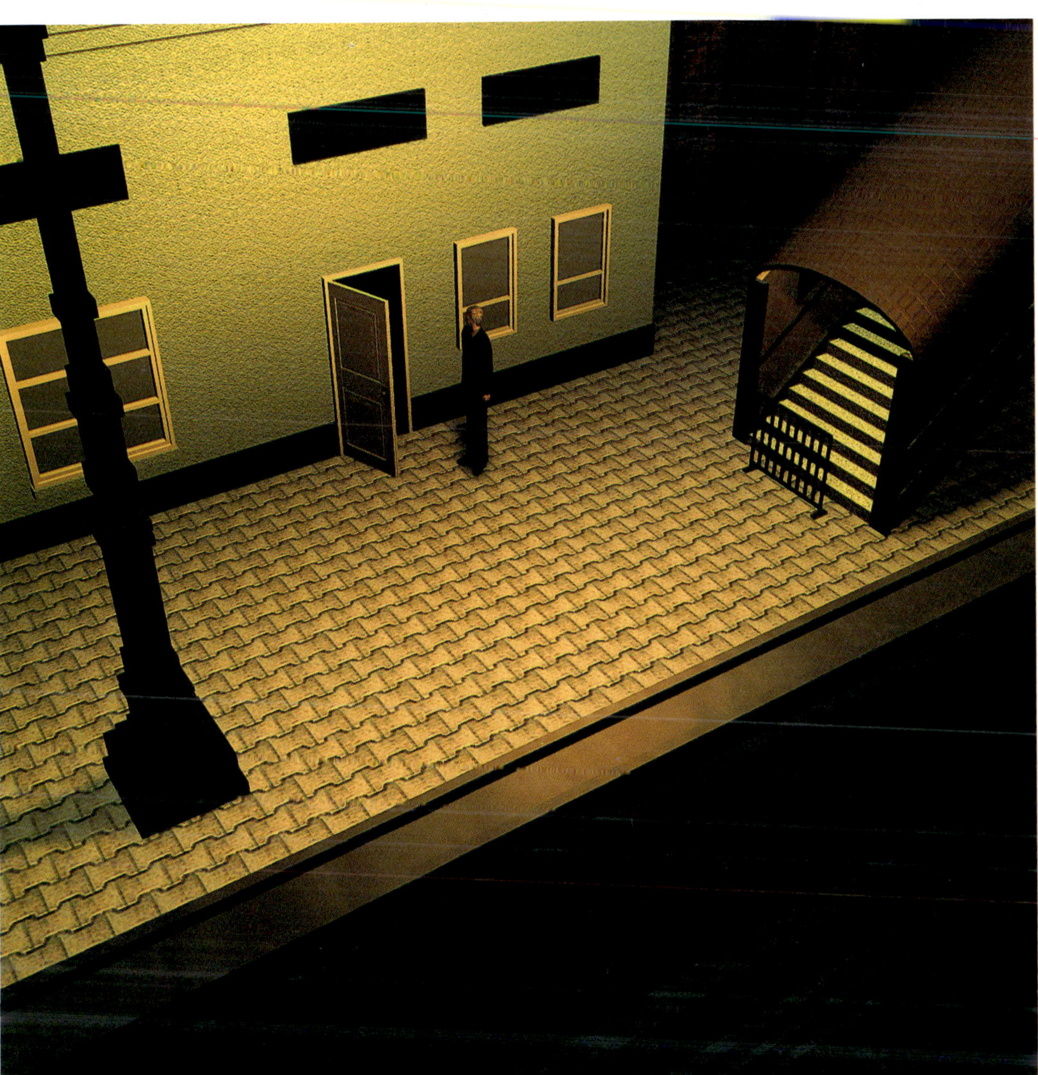

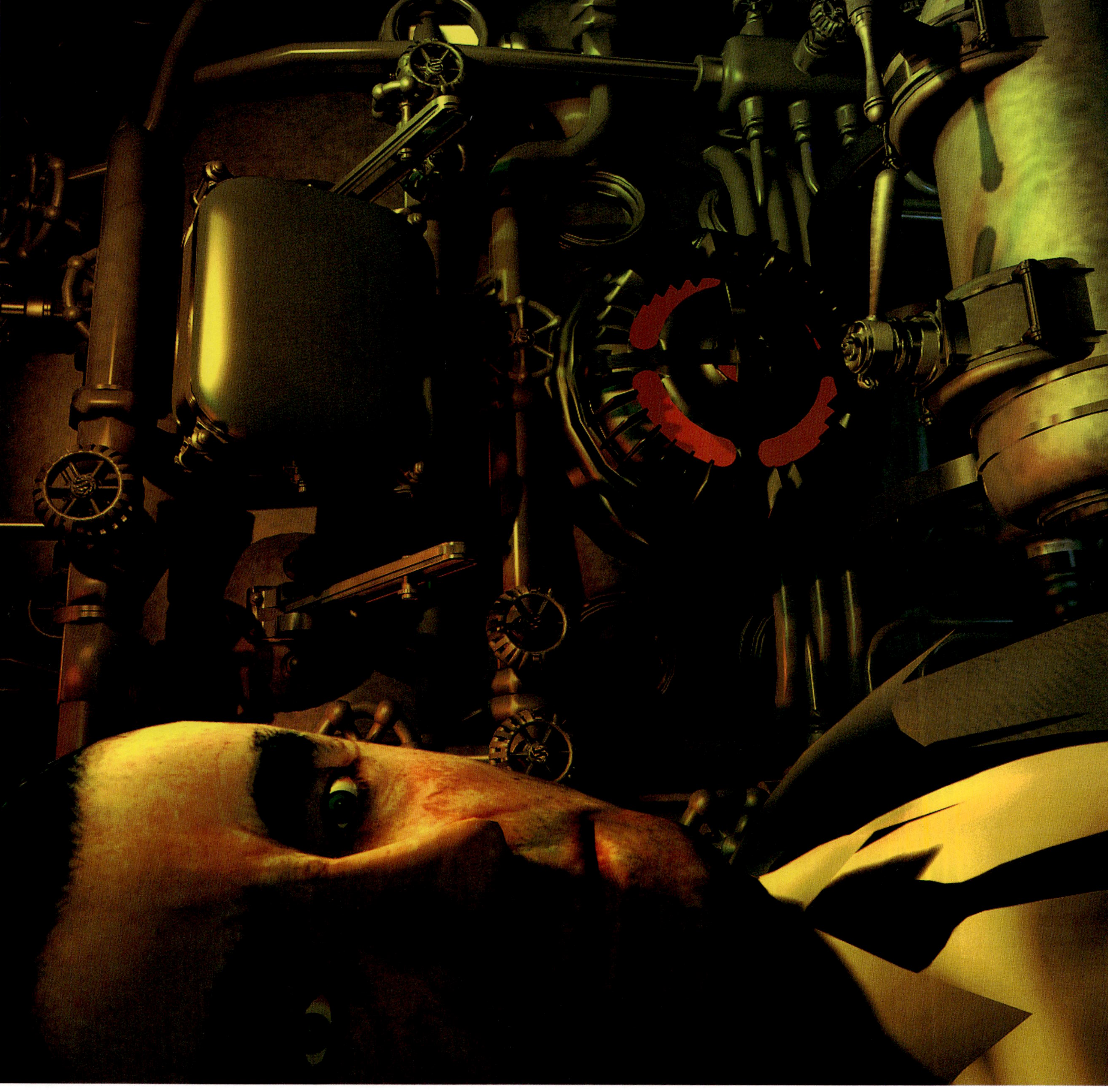

From eyeball to planet
No exit, no entrance
A loss of memory, or just its lack
Hear the machine engage, hear the response
Feelers of madness tickle the skull
Scintillating crystals of ore scale off
Mind and body split
Slowslop dismantled
And still Sensorama goes round and round

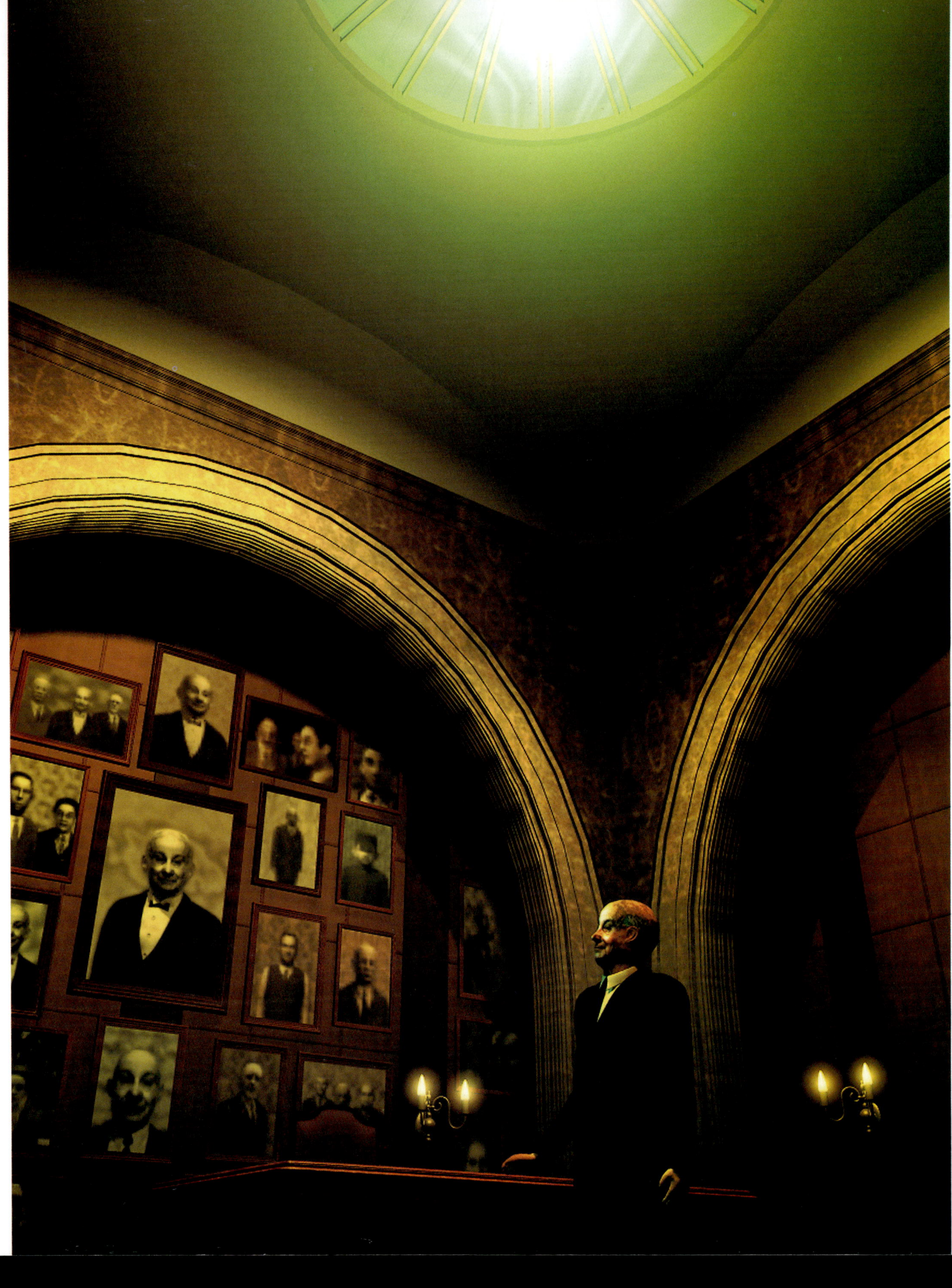

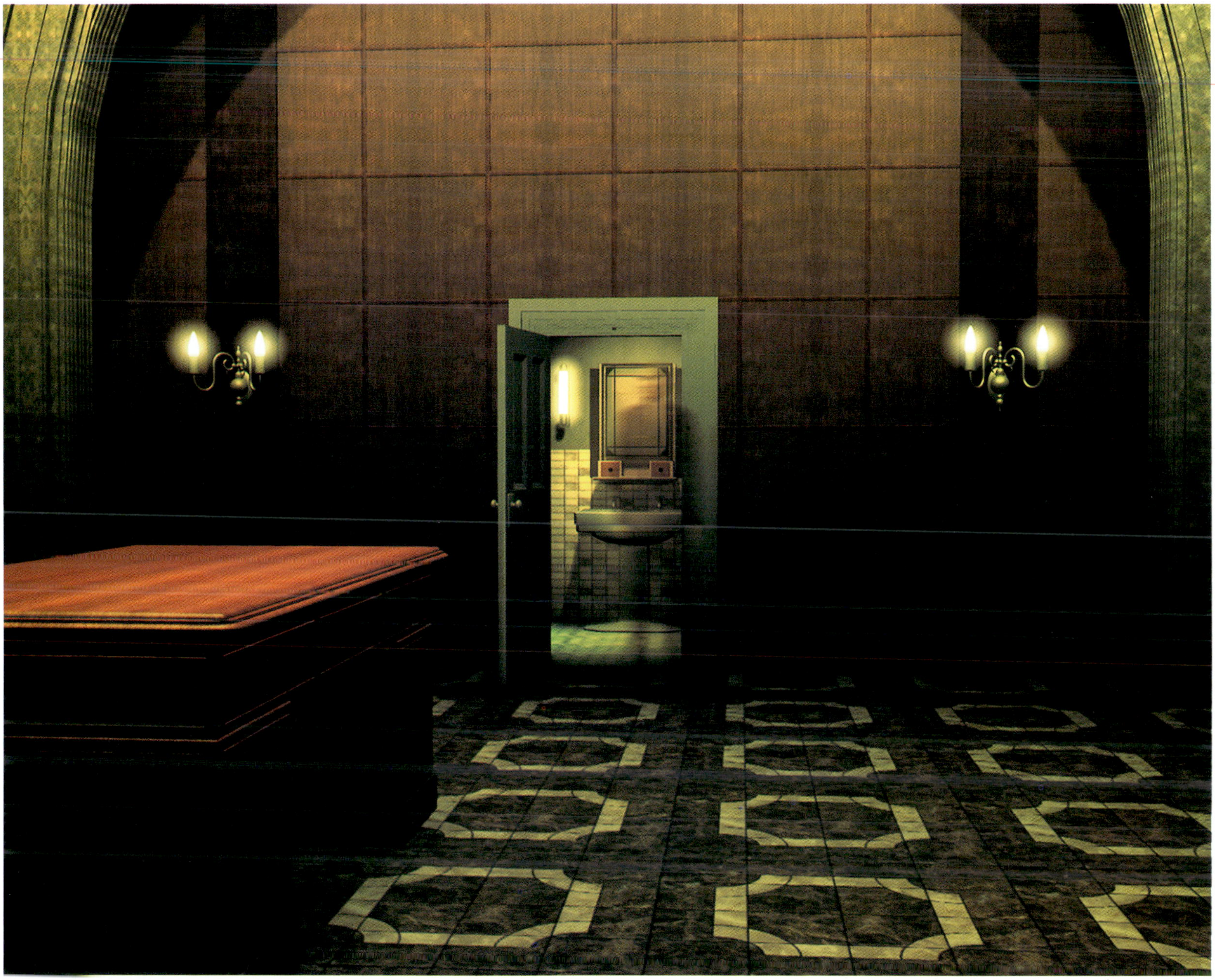

Year 12 of the Imperial Age

From eyeball to planet

Pale gray eyes stare into the void. Rigid body and face and skin. In the lavatory of an office at Army Intelligence Headquarters, a lead-gray corpse has been discovered. The discolored body of the Dictator. The corporeal substance of the Empire, gone forever.

No exit, no entrance

Imperial Guards place Slowslop in custody. Put him through three days of intensive interrogation in Room 305. A man of iron will, he keeps absolute silence. The attending physician injects truth serum hypodermically. Still does the Supreme Commander deny all.

A loss of memory, or just its lack

Interrogation and torture. He admits the existence of a plot for revolution. He denies the assassination of Orlovsky. The Imperial Guards decide to use the brainwashing machine. Sensorama in 306 now activated. A dissonant noise severs a fading consciousness.

Hear the machine engage, hear the response

The Version II starts up. Shafts of blue-white light. A locomotive's headlamp blinks on and off. Noise of the crowd, calling off of names, scream of metal on metal; explosions ring in raucous cacophony from the platform roof. Heartbeat keeps pace with hurtling locomotive.

Feelers of madness tickle the skull

On awakening he denies Orlovsky's murder, and the Guards resume electromagnetic radiation. Supreme Commander Slowslop begins to weaken. His patterns of thought now dysfunction. The Empire's audiovisual unlearning machine takes everything there is to be had.

Scintillating crystals of ore scale off

As it revolves there comes slowly before the eyes a skull-shaped piece of ore. Flaking crystal. A clotted sound, a metallic noise. Light-emitting crystal. From far off in the distance comes march music, army on parade. The Empire's red flag ripples in the wind.

Mind and body split

Gadgets scattered in the forest. Rusty metal, ore capsules. In the crimson sky floats the shadow of a diminutive being. A cloudburst beats down on the surface of a pool. Soil carried away. Torrents of muddy water. Iridescent patch of oil. Abandoned locomotive.

Slowslop dismantled

The Supreme Commander admits the crime. His motive unknown. The Guards continue their efforts to extract a confession. Into his dilated pupils a beam at peak power. Encircling the cerebrum, blue-white electromagnetic waves. A halo of light about his skull.

And still the Sensorama goes round and round

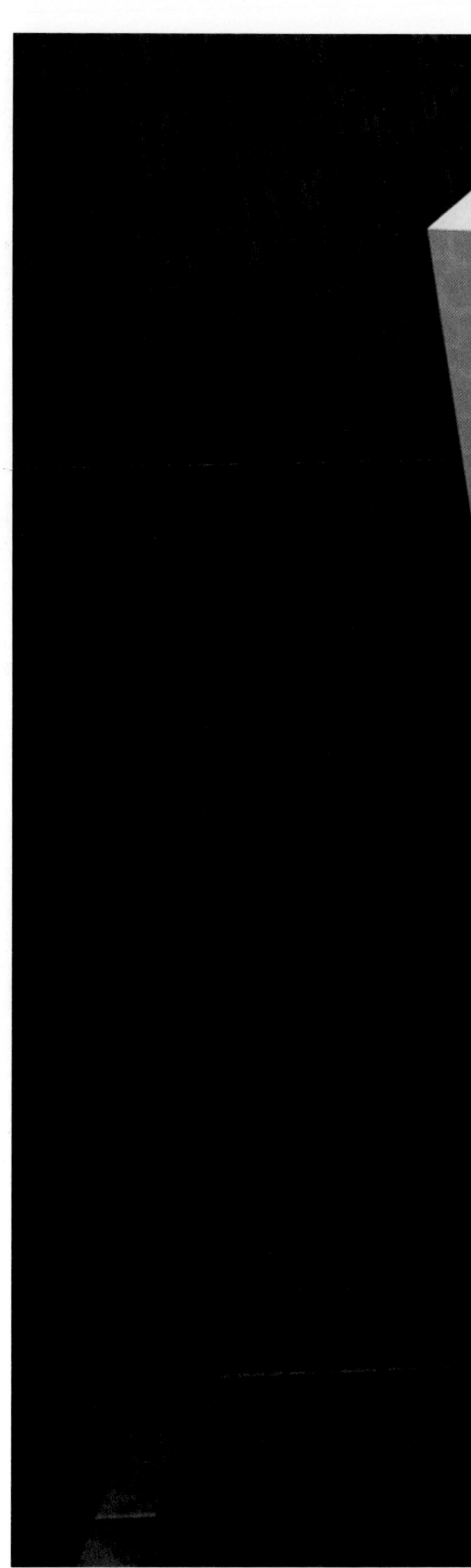

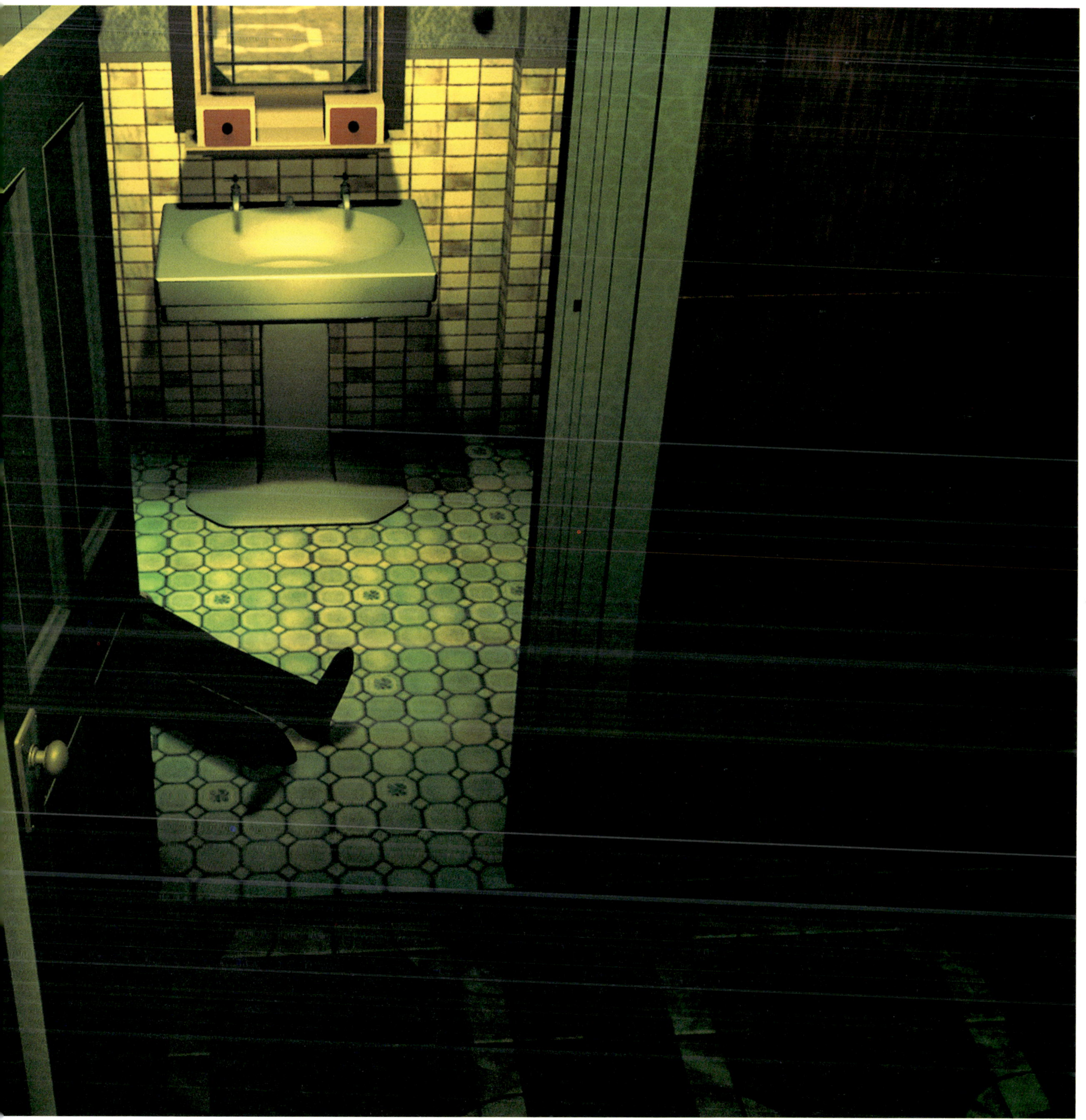

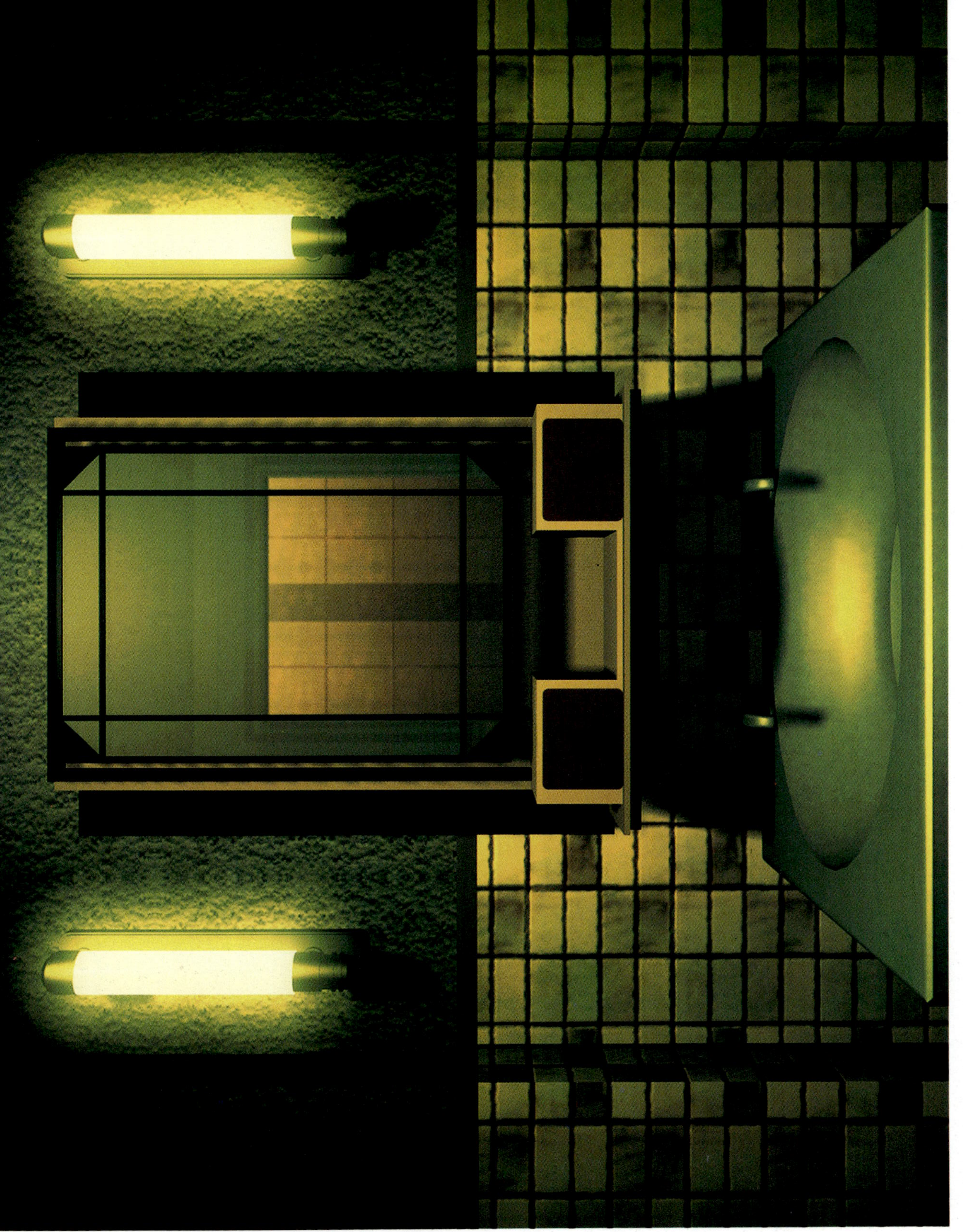

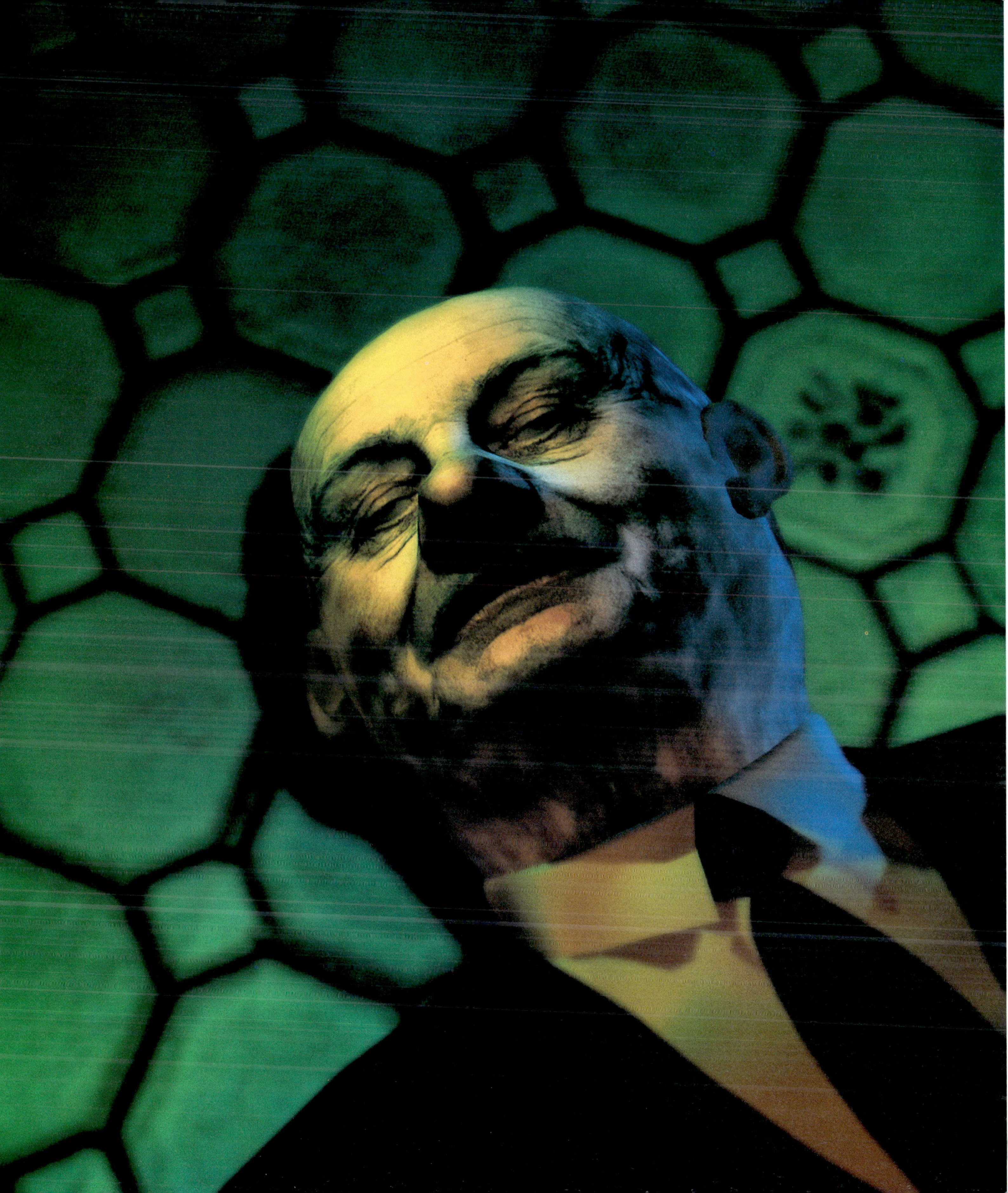

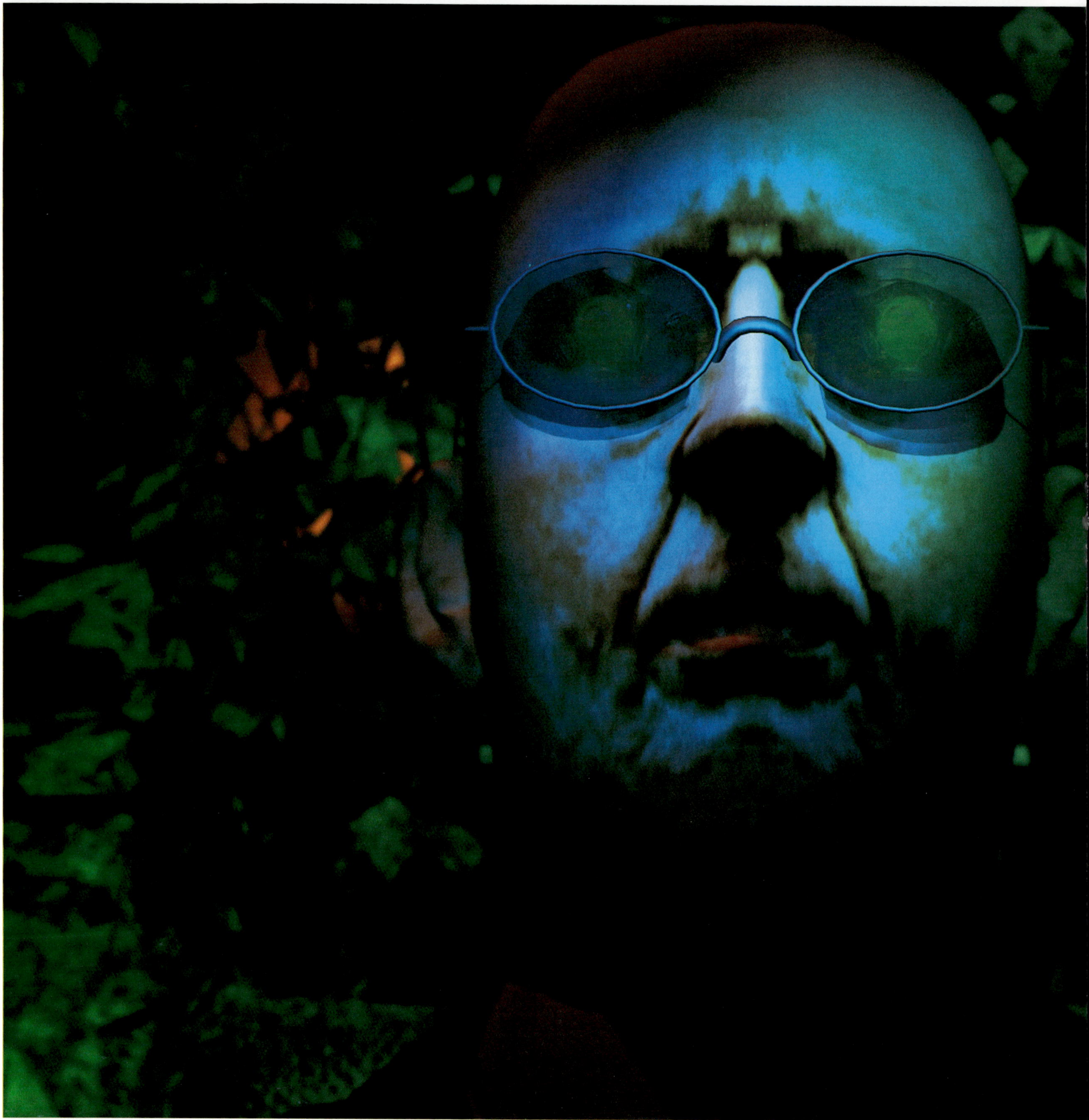

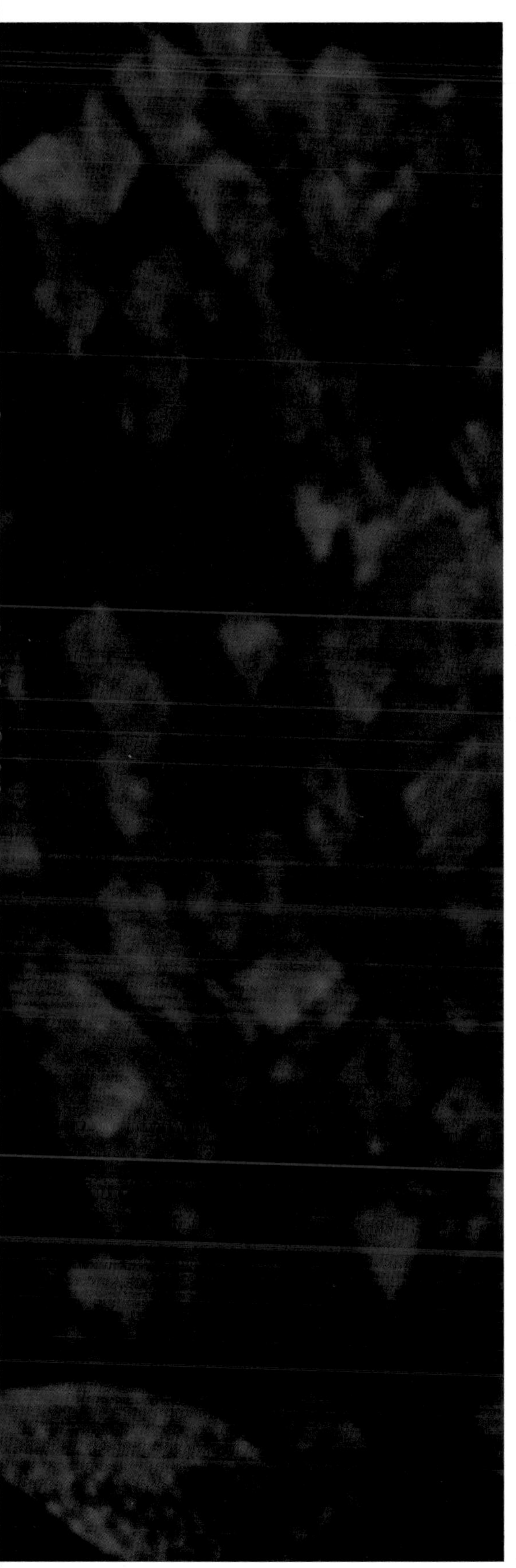

Orlovsky has breathed his last.

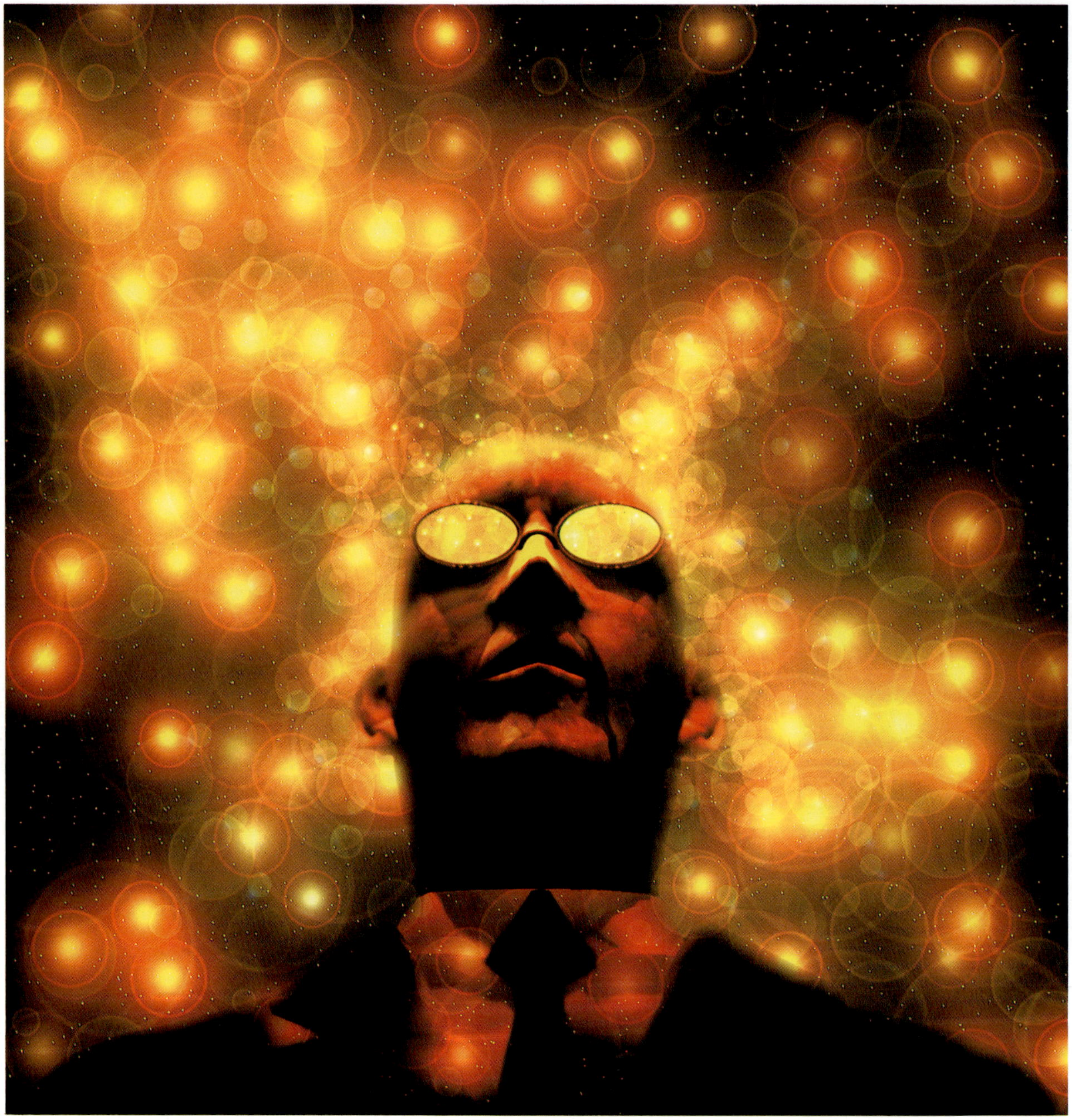

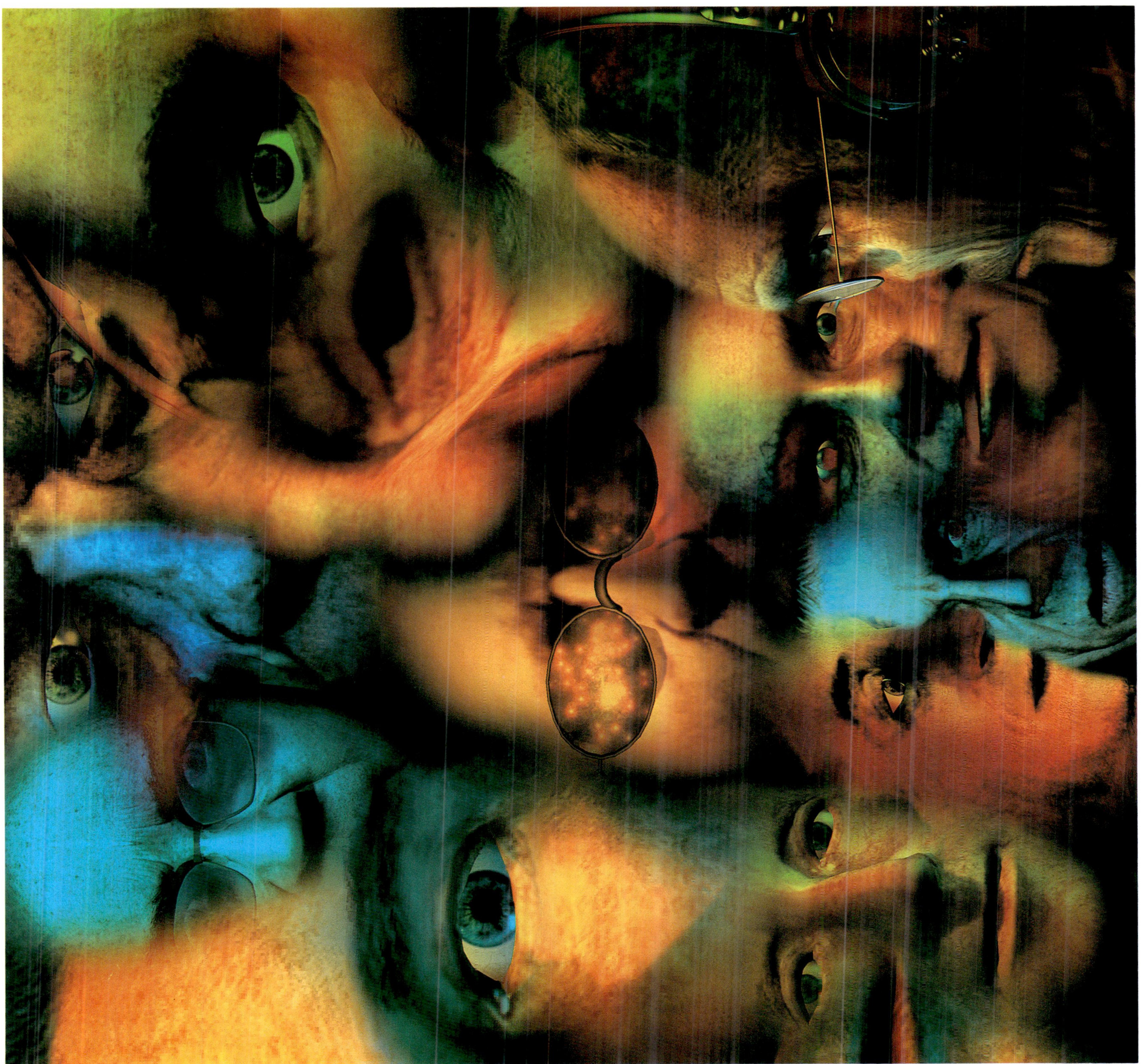

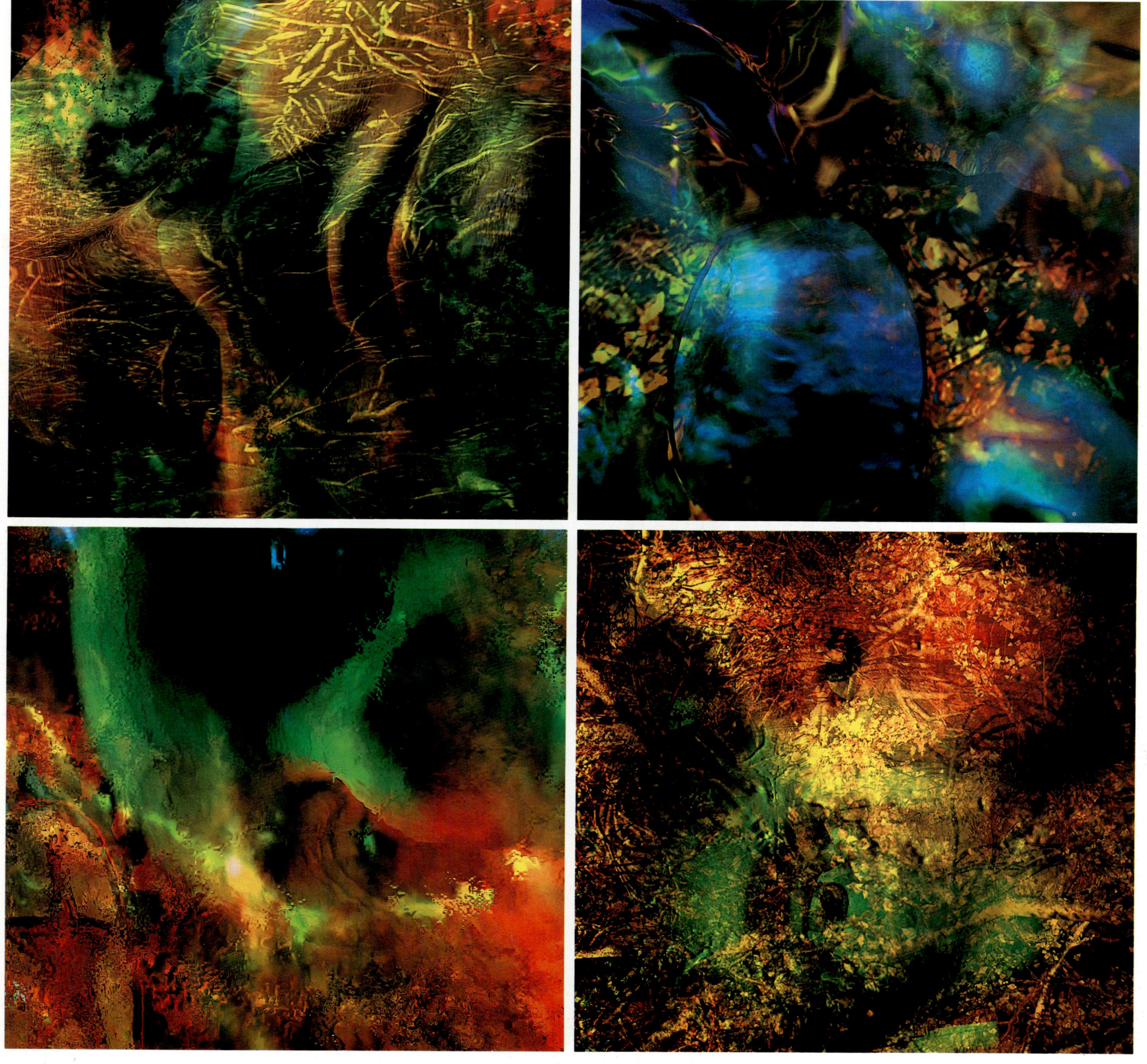

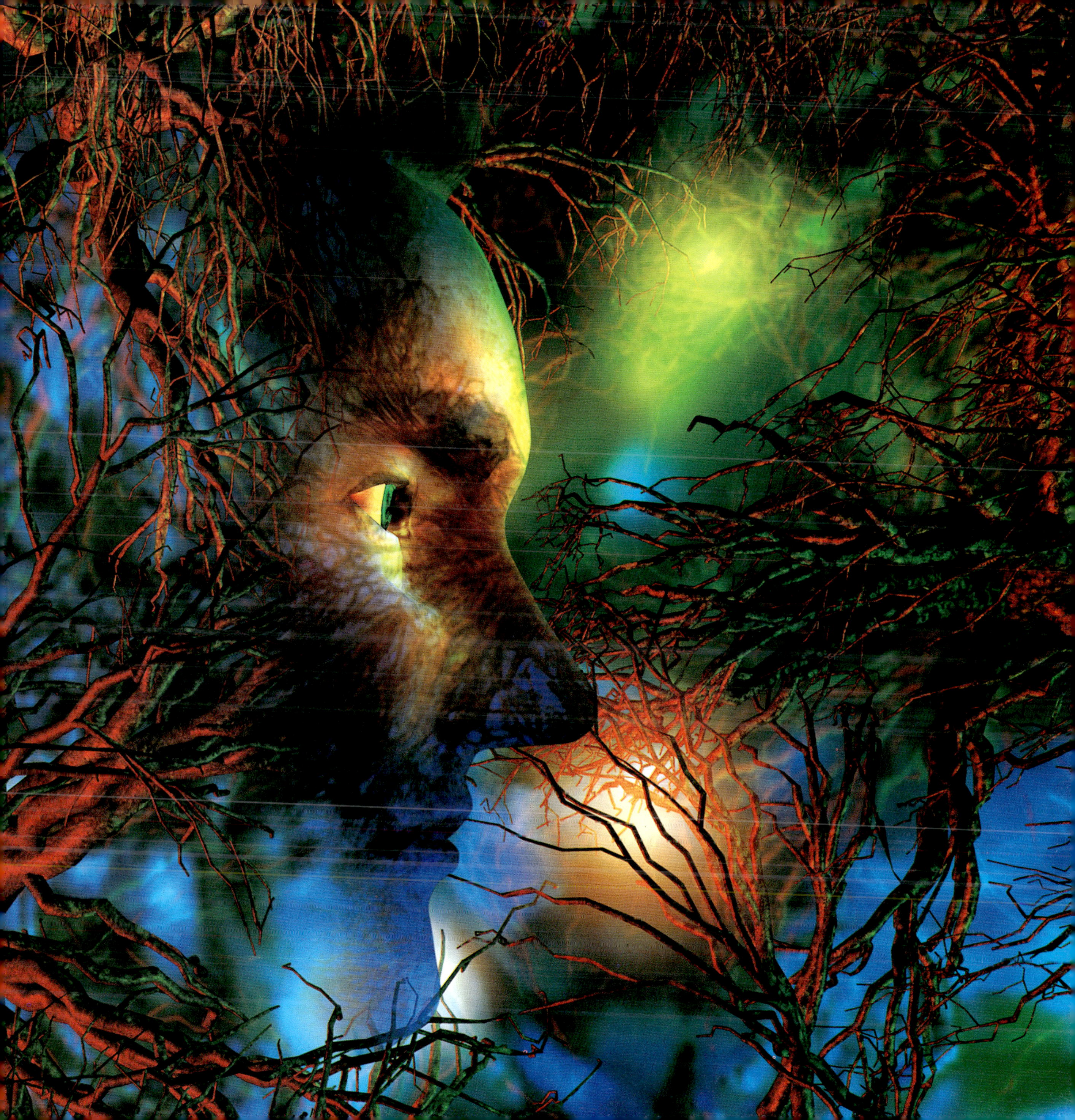

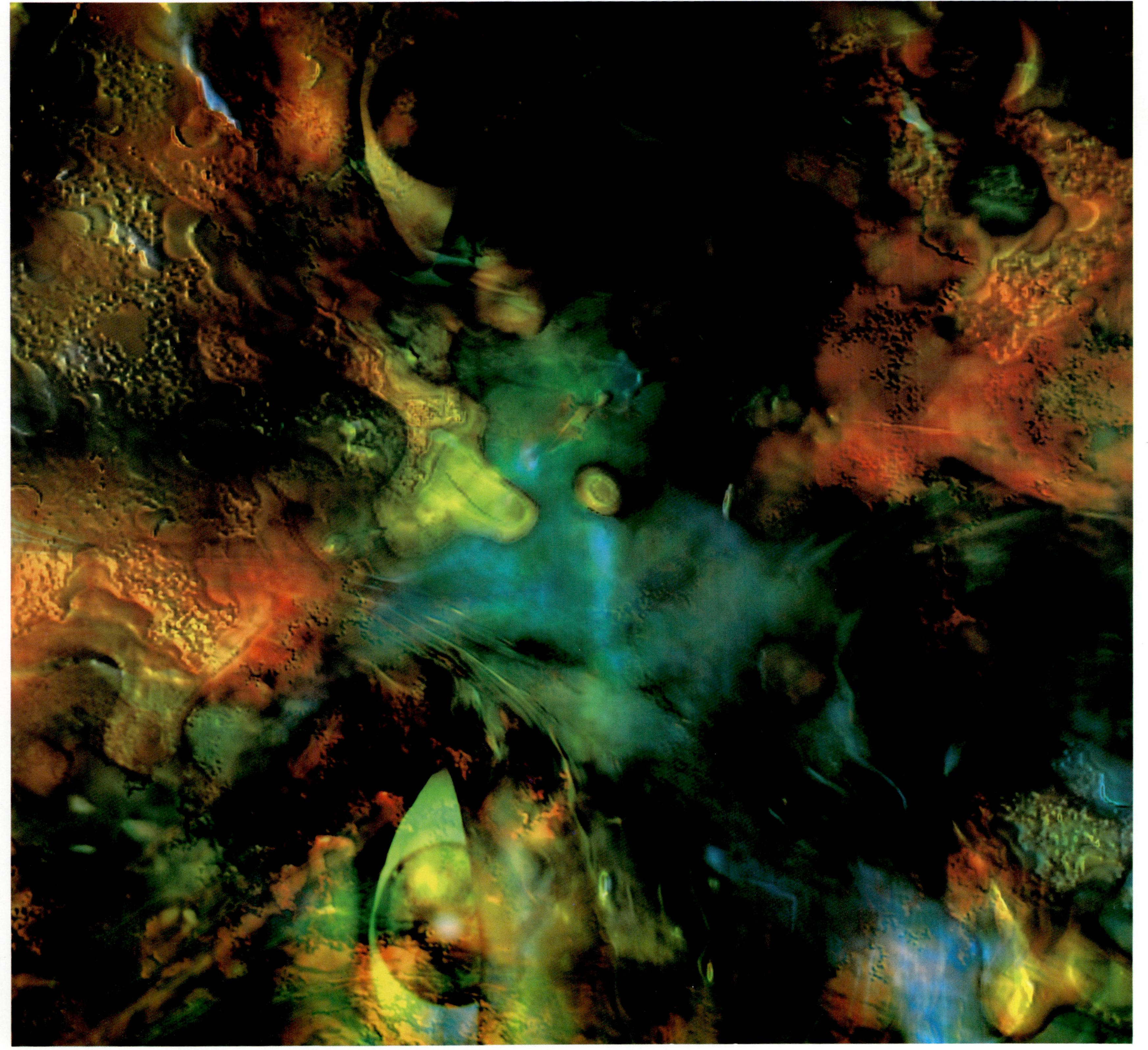

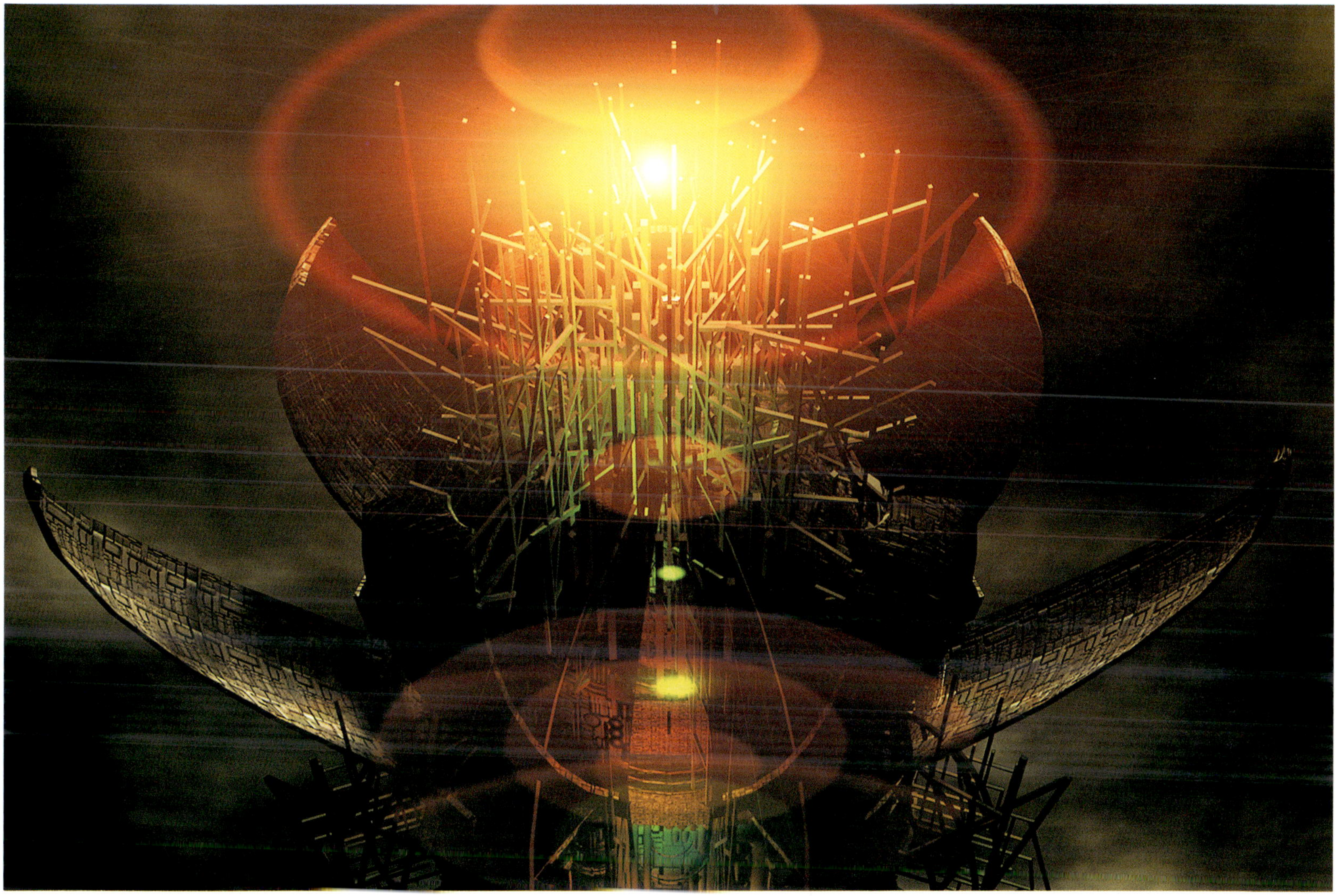

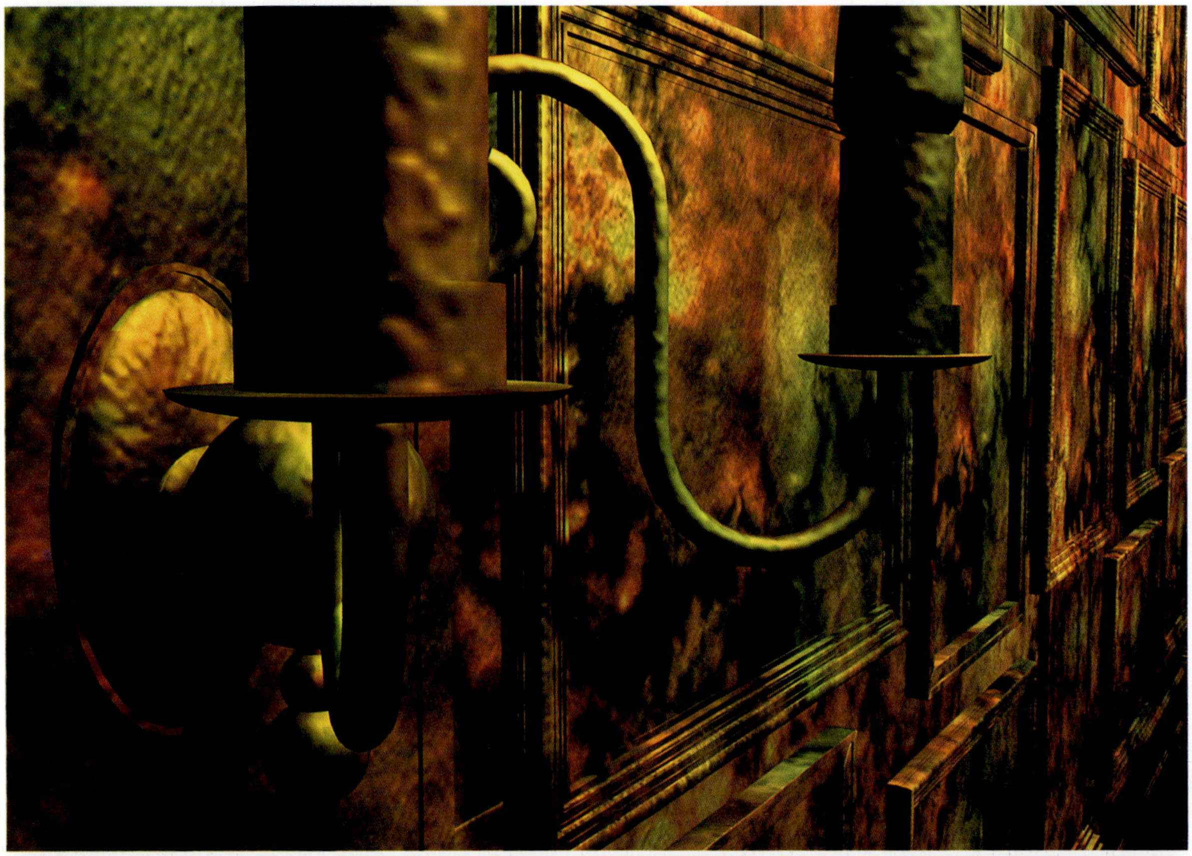

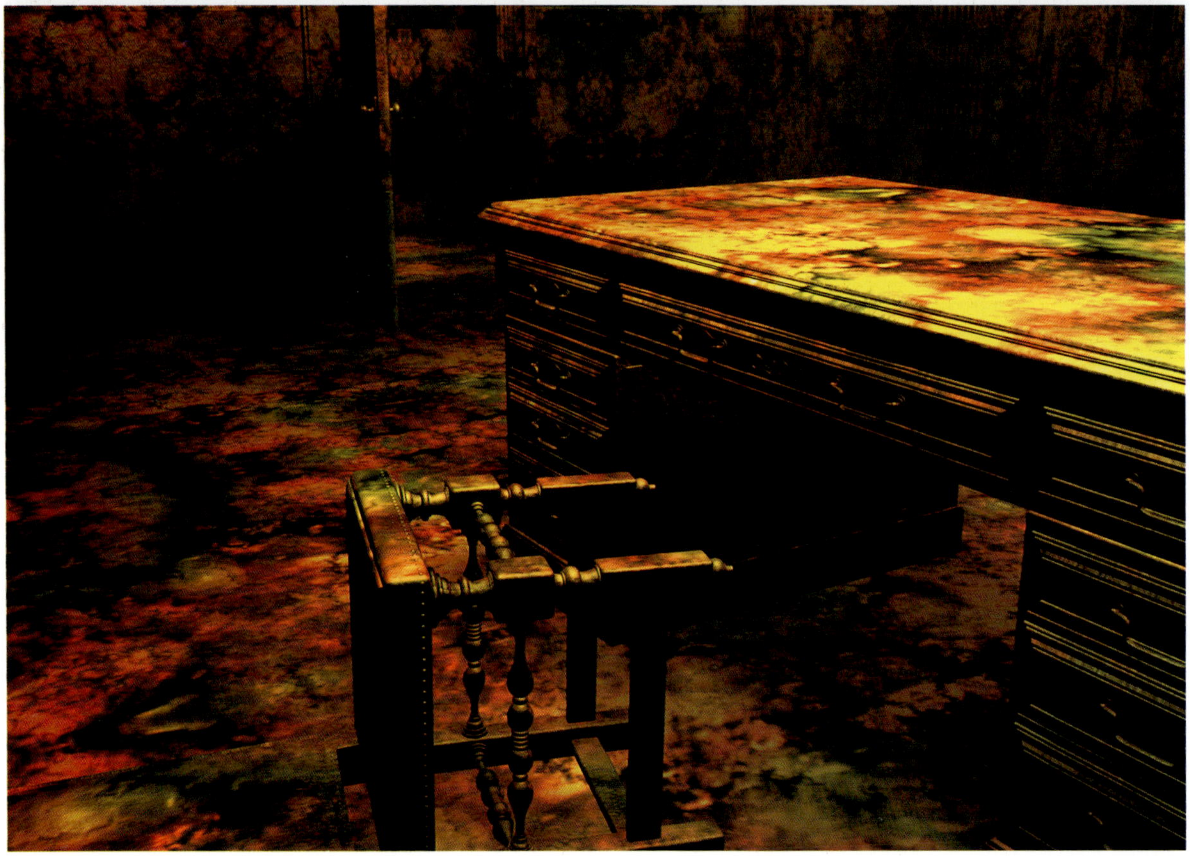

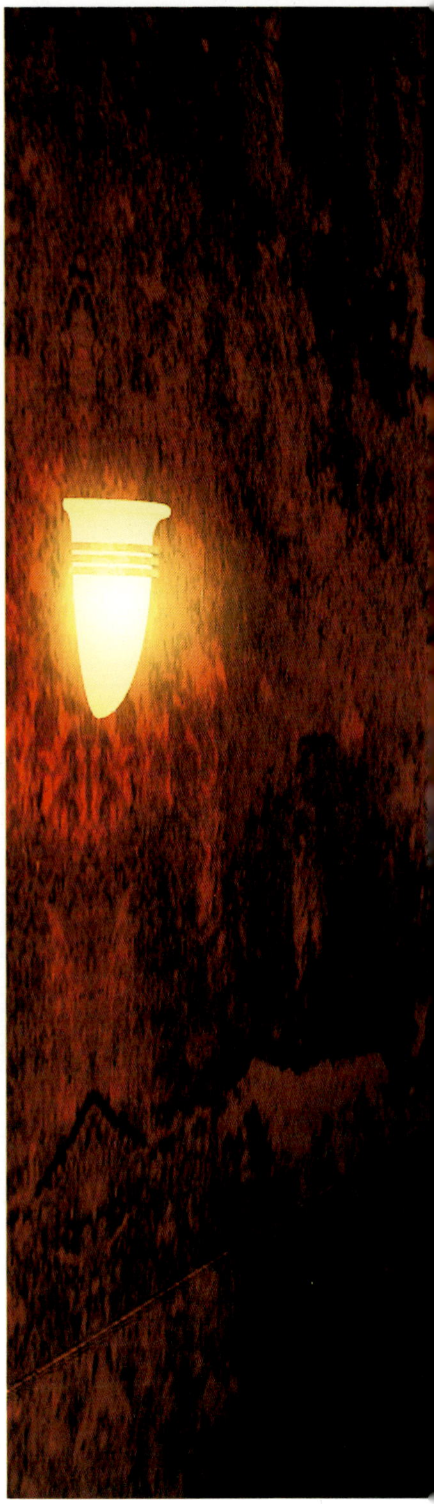

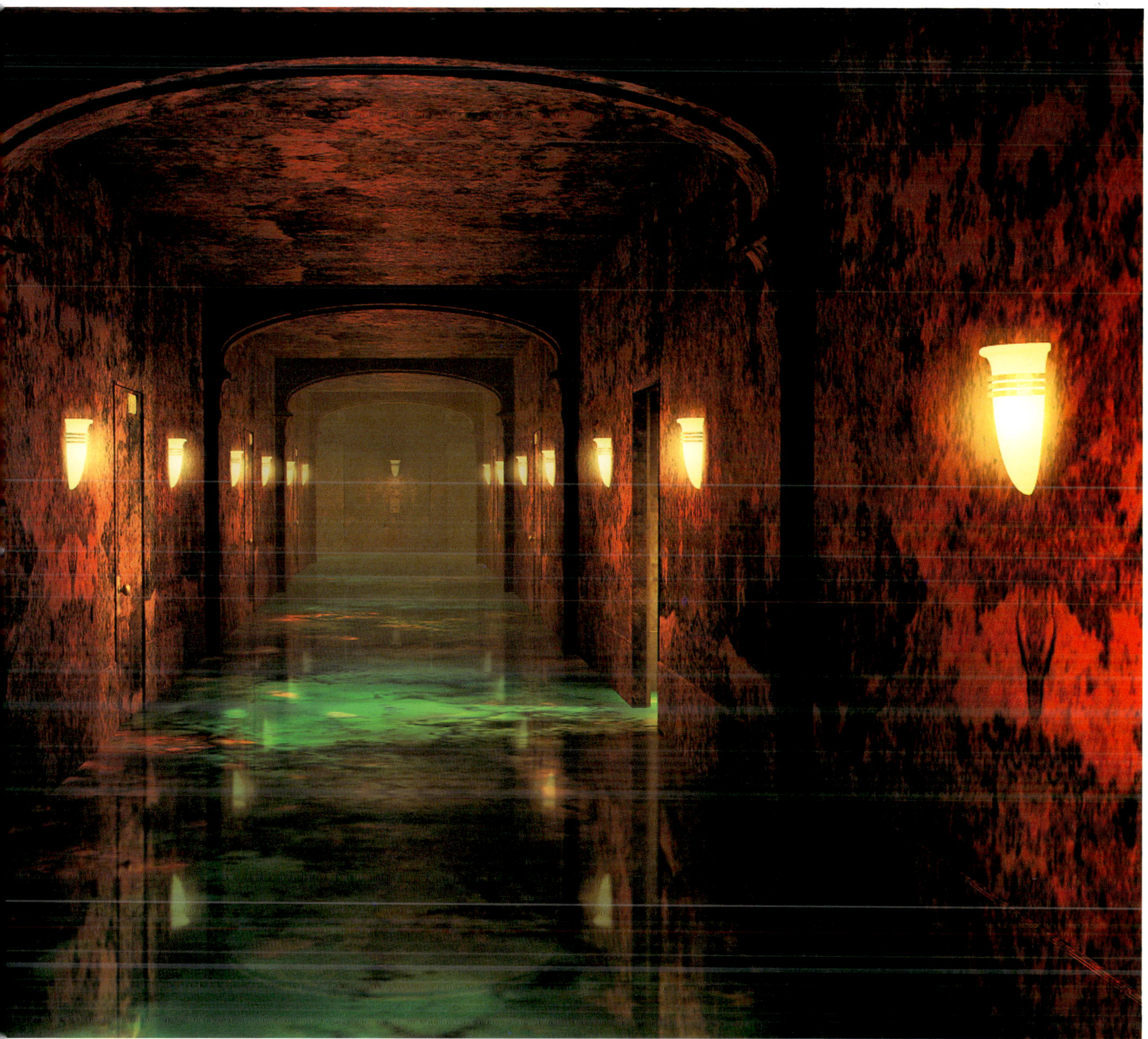

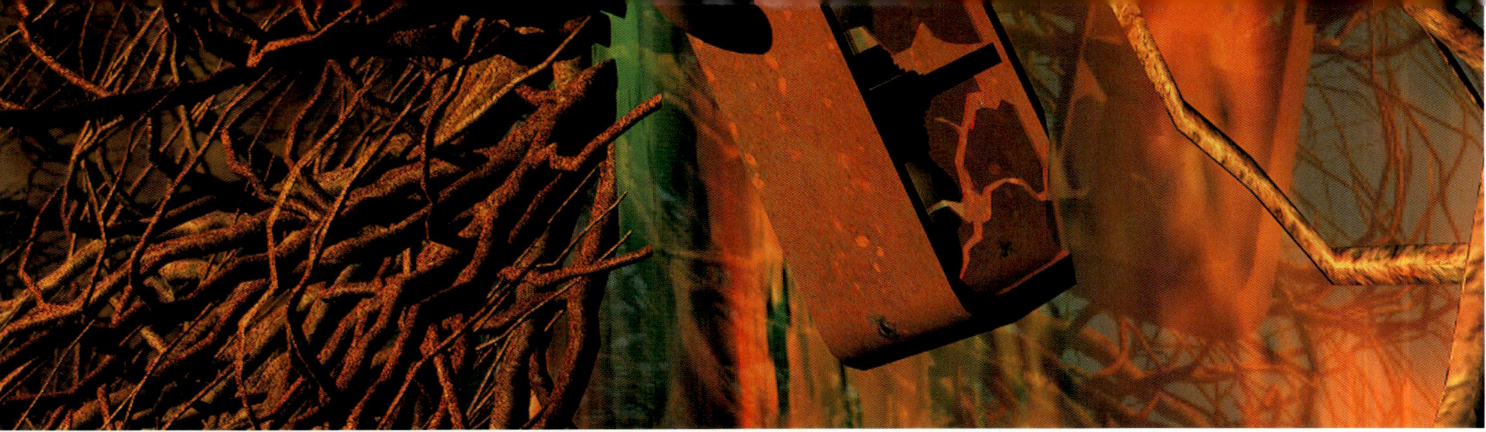

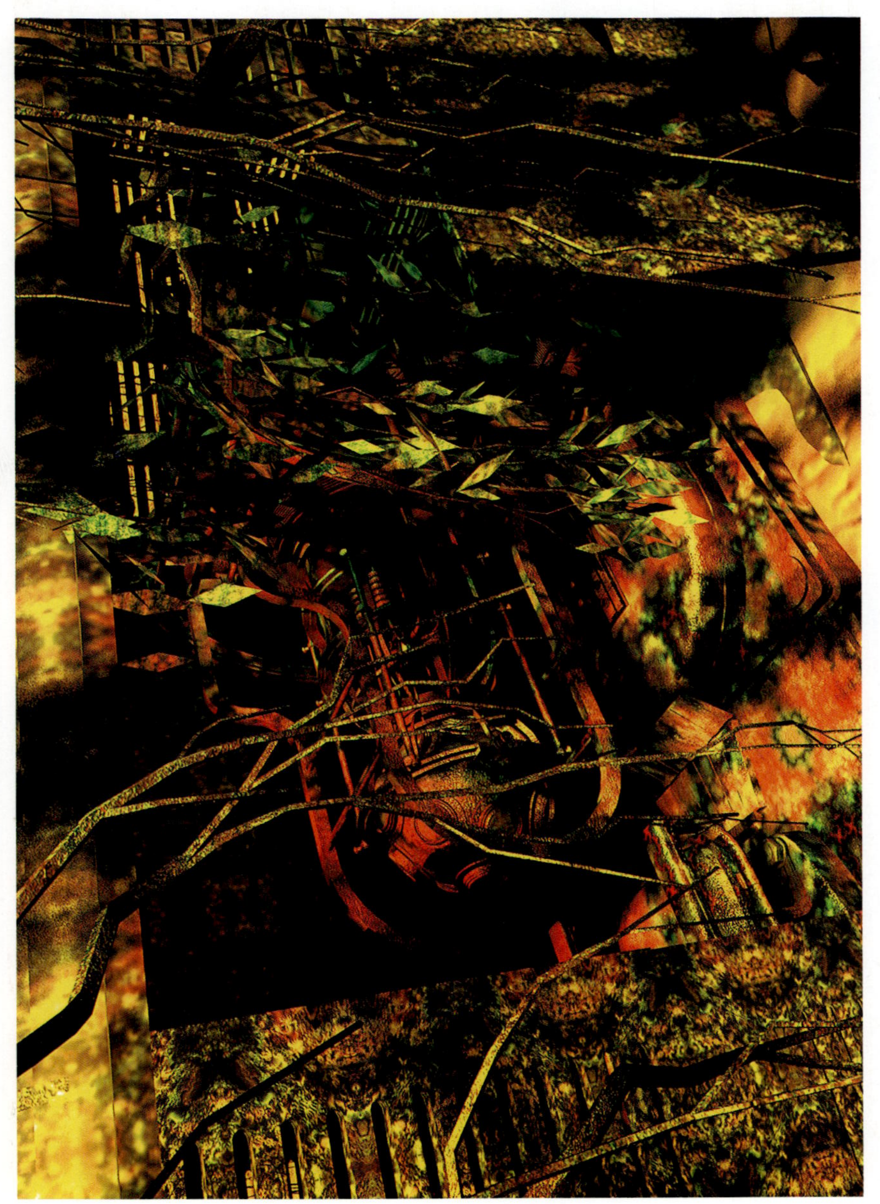

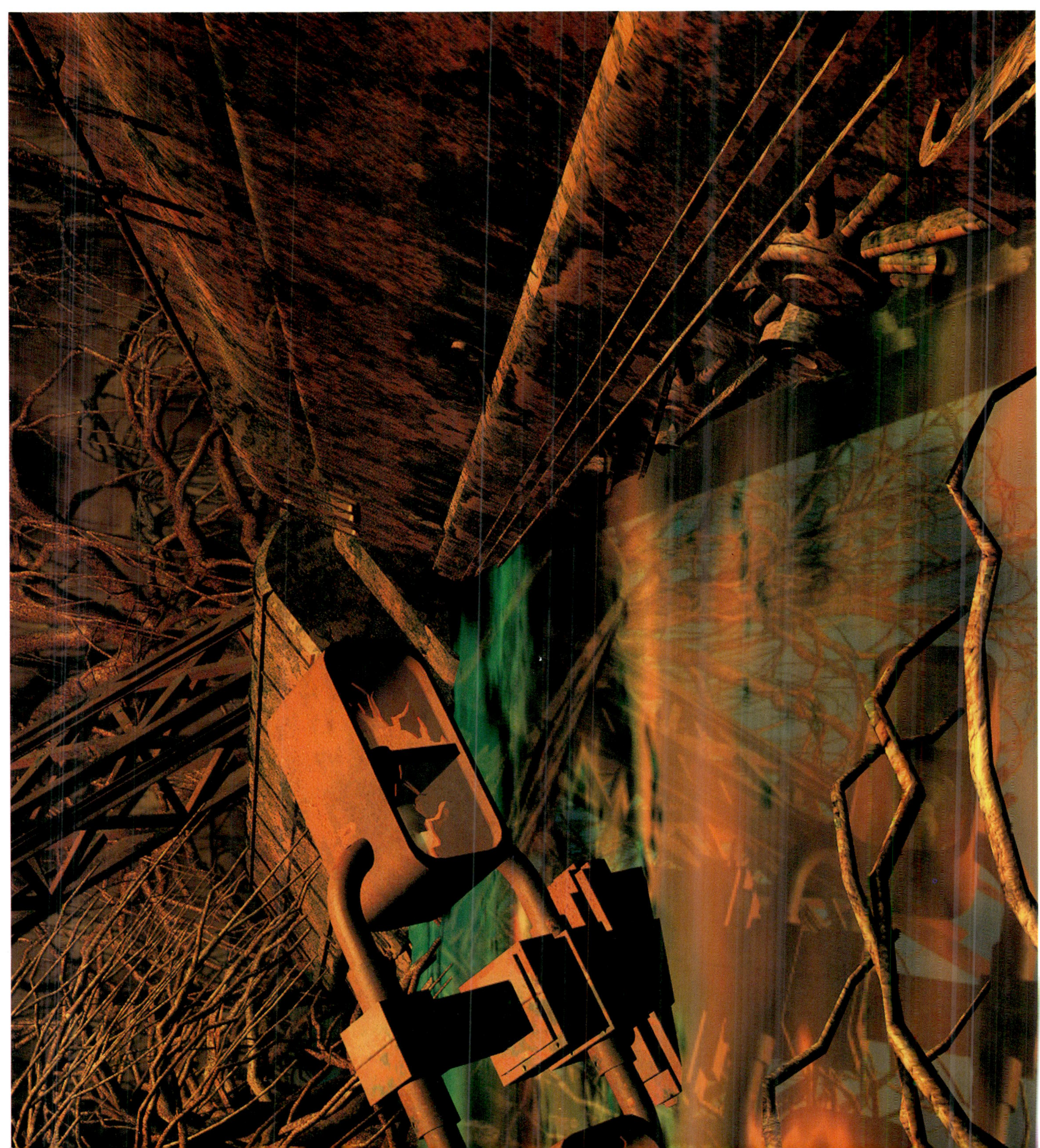

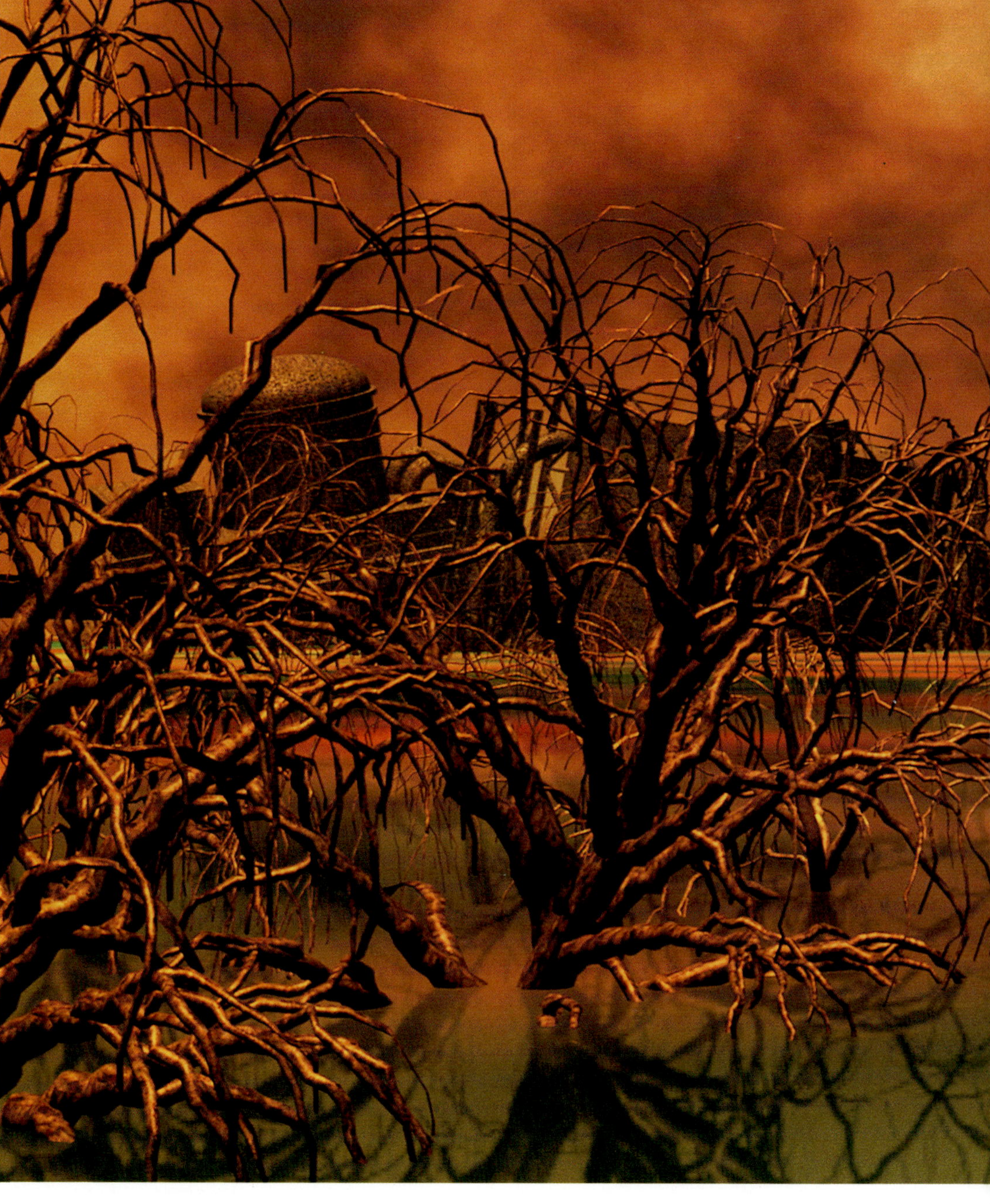

22 February, Year 12 of the Imperial Age

The relationship that one world maintains with another world is a matter of no interest to me. It seems to have all happened in the distant past.

I gave George's letter to Slowslop. He didn't believe a word of it. I, who was privy to all the secrets of Army Intelligence, was suspected of reactionary tendencies and sent to Room 306.

All kinds of images float in the blinding light. Fragments of memory break off and drop, drift about, fly off into the beyond. I had, of course, read George's letter, so I was able to endure the electromagnetic radiation with a measure of calm. I felt little physical pain.

After they finished with me I was released.

I got on the train and went all the way to East End. I found a room at a small inn and slept well that night. My intention was to stay there two or three days and try to sort things out.

On the third night I slipped out of the hotel and headed for intelligence headquarters in West End. I hid in the shadows, keeping out of sight of the guards. I know the headquarters building like the palm of my hand, so I waited until past midnight and then let myself in through Gondarev's old room. I went out into the corridor and down to the basement. That's where Orlovsky's office is. The door was unlocked. I opened it and went in. The overhead lights were off. Orlovsky was sitting in his chair bent over a report. I slipped around behind and strangled him. Then I opened the bathroom door and dragged in the corpse.

George gave up on the revolution. The real reason wasn't the comet. Somebody had to put a stop to it. Dictatorships just aren't right.

The next day the body was discovered. Slowslop was suspected. He managed to get away, but on the third day the Secret Police caught up with him and took him into custody. They put him on the Sensorama and interrogated him day after day. It's sure he ended up like Gondarev. I have no idea why I'm the only one released without a scratch.

On the seventh day I left the hotel and went looking for a house outside East End.

The days pass quietly. I have migraines but that's the worst of the aftereffects. Since the day I went on the Sensorama I've felt a sort of heaviness, like a mist inside my head, but I haven't lost my memory. I remember every detail of my past. I won't know about the hypnotic effects George mentioned until I see an airship in the sky.

Meteors reduced the Republic to ruins. It's impossible even to know if there were any survivors. Onegin has maintained silence. If George isn't mistaken, soon enough the whole world will vanish in a collision with the comet. Wrapped in a vague disquiet, I pass the days in idleness.

I walk in the woods. I stop...and think. How much is real? Where do my own memories begin? I cannot say if the green of trees that extends before my eyes or the rusting lightplane are illusions or not. Maybe I've already wandered into the realm of the mad.

Eyes are floating in the pool. On the lens are reflected the image of a planet. Gazing into the boy's unblinking eyes I await the instant that will be the last. When will it come?

(From the diary of Hausmann)

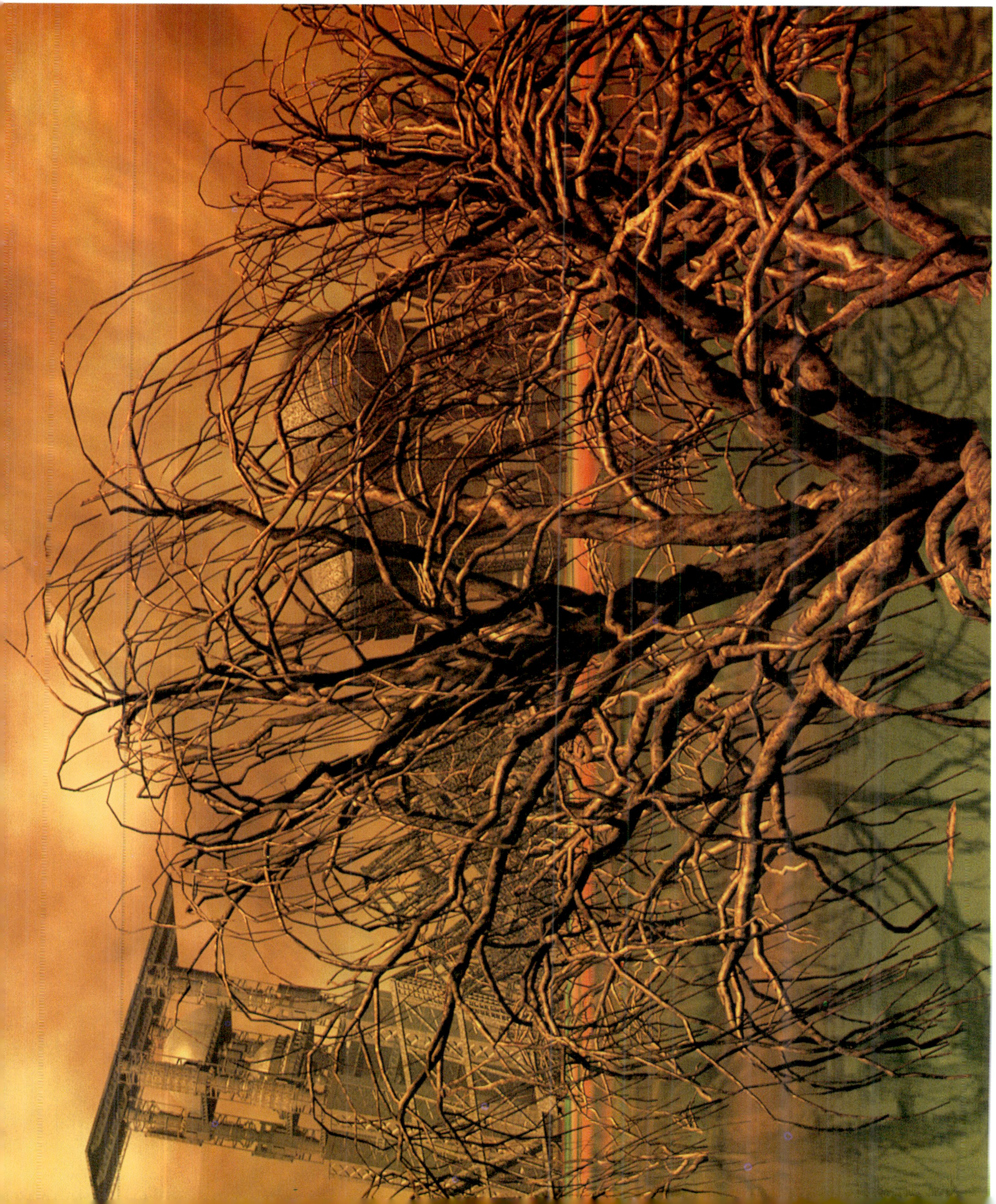

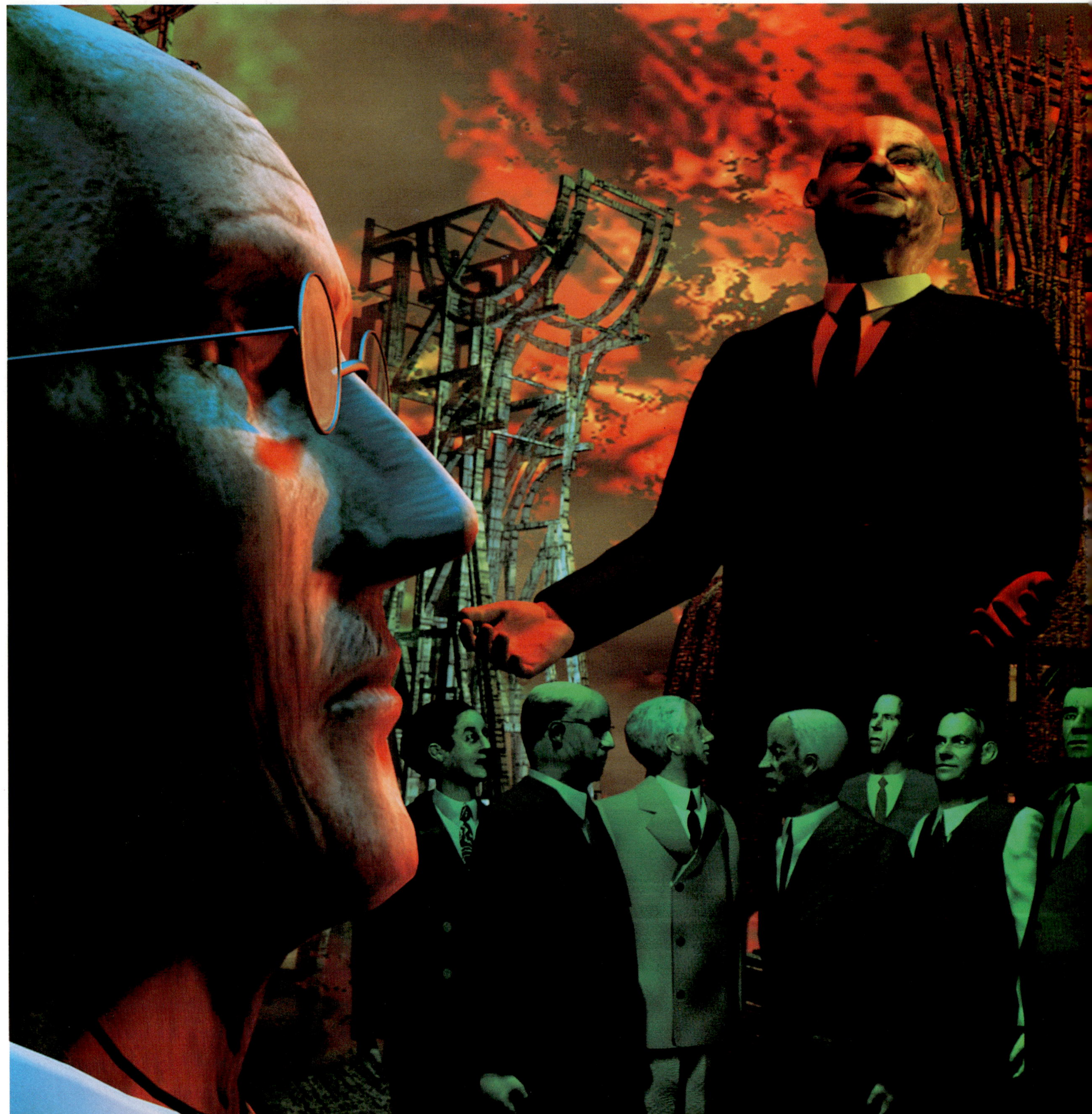

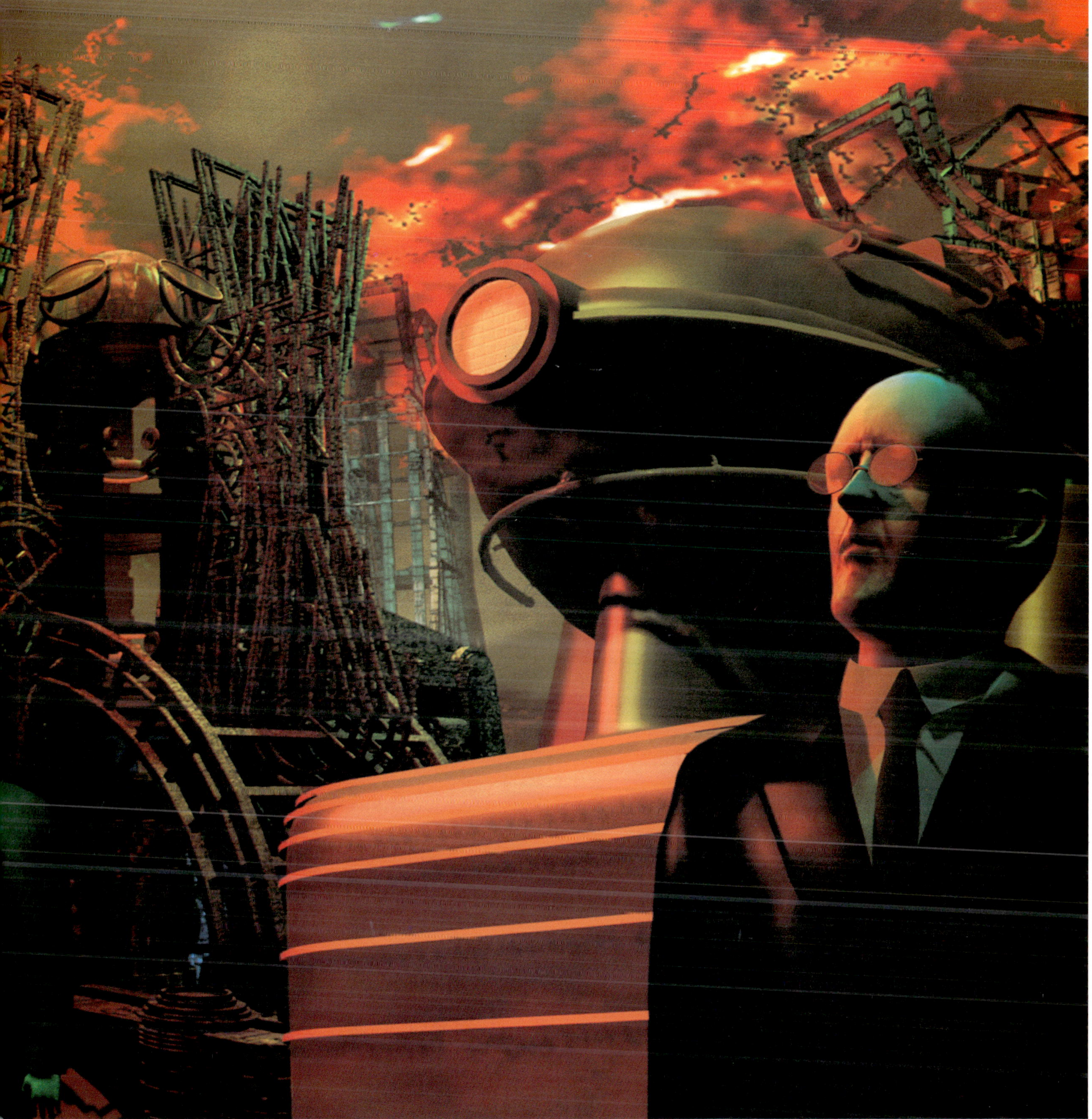

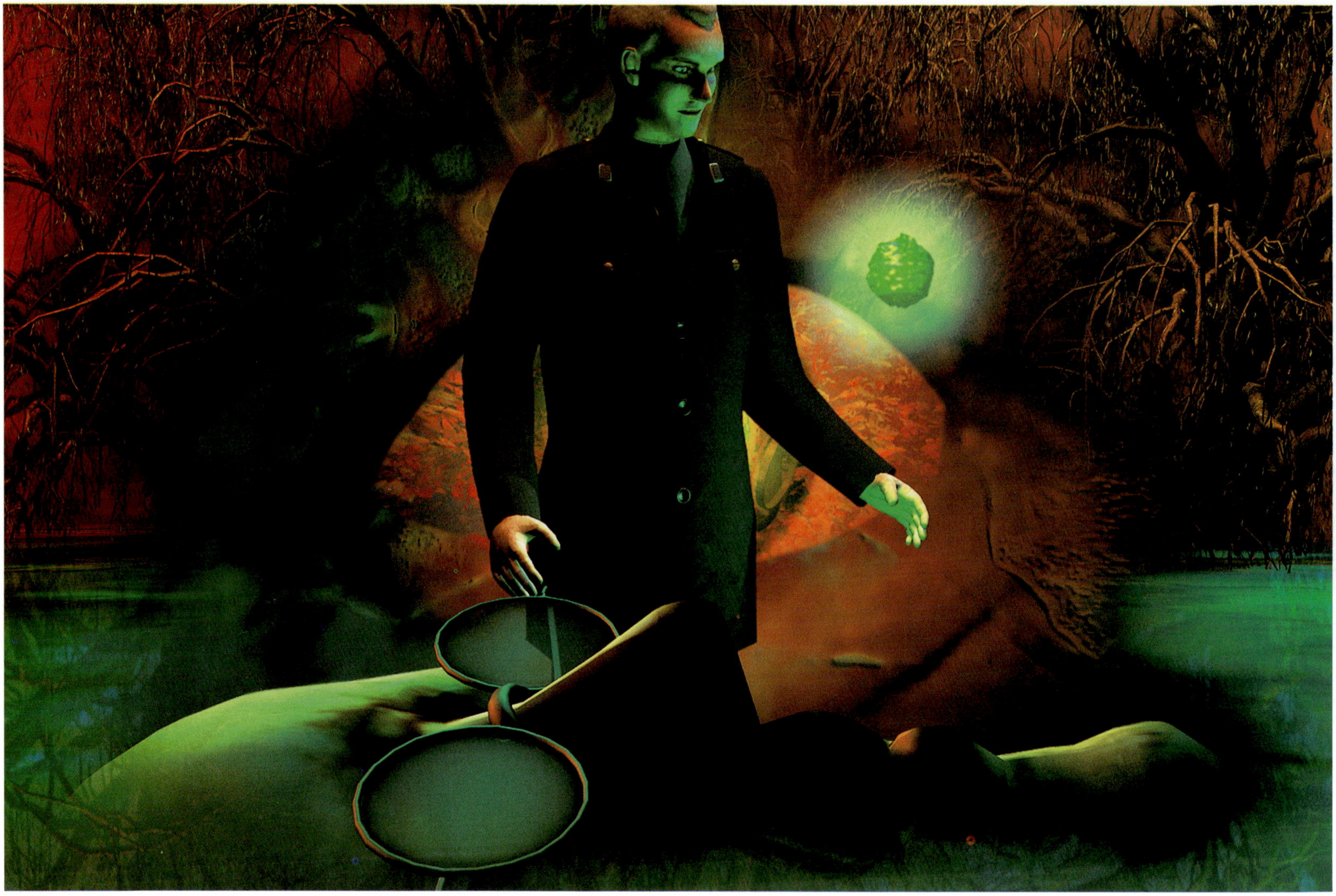

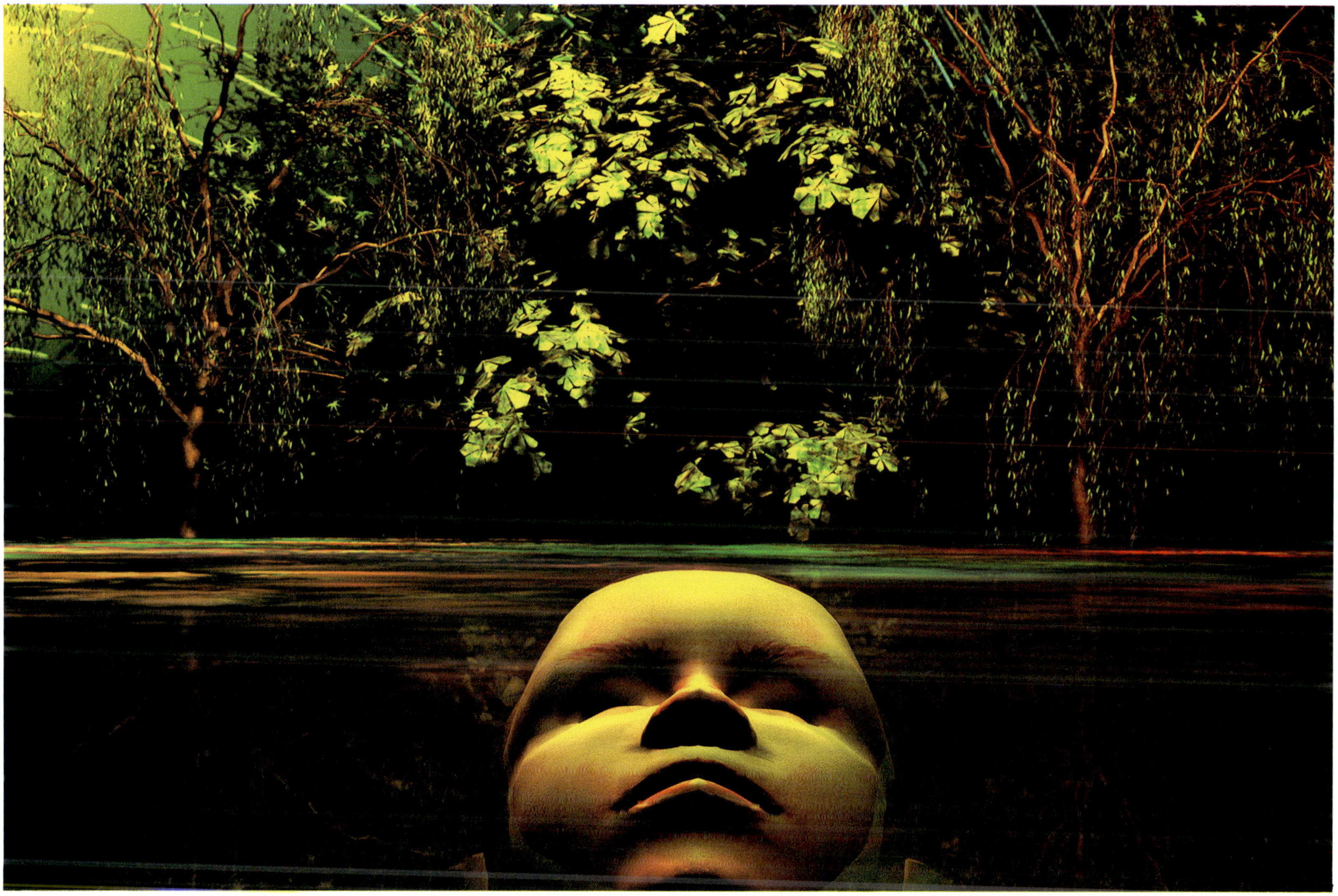

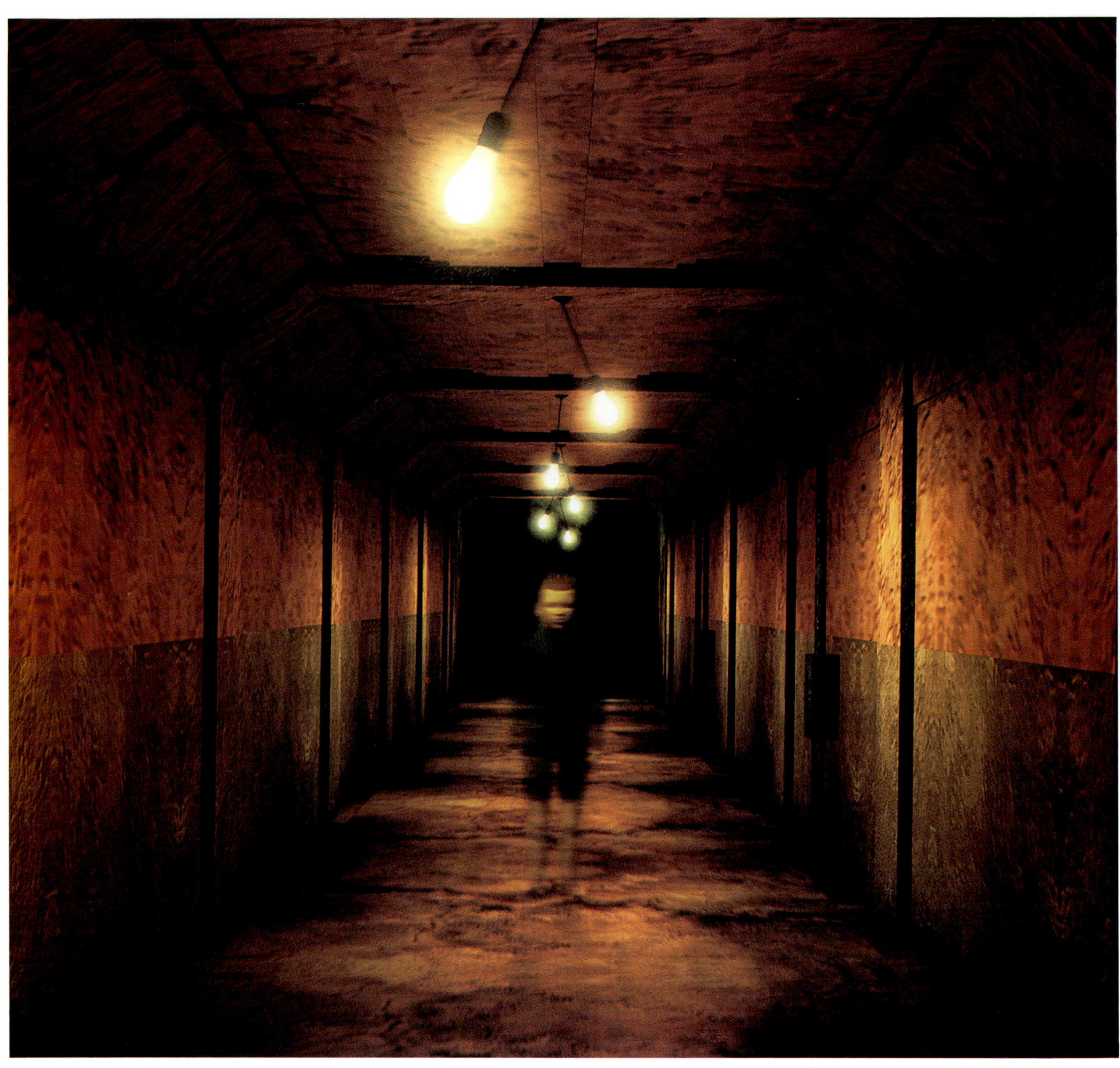

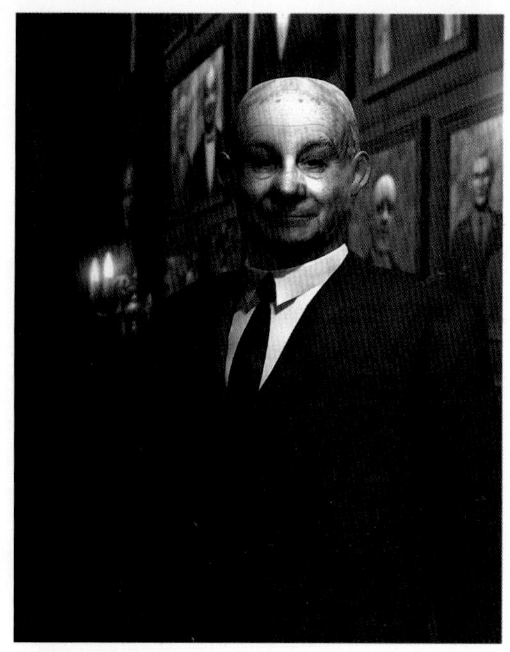

Paulo Orlovsky

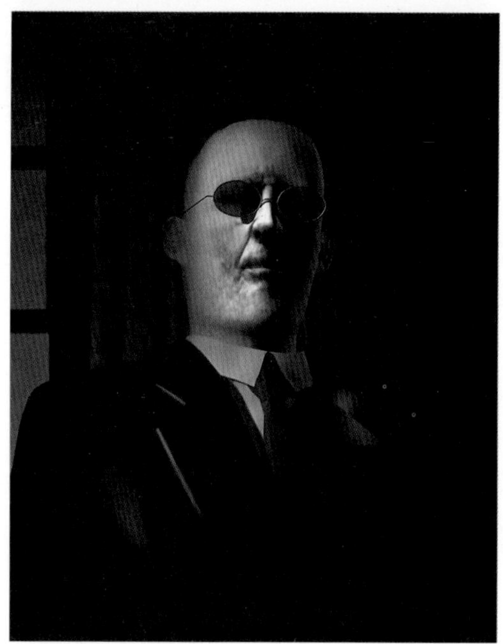

Theodore Slowslop

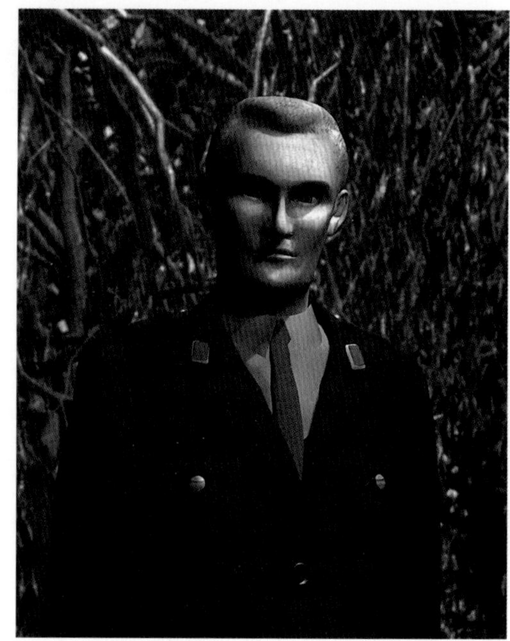

Louis Hausmann

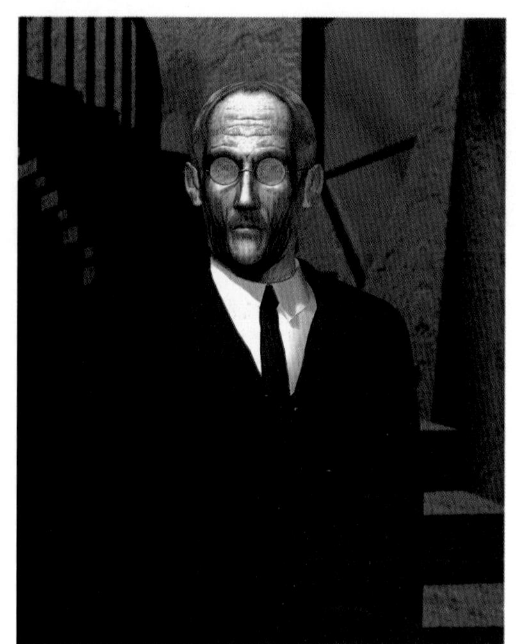

Ernst Onegin

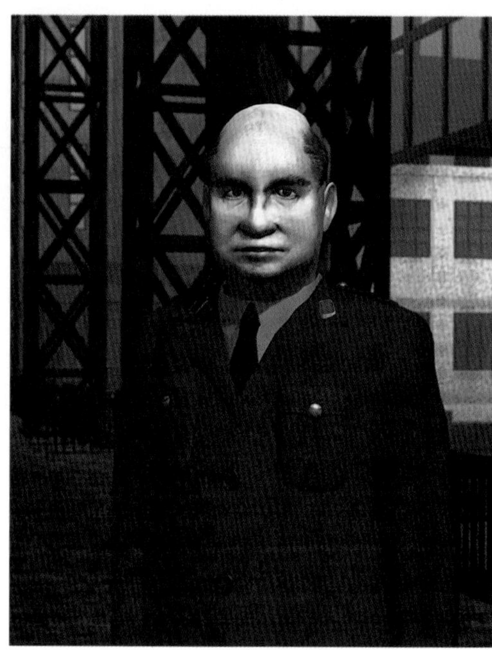

Oskar Gondarev

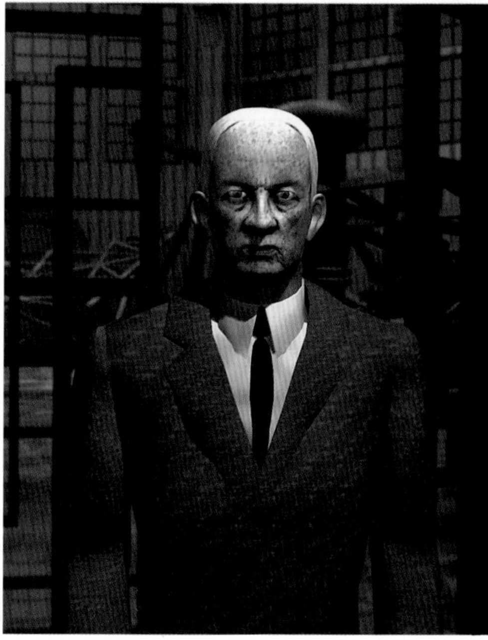

Horselover Frost

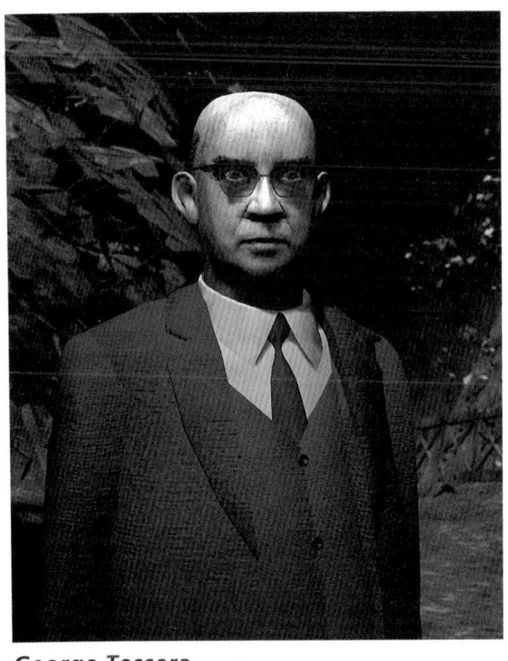
George Tessera

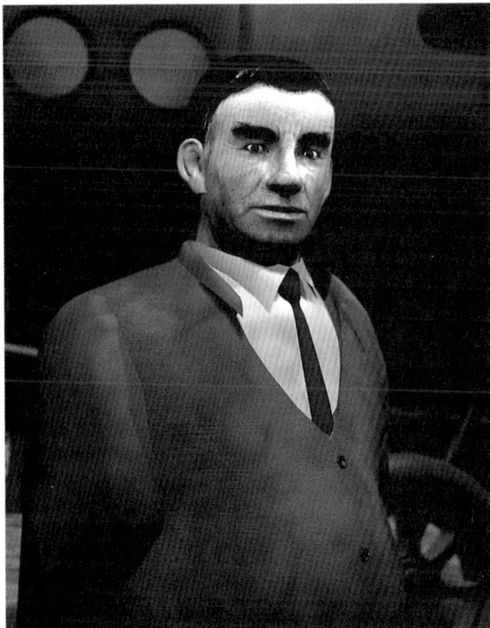
Wilhelm Draun

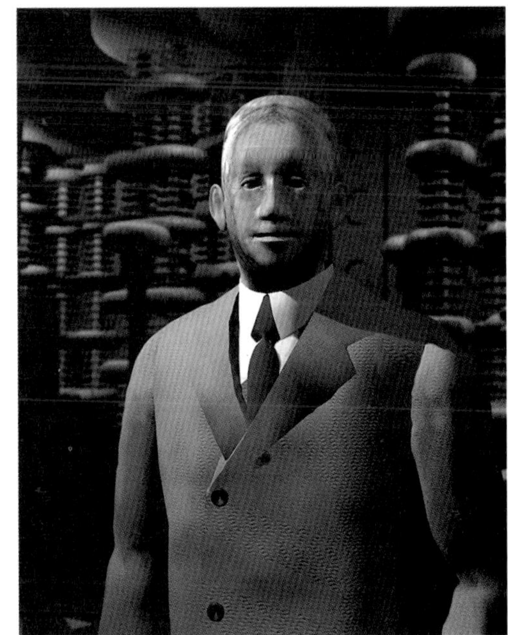
Charles Reif

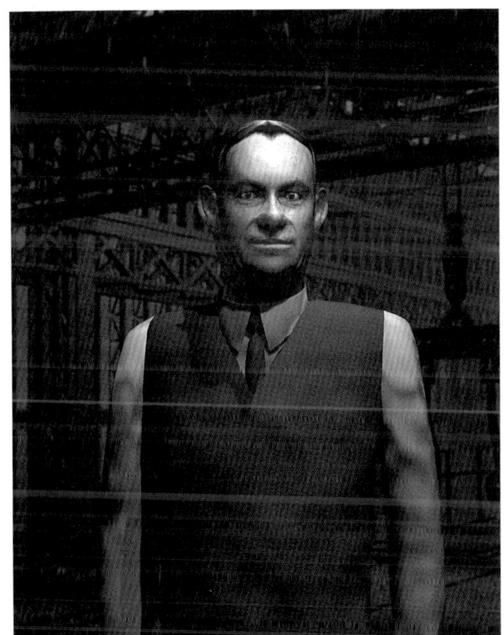
Thomas Reich

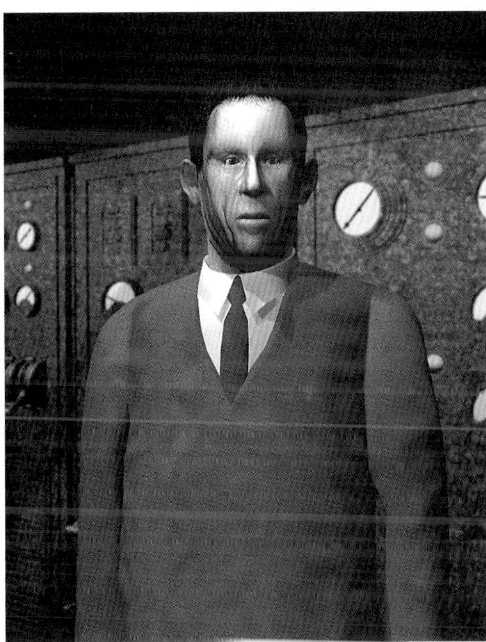
John MacNaughton

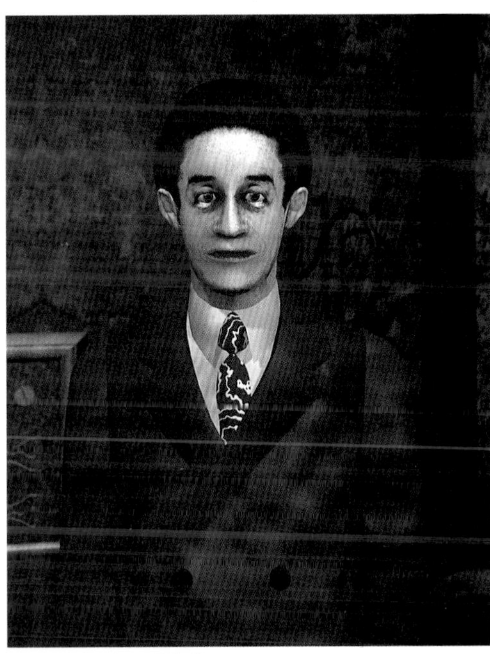
Constantine Wallace

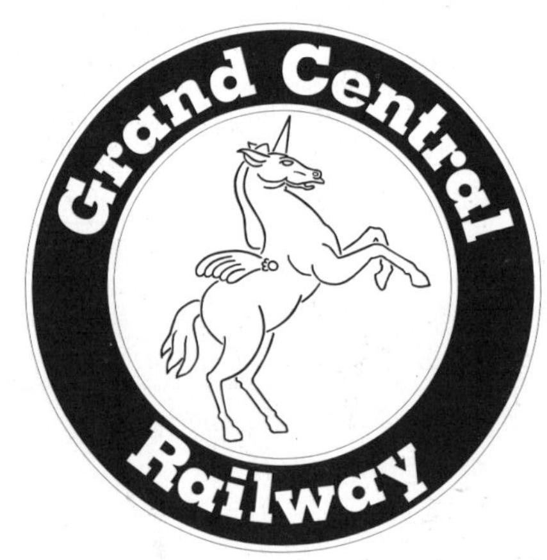
Grand Central
Railway